ASSIMILATION
AND ITS
DISCONTENTS

ASSIMILATION

AND ITS

DISCONTENTS

Barry Rubin

TIMES **T** BOOKS

RANDOM HOUSE

Grateful acknowledgment is made to the following for permission to reprint previously published material:
RAM'S HORN MUSIC: Two lines from "George Jackson" by Bob Dylan. Copyright © 1971 by Ram's Horn Music. All rights reserved. International copyright secured. Reprinted by permission.
SPECIAL RIDER MUSIC: Three lines from "It's Alright, Ma (I'm Only Bleeding)" by Bob Dylan. Copyright © 1965 by Warner Brothers Music. Copyright renewed 1993 by Special Rider Music. Two lines from "Highway 61 Revisited" by Bob Dylan. Copyright © 1965 by Warner Brothers Music. Copyright renewed 1993 by Special Rider Music. All rights reserved. International copyright secured. Reprinted by permission.

Library of Congress Cataloging-in-Publication Data
Rubin, Barry M.
Assimilation and its discontents / Barry Rubin.
p.   cm.
Includes bibliographical references and index.
ISBN 0-8129-2293-X
1. Jews—Cultural assimilation. 2. Jews—Identity. 3. Jews—Intellectual life. 4. Civilization, Modern—Jewish influences.   I. Title.
DS148.R83   1994
305.892'4—dc20   94-30991

FOR JUDY

The wise child asks: "What is the meaning of the rules, laws, and customs which the Eternal our God has commanded us?" . . . The contrary child asks: "What is the meaning of this service to you?" Saying *you,* he excludes himself. . . . The simple child asks: "What is this?" . . . As for the child who does not even know how to ask a question, you must begin for him. . . .

—The Passover Haggadah

I don't want to belong to any club that would have me as a member.

—Groucho Marx (also quoted by Woody Allen)

Rabbi Zusya said, "In the world to come, they will not ask me, 'Why were you not Moses?' They will ask me, 'Why were you not Zusya?' "

—Hasidic tale

CONTENTS

Introduction

If we act like other men, what shall we do on the day of the Lord? . . . If thou art of the opinion that there is no future world, and that the dead do not rise to new life, then why dost thou want thy birthright?

—*Jacob to Esau**

T HE SUBJECT of the Jews is nearly inescapable, though much of it concerns those escaping being Jews. How could it be otherwise with a highly literate, obsessively self-reflective people whose social and intellectual role far exceeds its numbers, whose survival and persecution has been so dramatic, and whose members are so unique yet—paradoxically—somehow seem to embody the human condition? And the issue of assimilation is always present—implicitly or explicitly, as subject or basis—in an outpouring of books, articles, films, music, or plays by and about Jews.

Yet it is quite different to see this phenomenon as a discrete historic process. The Jewish question has always given rise to a variety of answers. Whether or not contemporary Jews are aware of previous events and ideas, these still shape their lives and attitudes. The choices they have and decisions they make are often remarkably similar to those of their predecessors. Not only does a broader view of the assimilation process reveal what lies behind its many specific products, but it also brings to light fascinating individuals and experiences forgotten or suppressed despite their relevance for people today.

Jews were detached from the dominant society where they lived by

Midrash ha-Gadol, cited in Louis Ginzberg, *The Legends of the Jews* vol. 1 (Philadelphia, 1968), p. 320.

having a separate tradition—with its own worldview and past experiences—and by being in a different situation, that of assimilation itself. They saw the existing society's shortcomings more clearly, its advantages more originally, and its basic beliefs more skeptically. Thus arose the Jewish Variant: the twist, special spin, unique emphasis, or disproportionate preference that Jews put on any political or cultural concept or movement. Of course, anything Jews did was also done by others. Christians, too, changed religions, chose other identities, joined new causes, and so on. But this happened less deeply, thoroughly, and frequently among them in proportional terms and along somewhat different lines.

This book discusses these issues not in institutional or sociological terms but through the behavior of leading intellectual and cultural figures, the vanguard of assimilation and those most often agonizing over these problems in ordering their own lives. It compares the era of Jewish assimilation in Europe and America, examining how assimilation played a central role in Western history as well as in the lives and work of many great intellectuals, writers, and artists.

An author knows a subject is compelling when it seems omnipresent. For example, the April 1991 *Vanity Fair* alone contains four relevant articles concerning: Alfred Stieglitz, scion of a rich German Jewish family who founded art photography in America and wed Georgia O'Keeffe; Lady Mary Fairfax, whose family migrated from Poland in the 1920s and who became a powerful press lord and doyenne of Australian society; Charles Feldman, head of Famous Artists Agency and the great love of Jean Harlow; and the actress Ali MacGraw, whose Hungarian mother would never admit to being Jewish.

Many books could be filled with anecdotal material of this kind. Listening to the radio while writing, I heard a program about Muriel Spark, a leading British novelist who converted to Catholicism—though her son decided to be Jewish—and refused to discuss her Jewish background. I opened a new book by Mary Gordon, America's leading Catholic-oriented novelist, to find that her father, too, had been a convert. In films or television programs, intermarriage recurs as a remarkably common theme; Jerry Seinfeld and Roseanne Barr rule television comedy with extremely different styles. *Schindler's List* was the most important American film of 1994; a Jewish writer begins a *New York Times* lead story on crime with a Yiddish proverb. The 1994 world trade agreement was negotiated by Jews representing both the United States (Mickey Kantor) and Europe (Leon Brittan).

To pick two more random examples, three of four main articles in the July 22, 1990, *Washington Post* features section were about assimilating Jews who had made widely differing choices—Andrew Dice Clay, Sandra Bernhard, and Allen Ginsberg. That newspaper's October 18, 1992, reviews section is full of books by or about Jews: on sports and the American Jewish experience; a biography of Bill Graham, a Holocaust survivor and leading rock & roll impresario; the story of an upper-class New York family infected by antisemitism; a South African woman's group portrait of her set of Jewish friends; a Jewish couple's volume on foreign investments in America, analyzing problems of multiple loyalties and foreign influence paralleling issues in assimilation; and a Jewish author's book on politics in higher education, discussing multiculturalism in terms drawn from the integration of Jews into American society.

Despite such success for Jewish assimilation, the cost has been high. This book's title reflects this situation, recalling William Shakespeare's *King Richard III,* whose opening line—"Now is the winter of our discontent"—expresses ambiguity and dissatisfaction at the very moment his group's cause has triumphed. The same word appears in Sigmund Freud's *Civilization and Its Discontents,* which analyzes compromises required for survival in society that are both necessary and yet intensify certain personal problems. Franz Kafka, exemplifying a Jewish suspicion of contentment—as being a temporary, illusory state and also implying surrender to the dominant society—wrote, "While I was still contented I wanted to be discontented and with all the means that my time and tradition gave me, plunged into discontent—and then wanted to turn back again. Thus I have always been discontented even with my contentment."* The word *civilization* here also raises a question of which civilization assimilating Jews would join or build. The German Jewish poet Heinrich Heine called conversion a ticket to Western civilization while Freud himself saw education in that role.

Obviously all Western history of the last two centuries is not related to Jewish assimilation, but that assimilation was a leading factor in shaping the course and content of Western culture. Marx, Kafka, Freud, and many others did more than just describe or embody the contemporary Jewish situation, but much in their lives and thought reflected the issues of assimilation. Nor can one precisely define a Jewish style or ideology, but elements of

---

*Frederic Grunfeld, *Prophets Without Honor* (New York, 1980), p. 200.

such clearly exist, despite the fact that individuals used remnants from traditional Jewish life or thought intermingled with the unique assimilation situation and experience itself in reaching very different—sometimes opposing—conclusions.

The term *assimilation* is used here to mean a process of seeking integration in a larger society and increasingly taking one's ideas and customs from it. There is a spectrum of assimilationist solutions, with remarkable parallels among people who lived in different countries or centuries. The tug of past or lingering aspects of Jewish identity continue but become increasingly weaker. The ultimate result of ongoing assimilation is total assimilation through conversion, intermarriage, or fully entering another nation or ideological framework. This results in the disappearance of any Jewish identity or, indeed, anything distinguishing such people from the majority. As Jews do become totally assimilated, a powerful, positive, and productive psychological and intellectual force is lost.

Of course, everyone is influenced by the society in which he lives. A limited adaptation has been called "acculturation." But the idea of pluralism among members of the same society—especially beyond the purely religious sphere—is a fragile, relatively recent notion, itself an outgrowth of the Jewish debate over assimilation.

During most of their two millennia in the Western world, Jews assimilated only infrequently, remaining, despite persecution and murder, a tight-knit, relatively homogenous, autonomous community. The few converts there would quickly disappear into the dominant culture. Systematic and large-scale assimilation began only at the close of the eighteenth century. At that time, Jews began to be offered choices and opportunities in place of a way of life hitherto taken for granted.

That era saw a transition from a traditional Jewish society wrapped in religion, through a period of demoralization, division, and uncertainty, to a more complex solution of diverse religious interpretations and general acceptance that Jews are a people. Christians expected Jews to convert; leftists expected them to dissolve themselves in socialism; and liberals expected them to become equal but identical citizens. Each such resolution occurred in hundreds of thousands of cases. There also arose a distinctive assimilating Jewish subculture and massive participation in a wide range of intellectual and political movements, reflecting the dilemmas Jews were facing.

Decades of hope and progress alternated with years of frustration and backsliding. Among themselves, Jews had to choose among loyalties to nations—a Jewish one, or a dominant or minority group among whom they lived; religions—traditional or revised Judaism, atheism, some form of Christianity, or an exotic alternative; ideologies—Marxism, Zionism, liberalism, or conservatism; and castes—joining a sophisticated upper class to protect themselves from the prejudiced mob, a middle class offering relative anonymity and peace, or a lower class which they felt deserved justice and wanted to help overthrow the anti-Jewish rulers and system.

Should they conceal or take pride in being Jews, continue this line or break the long chain which had produced them? What loyalties, language, and beliefs should they espouse? How should they educate children or express themselves creatively? Should they seek a strategy to gain equality as Jews or stop being Jews in order to achieve equality as individuals? Should they blame the ruling society for oppression and defy or surrender to it? Or should they blame fellow Jews and try to change or denounce them? Was it better to accept the status quo or seek allies in trying to transform the existing society into one they could join?

The Haggadah of the Passover service gave a good model for this situation of choice. In it, the wise child asks, "What is the meaning of the rules, laws and customs?" His level of knowledge is less important than a willingness to learn and a desire to participate. In contrast, the evil child says, "What is the meaning of this service to you?" Saying "you," he excludes himself. Breaking with past generations and his own family, he walks away in disgust or indifference. Rather than being among those Jews who left Egypt, says the tradition, he would have stayed there to be assimilated in that society.

The simple son asks: "What is this?" Being as interested as the wise child in inquiring, he is not stigmatized but must simply be taught on a more basic level. The last is the one "who does not even know how to ask a question, you must begin for him," so totally detached as to be unaware that a history or people even exists. In all cases, the responsibility is on others to give instruction. Tradition suggests that those failing to provide instruction are equally at fault. The assimilation process produced all four types in profusion, though this last category would be its ultimate conclusion.

At the very least, those who are products of the assimilation process cannot understand themselves without comprehending this half-hidden factor. The objectivity of ideas or beliefs is compromised by the special circumstances that ensured their being chosen for that unique situation. This fact does not mean those views are inaccurate. Indeed, a special perspective may enhance an ability to find truth or achieve creativity. But if someone sees a certain color and declares his vision reality, it is important to know whether that revelation is due to keener vision or wearing tinted glasses.

Moreover, the patterns of Jewish experience—self-hate or self-affirmation; assimilation or identity; imitation or synthesis—are being duplicated by many other groups hitherto set apart by gender, race, recent migration, or lack of nationhood. An analysis of Jewish assimilation can make a valuable contribution to understanding the tribulations and decisions of different cultures in an era when conflicts of integration and coexistence are at the top of the intellectual, social, and political agenda.

The first part of this book traces the course of assimilation in Europe (chapters 1 and 2) and in the United States (chapters 3 and 4), describing parallels and differences. Chapter 5 summarizes central themes. The second part presents various factors in assimilation, including the political left (chapter 6), defection through conversion or intermarriage (chapter 7), joining other nations (chapter 8) or being anti-Jewish Jews (chapter 9); and the role of liberalism in facilitating either changing allegiance or endorsing a semi-assimilated ethnic identity (chapter 10). Chapter 11 considers how assimilating Jews relate to Israel and their own future.

I would like to thank Judith Colp Rubin for her careful reading of the manuscript and many helpful suggestions.

ASSIMILATION
AND ITS
DISCONTENTS

I

The House of Bondage: 1789–1897

The wise child asks: "What is the meaning of the rules, laws, and customs which the Eternal our God has commanded us?"

—*the Passover Haggadah*

THE LEVY FAMILY was having a concert party at its Berlin home in 1811, when the Prussian officer and poet Achim von Arnim arrived to pick up his wife. When Arnim made antisemitic insults to the guests and one of them, Moritz Itzig, challenged him to a duel, Arnim refused, saying that Jews had no honor. A few weeks later, Itzig encountered Arnim on the street and beat him with a cane. Shortly thereafter, when Napoleon invaded Prussia, Arnim stayed home. Itzig volunteered for the army and fell a patriot fighting for his country, which opposed emancipating the Jews, against France, which advocated it.[1]

Such were the contradictions Jews faced in that era: to die for countries that rejected them and to uphold the codes of societies refusing them equality, hoping that exemplary behavior would earn them freedom. Jewish civilization underwent a crisis in which its members had to decide whether they would use liberty to be Jews or as a way to escape that identity. While the community struggled toward redefinition, its declining power and prestige made many members defect to more self-confident faiths or doctrines. By concluding that Jews could not be intellectually modern or socially integrated without abandoning community and customs, assimilationists accepted their inferiority. For them, Judaism had become a misfortune not only due to persecution but because it was not seen as a cause worth upholding.

The number of Jews in the world decreased by 66 to 85 percent between the years 200 and 1200. By the mid-seventeenth century, they had declined from 7 to 10 percent to less than 1 percent of Europe's people. Nonetheless, the enormous pressures placed upon Jews by massacres and other mistreatment had little impact on the Jewish way of life. Jews stayed in their own society and civilization. "Conscious of their own worth," explained the Russian Jewish philosopher Ahad Ha-Am, Jews ignored what others thought of them and felt no sense of shame or humiliation. They just wanted to be left alone.[2]

But by opening the door to equality and challenging all tradition, the Enlightenment and French Revolution unleashed ideas many Jews were ready to heed. Inherited thoughts and customs were no longer a defense: on the contrary, they were assumed to be wrong by definition.[3] Those believing that being Jewish brought only punishment, humiliation, discrimination, risk, and exclusion from the West's cultural and material rewards had no interest in carrying this burden or passing the curse to their children. As Ahad Ha-Am asked in the 1890s, how could they "justify their obstinate clinging to the name of Jew . . . which brings them neither honor nor profit—for the sake of certain theoretical beliefs which they no longer hold? Since we no longer treat the outside world as a thing apart, we are influenced, despite ourselves, by the fact that the outside world treats us as a thing apart." When a Russian writer asked, "Since everybody hates the Jews, can we think that everybody is wrong, and the Jews are right?" some Jews agreed.[4]

By the mid-1800s, in Theodor Herzl's words, it began to "appear not customary, not proper, and not desirable to emphasize one's Jewishness."[5] The community's physical and spiritual survival seemed threatened less by the old shadow of murder than from the new prospect for voluntary desertion. Previously, only religious conversion could integrate Jews into society, at the cost of a direct, conscious betrayal of roots, family, and self. Now, secular European thought let them merely change customs with apparent ease and a clear conscience that they were contributing to human progress. For Jews as individuals, assimilation had become more attractive; for the Jews as a group, it would be fatal.

Indeed, by the 1880s, assimilation was making such deep inroads that the poet Judah Leib Gordon asked, "And our sons? The generation to follow us? From their youth on they will be strangers to us. . . . Perhaps I am the last of Zion's poets; And you the last readers?" Ahad Ha-Am spoke in similar terms, "All our greatest artists, thinkers, and writers . . . leave our humble cottage as soon as they feel that their exceptional abilities will open the doors of splendid palaces." Other civilizations "grow rich by our poverty, prosperous by our decay; and then they cry out on this despicable nation, which has not a single corner of its own in the temple of modern culture!"[6]

Yet the Jews had built far more than a corner of Western culture. They had founded the first monotheistic religion, of course, but their survival for three thousand years cannot be explained in purely religious terms. The key to that enigma was their concurrent invention of the world's first nation, long before that concept could be expressed: a people bound together not just by common ruler, religion, or ancestry, but also by a culture, ideology, and set of mutual obligations creating a community consciously resolute to preserve its solidarity. Modern nomenclature obscures this fact by replacing the national name—Hebrews or Israelites—for Jews, which seemingly refers only to religion.[7]

Most Jewish doctrine and religion was directed at creating and preserving the nation, with a remarkable amount of success. Of all the ancient tribes and kingdoms, only the Jews preserved their identity from civilization's dawn to the present, despite such national traumas as the fall of the First Temple in the seventh century B.C.E., the Roman conquest and destruction of Judea in 70 C.E., periodic massacres from the eleventh to seventeenth centuries, and, most recently, the Shoah.

From the start, Jews had to justify resisting submersion into other groups as the temptations of assimilation appeared in forms that would recur. The Bible candidly shows the ability of surrounding societies to seduce Jews culturally or romantically. Repeatedly Jews are recalled to distinctiveness as a people who dwell alone, even amidst others. The Bible virtually ignores afterlife or heaven but is full of national history and injunctions to maintain identity and avoid assimilation. It describes the Jews' rise from a single family to a tribe, confederation, and finally nation-state whose culture and religion brimmed with survival mechanisms. "You will be to me," God says, "a kingdom of priests, and a holy nation."[8] The punishment for abandoning such rites as Passover or the Yom Kippur fast was to be "cut off" from the nation. Jewish religious practices were equally national customs. The First Commandment ordered them to reject other nation's deities lest the Jews be wiped "off the face of the earth."[9] They were enjoined to recall their history and pass on their identity from generation to generation.[10]

By the same token, though, Jews did not survive merely due to exclusion or persecution but in affirmation of their own religious, cultural, and intellectual civilization. "The consciousness of [exile]," wrote the scholar Abraham Halkin, "did not prevent the Jew from going about the ordinary business of living, even seeking happiness.... Yet the Jew never forgot it."[11] Only assimilating Jews who no longer knew these self-affirming aspects could claim that external pressure alone prevented the Jews from disappearing. Persecution was not the root of Jewish distinctiveness but the result of the majority's refusal to accept it. To stir Persia's monarch against the Jews, the court official Haman told him, "There is a certain people, scattered and dispersed among the other peoples in all the provinces of your realm, whose laws are different from those of any other people and who do not obey the king's laws."* Indeed, in medieval Islamic Spain and modern Europe, by discarding religion and ethnic identity assimilating Jews actually increased their own persecution.

The biblical story of the Jewish sojourn in Egypt is a model assimilation tale. Sold into slavery by his brothers, Joseph interprets Pharaoh's dream of impending famine and gains the highest office, though jealous aristocrats point out that he "cannot even speak the language of our land." Joseph disregarded his background, having found like many later Jewish migrants that intelligence and talent could raise him from penniless refugee to wealth and success. He even thanked God for having "caused me to forget my father's house," but called his sons from a mixed marriage by names juxtaposing successful assimilation with the sadness of exile: Manasseh (God has made me forget completely my hardship and my parental home) and Ephraim (God has made me fertile in the land of my affliction). When famine forces his brethren to come to Egypt seeking food, Joseph so identifies as an Egyptian as to follow their custom of refusing to dine with Hebrews. But on hearing his brothers repent for having treated him so badly, Joseph recognizes his own betrayal of group loyalty and saves them.[12]

After the Jews moved to Egypt, though, their very success at assimilating—as it would again three thousand years later in Europe—made the majority resent their prosperity, fear their aims, and oppress them.[13] Only when Moses, so assimilated as to hide his very origin, rebelled at this subjugation did liberation begin.[14] Even then, despite many signs from God, the freed slaves still yearned for Egypt's fleshpots to the day they entered the promised land.[15]

*Esther 3:8.

In Egypt and everywhere else they went, Jews faced the temptation of intermarrying with the local people and thus being lured into joining another nation and religion. This is a constant biblical theme, as when a plague broke out to punish those Jews "whoring with the Moabite women, who invited [them] to the sacrifices for their god."[16] Such activity was rejected not on racial but on national and religious grounds: "Thy daughter thou shalt not give unto his son, nor his daughter shalt thou take unto thy son. . . . For thou art a holy people unto the Lord thy God."[17] The two biblical books named for women, Ruth and Esther, both deal with intermarriage: the former of a faithful convert whose descendants would include King David and the Messiah; the latter by a Jew who became queen to save her people.

Abraham insisted his son Isaac not take a Canaanite bride but only one from his own people. Even in ancient days, Jewish mothers worried lest their son wed a shiksa: "Rebecca, weary of her life on account of the woman chosen by her older son [Esau]," says rabbinic tradition, exhorted Jacob to follow Isaac's example. Still, Jewish kings, including Solomon, repeatedly ignored this injunction and married foreign—i.e., non-Jewish—women who led them to venerate other Gods.[18] By inducing King Ahab to idol worship, his wife, Jezebel, brought about his dynasty's downfall.

The ensuing defeats and exiles, however, did not divert Jews from a persistent loyalty to God and to each other, believing that no matter how long one was separated from people or land, repentance and return was possible. The 44th Psalm is typical in this regard: "Thou hast cast off and brought us to confusion . . . and has scattered us among the nations. . . . Yet have we not forgotten thee, neither have we been false to thy covenant." Even the ancient rabbis knew this peculiar fortitude had to be justified. They cite Esau as telling Jacob that the Jews were foolish to be different from others. Jacob replied that if Esau did not believe in the Lord or judgment, "Why dost thou want thy birthright? Sell it to me, now, while it is yet possible to do so."[19] If one rejects the inheritance, it is worthless and might well be bartered, even for a single meal.

In practice, the precept was that Jews might adapt others' more superficial customs and ideas if they stayed within the Jewish community and upheld its basic principles. Thus, ancient Jews borrowed much from Greek culture—clothing, language, names, and literary forms—while retaining a separate identity. Those living outside their own land preserved their communities and laws, continuing to regard the land of Israel as their country.

Jews like Philo, living in the Greek city of Alexandria, wrote plays, poems, or philosophy in Greek style using Jewish material and ideas. He explained that Jews were both loyal citizens and a distinct people who viewed Jerusalem as "their mother-city" and the other places they lived as "their fatherlands."[20] But his own nephew assimilated so completely as to become the Roman general Tiberius Julius Alexander, an especially brutal suppressor of the Jewish nationalist revolt in the land of Israel.

After Jerusalem fell and the exile began, the rabbis recast Judaism to save it. With remarkable effectiveness they used the Bible as what Heinrich Heine would call a "portable fatherland," building a society and body of knowledge across frontiers and despite ferocious persecution. Jews were massacred throughout Europe during the Crusades and expelled from England in 1290, from France in 1394, Prague in 1400, Vienna in 1421, Tyrol in 1475, and from many other places. Martin Luther's praise for Jews when he began his Protestant movement in the 1500s turned into hysterical antisemitism when they did not join him.

This pressure prompted some conversions, whose offspring reportedly included a twelfth-century pope and St. Teresa of Avila. Usually, though, Jews resisted joining what was not just another faith but the one oppressing and degrading them. Tens of thousands died rather than abandon their religion. A single convert could, from fanaticism or hope of gain, imperil whole communities by claiming the Talmud was anti-Christian or that Christian blood was used to make Passover matzo. This danger, however, also strengthened the community's solidarity and contempt for converts.[21]

Only in Spain was there large-scale assimilation which, prefiguring later events in modern Europe, further inflamed hatred. Although Muslim rule there let Jews create a sophisticated Hebrew culture and a few Jews to reach high political posts—like Shmuel Hanagid, Granada's chief minister in the early eleventh century—their status was insecure. Hanagid's son and six thousand other Jews were massacred by Muslims in 1066. Moses Maimonides, the era's greatest Jewish thinker, left Spain forever in 1148 when a militant Muslim sect forced Spanish Jews to convert. Having witnessed such events, he sympathetically wrote Yemen's Jews in 1170 that it was acceptable to profess conversion to Islam to avoid execution, while practicing Judaism secretly until they could flee to lands where they could once again practice their religion openly.

As Christians recaptured Spain, they, too, demanded that Jews convert or die, both fates that befell hundreds of thousands in the pogroms of 1391. Thereafter, at least six of eighteen Spanish bishops were from once-Jewish families. Rabbi Solomon ha-Levi of Burgos had become Pablo de Santa Maria, bishop of Burgos and persecutor of those who remained Jews. When the last Muslim stronghold fell in 1492, the Catholic monarchs ordered all Jews to leave Spain or convert. About half the Jews fled; the rest became Christians, though a few continued to practice Judaism secretly. Jealous of all the converts' success and doubting their sincerity, the church tortured and murdered thousands of them.

The disaster in Spain was only one element in the decline of Judaism's fortunes. As Jews were increasingly confronted by change, events made them more suspicious of it. Jewish law and thought often tended defensively toward a narrow legalism. The 1648 massacres in Eastern Europe devastated Jewish communities there, and the failure of the self-proclaimed messiah Sabbatai Zvi during the next two decades demoralized the survivors. Between 1634 and 1700 almost twelve hundred Jews were baptized in Rome alone, in larger proportions than ever before.[22]

Among those few secret Jews surviving the Inquisition in Spain and Portugal, several thousand eventually reached Amsterdam. Having shuttled between Christianity and Judaism, forced to profess ideas they did not believe, and familiar with both systems, some came to doubt religion altogether. The day was passing when people had to regard their own doctrine as the only truth, their group as repository of all virtue, the existing order as the only conceivable one, or received ideas as always correct. The philosopher Baruch Spinoza, among the first Jews to be so exposed to European knowledge, argued that the Bible was written by the ancient Hebrews, not by God. Expelled from the Amsterdam synagogue in 1656, he made no effort to reverse the expulsion but simply lived in the Christian world without converting, a forerunner of modern Jewish intellectuals.

Generally, though, social or intellectual interchange between Jews and Christians was still limited. Jews had little interest in Western education or culture, identifying both with a hostile, spiritually inferior Christianity. When the young Solomon Maimon was dazzled by a magnificently dressed Polish princess in the 1760s, his father whispered to him, "Little fool, in the other world the princess will kindle the stove for us."[23] Christians felt the same way about this world, making Jews pay special taxes, live in ghettos locked at night, and face marriage restrictions to keep their numbers down as in Pharaoh's Egypt. In those days, one of them wrote, a German Jew "had no fatherland" and his "birthplace was more foreign to him than any foreign land."[24]

The Enlightenment, created by Christians struggling with their own tradition—against backwardness and the power of kings, nobles, and popes—inevitably appealed to Jews victimized by the same system. For them, to join this effort was a matter of self-interest and a seeming solution to the Jewish problem. Moses Mendelssohn did the most to expose Jews to this new European civilization and Christians to the startling idea that Jews might be equal. Born in 1729, this noble-faced hunchback taught himself German and Western philosophy in Berlin. The Christian writer Gotthold Lessing publicized him as a kind, brilliant man who proved that Jews could be civilized, after all. For his part, Mendelssohn sought to show that a Jew could master European thought and customs while remaining religiously observant, that there was no conflict between obeying Jewish law and being a good citizen. Influenced by Maimonides and Spinoza, Mendelssohn insisted that Judaism was a rational religion that need not fear more education or new ideas. Ritual must be kept because it was ordained by God and preserved the Jewish people, but reason could be used as a guide for ethical behavior.[25]

Mendelssohn's labor was the beginning of a long battle to improve the Jews' image among Christians so that virtue and achievement could win the Jews acceptance. In 1769, this effort faced a crisis when a Protestant minister insisted that Mendelssohn either publicly refute the truth of Christianity or convert. Mendelssohn had to avoid insulting Christians while defending Judaism, knowing that the slightest mistake could undo all his progress and even endanger his people. His dignified response that Judaism was valid for Jews won him respect. To help Jews enter the mainstream society, he translated the Bible into German and used it to tutor his own children. He campaigned for equality; boosted German over Yiddish and the Bible over the Talmud; defended Jewish communities; and helped found the Berlin Jewish Free School to teach both secular and religious subjects.

Samson Raphael Hirsch, founder of modern Orthodoxy, later praised Mendelssohn for showing that "one can be scrupulous in religious observance but be nonetheless a highly esteemed man and shine out as a German Plato."[26] But this was a tough balancing act and, on Mendelssohn's own terms, it failed. Once the shell of observance cracked, its contents could not be saved. Contrary to Mendelssohn, many assimilating Jews would conclude that reason and religion conflicted or at least that their own creed was obsolete. Although only about 1 percent of Jews converted, those who did tended to be the most wealthy, Western-educated elite.

Mendelssohn's own pupil, David Friedlander, went so far as to propose in 1799 that Jews convert in order to gain equal rights. When a Christian proposed to him that the Jews reestablish a state, Friedlander said that centuries of oppression had atrophied their urge for freedom and destroyed any spirit of unity.[27] Mendelssohn was even unable to pass on his beliefs to his own children. His daughter despised Judaism; she became a Protestant in 1804, then a Catholic four years later. She left her husband—a fellow convert—for a Catholic reactionary opposed to Jewish emancipation, taking along her two sons, who became devoutly Christian painters, pouring into that religion a passion hijacked from Judaism.

When Mendelssohn's son, Abraham, baptized his children without himself converting, his brother-in-law wrote him, "Do you really think you did something wicked when you gave your children the religion which you regard as better for them? It is rather a form of homage which you and all of us are rendering to the efforts of your father in behalf of true enlightenment. He would perhaps have acted as you did for your children and I for my person. One can remain true to an oppressed, persecuted religion and can even force it on one's children with the prospect of a lifelong martyrdom—as long as one regards it as the sole means of salvation. But to do so when one no longer believes this, is barbarism."[28]

Indeed, Abraham Mendelssohn largely agreed with this assessment. "Some thousands of years ago," he told his daughter, "the Jewish form was the reigning one, then the heathen form, and now it is the Christian."[29] In 1822, he and his wife also converted. One of their children, Felix Mendelssohn, became a pious Catholic composer, of whom the convert Heinrich Heine would write the nearly converted socialist Ferdinand Lassalle in 1846, "I cannot forgive this man of independent means for putting his great, his prodigious talents at the service of [Christian] zealots" who opposed democracy and equality for the Jews.[30]

But this new era of Judenschmerz, of sorrow at being a Jew, was fully launched by political events. More centralized or democratic states rejected both Jewish autonomy or feudal anti-Jewish laws as restricting their power. The French Revolution gave Jews equal citizenship in 1791 but only in exchange for full assimilation under the formula, "The Jews should be denied everything as a nation, but granted everything as individuals." Napoleon called a meeting of leading Jews to declare allegiance to France and to insist that Judaism was a religion, not a nation. Most French Jews fulfilled Napoleon's hope that they would quickly disappear through assimilation.[31]

After conquering Prussia in 1812, Napoleon extended emancipation to

German Jews, repealing residency and job restrictions. Yet patriotic Jews like Moritz Itzig joined Prussia's army in battle against both Napoleon and their own interests. When France was defeated, Prussia rescinded Napoleon's decree. Jews who had thought themselves on the verge of achieving equality sank into desperation. In Berlin and Vienna, the Jewish elite was expelled from the intellectual salons it had created, where conversation had often led to conversion. Between 1780 and 1806, of a group of twenty Jewish women who socialized with the aristocracy, at least seventeen converted, and ten married gentiles.[32]

In this era, each Jew could refuse the chance to cross over and remain a pariah or do so, knowing, as German-born Jewish political theorist Hannah Arendt wrote, that he "had betrayed his people, denied his origin, and exchanged universal justice for personal privilege." Solomon Maimon, a self-taught philosopher respected by Kant, wrote that he had "happily emancipated myself from the fetters of superstition and religious prejudice . . . in which I had been brought up. . . . I could not return to my former barbarous and miserable condition, deprive myself of all the advantages I had gained, and expose myself to rabbinical rage at the slightest deviation from the ceremonial law or the utterance of a liberal opinion."[33]

One of the Berlin salon's leading figures was Rachel Levy. Itzig had confronted Arnim at her house and she was patron to Germany's most beloved writer, Goethe. Still, she knew being a Jew limited her prospects. There was no reason to stay in "the religion of your birth." It was better to join an aristocracy whose customs, views, and culture were superior, she wrote in 1771. Levy thought being a Jew was "loathsomely degrading, offensive, insane, and low," compelling her "to live unknown among the unworthy," shutting her out of German life and culture. A count broke off their engagement because his family objected. Another Christian she adored told a friend, "Never has a Jewess—without a single exception—known true love," while writing her a few days later that no one knew as well how to love as she. In 1814, she finally converted to marry the reactionary diplomat Karl August Varnhagen von Ense, who served a regime opposing Jewish emancipation.[34]

"Unfortunately," she wrote, as if in response to Mendelssohn, reason could "free isolated individuals only." Removing "the infamy of birth" required transforming oneself and changing allegiances. In the end, her only link to Jewishness would be "solidarity with all those who likewise wanted to escape."[35] As with many later Jewish intellectuals, Levy cited her choice as proof of freedom and open-mindedness, though it required the most rigid bondage and sanction of prejudice. Once converted, though, she waxed nostalgic on what she had formerly thought "my greatest disgrace, my bitterest pain and misfortune, namely to have been born a Jewess, I would not now dispense with at any price."[36] But, aside from memory, she had already dispensed with it.

Other Jews equally traumatized by Prussia's reversal of Napoleon's brief emancipation—Karl Marx,* Ludwig Börne (born Loeb Baruch), Heinrich Heine (born Haim Heine), and Moses Hess—became political thinkers obsessed with the link between the Jewish question and political change. Knowing that conversion was prompted by the necessities of livelihood, they inclined toward economic determinism. "Just as Jewish businessmen were compelled to remain Jews in order to acquire more wealth," Börne wrote, "Jewish intellectuals had to abandon Judaism so as not to starve."[37] Equally, they harshly criticized German society for denying Jews equality. As atheists and radicals they had guilty consciences at gaining freedom by betraying their principles, grabbing the privileges of a Christianity they disbelieved.

Börne, a champion of democracy and reform, was born in Frankfurt in 1786 and baptized in 1818. His political views forced him into a long exile in France, where he died in 1837. But even conversion did not free him of his past: "Some reproach me with being a Jew," he recounted, "some praise me because of it, some pardon me for it, but all think of it."[38] He and his radical friends were dismayed at the strong resistance to Jewish emancipation, but this very struggle for change led conservatives to redouble their attacks on Jews as a subversive force. Börne appealed to German reason and self-interest: "Hate the Jews or love them, oppress them or elevate them. . . . [But] see how far you get with the freedom of Germany so long as this freedom is not to be for all." By keeping Jews subordinated, Germans "will discover that they . . . as well as the jailed, may not leave prison.† . . . Neither group is really free."[39]

The idea that the masses had common interests with the Jews would often be repeated by Jewish assimilationists speaking as Marxists, liberals, or patriots. Actually, their needs and goals often conflicted. Börne saw this situation as irrational but hard to change: "The poor Germans! Living on

*On Marx, see chapter 6.
†Bob Dylan would use the same concept in a song a century and a half later: "Sometimes I think this whole world is one big prison yard./Some of us are prisoners the rest of us are guards."

the first floor, and oppressed by the seven stories of the higher classes," they felt better disparaging "people who live even further down, in the basement. That they are not Jews consoles them for the fact that they are not even court [officials]." Addressing Germans, he wrote, "You have deprived the Jews of air; but this saved them from putrefaction. You have strewn their heart with the salt of hate; but this has preserved it fresh. You have locked them up all winter long in a deep cellar . . . but you yourself, exposed to the frost, are half frozen. When spring comes, we shall see who blossoms earlier, the Jew or the Christian."[40] But antisemitism was increasingly inspired by just such a view of Jews as dangerously strong.

Heine exemplified the blend of self-hatred and bitter pride found in so many assimilating Jews. When he told fellow students at the Catholic school he attended of his Jewish background, their ridicule led to an altercation. Blamed for the disorder, he was beaten by a priest. To separate himself from Jews and become accepted by German society, Heine studied its lore, made gentile friends, and wrote poems designed to be typically German, some of which he published anonymously in an anti-Jewish newspaper.

"What a tragic story," he wrote, "is the history of the Jews in modern times! And if one tried to write about this tragic element, one would be laughed at for one's pains. That is the most tragic thing of all."[41] Nonetheless, the history of the Jews as a people seemed a promising alternative to the definition of Jews as a religion. Heine joined the Society for the Culture and Science of the Jews, established in Mendelssohn's spirit in 1819 to study Jewish life, teach Jews about the outside world, and defuse anti-Jewish prejudice.

Like Heine, the society's president Eduard Gans argued that for the Jews "to merge does not mean to perish. Only the obstinate, self-centered independence of the Jews will be destroyed, not that element which becomes a part of the whole; serving the totality." A month after the first meeting, Gans applied for an appointment to the University of Berlin's law faculty. On being rejected, he wrote, "I belong to that unfortunate class of human beings which is hated because it is uneducated, and persecuted because it tries to educate itself."[42] Both Heine and Gans converted to Christianity in 1825. Immediately afterward, Gans obtained a university post. Heine expressed his disgust for Gans—and himself—in an unpublished poem: "So you crawled to the cross that you despise, to the cross that only a few weeks ago you thought of treading under foot. . . . Yesterday a hero and today already a rascal."[43]

"I would much rather have heard that he had been stealing silver spoons," Heine wrote about Gans. Like Börne and Marx, Heine saw the decision to convert in economic terms: "I assure you, if the law permitted the theft of silver spoons, I would not have been converted." He spoke bitterly of baptized Jews "hopeful of obtaining a position." In a sense, such a craven step could be held as proving Heine's low opinion of Jews as greedy "people who understand arithmetic."[44]

But Heine could also claim that his assimilation fooled the bigots. In his poem "Donna Clara," a knight proclaims his love for an antisemitic Spanish aristocrat who asks her mysterious suitor's name. He replies, "I, Senora, your Beloved, / Am the son of the renowned, / Famed and scripture-learned Rabbi, / Israel of Saragossa!" In another story Heine wrote, "What does it matter who is beneath the mask?" At a ball, "a costume covers all pretensions and brings about the most beautiful equality and the most beautiful freedom—the freedom conferred by masks."[45]

Antisemites, though, had their own interpretation of such cynicism. If Jews could profess a Christianity in which they did not believe, they would hardly be so altruistic as to dissolve themselves. Behind their masks, they must be planning to seize power under a capitalist, communist, or democratic banner to foist on society their secularism and internationalism. For Jews, the decision whether to don the mask or fling it off was a continuing dilemma, whereas the idea of such a choice rarely occurred to members of the majority community, who took for granted that they could only be themselves. For a man in Heine's position, the danger was that being Jew, Christian, or cynic, German, Frenchman, or universalist, might all be masks rather than identities.

Heine's guilt made him devalue his own conversion. He wrote a Jewish friend, "I regret that I've been baptized. I don't see that it's helped me very much.... I am now hated by both Christians and Jews. I have become a true Christian—I now sponge on rich Jews.... I often get up at night and stand before a mirror and call myself all sorts of names." On the other hand, he pitied those poor people: "Who groan beneath the heavy, threefold evil / Of pain, and poverty, and Judaism.... The most malignant of the three the last is: / That family disease a thousand years old, / The plague they brought with them from the Nile Valley.... Will Time, the eternal goddess, in compassion / Root out this dark calamity transmitted / From sire to son?—Will one day a descendant / Recover, and grow well and wise and happy?"[46]

The contradictions of the times and his situation made Heine reject religion while accepting Christianity, and proclaim himself an international-ist while insisting he was a German patriot. In letters to Jews, Heine spoke as a Jew and denied a belief in Christianity; writing to Christians, he sounded like a fervent Christian and antisemite, ridiculing Jews as crude, big-nosed, unsanitary pawnbrokers or peddlers who spoke crude Yiddish rather than proper German.[47]

Under such conditions, the equidistant alienation of many Jewish intel-lectuals was inevitable. Heine wrote of one town, "The Jews here are, as everywhere else, insufferable usurers and scoundrels. The Christian mid-dle classes are distasteful, and animated by a singular hatred. The upper classes are even worse." His poem, "Testament," asked: "Who needs my religion most? / My faith in Father, Son, and Ghost? / Let the Rabbi of Posen, the king of China / Cast lots for the piety of Heine!" A poem about a medieval religious disputation takes no side between Jew and Christian but ends with the aristocratic judge saying: "Which is right I hardly know— / But, to tell the truth, I think / That the rabbi and the friar, / That they both—forgive me—stink."[48]

Still, once baptized, Heine had to regard any continued effect of Juda-ism on him as transcending religion. He read the Jewish Bible—ironically in Luther's translation—and had sentimental memories of youthful Jewish studies, holidays, and cooking. He spoke of his concern for imperiled Jews, but carefully insisted that he felt equal solidarity with any other threatened or oppressed group. He glorified ancient Israel and Jewish ethics, while calling Jews money worshipers and contemptibly servile. He expressed loyalty to democratic ideals and Germany, though, calling himself a "good soldier in the war of liberation fought by all mankind."[49]

Similarly, while claiming that he made "no secret of my Judaism," which he had "never left," he also spoke as an enthusiastic Christian of Jesus, "What a beautiful figure is this Man-God! How narrow in compari-son appears the hero of the Old Testament! . . . Moses loved his people . . . Christ loved humanity. [Jesus] demolished the ceremonial law, which had no further meaning or use. He even passed final sentence of death on Jewish nationalism," offering all nations what "had once belonged only to the chosen people." Heine heaped praise on the antisemite Martin Luther. Even God, like Heine, was portrayed as an embarrassed convert who in his new cosmopolitan, universal guise secretly resented "the poor Jews be-cause they knew him as of old, and every day in their synagogues insist on reminding him of his erstwhile obscure national connections. Perhaps the old gentleman wishes to forget that he is of [Jewish] extraction."[50]

This ambiguity was expressed in one of Heine's stories where the main character says that Judaism "brings nothing but shame and abuse. . . . I avoid everything that reminds me of it." But he also knew something had been lost, "An old Jew with his long beard and ragged coat . . . feels happier than I do with all my accomplishments," because each Sabbath he forgets his sorrows, eats well, and rejoices with such contentment that he would not change places with even the richest or most cultured man. In similar terms, Heine compared Berlin's modern Jews to Poland's backward ones: "We no longer have the strength to wear beards, to fast, to hate, and to suffer hatred." Polish Jews looked filthy and repulsive, were uncultured, and displayed "revolting superstition"; they also enjoyed an admirable inner unity and freedom.[51]

Heine embodied the conflicts felt by assimilating Jews. Since they both craved and felt deprived of full membership in German society, they identified with it as patriots and dissociated with it as universalists. "I love Germany and the Germans," wrote Heine, "but I love no less the inhabitants of the rest of this earth, whose number is forty times greater." This attitude made him worthier "than those who cannot pull themselves out of the swamp of national egotism and who love none but Germany and the Germans." Yet he also insisted on his patriotism: "I could never renounce a German cat or a German dog, however insupportable their fleas and fidelity might be to me." Unfortunately, humanity was indifferent to this attachment while Germans—or other nations addressed by such an argument—thought it seditious.[52]

Similarly, Heine could subordinate Jewish interests while seeing the Jews as vanguard once they finally realized "they will achieve full emancipation only when the emancipation of the Christians is completely won and secured. Their cause is identical with that of the German people, and they should not need to demand as Jews, what has long been due them as Germans." The Jews' mission was to bring "the worldly Savior" of political and social progress. Despite Heine's willingness to diminish only Jewish interests, his enemies saw him as a Jew; and when Germany sought a redeemer it was one sworn to exterminate the Jews.[53]

"A baptismal certificate," said Heine, "is a ticket of admission to European culture."[54] Yet one of his comrades, Moses Hess, suggested a different route. He was far more integrated into the Jewish worldview from which his compatriots' parents had already broken. His father headed the Cologne Jewish community, his religious grandfather cried when speaking of the Temple's destruction and the Jews' dispersion, while Hess himself received a traditional religious education as well as a German one.

At first, Hess sought to be liberal, socialist, and German, urging the Jews to disappear through assimilation, changing his own name from Moses to Moritz. But experience disillusioned him. His music for a patriotic German song was scornfully rejected because he was a Jew. Hess began to grope for a new approach: instead of vanishing, Jews could modernize within the context of their own culture, as a nation among other reviving nations.

Their ancient state, "continues to live until this very day in the feelings of its scattered members, [a] despised people, which has remained loyal to its old customs . . . reawakens now, after a long sleep, to a higher consciousness, [a place] in the great renaissance of the nations."[55] His book *Rome and Jerusalem* (1862) drew inspiration from the recently triumphant Italian nationalist movement which revived and united that historic people. At the time, Hess was almost unique in combining traditional Jewish and modern European thinking, though Heinrich Graetz employed similar ideas in his influential *History of the Jewish People* (1853–76), suggesting that history had made Jews into a legitimate nation.

Unfortunately, few German Jews achieved the balance favored by Mendelssohn. The great majority were either so embedded in traditional Jewish religious thinking as to rebuff change completely or so steeped in European ideas as to reject any Jewish identity altogether, seeking to assimilate through liberalism, socialism, patriotism, or by making Judaism imitate Christianity. The latter group could well claim that history was on its side in the mid-nineteenth century, as signs of popular democratic revolution revived Jewish hopes.

In 1848, there were pro-democratic uprisings in almost every European capital. Attacking the reactionary order denying the Jews equality, these seemed proof of the common interests described by Borne, Heine, and Marx. Jews became leaders in these insurrections: in France, the new minister of justice Adolphe Cremieux; in Austria, Adolf Fischhof and Joseph Goldmark; in Prussia, the parliament's vice-president Gabriel Riesser; and many others.[56]

Most of these figures followed the strategy prescribed by radical Jewish intellectuals. Fischhof's call for revolution advocated universal assimilation instead of ethnic nationalism: "Ill-advised statesmanship has hitherto kept apart Austria's nationalities. They now must find their brotherly way to one another and increase their strength by unity." He advocated communal rights for these nations, but did not number the Jews among them. "If it be true that we are awaiting the coming of a messiah," Goldmark announced, he was about to arrive. "If we are no longer oppressed, we need no messiah."[57]

As leaders of a national movement, they felt required to exclude any Jewish interest or influence from their personal history. As one put it, "Being simultaneously a Jew and a German, the Jew in me can never be free without the German, nor the German without the Jew." Even a rabbi in Austria's parliament declared, "What shall be done for us now? Nothing! Everything for the people and the Fatherland. . . . No word about Jewish emancipation unless others speak up for us. . . . First the right to live as men, to breathe, think, speak, first the right of a citizen . . . afterwards comes the Jew. They should not reproach us that we always think first about ourselves!"[58]

But the revolution's enemies and some of its supporters did so anyway: the former associating Jews with the pro-monarchy Rothschilds; the latter with radicalism. Antisemitism among the masses was matched by non-Jewish leaders' lack of interest in Jewish emancipation. After suppressing the revolt, restored regimes repeated the pattern of three decades earlier, renewing anti-Jewish restrictions as soon as they felt securely in power again. To make matters worse, Jews were caught between other nations' quarrels as they advocated Hungarian culture among the Slovaks, Serbs, Croatians, and Romanians; German among the Czechs and Poles, and so on. "With whomever they side," complained a Viennese Jewish journalist, "they find a powerful party opposing them."[59]

In England, Jews had a more serene situation. Their leader for four decades after 1824 was Moses Montefiore who, like Moses Mendelssohn in Germany, battled for Jewish rights while remaining observant. He wrote in 1836 of his resolve "not to give up the smallest part of our religious forms . . . to obtain civil rights."[60] In the long run, though, many of his descendants converted, one becoming the Anglican bishop Hugh Montefiore.

Benjamin Disraeli, the best-known Jew in Britain, resembled Heine in his bitter, sentimental pride. Baptized at age thirteen, he flaunted a background too well known to hide. Disraeli's flair for showmanship and England's relative tolerance brought him huge success. Having abandoned a religion combining tradition and justice, he urged Britons to maintain their own institutions while showing practical compassion for the poor. He supported the legal change that finally made unconverted Jews eligible to serve in Parliament in 1858, twenty-one years after he was first elected.

Visiting Jerusalem, he was entranced by a romantic vision of his lineage. As a convert, Disraeli, like Heine, could lecture Christians on their own religion. "Christianity is Judaism for the multitude, but still it is Judaism." His novel *Alroy* (1833) portrayed a medieval Jewish prince's foiled attempt to re-create a Jewish kingdom. In *Tancred* (1847) the hero, a British aristocrat, seeks transcendent religious experience. "We shall soon see a bishop at Manchester," he is told. "But I want to see an angel at Manchester," he replies.* Arriving in the holy land, he concludes that only those of "the holy race" can achieve this blessing.[61]

Disraeli proudly proclaimed himself "descended in a direct line from one of the oldest races in the world . . . who had developed a high civilization at a time when the inhabitants of England were going half-naked and eating acorns in their woods."[62] Many Jews saw such outspoken comments as provocative, especially those wealthy ones quietly joining an elite whose customs interested them far more than their own history. "There is only one race better than the Jews," stated one of them, "and that is the Derby." Still, in 1833, the first unconverted Jew was allowed to be a lawyer; in 1855, one became Lord Mayor of London, in 1858 Lionel Rothschild entered the House of Commons, and in 1885 Nathaniel Rothschild became the first Jewish peer and member of the House of Lords.[63]

In other countries, too, legal discrimination diminished. Jews were made full citizens of the Austro-Hungarian Empire in 1867 and in Germany three years later. German Jews felt, one of them wrote, joy and hope "almost beyond description."[64] Jews rushed to take up this opportunity, moving to cities and becoming doctors, lawyers, and journalists. Paul Reuter founded a news agency; Giacomo Meyerbeer's operas were so successful that Prussia's king made him director of the Berlin opera house despite the composer's refusal to convert. Gerson Bleichroder, whose grandfather had been refused permission to live in Berlin, became its leading banker. Jewish heiresses were welcome to wed aristocrats and renew their capital as long as they converted. Even the anti-Jewish Christian Conservative Party was led by a convert, Friedrich Stahl, a University of Berlin law professor who claimed that only a Christian state could govern the German people.

Yet while many individuals' lives and expectations improved, their entry into professions and cultural pursuits brought complaints of Jewish domination. The affluence of the Rothschilds and other Jewish bankers created a legend of financial power further inflaming antisemitism, though

*See Franz Kafka's parallel episode with an angel, chapter 3.

such personal fortunes did not bring Jews any political influence as a group. At the same time, emancipation weakened Jewish communities, no longer at the center of members' lives but a sideline at best. The assimilationists' need to prove themselves loyal citizens made them deny Jews were a nation in exile. The liberal and Jewish leader Gabriel Riesser said that German Jews were closer to Germans than to Jews of other lands. "We are not immigrants, we are born in Germany and, therefore, have no other claim to a home: we are either Germans or homeless."[65]

Persecution, however, was intensifying international Jewish cooperation at the moment many Jews were denying that any such connections existed. In 1840, when a Catholic monk disappeared in Damascus, local Christians accused Jews of murdering him to use his blood to make Passover matzo. Several Jews were seized, imprisoned, and tortured (two of them to death). In many countries, Jews protested, rousing the British, United States, and even Russian governments to action. A delegation led by the British Jewish leader Montefiore and his French counterpart Cremieux obtained the surviving prisoners' release.

Eighteen years later, a Jewish child, Edgar Mortara, was baptized by his Catholic nurse in Italy and kidnapped by the Vatican. Despite Jewish protests, he was raised as a Catholic, becoming a priest and fanatical advocate of Jewish conversion. This occurrence endangered every Jew; it can be regarded as parallel to the contemporaneous Dred Scott case in America, whose outcome decreed that blacks had no rights that had to be respected by whites. The kidnapping and other such events led to the creation of the French Alliance Israelite Universelle in 1860 and the British Board of Delegates organization in 1871.

The definition of Jewish religion was also hotly debated in this era. Those saying Jews were just a religious group with no national attributes were also ready to adjust tradition to the norms of societies they sought to enter. The Reform movement appealed to assimilating Jews by Christianizing Judaism itself. Allusions to a Jewish people and its hope to return to the ancient homeland were dropped from the prayerbook. German replaced Hebrew, services were sometimes held on Sunday, and all synagogues were called "temples" to negate the centrality of the Temple in Jerusalem.[66] The Reform movement interpreted dispersion not as exile but as a divinely ordained mission to carry an ethical message to all humanity. This idea reversed the purpose of Jewish religion and culture from preserving the Jews as a people to making them the world's servant.

The effect of this view was epitomized by Abraham Geiger, Reform's

founder, during the 1840 Damascus crisis: "It is quite honorable that eminent people are manifesting solidarity with their persecuted brethren, but
... in my eyes it is more important that Jews in Prussia should be allowed to
become pharmacists or lawyers than that Jews in Asia or Africa be rescued."
As Hess argued, dissolving the national bond jeopardized Jewish survival:
No "fabricated prayerbook" could replace "the moving Hebrew prayers,
which express the pain and agony over the loss of the national home—
prayers which have created and preserved over thousands of years the
unity of our tradition and are even today the link that binds all Jews together all over the world."[67]

But now high hopes faded and prescient Jews began to doubt whether
there was any escape at all from their dilemma. One of Germany's most
famous novelists in those years was Berthold Auerbach, who wrote about
peasant life in his rural home area. In an 1869 letter to Cremieux, he expressed the common attitude among assimilating Jews that their task was to
join and elevate the countries where they lived, "to help establish the life of
state and nationality on a superior plane, not on the basis of blood descent
but on that of the spirit." He also implied that local assimilation might coexist with an underlying unity: "The Jews are like the Bible which, translated into all national languages, nevertheless remains the same immutable
content."[68]

But a decade later, Auerbach was in despair. The growing new antisemitism portrayed Jews as a race and assimilated Jews as even more dangerous than their caftan-wearing Orthodox ancestors, since they could
more easily hide their "true nature" and use success to subvert society from
within. After a half century of struggling to prove Jews were good Germans, and showing how a Jew could write with such feeling for German
life, Auerbach concluded, "In vain have I lived and worked!"[69]

"It's like blacks calling themselves whites," said the composer Richard
Wagner of emancipated Jews. Yet even Wagner could not dispense with
such useful creatures. He praised one Jewish conductor in 1841 by saying,
"Without Meyerbeer, I would be nothing." Hermann Levy, a rabbi's son,
conducted the premiere of *Parsifal* in 1882. Another Jewish musician lived in
Wagner's home, suffered his insults, and shot himself in despair when his
hero died. Even Wagner's impresario was a Jew. Wagner hated the music
written by Mendelssohn, Meyerbeer, and Offenbach, but assimilating Jews
liked Wagner's operas. Wagner's hypocrisy and his Jewish admirers' fool-
ishness was much ridiculed at the time. Yet Jews' affinity for Wagner made

sense even as it exposed the inescapable contradiction in their position. If Wagner expressed the essence of the German soul, Jews seeking to be German had to enjoy his work. By applauding the music they sought to prove him wrong about them.[70]

A parallel dilemma occurred with the German Christian novelist Theodor Fontaine who, despite his many devoted Jewish readers, claimed that Jews had failed to assimilate: "They are irritants everywhere. . . . Despite all its gifts, it is a horrible people . . . afflicted from its very origins with a kind of conceited vulgarity, which the Aryan world cannot get along with." He called one man, whose family had long ago converted, a "typical Jew" who could not "get rid of his Jewish mentality."[71]

The upsurge of antisemitism in Germany, Austria-Hungary, and Russia was fueled by economic crises during the 1870s, 1880s, and 1890s. Few Jews there escaped experience with antisemitism, what Walter Rathenau called, "a painful moment that he remembers all his life: when for the first time he becomes fully aware that he came into the world as a second-class citizen, and that no amount of ability and no personal merit can free him from this situation."[72] Many Jewish university students changed names and shunned relatives to hide their background. The Union of German Students was founded in 1880 as explicitly antisemitic; the more moderate Congress of German Fraternities voted in 1896 to accept no Jews. But when some Jewish students started their own fraternities, others opposed doing so as an apparent admission of assimilation's failure.

Conditions in Russia and Eastern Europe were far worse. The historian Lewis Namier compared Jews there to an iceberg: partly submerged and still frozen; partly evaporated away by assimilation; and the rest having melted to form waves of political turmoil. To escape discrimination barring them from the main cities, about forty thousand Jews had converted in St. Petersburg and Moscow alone by 1839, and every tightening of residency restrictions added more.[73]

The regime forced Jews who would not convert to live in a swath of western Russia where about five million of them were concentrated by century's end. A lively Yiddish and incipient Hebrew culture, simultaneously preserving and modernizing Jewish life, grew in these mud-streeted villages. Tradition had taught Russian Jews to seek knowledge but restricted their freedom to do so. Now literary classics and scientific works were translated into Yiddish, becoming, publishers boasted, better than the originals. Yiddish writers criticized their people's backwardness, skewering pious reactionaries as hypocrites, the rich as pretentious, and young secular intellectuals as naïve.

Oppressed by government and neighbors, barred from most professions, and deprived of educational opportunities, many concluded the only choices were emigration or overthrowing the czar. On March 1, 1881, Czar Alexander II was assassinated by a radical group, a few of whose members were Jews. Six weeks later, officially sanctioned anti-Jewish pogroms began, killing hundreds and destroying homes and businesses. Russian liberals and radicals remained silent or even praised the upsurge as revolutionary. New laws tightened the ban on Jews living in most of Russia without special permission. Hundreds of thousands were expelled. The number of Jewish students in high schools and colleges was reduced. A statement made by the czarist minister Konstantin Pobyedonostzev proved prophetic: "A third of the Jews will emigrate, a third will be converted and a third will die."

Small Zionist groups from Russia founded their first settlement in the land of Israel in 1878. But about two million Jews crossed the Atlantic; others left rural areas for German or Austrian cities whose already partly assimilated Jews often shared the majority's disdain for the immigrants' accents, dress, or religious practices and feared that these newcomers might undermine their own security by provoking antisemitism. "Those Jews may be registered with the police as Jews," a German Jewish newspaper complained in 1872, showing how far assimilation had progressed, "but their way of living is thoroughly un-Jewish."[74]

For those remaining in Eastern Europe, growing insecurity shook their faith in assimilation. Isaac Elhanan Spector, a modernizing rabbi, wrote in his post-1881 memoirs: "The spirit of freedom which swept across the land . . . was delusive. Many people, sensible ones at that, thought the days of darkness were over. The sun of knowledge would purge men of evil, no man would harm another because of his beliefs or views, hatred for different religions and nationalities would disappear without trace."[75] Intellectuals like Peretz Smolenskin, who had claimed Jewish tradition created bias and that educational attainment would dissolve it, found the pogroms "a cruel shock. Almost overnight, religious bigotry and intolerance, bureaucratic harassment and official connivance in the pogroms seemed to obliterate twenty years of slow progress. . . . Beneath the thin veneer of relative tolerance an abyss of deep hatred continued to exist."[76]

In Odessa, Russia's most liberal, Western-oriented city, intellectuals like Smolenskin rethought their stance. One of his comrades, Moses Lilienblum, called for reestablishing a Jewish state, declaring, "I am convinced that our misfortune is not the lack of general education but that we are aliens. We will still remain aliens when we will be stuffed with education as a pomegranate is with seeds."[77] Leo Pinsker, a doctor and Crimean War hero, wrote a Zionist book, *Auto-Emancipation,* in 1881. Still another Odessa man, the essayist Ahad Ha-Am, advocated both a Jewish state and a struggle against the "inner slavery and spiritual degradation" of assimilation. To learn from Europe was good; to surrender one's own culture and religion to be European, odious. He moved to Tel Aviv in British mandatory Palestine in 1922.[78]

But while Russia was a predictably reactionary country, events in France, the birthplace of Jewish emancipation, were even more alarming for the cause of assimilation. Captain Alfred Dreyfus, a Jewish officer in the French army, was falsely accused of selling military secrets to Germany in 1894. Dreyfus was the very model of an assimilated gentleman, completely secular, and every inch a French patriot. Nevertheless, in a wave of hysteria Dreyfus was convicted and sentenced to life imprisonment on Devil's Island. Anti-Jewish riots and demonstrations broke out throughout France, with crowds screaming "Death to the Jews!" And this was happening, wrote the Viennese journalist Theodor Herzl, "In France. In Republican, modern, civilized France, a hundred years after" its revolution promised emancipation.

Two years later, a French spy found a German document showing the guilty man was another officer, a dissipated, debt-ridden aristocrat. Dreyfus's innocence was championed by Socialist leader Jean Jaurès, radical politician Georges Clemenceau, and the writers Anatole France and Emile Zola. But French Jews were generally too intimidated to speak out. For five years, Dreyfus suffered on Devil's Island. By the time he obtained a new trial, his health and spirit were broken. The army—a general warned, "Either Dreyfus is guilty or I am"—pressed the court into reaffirming his guilt. But citing "extenuating circumstances" it reduced his sentence and he was soon pardoned and released.* The case, Hannah Arendt later wrote, showed that every Jew, no matter how assimilated or wealthy, was still something of a "pariah, who has no country, for whom human rights do not exist, and whom society would gladly exclude from its privileges. No one, however,

---

*Dreyfus's family was a paradigm for the Jewish experience in Europe: his great-grandfather was a kosher butcher; his granddaughter, a member of the Resistance, died in Auschwitz.

found it more difficult to grasp this fact than the emancipated Jews themselves."[79]

The accumulation of both disappointments and knowledge from the assimilation process now produced a new approach to the Jewish question. Zionism combined the traditional Jewish religious concepts of peoplehood and exile with the modern European idea of nationhood based on history. It was an idea already voiced by Hess, a few rabbis, and some intellectuals in Russia. But Theodor Herzl, whose life was a prototype of successful assimilation and spiritual discontent, actually launched the ideology and movement.

Herzl was born in 1860 in Budapest, a city midway between western and eastern Jewry, to a family halfway on the path from tradition to assimilation. The Herzl household observed basic rituals and festivals—particularly Hanukkah and Passover—but the children had little religious instruction and were not taught Hebrew. Theodor had a bar mitzvah but in a ceremony called—to imitate Christian practice—a confirmation. He attended religious school but felt no emotional stirring. Herzl's Orthodox grandfather was interested in the idea of a Jewish return to Zion, but two of his uncles had converted.

In 1878, Herzl's family moved to Vienna, Austria-Hungary's political and cultural capital. As a college student there, Herzl was a typical alienated, middle-class Jew sincerely seeking to conform with his peers, which required an interest in drinking, gambling, dueling, and the theater. Like many Viennese Jews, Herzl at first favored German nationalism as a way to unite with neighbors despite religious differences. He wrote in his diary of a common conflict: "the Jewish Question grieved me bitterly [but sometimes] I would have liked to get away from it—into the Christian fold, anywhere." But he also saw this was futile. He joined a fraternity, then resigned when it adopted an antisemitic policy in 1883. Beginning a law career the next year, he found advancement was blocked for a Jew. Rather than converting, he changed professions to become a playwright and journalist.

Since being a Jew and being accepted into the dominant society were contradictory, successful Jews chose to dissociate themselves from that unpopular group. As Herzl's boss on the *Neue Freie Presse* expressed this philosophy, "I am not pro-Jewish; I am not anti-Jewish; I am a-Jewish." Although he moved in Vienna's highest cultural circles, personal success did not eliminate feelings of exclusion, insecurity, and alienation. Constantly pressed to choose between his people and self-interest, Herzl was unwilling to abandon and unable to escape his community. Concluding that assimilation destroyed dignity and inflicted psychological harm as a denial of one's self, Herzl—like his fellow Viennese Jew Sigmund Freud—was trying to comprehend the forces underlying Europe's social change and political precariousness.

Herzl observed that, contrary to assimilationist predictions, antisemitism was escalating rather than disappearing. West European societies seemed unable—and East European ones unwilling—to accept Jews as equal citizens. If other peoples sought a renaissance by reviving their traditions and gaining a state, the much older Jewish nation might have its own liberation movement. In one of his plays, Herzl shows a Jew learning from a Christian "how to bow without cringing, how to stand upright without defiance." In a talk with the Jewish sculptor Samuel Beer in 1894, Herzl said that Jews were still not accepted despite their achievements. Suddenly he realized that perhaps they should not subordinate all for the sake of approval. He began writing about this problem from a new approach. A few days later, the Dreyfus case exploded on the French political scene, sadly confirming his view.

The publication in 1896 of Herzl's book *Der Judenstaat* brought him overnight fame and leadership in a movement born from material conditions but given life by his pen. Some of his friends thought he had lost his mind, yet Herzl was well suited for this task of leadership. Handsome, witty, and elegant, Herzl was a Jew who even antisemites had to admit was a gentleman and one to whom the gates of palaces would open. His full black beard and dark melancholy eyes made him appear like a biblical figure, embodying the unity of tradition and modernization he urged.

His movement saw Jewish history in a new way even when using its most customary images. Religion was credited with preserving Jews for two millennia but not as sole root or reason for their existence. The task, said Herzl, was to re-create "that equilibrium that our great ancestors possessed in their inner being," so damaged in more recent times by religion's decline and a new sense of inferiority. The very process of rebuilding a sense of national solidarity would reconstruct the Jewish people's character and fortunes, gaining them respect and making them productive.

While humanity was barely beginning an age of nationalism, the Jews' own situation inspired many Jewish intellectuals to boast of a universalism that saw any patriotism as a regressive step. Herzl wrote, "I do not dispute this point of view. I simply believe that if all our contemporaries actively espouse nationalism to our detriment, it would be foolish of us to reject this idea which could afford us protection." The Jews need not strive to be superior, they would be glad to achieve equality with the world's other peoples rather than be at their mercy.

Similarly Herzl denied that the purpose of exile was to spread ethics and monotheism, sarcastically noting that bourgeois Jews promoted this idea but the masses suffered for the myth "that the Jews have to live dispersed among the nations in order to instruct them. If the nations had not hated and despised us anyway they certainly would have had to laugh at us for such arrogance." The Jews' situation was neither a divine mission to be obeyed nor a misfortune to be passively accepted but a tragic exile to be reversed. Judaism mourned for a lost, God-given homeland, taught the destroyed Jerusalem Temple's ritual, followed that land's seasons, and prayed for the holy city's restoration. The Passover service ended with a pledge, "Next year in Jerusalem!" In his speeches, Herzl invoked one of the most heartfelt Jewish prayers: "If I forget thee, Oh Jerusalem, let my right hand wither!"

This nationalist interpretation understood antisemitism as deriving from deep, virtually ineradicable factors in Europe's culture and history. No display of Jewish virtue, eagerness to assimilate, education or revolutionary change would alter these attitudes. To conservatives, Jews were radicals; to socialists, they were plutocrats. Antisemitism's material basis was that Jews were different. As in Pharaoh's Egypt, the more Jews living in any country, the more the majority would fear, mistrust, hate, and envy them.

Herzl's view of antisemitism proved accurate. Modern times had brought remarkable improvements in transport and communication, he wrote in 1898. "But one thing only is still as it was when the Turks conquered Byzantium, when Columbus set sail ... when men rumbled over the highway in stagecoaches—and that single thing is the plight of [our] ... people.... After a short breathing space for us modern 'emancipated' Jews, bad times have come again ... not only in the backward countries ... but also in those that are called civilized." Neither wealth nor patriotism, socialist fervor nor scholarly achievement, fine manners nor high connections could inoculate any Jew from the threat of antisemitism. "Even if your present situation is satisfactory and you can eat your supper in untroubled leisure," he warned, the situation might not always be so good. Preparing for the storm about to strike the Jewish people was as essential as buying a winter coat before the snow fell.[80]

"We have honestly endeavored everywhere to merge ourselves in the social life of surrounding communities and to preserve only the faith of our fathers," Herzl wrote. "We are not permitted to do so. In vain are we loyal patriots, our loyalty in some places running to extremes; in vain do we make the same sacrifices of life and property as our fellow-citizens; in vain do we strive to increase the fame of our native land." Jews were treated like strangers in places where they had lived for centuries.[81] The way to explain this problem was as a normal contrast among nations rather than as a case of religious heresy, political conspiracy, economic greed, or racial inferiority. Jews were neither saints nor demons but simply themselves: a people with a history, religion, culture, linguistic heritage, and other characteristics.

Understanding this fact was their "last chance before disappearing." Zionists, Herzl wrote, did not demand that all humanity unite, did not seek to "wear the mask of any other nationality," did not work for revolutionary upheaval.[82] The fundamental Jewish interest lay not in being liberal reformers, local patriots, or revolutionaries—stances that antagonized as many neighbors as they pleased. Those Jews wishing to do so could assimilate; those who wanted to should be free to live in their own state. It was an argument like that of other contemporary nationalist movements. A nation that once governed itself on its own land had been displaced. Yet defeat and suffering had not destroyed a sense of identity and an urge to struggle for renewal in its people's hearts.*

Many Jews, however, opposed Zionism. The most religiously conservative insisted that only the Messiah could ordain a return to the land of Israel; the radicals expected salvation from socialist revolution. Some rich and middle-class Jews, who sought to conceal their identity, reduce it to a marginal religious factor, or disown it altogether, feared such a movement would inflame antisemitism and might cost them their positions in the countries where they lived. Scientists, professionals, and artists worried lest identification with a Jewish people might narrow their horizons or damage their careers. Most of all, the movement had to show the many who were sympathetic but thought a Jewish state an impossibility that their goal was no fantasy. Herzl's statement, "If you will it, it is no dream," had a double meaning. Not only did success entail a great practical effort, it also required a vision worthy of realization.[83]

---

*Other nationalist leaders had similar problems to an extent forgotten today, when the existence of countries like Hungary or Poland, Germany or Italy, Turkey or Syria is taken for granted. Loyalty to local rulers, multinational states, or religious identities was often so powerful that it took decades to persuade or compel people to change their views.

Herzl stressed that Jews were not rejecting Europe, only reacting to its rejection of them. To be a nation, after all, was the way European civilization was organized. By incorporating this idea, Jews would be finding their own place in that world. "To cure the age-old misery the most modern means are called for." Only the assimilation process itself had given rise to the notion that a Jewish identity must be jettisoned by a modern, civilized individual.[84]

In August 1897, at the first world Zionist congress in Basel, Switzerland, Herzl's appearance on the platform set off fifteen minutes of applause and weeping among delegates from over a dozen countries. "At Basel I founded the Jewish state," he wrote in his diary. "If I said this out loud today, I would be answered by universal laughter. Perhaps in five years, and certainly in fifty, everyone will know it."[85] Almost exactly fifty years later, Israel declared its independence. As one people and one nation, Herzl argued, Jews must work together despite divergent beliefs. Though he was an agnostic, Herzl attended services in Basel to underline his point that Jewish holidays and religious customs were a vital part of the national identity. "Zionism," he explained, "is the return to Judaism even before the return to the Jewish land." The meeting passed a resolution that it would "do nothing that contradicts the Jewish religious laws."

Knowing that the Jews' reputation for financial and political power was both a major cause of antisemitism and largely an illusion, Herzl tried to make it an asset in their own interest. He met with the Ottoman sultan, the German kaiser, Russian cabinet ministers, and other notables, offering Jewish support in exchange for their assistance. This effort laid the basis for the 1917 Balfour Declaration as a charter for a Jewish homeland.

To assimilationist Jews horrified that the new movement confuted their efforts to bury Judaism's national aspects, Herzl asked, "What [have they] done in all these years to relieve the frightful distress of our brothers[?] Where are the results of their work? . . . I am convinced that those Jews who stand aside today with a malicious smile and with their hands in their trousers' pockets, will also want to dwell in our beautiful house."[86] Although the main argument against it was that it was an impossible, impractical dream, Zionism ultimately proved far more practical than its critics' views, which seemed so pragmatic but failed so catastrophically.

With the eight years left to him before his death in 1904 at the early age of forty-four, Herzl united diverse sections of the Jewish community behind his idea, made the movement respectable among non-Jews, put its demands on the international agenda, helped accelerate a cultural renaissance, and built institutions able to carry the struggle to success. The first Zionist congress was held in the centennial year of Mendelssohn's death and Heine's birth. After a century of the experiment in assimilation, Herzl concluded that "The Jews have three roads before them: One is apathetic submission to insult and poverty; another is revolt, outspoken hostility to an unjust social system." The third was to organize themselves, proudly proclaim their heritage, and build a future of their own making.[87] The debate among European Jews over these alternatives would continue for another half century.

2

The Burst Cocoon:
Europe 1897–1940

If the question were put to him: "Since you have abandoned all these characteristics of your countryman (language, religion, nationalism), what is there left of you that is Jewish?" He would reply, "A very great deal, and probably its very essence."
—*Sigmund Freud, introduction to the Hebrew edition of* Totem and Taboo

ARTHUR SCHOLEM was a very angry man on February 15, 1917. His son Werner had been charged with treason for demonstrating against Germany's war effort; another son, Gershom, still living at home, was a Zionist. Arthur sent Gershom a registered letter, addressed to his own house, giving the boy two weeks to move out. Socialism and Zionism, Arthur wrote, were anti-German activities that he would no longer permit under his roof.

He should have been used to incongruities: his mother owned a kosher restaurant, but his father had renamed himself Siegfried in honor of Wagner's opera. In the Scholem house, customs were similarly mixed up. Arthur forbade Jewish expressions, but his wife used them anyway. Friday night was a family night when prayers were said but only partly understood, and Arthur scorned Jewish law by using the Sabbath candles to light a cigar after the meal.

On Passover, the family ate both bread and matzo. Arthur went to work on Yom Kippur and did not fast. He praised the Jewish mission to spread monotheism and ethics, and he disparaged conversion. But the family celebrated Christmas as a German national festival and sang "Silent Night." Arthur insisted on his German identity, but almost all his friends were Jews, and no Christian ever set foot in his home. And when Gershom became a Zionist, his parents bought him a portrait of Herzl and put it under their Christmas tree.

As a result of this mélange, Arthur's four sons personified the quartet of the Passover Haggadah, becoming, respectively, a right-winger; a Communist member of Parliament; a centrist like Arthur; and a Zionist professor who moved to Jerusalem. Decades later, after the Shoah, the first brother continued to call himself a German nationalist. When asked how he could think that way after Hitler, he fumed, "I'm not going to let Hitler dictate my views to me!" Werner, the Communist brother, married a Christian and his own assimilationist father boycotted the couple. Forty years later, after Werner's death in a Nazi concentration camp, his widow converted to Judaism.[1]

The Scholems were by no means atypical: diverse individual stands toward assimilation divided many families; each Jew's contradictory feelings split his own psyche. If being a Jew was purely a matter of religion, those ceasing to believe or practice that doctrine could not be Jews. But if it was more than a religion, antisemites could be right in considering Jews an alien group whose assimilation was impossible. If Jews asserted their own identity, it would seem to prove the antisemites' charge that they were not truly assimilated; but to hide or deny their background incurred a heavy psychological price. Much of twentieth-century European history grew from these paradoxes.

Jews, as their very success showed, did not act quite like non-Jewish counterparts; their beliefs and culture mutated into something paralleling but also different from the wider culture. No matter how much they universalized or abstracted it, their starting point was inevitably marked by their inheritance, personal experience of breaking with that tradition, and fate in being half rejected, half integrated into the societies where they lived.

Together, these influences set specific emphases and bearings for their lives and creations, though Jewish assimilationists heatedly denied it, especially since antisemites claimed this as proof that Jews were not carbon-copy Germans or Russians but aliens with their own agenda. As earnest as Jews were about assimilation, most European nations disbelieved them, understandably incredulous that any group would willingly give up its culture, history, religion, and identity. No matter how much the most urbane Jew detached himself from the community, he was still held accountable for the actions of any other Jew. Every Jewish writer, artist, or thinker knew he was being watched to see if he was transcending the ghetto's narrow limits, embracing a world—or at least nation—that his people had not created.

In response, assimilationists became achievement oriented, insisted on their sincerity, rejecting all the more heatedly any Jewish identity. Understandably they wanted to be judged as individuals, not as members of a group—especially one treated as inferior. The writer Arthur Schnitzler, himself a convert, has a character describe how he "felt himself akin with no one . . . in the whole world: with the weeping [Zionist] Jews as little as with the bawling Pan-Germans in the Austrian Parliament; with Jewish usurers as little as with noble robber-knights; with a Zionist bar-keeper as little as with an [antisemitic] grocer."[2] But rather than having discovered sublime truth, such a person was as driven by his own group's ethos as was everyone else. After all, to think oneself above all communities was a typical belief of Jewish assimilationists, quite atypical of Austrians as a whole.

This blend of rebellion and conformity, of overconfidence and self-hatred among Jewish intellectuals is well illustrated by Lewis Namier. He rebelled against his wealthy Polish Jewish family, which had converted to Catholicism. It had cut off the past; he became a historian. His relatives sought respectability; he became iconoclastic. They buried their Jewishness; he advertised it but looked down on most Jews. Moving to England, he became assimilated in its world of gentlemanly scholarship, but his romantic temperament made him enjoy shocking the staid British. During an argument about colonial policy, Namier stood up, glared around the room, and said loudly, "We Jews and the other colored peoples think otherwise!"[3]

While flaunting his Jewish allegiance and flamboyant outsider status, Namier deeply craved acceptance. His subject was British political history, as if to prove he could know his new society better than its native-born inhabitants. Despite all his worldly success, he was a lonely man who said he had no roots and was a stranger everywhere. He was so hurt when passed over for an Oxford endowed chair that he converted to Christianity.[4]

By so dividing loyalty and confusing identity, wrote the Polish Jewish scientist Leopold Infeld, the assimilation process "deformed character." Though rejected by Polish society, Infeld returned to that country he loved in the late 1940s after many years in America. He despised the Jewish identity into which he was born: "The ghetto is full of misery, dirt, sadness. . . . I tried hard, and often cynically, to burn out of me the traces left by my upbringing. Every successful step outside was bound to increase my contempt for the small, sad world from which I came and my desire to erase its visible signs."[5] Like an escaped convict, he tried to shed "his prisoner's garb and rid himself of the chains still hanging about his ankles." Yet he felt "a curious mixture of hate and love. I could say to myself, 'What do I care about Jews? I am above racial, religious problems and prejudices.' But all my continued attempts to tear off the bonds only prove that these bonds exist, and they will exist to the last day of my life."[6]

Many Jews of Infeld's generation were also attracted to a powerful, modern European civilization and repelled by a Jewish identity that now appeared to them little more than an inferiority complex and a culture whose age and religious content made it seem all the more backward. Being Jewish brought penalties and humiliation without material rewards. The Orthodox approach was seen as archaic and requiring a level of knowledge many assimilating Jews now lacked. Tradition purposefully stultified to defend itself by building higher walls against the outside world. Orthodoxy was often less imbued with the Torah's spirit than with legal details. Rabbis used social coercion to enforce conformity. Many youths felt piety synonymous with reactionary, equating abuses with Judaism as a whole. Little Jewish literature existed in English, Russian, German, or French, which made a deeper understanding of Judaism inaccessible to those ignorant of Hebrew. The watered-down Reform version offered little spiritual comfort or emotional involvement.[7]

So powerful was the appeal of mainstream European culture that parents trying to force children into tradition often failed. A German Jew wrote that his father's attempt to make him into a great Talmud scholar, "achieved the opposite of what he intended." After being ordered to stop attending the theater and opera, he ran away from his yeshiva's "stifling atmosphere. . . . For the next thirty years—recalling the torments of my youth—I could not bring myself even to take a peek into a Hebrew book." This rebellion "marked the beginning of my inner independence from my father, who until then had determined how my life would be shaped, without regard for my wishes and inclinations."[8]

Urban, middle-class European Jews generally put their faith in an assimilationist covenant promising acceptance in exchange for surrendering their religion and customs, gaining a Western education, and adopting the dominant culture. The ferocity of their feud with tradition would fade as its power over them declined. No matter how secular they became, they had once studied the sacred texts, knew their languages, and could look back on a childhood in that universe of customs and sensibility. After the 1890s, though, a new generation whose parents had already abandoned tradition had no such memories. They were rebelling against a spiritual vacuum and symbols too stripped of meaning to merit respect. They either had no religious instruction or it was so poor, so openly self-ridiculing, as to alienate them further.

As so often happens, social and intellectual revolt was a byproduct of familial rebellion.* Gifted sons turned against Orthodox fathers to become assimilated, or against assimilated fathers to be radical. Gustav Mahler's father read French philosophers; Victor Adler's father, though religious, was a revolutionary democrat.[9] Both sons converted to Christianity. Such people reacted against bourgeois success, wrote the critic Walter Benjamin, as he did himself, by "building their counterworlds in spiritual protest, they incisively shaped the future of science, philosophy, and literature."[10]

Vienna, Austria-Hungary's capital, was a center of cultural creativity and a distinct Jewish assimilationist civilization. The city's Jewish population increased sevenfold between 1857 and 1867, the year Austrian Jews were granted full citizenship. By 1880, Jews made up 10 percent of its residents. As in other European cities, many were recent migrants from the rural east whose traditional religious ways divided them from both the Christian majority and from more integrated Jews, who feared this influx menaced their own status. But whether veterans or new arrivals, they took advantage of new opportunities with ambition, vision, and zeal. Still barred from some jobs and flooding into others, assimilating Jews emerged as a society different from both Christian Austrians and traditional Jews. Whether converted or not, they straddled two identities, keeping to their own neighborhoods and groups. The Austrian writer Stefan Zweig, like Freud, said that 90 percent of his friends were Jews. Jews found it easier to adopt gentile culture than to make gentile comrades.[11]

The conversion rate in Vienna was Europe's highest, among thousands of Jews indifferent to their heritage, tired of discrimination, eager to obtain civil-service and teaching posts barred to unconverted Jews, or wishing to marry Christians.[12] What is surprising, however, is not how many Jews converted or drifted away but how many did not do so. Some could not forget that they were Jews; more were not permitted to forget. When Al-

---

* "'Some time ago I stopped identifying all the evils of life with my father and therefore with being a Jew." Herman Wouk, *Marjorie Morningstar* (New York, 1957), p. 177.

bert Einstein moved from Switzerland to Germany in 1914, he later wrote, "I discovered for the first time that I was a Jew. I owed this discovery more to the gentiles than Jews."[13]

"I'm not baptized," said one of Schnitzler's assimilationist characters, "but on the other hand I am certainly not a Jew either . . . for the simple reason that I never felt myself to be a Jew."

"If someone were to bash in your top hat [since] you have a somewhat Jewish nose," replied another, "you'd realize pretty quick that you were insulted because you were a Yiddisher fellow."[14] Viennese assimilationists might treat their Jewishness as irrelevant, but others still considered them to be Jews. Jews did not have a persecution mania, wrote Schnitzler, discrimination was real. Any club they joined or party they backed was tagged as a Jewish one or pushed Jews out to avoid that stigma. Rabbi Joseph Bloch complained in the 1880s that Jews in public life "forgot that they were Jews and thought their enemies would not remember it either." Writers, editors, and journalists lived "in perpetual fear of being labeled as Jewish" and so avoided defending Jewish causes.[15] The same factors applied to the many Socialist leaders (Rudolf Hilferding, Otto Bauer, Max and Friedrich Adler) who, Jews by origin, tried to distance themselves from that community.[16]

The same pattern prevailed in Germany. When Börne, Heine, and others founded Young Germany to extol democracy, enemies dubbed the group Young Palestine. Now the Independent Students Association, which rejected discrimination, became known as the "Jews' Club," despite its Christian majority. Stefan George, the humanist who had many Jewish followers (and whose non-Jewish devotees were among the most courageous anti-Nazis), was careful to keep them in the minority. The liberal Democratic Party, many of whose founders and voters were Jews, became known as the "Jew Party" and declined until, in 1930, it merged with an antisemitic party.[17]

Contrary to expectations, then, assimilation could intensify danger. Frock-coated Jewish lawyers and writers were as disliked as black-coated Jewish moneylenders or rabbis. Assimilated Jews were a separate caste hated by envious rivals. An antisemite in a satirical Viennese novel explained, "We must give up either our Christian ways, our own life and customs, or the Jews. The trouble is simply that we Austrian Aryans are no match for the Jews, that we are ruled, oppressed, and violated by a small minority because this minority possesses qualities which we lack."[18]

It was becoming evident that Christian societies that once demanded the Jews merge and disappear were now rejecting them as full members. In addition, Jews were also starting to debate the price for gaining equal rights. "Neither assimilation, Zionism, socialism, conversion, nor self-hatred would bring closer the days when Jews could breathe easily without persecution," historian Robert Wistrich wrote.[19] Antisemitism was aroused by the fact that Germans believed the most traditional and most assimilated Jews were in league against them.

In reaction to such experiences, some Jews became increasingly skeptical of assimilation or alarmed at its destructive—perhaps fatal—effect on their collective survival. The year 1897 may be viewed as a turning point in this process: the first Zionist congress was held; the Jewish Socialist Bund was founded in Russia; Sigmund Freud joined the Jewish fraternal organization B'nai B'rith, during what he called his "year of decision" in creating psychoanalysis; the antisemite Karl Lueger became Vienna's mayor; and the composer Gustav Mahler as well as the writer Italo Svevo, perhaps Italy's greatest novelist, converted.

In that year, too, the Viennese Jewish parliamentary deputy Joseph Karels complained to his colleagues, "When you consider the way in which the poor Jews strive to gain your favor in the ranks of the Germans, how they try to accumulate the treasures of German culture, how they work in the sciences, some perhaps dying young as a result—and all the thanks they get is that they are not even accepted as human beings."[20]

As he suggested, Jews throughout central Europe fell in love with German culture. To them, Kant, Schiller, Goethe, and Lessing became the new prophets of all that was sublime and beautiful in life. "For many Jews," wrote Gershom Scholem, "the encounter with Friedrich Schiller was more real than their encounter with actual Germans."[21] They considered themselves to be the guardians of German culture's best values, as one German Jew said in 1912, "administering the spiritual property of a nation which denies our right and our ability to do so."[22]

The most assimilation-oriented, noble sentiments provoked rather than defused antisemitism. It was hard to respect or trust someone who surrendered too easily. Each idea or specific aspect of their culture the Jews seemed to appropriate made many Germans jealous and persuaded some to renounce these concepts altogether. Others resented it when Jews seemingly told Germans how to live. They wanted the Jews to disappear, not to dissolve themselves by assimilation into a new cosmopolitan, secular, liberal, or socialist order. For their part, non-Jewish allies proved inconstant.

"Who created the Liberal movement in Austria? . . . the Jews," wrote Schnitzler. "By whom have the Jews been betrayed and deserted? By the Liberals." The German nationalists, Socialists, and Communists would follow the same pattern: "As soon as you've drawn the chestnuts out of the fire they'll start driving you away from the table. It always has been so and always will be so."[23]

Formerly ridiculed as ragged and backward, Jews were now attacked for being prosperous and educated, accused of imposing a foreign culture on the German people. Once derided as adherents of a contemptible religion, nonpracticing or even converted Jews were now jeered as an inferior race. As assimilationists celebrated their success, wisps of smoke already signaled the fire that would burn to the ground the edifice they had built.

Yet between the first portents of disaster in the 1890s and the onset of their annihilation in 1938, Vienna's Jews created many cultural treasures during an era which—like the times of democratic upsurge one hundred and fifty years earlier—began with great hope. His generation, said the composer Ernst Bloch in 1912, anticipated messianic change. Freud wrote, "Every diligent Jewish boy carried a minister's portfolio in his satchel."[24] Whereas Heine called conversion his ticket to Western civilization, Freud noted that learning was replacing baptism, though even in his day one had to convert to become a full professor in Vienna, one reason he chose a career outside the university.[25]

In the end, trying to assimilate through education and cultural achievement again made the Jews distinct in being so successful and oriented toward intellectual matters. On Schnitzler's 1891 list of Vienna's literary leaders, at least sixteen out of twenty-three were of Jewish descent. From the late 1880s to 1904, 24 to 33 percent of Vienna university students were Jews, a figure kept down by admissions quotas. About 75 percent of lawyers and well over half the doctors and journalists in Vienna were Jews. Between half and two-thirds of Vienna's educated class were Jews or recent converts.[26]

These people were, as Schnitzler wrote, either "ashamed of being Jews, or . . . proud of it and were frightened of people thinking they were ashamed of it."[27] To all the inner Jewish psychic and familial tensions were added political and social pressures. Caught between such forces, it is not surprising that Viennese Jews both invented psychoanalysis and furnished its patients.

The Viennese Jewish novelist Joseph Roth satirized these attitudes in a book appropriately entitled *Flight without End*, with anomalies like a Jewish club with a quota on accepting Jewish members and a Jewish woman who became depressed when anyone told a joke, lest it ridicule Jews and she had to decide whether to laugh. Since certain German army units tried to bar Jews, some rich Jews tried to place sons in them, thinking it a status symbol to gain entrance to an otherwise Jew-free place. Jewish student fraternities emulated Christian ones by dueling and, since the non-Jewish clubs refused to duel Jews, had to beat each other up.[28]

Such contradictions suffused the dilemma of assimilationist Jews in Vienna. They had become wealthy and successful without being truly secure or accepted. They were the city's cultural glory without being its pride. They abandoned old customs but could not quite make the new ones their own. The perfect case was a contemporary novel's Jewish hero who sought to prove his Viennese identity by singing a folk song in perfect local dialect, only to be congratulated by critics who declared that they never knew Jews could sing Viennese songs so well. Do what he could, he could not be completely and purely a Viennese.[29]

Thus, rather than integrating them, the assimilation process gave Jews distinct professions and ideas. No longer distinguished by clothes, kosher food, or Sabbath observance, they were now set apart by disproportionate tendencies toward humanism, secularism, liberalism, socialism, and modernism. Breaking with their own old ways made them irreverent toward conventions, especially those, like church-oriented painting or music, conflicting with that Jewish background. Still, while a Jew might act the bohemian aesthete, intellectual, or aristocrat, the cafés where he went to play those roles were full of other Jews doing the same thing. The critic Karl Kraus quipped that even if Jews became nearly indistinguishable from Christian counterparts, they could always be told apart by the great emphasis they put on that fact.[30]

The popular composer Gustav Mahler and the social critic Karl Kraus, both converts, illustrated the Viennese Jews' dilemma. First, some non-Jewish counterparts rebuffed them. A friend of Mahler's urged his Christian fiancée to break the engagement since she was "a fine girl . . . racially so pure." The humanist poet Rainer Maria Rilke warned Kraus's wife-to-be of a "last ineradicable difference" between them.[31] Second, Mahler and Kraus were ill at ease with themselves. Despite personal success and conversion, Mahler felt "thrice homeless: as a Bohemian among Austrians; as an Austrian among Germans; and as a Jew everywhere in the world. Everywhere I am regarded as an interloper, nowhere am I what people call 'desirable.' " Mahler, his wife commented, "had no wish to be reminded of origins, family, race, those emblems of the weight of the earth."[32]

Kraus obsessively exposed other people's hypocrisy in *Die Fackel,* his controversial, popular magazine published between 1899 and his death in 1936. But he, too, had things to hide. In a 1913 essay he insisted that whatever Jewish characteristics were, he did not possess them. Kraus once described Herzl as a tool of antisemites for calling attention to such distinctions. Like many Jewish intellectuals, he could dissect the origins of someone else's thought but, looking in the mirror, saw only a man who had given birth to himself. Kraus's bitter, sarcastic polemics, said Walter Benjamin, "came from the gun he held to his own heart." Kraus confirmed this,* "Antisemitism is the mentality . . . that means seriously a tenth part of the jibes that the stock-exchange wit [an antisemitic way of saying a Jew] holds ready for his own blood."[33]

Despite Kraus's denial, his own cultural products and those of other assimilating Jews were infused with Jewish characteristics. "Everything—language and fact—falls for him within the sphere of justice," explained Benjamin. "To worship the image of divine justice in language—even in the German language—that is the genuinely Jewish somersault." The poet Hugo von Hofmannsthal's only direct reference to his heritage was the line, "Weariness of long forgotten races, I cannot brush off my eyelids." The philosopher Ludwig Wittgenstein, from a converted family, wrote in his diary, "Amongst Jews 'genius' is found only in the holy man. Even the greatest of Jewish thinkers is no more than talented. (Myself for instance.)"[34] Others left traces even in scientific work, like the anthropologist Franz Boas and sociologist Emile Durkheim, who insisted that environment, not race, shaped character—a crucial axiom for the possibility of assimilation.

Schnitzler depicted Jews' "eagerness to assimilate to an environment that despised them" in his 1908 novel, *The Road to the Open.* A Jewish character complains of Christian friends "who gorge themselves sick at Jewish houses and then [criticize] the Jews as soon as they get on the doorsteps." They should at least wait a few minutes longer, he adds with Viennese irony. The novel features a dialogue between a Zionist, Leo, and an assimi-

---

*Compare to Norman Mailer: "No antisemite can begin to comprehend the malicious analysis of his soul which every Jew indulges every day." Abraham Chapman, *Jewish-American Literature* (NY, 1974), p. 626.

lationist, Heinrich, observed by George, a Christian aristocrat. Leo remarks, "One really can't bear a grudge against these people if they regard themselves as the natives and you and me as the foreigners," for that only reflected reality.[35]

Heinrich responds, "My home is here, just here, and not in some land which I don't know, the description of which doesn't appeal to me the least bit and which certain people now want to persuade me is my fatherland on the strength of the argument that was the place from which my ancestors some thousand years ago were scattered into the world."

Leo says that Heinrich merely mistakes the accident of birthplace for the essence of identity. If he moved elsewhere, he would speak a different language and write about other subjects.

Establishing a Jewish state, answers Heinrich, would defy progress, which requires abandoning "customs which you have now ceased to observe and some of which seem as ridiculous and in as bad taste to you, as they do to me." What they had in common was that "you will never migrate to Palestine all your life long, even if Jewish states were founded and you were offered a position as prime minister . . . [and] in spite of my complete indifference to every single form of religion I would positively never allow myself to be baptized," even to escape discrimination.

Leo asked what he would do if Jews were again massacred. That would never happen again in Austria, objected George, and the trio laughed together at his pledge on behalf of all Christendom. Yet such days did come again in those characters' "life-time."

No one was more aware of this fear than Franz Kafka, born in Prague in 1883. Viennese assimilationists might camouflage themselves in a hegemonic German culture, but in Prague loyalty to things German set Jews apart from the Czech majority. In the imperial capital, Schnitzler could find fulfillment in an audience's cheers; Kafka's banal life as insurance clerk made him yearn for the ethereal while his role as the firm's token Jew gave daily experience of what literary scholar Robert Alter called an "awareness of Jewishness as a condition of being unwanted, mistrusted, transparently dependent on the favor of others."[36]

In contrast to Schnitzler's Heinrich, Kafka had difficulty seeing his hometown as his home, "The unhealthy old Jewish town within us is far more real than the new hygienic town around us. With our eyes open we walk through a dream: ourselves only a ghost of a vanished age."[37] In his stories, this sense of displacement is extended to the whole world, where, the lightly disguised wandering Jew knows, "No one will come to help me . . . every door and window would remain shut, everybody would take to bed and draw the bedclothes over his head."[38]

Whatever Kafka's universal implications, his stories obviously reproduced problems and situations faced by contemporary Jews. Though ultimately failing, Kafka wanted to escape, not celebrate, alienation. He became interested in Yiddish and dabbled in studying religious texts; toyed with learning Hebrew, becoming a Zionist or emigrating. But he remained too indecisive even to marry and maintain the Jewish line he wanted so badly to extend intellectually. He imagined a patriarchal Abraham in his own image, ready to serve God "with the promptness of a waiter" but unable to get away from his busy shop, or simply refusing to believe that God wanted him,* fearing, "the world would laugh itself to death" at his presumption.[39]

His short stories are often parables replicating the Jewish duality that assimilation sought to deny: the existence of choice about what others took for granted, a sense of being in two places or being two people at once: new city and ghetto; Prague and Jerusalem; German culture and Jewish culture; Czech or German loyalty; Jew and citizen of Western civilization; Israelite and cosmopolitan member of the human race. Falsely accused, the Jew would be put on trial (*The Trial,* 1915); no matter what strategy was attempted, he would be denied access to the sanctuary (*The Castle,* 1922). With Kafka's x-ray vision, all becomes arbitrary:

> Why, by the way, was I so intent on staying with him? . . . I'll stay with him and slowly he'll draw the dagger . . . and then plunge it into me. . . . Why is it that around me things sink away like fallen snow, whereas for other people even a little liqueur glass stands on the table steady as a statue? . . . Just look at yourself! The entire length of you is cut out of tissue paper, yellow tissue paper, like a silhouette, and when you walk one ought to hear you rustle. . . . What makes you all behave as though you were real? Are you trying to make me believe I'm unreal, standing here absurdly on the green pavement? You, sky, surely it's a long time since you've been real, and as for you Ringplatz [Prague's main avenue], you never have been real. . . . It's negligent of me to go on calling you so-called moon, moon. Why do your spirits fall when I call you "forgotten paper lantern of a strange color"?[40]

---

*Bob Dylan echoes the thought in his song "Highway 61 Revisited": "God said to Abraham, 'Kill me a son' / Abe says, 'Man, you must be puttin' me on.' "

He presents Jews in Aesopian guise, as an apparently inferior species that nonetheless prefers its own way and views assimilation skeptically. In one story, an ape imitates human customs to try to regain his freedom, not because he thinks humans superior but merely "because I needed a way out, and for no other reason."[41] In another, canines "are drawn to each other and nothing can prevent us from satisfying the communal impulse; all our laws and institutions, the few that I still know and the many that I have forgotten, go back to this longing for the greatest bliss we are capable of, the warm comfort of being together." Although widely dispersed and diverse, their "one desire is to stick together," though many of them now obey laws that are not their own and are even directed against them.[42]

These laws and slanders would eventually be activated, as in *The Trial*, where the lies told about Joseph K. led to his arrest "without having done anything wrong."[43] For the hunted mouse folk in "Josephine the Singer," life was "very uneasy, every day brings surprises, apprehensions, hopes, and terrors, so that it would be impossible for a single individual to bear it all did he not always have by day and night the support of his fellows."* Josephine's crooning—like religion—both comforts and endangers them: "When we are in a bad way politically or economically, her singing is supposed to save us, nothing less than that, and if it does not drive away the evil, at least gives us the strength to bear it."[44]

Another Kafka theme was tradition's weakening by a people's decay and amnesia or by God's silence and distance. "What is the Talmud if not a message from the distance?" he asked, but, "It is an extremely painful thing to be ruled by laws that one does not know," he wrote.[45] Jews are like denizens of a frontier town so remote from the capital as to have forgotten their own laws and to know no longer whether the king is dead or ignores them: "Over and over again it must be repeated. There is perhaps no people more faithful to the Emperor than ours . . . but the Emperor derives no advantage from our fidelity."[46]

Yet how they could stay faithful was another question and while anything seemed possible, Kafka could not decide what should be done. His generation was like ambivalent caterpillars, "With their posterior legs they were still glued to their fathers' Jewishness and with their waving anterior legs they found no new ground. The ensuing despair became their inspira-

---

*Comparing Jews to mice, a theme used by Kafka, Steven Spielberg's film *An American Tale*, and Art Spiegelman's book *Maus*, projects a weakness that can be a source of sympathy or contempt.

tion." The result was not German literature but Jewish literature written in German.[47] With legs waving in all directions, more than one kind of metamorphosis was possible. If one might wake up to find himself a German or Jew, Christian or Marxist, he could also arise as an insect, as did Gregor Samsa in Kafka's story of a young man who is transformed into an insect.

Such morsels of the supernatural could break into orderly Prague.* Even bereft of the old map, one might still seek God. Half asleep in a friend's guest bedroom one night, Kafka saw an angel enter through the ceiling with an important message for him. He soon realized it was only a ship's figurehead hung on the wall. The hilt of its sword had been made into a candle holder. So Kafka climbed on a chair, put a candle in, lit it, and then sat late into the night under the angel's faint flame.[48] Even a religion in which one no longer believed could help light the way.

But as Kafka hinted, the Western Jew had lost his old place without gaining a real new one. Obsession with fashion now outbid preoccupation with eternity; new novels triumphed over old prayers; legend fell before science; laws exacting self-discipline gave way to the thrill of freedom. Yet in the process, life was also spiritually drained. Whatever the material gains, assimilating Jews had sacrificed what Albert Einstein called in 1921 "an enviable state of psychological equilibrium." The ghetto, proclaimed social critic Max Nordau in 1897, had also been a refuge where "the opinion of the outside world had no influence.... One tried to please one's co-religionists, and their applause was the worthy contentment of one's life." Ghetto Jews lacked much, explained the historian Louis Namier, but "had one great advantage over us—each of them belonged in every fiber of his being to a community in which he was wholly absorbed, in which he felt himself a fully privileged member."[49]

If some of these problems described by assimilating Jews were also elements of the general human condition, they coincided most immediately with Jewish culture and assimilation. No one more clearly illustrates this fact—and the rise of a new type of Jewish identity among those rejecting both tradition and full assimilation—than Sigmund Freud. It was not "entirely a matter of chance that the first advocate of psychoanalysis was a Jew," as Freud himself explained. "To profess belief in this new theory called for a certain degree of readiness to accept a position of a solitary opposition—a position with which no one is more familiar than a Jew."[50]

*See Disraeli's parallel remark about Manchester on p. 18.

Precisely because psychoanalysis was so beleaguered and so much less science than unprovable surmise, Freudians, like Marxists, feared their claim to uncover universal, timeless truths would be ridiculed as the product of a particular group and situation. Thus, Freud and the movement sought to play down its overwhelmingly Jewish composition and the roots of many of its ideas in the assimilation process. Psychoanalysis advocated the painful uncovering of a past that one would prefer to keep hidden, a perfect analogy for the crisis of assimilation. Freud proposed that only by digging out the past, facing it, and integrating it into the consciousness could one's problems be resolved.

But Freudians—and Marxists, too—were loath to use their analytical tools on themselves. Detaching Freud's views from his origins should be as alien to psychoanalysis as it should be for Marxism's materialist philosophy to deny the importance of its founder's social position. For as Marx wrote—but ignored in his own case—even the educator must be educated. Ideas come from somewhere, and the past is not so easily jettisoned. One of Freud's examples of a revealing slip of the tongue was about a Jewish convert who referred to his children as *"Juden"* (Jews) instead of *"Jungen"* (young ones).[51]

Freud himself affirmed his identity, though he had more trouble in defining it. "My parents were Jews," he wrote, adding, "I, too, have remained a Jew," a wording that showed this was a choice one could not take for granted. Sigmund's parents were raised as Orthodox but became Reform. He was antireligious, his sole affiliation being with the secular Jewish fraternal organization, B'nai B'rith. "I never understood why I should be ashamed of my descent or, as one was beginning to say, my race."[52]*

"This is what I believe," he assured his future wife, who came from an Orthodox family, during their courtship: "Even if the form wherein the old Jews were happy no longer offers us any shelter, something of the core, of the essence of this meaningful and life-affirming Judaism will not be absent from our home."[53] He had not intermarried and did submit—albeit reluctantly—to a religious wedding. But he would not let his wife observe Jewish holidays and brought up their children with no religious instruction at all. He later even claimed to have forgotten any Hebrew and to know nothing about Judaism.

Freud wrote a friend about an Orthodox youth he saw on a train as a

*See chapter 5.

typical Jew, "cunning, mendacious, kept by his adoring relatives in the belief that he is a great talent, but unprincipled and without character." He
discovered that the boy "hailed from [a Moravian town]: a proper compost
heap for this sort of weed."[54] Yet a psychoanalyst might do a double take
here. Freud, too, was a young man at the time, whose family came from a
similar town and thought him, too, a genius. Glaring contemptuously at
this paragon of traditional Judaism, Freud saw himself as he might have
been or as non-Jews saw him, stirring his angry need to prove his own degree of assimilation by denying any similarity.

A parallel experience occurred when his father recounted how he once
went for a walk in his hometown, "beautifully decked out, with a new fur
cap on my head. Along comes a Christian, knocks off my cap into the muck
with one blow, and shouts, 'Jew, off the sidewalk!' " Freud asked, "And what
did you do?" "I stepped into the road and picked up my cap." This response, he wrote, "did not seem heroic to me."[55] In contrast to this weakness, Freud wanted to be bold, both physically and intellectually. When
called a "dirty Jew" on a train, he recounted, he stood up to the bully. His
own son would have a memory of a father who charged antisemites swing-
ing his walking stick. And that son would fight two duels to defend his own
honor while a university student.[56]

Freud's famous statement that he was "a godless Jew"—often interpreted as showing his distance from Judaism—clearly defined himself as
both atheist and Jew. To Freud and Jewish intellectuals of his time, religion
was a mark of backwardness and superstition even more than to Christian
counterparts. Jews and Christians might then meet as equals on the field of
rational scientific thought, though Freud himself doubted the latter would
abandon a religion so thoroughly reinforced by the surrounding culture.
But during Freud's time, Jewishness was taking on national connotations as
the Jewish people, literature, and Hebrew language were revived by the
most outspoken atheists trying to refurbish a religious legacy with a secular
historical one. His ambiguity, like that of many others, arose from a contempt for traditional, religious, "ghetto" Jews combined with an affinity for
proud, secular, nationalist Jews.

In this era, lack of adherence to Judaism was not necessarily the preface
to total assimilation. The anticlericalism of French intellectuals did not
make them less patriots; on the contrary, it intensified their national identity. As this role model spread among Jews and antisemitism mounted,
Freud could state by 1931, "I am a fanatical Jew. I am very much astonished

to discover myself as such in spite of all efforts to be unprejudiced and impartial."[57] His identity had overcome even his scientific perspective on life.

Indeed, Freud's friends were mostly Jews, and in this circle he used Yiddish phrases, Jewish jokes, and biblical references. To his leading disciple in Berlin, Freud wrote, "It is kindred Jewish traits that attract me in you." Freud also manifested the counterlife syndrome so frequent among assimilating Jews. He collected antiquities, which put him "in high spirits and speak of distant times and lands." He felt "strange secret yearnings . . . perhaps from my ancestral heritage—for the East and the Mediterranean and for a life of quite another kind," words reminiscent of Disraeli's. After seeing Herzl's play "The New Ghetto," Freud dreamed about "the Jewish question, the worry about the future of one's children, whom one could not give a homeland." He was sympathetic to Zionism, referring to "our" Hebrew university in Jerusalem and "our" settlements. From Rome, he sent a postcard of the arch marking the Roman triumph of Jerusalem two millennia earlier, writing, "The Jew survives it!"[58] His flamboyance, passion for knowledge, and a creative bent he called a "succession of daringly playful fantasy and relentlessly realistic criticism" were common attributes in Jewish intellectual life.[59]

Freud also had many German traits, from a stiff, methodical character to a love for dressing in lederhosen and feathered hat to take nature hikes. As he asserted in 1926, "My language is German. My culture, my attainments are German. I considered myself German intellectually." Antisemitism made him feel more Jewish, but if Jews behaved inappropriately Freud felt his desire to be accepted as German thwarted, as when a Jewish boy at a spa where he was vacationing spilled water on a guest in front of gentiles. A well-meaning German lady praised his own well-behaved brood by saying, "Your children, Herr Professor, look so Italian." Not good enough to be Germans, perhaps, but not so bad as to be Jews.[60]

Many of Freud's ideas deal with aspects of life and thought especially intense in the assimilationist milieu. Character is shaped by one's past, despite attempts to bury it. To see parent/child relations dominated by antagonism paralleled the intergenerational disputes over the degree of assimilation that touched all Jewish families in that era. After all, continuity is also a powerful force. An Austrian Christian pursuing a centuries-old way of life would be less inclined to think in such terms, whereas the last Jew in a family line murdered the memory and life work of a string of ancestors going back three thousand years.

In examining aggression, Freud could not forget past atrocities toward Jews resulting from irrational hatreds, which taught "the narcissism of small differences, people seem to enjoy persecuting or at least ridiculing immediate neighbors and Jews had been a favored target.... Unfortunately, all the massacres of Jews in the Middle Ages were not enough to make that age more peaceful and more secure for their Christian comrades." "A religion, even when it calls itself the religion of love," Freud noted, "must be hard and loveless against those who do not belong to it."[61]

Whatever Freud's personal pride in being Jewish, though, he felt any ethnic identification would poison the psychoanalytic movement. So Freud—like the Jewish leaders of Marxist parties—set out to find an Aryan prince as successor. "Don't forget," he wrote a disciple, that the acceptance of psychoanalysis by Carl Jung, a Christian and a minister's son, was "all the more valuable [to save] psychoanalysis from the danger of becoming a Jewish national concern." He told another that the Aryans "are fundamentally alien to me," but, in dealing with Jung as in assimilating to German culture, "We must, as Jews, if we want to join in anywhere, develop a bit of masochism."[62]

Freud took this stance even though he knew of his designated protégé's antisemitism. At the 1910 psychoanalytic congress, he told Jewish followers at a secret meeting of his readiness to retire in favor of Jung. As Jews, they were "incompetent to win friends for the new teaching. Jews must be content with the modest role of preparing the ground.... We are all in danger." Only Jung could save them. Soon, though, the two men quarreled on key issues. Freud concluded that his effort to assimilate the "goyim" into psychoanalysis had failed. Jews and Christians "separate themselves like oil and water."[63] After a Jewish psychologist, once romantically involved with Jung and yearning to have an "Aryan-Jewish" child, married a Jew, Freud wrote her in 1912, "I am, as you know, cured of the last shred of my predilection for the Aryan cause." He hoped her baby would become "a stalwart Zionist. He or it must be dark in any case, no more towheads. Let us banish all these will-o'-the-wisps! . . . We are and remain Jews. The others will only exploit us and will never understand or appreciate us." By 1915, he wrote of Jung's "antisemitic condescension toward me."[64]

Long before the Nazis took power, Freud was disillusioned about assimilation. When an interviewer said Jews were overintellectualized and psychoanalysis bore that mark, Freud responded, "So much the better for psychoanalysis then!" He had defined himself "in his essential nature a

Jew" and this ultimate rationalist was willing to ponder that "miraculous thing . . . which—inaccessible to any analysis so far—makes the Jew."[65]

But most Jewish intellectuals were still attracted either to assimilation or to leftist causes. Jewish politics and self-image were only gradually being remade. One of the architects was Max Nordau, born Simon Südfeld, a rabbi's son, in Budapest in 1849. As a youth, he broke from Judaism "and since then I have always felt as a German, and as a German only." Changing his name from one meaning "south field" to the German word for "north" seemed to mark a switch from a Mediterranean to Aryan allegiance.[66]

Like Freud and Herzl, Nordau began as a German nationalist. Believing that the main human impulse was a desire for community, he thought to find it in a union with German culture. In an 1887 novel his hero returns to his beloved Germany after many years abroad, speaking in terms that might have easily been applied to Judaism: "I reproach myself for having emigrated. It is convenient to turn one's back on one's country and to search for more pleasant circumstances abroad. . . . Only a self-seeker deserts his people in its struggle against pressure and darkness and that one has no right at long distance to play the happily redeemed and criticize conditions at home while those who remained behind fight bitterly to improve conditions."[67]

Nordau also expected the spread of learning and science would solve the world's problems. But hints of a reconsideration appear in his 1894 play. When the ambitious main character hides his humble origins, a friend urges, "You must feel all of yourself as possessing worth, including your origin. For that you have hitherto not been courageous enough. But you must learn it." After seeing the Dreyfus trial and meeting Herzl, Nordau was ready for that step. "Jew-hatred is not the result of antisemitic lies and insinuations," he wrote, "but on the contrary, the lies and insinuations are the result of the antisemitic feelings."[68]

Elected vice president at the 1897 Zionist Congress, Nordau took up the task of rallying Jewish pride and self-respect trampled by millennia of persecution: "It is the greatest triumph for antisemitism that it has brought the Jews to view themselves with antisemitic eyes. The Jews consider themselves as pariahs." So overwhelming was the assimilationist impulse that barely one-fifth, Nordau estimated, of those who won prominence in science, literature, the arts, or politics, remained Jews. Whereas their ancestors had kept the faith in the face of torture and death, the new generation relinquished it for personal advantage. Rather than a way to gain the right "to live more freely as Jews," assimilation had come to mean the surrender of Jewishness in order to adjust to the countries where they lived.[69]

If Jews were treated as equal citizens, they could keep an ethnic identity while fulfilling all obligations to that country. They would remember their membership in a people with a great past and, perhaps, a glorious future. But if the nationalist interpretation did not gain hegemony among the Jews, Nordau wrote in 1920, the people would not be saved from spiritual and probably physical extinction. The choice was between "Zionism and death."[70]

This slogan would prove literally true in the friendship of Gershom Scholem and Walter Benjamin. They met in 1915, both rebels against German-Jewish bourgeois backgrounds. Like many young Jews moving to the left, Benjamin came from the more affluent, assimilated family. One crucial incident for him seemed like a Kafka story or case for Freud. Urged by relatives to attend synagogue, Benjamin could not find the building. He attributed this forgetfulness to my "dislike of the impending service, in its familial no less than its divine aspect." Suddenly he was "overcome . . . by the thought 'Too late, time was up long ago, you'll never get there' and . . . by a sense of the . . . benefits of letting things take what course they would; and these two streams of consciousness converged irresistibly in an immense pleasure that filled me with blasphemous indifference toward the service, but exalted the street in which I stood."[71]

This exaltation led Benjamin to his main intellectual project: an attempt to grasp a sense of place, not a Jewish place—for which he had no ardor—but the more immediate geography of Berlin and Paris. In personal terms, though, Benjamin continued to be lost. While Scholem moved to Jerusalem in the mid-1920s, Benjamin became interested in Marxism and toyed with joining the Communist Party. Moscow and Jerusalem were not just opposite poles but both alternatives to a German bourgeois life lacking emotional or intellectual enthusiasm. Jerusalem was the more radical choice, requiring a far more thorough personal reevaluation. After all, intellectuals were less committed to the customs and comforts of social class than they were to German culture.[72]

Like Benjamin playing hooky from synagogue, a desire to break with family and religion begat an alienation that sought a resolution by joining some other community. This had been Nordau's path toward the kaiser's empire, as it had been Freud's in seeking the kingdom of science, or for many others hoping to ascend to the dictatorship of the proletariat. "You are endangered more by your desire for community," Scholem wrote Benjamin, "even if it be the apocalyptic community of revolution, than by the horror of loneliness that speaks from so many of your writings."[73]

The behavior of intellectuals in those years was fraught with contradiction. They wanted to leave the Jewish community because they thought it backward but also disassociated themselves because to do so was to their advantage. They wished to assimilate to the places where they lived, but the very existence of this conscious desire branded them as Jews. Distancing themselves from all community to be cosmopolitan and humanist only made them more alienated and incapable of comprehending other people's motives. They held apart from commitment to purify the objectivity of their thought but then abandoned critical faculties in running to join other groups. Hannah Arendt exemplifies this attitude in attributing to Benjamin "the bitter insight that all solutions were not only objectively false and inappropriate to reality, but would lead him personally to a false salvation, no matter whether that salvation was labeled Moscow or Jerusalem."[74] But in the 1930s, the choice between Berlin, Moscow, or Jerusalem was not equally false. The wrong decision would mean torture, futility, and death.

Such was Benjamin's case. When Hitler took power, he fled to Paris. Scholem again encouraged him to come to Jerusalem, even arranging a stipend for him to study Hebrew and the promise of a job. But Benjamin confessed to "a pathological vacillation."[75] As the German army occupied France in 1940, Benjamin crossed into Spain carrying a U.S. visa, his ticket to sanctuary. Faced with an official's threat to send refugees back to France—rescinded a few hours later—Benjamin committed suicide. In those years, he would not be the only one to die partly of unrequited assimilation.

In the decades before Hitler took power, the vast majority of German Jews sincerely sought to assimilate and thought they were succeeding. German Jewish leaders tried to refute antisemitic propaganda rationally, as German culture taught them, presuming it was an aberration. But Jews were the ones isolated in their own concept of Germany. They were understandably deceived by previous progress, their deep sense of being German, and an emphasis on democratic aspects of German culture.

This view was presented, for example, in an 1890 article, "The Chosen People, or Jews and Germans," by Professor Heymann Steinthal of the University of Berlin and the Institute for Jewish Science. His own career seemed to prove the feasibility of coexistence. No longer a people in their own right, he wrote, Jews had to "promote with all our might the . . . moral and spiritual aims of the peoples among which we live, and to cooperate in their national task."[76] Proponents of a German-Jewish synthesis claimed that Jews would prove themselves good Germans by excelling in morality, bravery in battle, and contributing to progress.

The philosopher and political activist Gustav Landauer, too, felt multiple identities he believed could coexist. Humanity was like a garden, he said in 1914, and not all trees were alike. If someone felt a special sense of unity with others, he would not easily be talked out of it. There were not "so many communal relationships which reach back for thousands of years that I should gladly dispense with one of them."[77] He thought his combined German and Jewish identities "do each other no harm but much good," like two brothers who lived in harmony together despite differences, "even so do I experience this strange and intimate unity in duality as something precious." But as in the Bible, fratricide was also a possible outcome. After Landauer led a failed 1918 leftist revolt, German officers murdered him. His dying words were, "I've not betrayed you. You don't know yourselves how terribly you've been betrayed."[78] But these Germans were not deluded: they were merely following their own interests rather than Landauer's views.

Such Jewish theologians as Hermann Cohen agreed with Landauer's view of identity, though not with his radical politics. The Jews' mission to promote ethics, Cohen said in 1916, justified their existence as a separate group. Since Cohen saw the synagogue as the church's conscience, prodding it to continue spreading monotheism, Jews existed for the effect they had on Christians rather than for some value in themselves. Thus Jews had a subordinate fate and it was quite logical for Cohen to complain about Zionism: "Those fellows want to be happy!"[79]

The man to whom Cohen made that last remark was Franz Rosenzweig, whose great-grandfather had directed Mendelssohn's Jewish Free School and whose cousins were now fervent Christians. "We are Christians in every respect," he wrote his parents in 1909. "We live in a Christian state, attend Christian schools, read Christian books, in short, our whole civilization is fundamentally Christian."[80] Like many Jews, Rosenzweig was an atheist regarding Judaism but a potential believer concerning Christianity.

On one hand, Rosenzweig thought no modern scholar could take religion seriously. On the other hand, he was impressed by the faith of a Christian friend of Jewish descent. In 1913, he decided to spend one last Yom Kippur in a small Orthodox synagogue before converting. A profound spiritual experience that day changed his life, and he became a Jewish theologian. Vienna-born Martin Buber, influenced by Hasidism during visits to Eastern Europe, also mixed tradition and modernism, along with Zionism. For him, choosing a Jewish over a German identity was to strive for a oneness in character echoing the link between humans and God.[81]

Such religious reawakenings were rare. But equally the view of Steinthal and Cohen—dominant as it was among Jews—ignored their real lives of unease in German society. When he was eighteen, Hans Morgenthau, later a leading theorist of international affairs, wrote that his life's goal was "to feel that the burden of antisemitism be lifted from my shoulders." Another young Jew noted, "Every Christian citizen immediately belonged and, until proven otherwise, was considered decent; the Jew had to first legitimize himself and prove his decency."[82] Philipp Lowenfeld, a lawyer, recalled no one at school or home ever mentioned the existence of Zionism or "a genuine Jewish national consciousness." He once overheard his father grudgingly say privately that he felt more Jewish every year. "But almost no one was ready to admit that in those days."[83]

The combined lack of self-confidence, the enveloping Christian society, and an ideology preaching submissiveness led to bizarre juxtapositions. A group of well-meaning young German Jews planning social work among poor Jewish immigrants debated whether they should hang a painting of the Virgin Mary at the settlement house—not as a religious statement but as a way to show uncultured newcomers a fine example of enlightened art.[84]

Even by the early 1920s, wrote Scholem, "It was impossible to ignore the huge, blood-red posters with their no less bloodthirsty text" announcing Hitler's speeches. Yet fear and hope blinded most Jews to the threat from fascism. Instead they felt anger at anyone who brought up that subject, preferring to believe in the possibility of integration into that hostile environment. Recognizing the extent of German antisemitism would have meant abandoning that dream.[85]

But there was more than one dream available to European Jews in those decades. Some flitted from solution to solution, seeking a home but incapable of settling anywhere, linking restlessness to liberty or creativity. Perhaps this quest's champion was the writer Arthur Koestler. "Since my school days," Koestler wrote, "I have not ceased to marvel each year at the fool I had been the year before. Each year brought its own revelation and each time I could only think with shame and rage of the opinions I had held and vented before the last initiation."[86] He represented the worldview of a whole caste of assimilating Jews, "steeped in German culture, supporters of the Weimar democracy, yet immune against German chauvinism through a hereditary Judeo-cosmopolitan touch. We were fervently anti-war, anti-militaristic, anti-reactionary. . . . We were very enlightened and reasonable. Only, we failed to see that the age of Reason and Enlightenment was drawing to a close."[87]

Born in Budapest to an assimilated family, Koestler became a romantic, right-wing Zionist and lived in Palestine between 1926 and 1929. In a novel on his adventures there, *Thieves in the Night,* he was self-consciously impartial. The main character, notably named Joseph, is half-Jewish, half-English.[88] Next, he became a Communist and spent 1932 in the Soviet Union. Disillusioned by Stalin's purges, he left the Communist Party in 1938 and wrote *Darkness at Noon.* His comment on being a political exile in Paris—a Frenchman would embrace you then leave you "shivering in the street, condemned to remain forever a permanent tourist or permanent exile"— defined well his personal situation. When Germany invaded, France threw him in a detention camp under awful conditions. A study of Eastern mysticism led to *The Yogi and the Commissar;* another impulse made him claim all Jews were descended from a Turkish clan, *The Thirteenth Tribe.* He finally became an advocate of suicide for the ill and elderly, and followed his own advice.[89]

Other Jews completed the project Rosenzweig had planned by converting or intermarrying in such large numbers that, between 1871 and 1933, the proportion of Jewish children in Germany fell by half. When the Berlin Jewish community's newsletter began printing new converts' names in 1910, some threatened to sue. But nothing would rid Jews of their taint. The great sociologist Georg Simmel—son of converts, married to a Christian, and totally indifferent to Judaism—was denied a full professorship in Germany for thirty years because he was considered a Jew.

Despite his own youthful conversion, Arnold Schoenberg, a founder of modern music, angrily reacted to similar discrimination. "What," he asked in 1923, "is antisemitism to lead to if not to violence?" He praised less assimilated Jews who had remained "uncorrupted and unbroken." A decade later, he chose to join them, formally returning to the community in a ceremony held in Paris. Rejected by Germany, he had decided "to work in the future solely for the national state of Jewry."[90]

But many Jews blamed themselves for antisemitism, not just from self-hatred but also from a hope that if they caused the problem they could also solve it. Walter Rathenau, well-integrated into German society as a powerful business executive, officially withdrew from the Jewish community in 1895. By staying distinctive, he warned in 1911, Jews induced antisemitism. To be accepted by fellow Germans, they must discard all ethnic traits and merge totally, a step upward since German civilization was superior to their own. Rathenau proclaimed, "I have . . . no other blood than German, no other stem, no other people. . . . I share nothing with the Jews [except] what every German shares with them. . . . I am hurt more if a Bavarian declaims against the Prussians than if he does so against the Jews." Jews had to show superior morality by helping others while demanding nothing for themselves.[91]

It was a logical theory: if Jews wanted neighbors to stop being insular, they must give up their own ways. Yet Rathenau failed to understand how assimilation also fueled antisemitism. His political enemies blamed "the Jews" for the policies he advocated. Rightists murdered Rathenau soon after he became Germany's foreign minister in 1922. The Nazis later used his words as proof of Jewish inferiority and his life to show that treason by the Jews caused Germany's defeat in World War I.

Equally tragic was the life of the writer Theodor Lessing, a German superpatriot who thought history had made the Jews ugly and obsolete. By the 1920s, inspired by Zionism and disillusioned by assimilation, he totally changed his view, seeing German society as hostile no matter what Jews did. "We were told: you are parasites on the land of others—and so we tore ourselves loose. . . . We were told: you are decaying and becoming cowardly weaklings—and so we went into battles and produced the best soldiers. . . . We were told: have you not yet learned that your preserving your distinctiveness is treason against all international pan-human values?" Jews should instead be proud to be "a link in a chain that reaches back to Saul and David and Moses. By regenerating himself and by assuming his share of the suffering and struggle that fall to the lot of Jews, let him pave the way for a brighter heaven for his children and the children of his people."[92] In 1933, he was murdered by the Nazi regime's agents in order to still his voice.

Jacob Wassermann, a best-selling novelist, also spoke in terms verging on the antisemitic: "Let the Jews be killed or exiled, let them be made the bugaboo of children and an object of scorn: all this would be less fatal for the culture of mankind than if the Jews themselves were to give up the role which they have hitherto played in the world arena, in accordance with their mission and destiny." Every European village, he proclaimed, meant more to him than the soil of the so-called Holy Land. Jews living in Germany had been improved by German culture, but East European Jews were inferior "profiteers and speculators" who had nothing to do with him, whose family had lived in Germany for six centuries. His most famous book, *Caspar Hauser* (1908), was about a mysterious foundling of unknown antecedents who became a saintly figure. The plot seemed to fulfill the common Jewish assimilationist wish to be one's own ancestor, free of identifying marks of race or religion, admired by all as a universal symbol of ethical, altruistic perfection.[93]

But long before Hitler took power, Wassermann deduced that the Germans would not allow assimilation. His 1921 book, *My Way as German and Jew,* concluded: "Vain to adjure the nation of poets and thinkers in the name of its poets and thinkers. Every prejudice one thinks disposed of breeds a thousand others, as carrion breeds maggots. Vain to present the right cheek after the left has been struck.... Vain to act in exemplary fashion.... Vain to seek obscurity. They say: The coward!... Vain to go among them and offer them one's hand. They say: Why does he take such liberties, with his Jewish obtrusiveness? Vain to keep faith with them, as a comrade-in-arms or a fellow citizen. They say: He is Proteus, he can assume any shape or form. Vain to help them strip off the chains of slavery. They say: No doubt he found it profitable. Vain to counteract the poison. They brew fresh venom. Vain to live for them and die for them. They say: He is a Jew." No sacrifice would suffice, no plea would bring about the Jews' assimilation as equals. Though he "bore a color and stamp of German life" and foreigners saw him as a German writer, Germans saw him as "a product of Jewish cleverness in adaptation and disguise, of the dangerous power of deluding and ensnaring."[94]

Ernst Toller thought obsessively of this problem. As a young German patriot, he rushed to fight in World War I. Disenchanted, he helped lead a 1919 leftist uprising in Bavaria and spent five years in prison. Next, he became a playwright preaching world brotherhood and pacifism. In the end, he lamented that his acts had subverted the Weimar Republic and helped Hitler gain power. In his autobiography, *I Was a German,* Toller described his family's progression from Orthodox grandparents, to Germanophile father, to a boy who felt pain when German playmates called him a Jew and "overwhelming joy" when he passed as an Aryan. To prove himself German, he was ready "to repudiate my mother." But wasn't Germany also his homeland, shaping his spirit and language? "A Jewish mother brought me into this world, Germany has nourished me, Europe has educated me, my home is this earth, and the world my fatherland." He wanted to give them all equal loyalty, "Must I succumb to the madness of my persecutors and accept Jewish instead of German arrogance?" The catch for Toller was that he accepted his persecutor's rules, fearing that failing to fill all these roles would prove them right about his true identity. Unable to resolve this contradiction, he committed suicide in 1939.[95]

Jews like Toller or Walter Benjamin, feeling excluded by German nationalism, sought to attain an internationalist and saintly persona instead. If one could not integrate into Germany, the object of assimilation must be broadened to encompass the whole world. To prove Jews were not inferior, they tried to act, as Wassermann put it, in "exemplary fashion."

That approach was represented by Stefan Zweig, a best-selling novelist and biographer born in 1881. Like many assimilating Jews before him, Zweig wanted to be a bridge between nations by imparting their cultures to each other. Similarly he was compelled to avoid Jewish themes for the superbly ironic reason that such topics would detract from his cosmopolitanism. By 1937, rising antisemitism made him finally affirm his Jewishness in a short novel, *The Buried Candelabrum*. Zweig and his wife committed suicide in Brazil in 1942; his final note stands as an epitaph for the assimilationist experiment. Having seen Europe destroying itself and exhausted by years of wandering as a man without a country, he could go on no longer: "I knew that all behind me was dust and cinders, the past solidified into bitter salt.... Now I do not belong anywhere, everywhere a stranger and at best a guest."[96]

Failing to find such refuge, Kafka's three sisters along with four of Freud's six siblings died in concentration camps. Freud and Einstein were saved from the same fate only by their attainments in Western intellectual civilization, which rescued them from their inability to assimilate into the society where they lived. But they were among a small minority.

"Man can flourish only," Namier claimed, "when he loses himself in community. Hence the moral danger of the Jew who has lost touch with his own people and is regarded as a foreigner by the people of his adoption.... The result is a want of solid foundations in the individual which in its extreme form amounts to moral instability."[97] Truly these generations were unstable and suffered a great deal. But they also achieved more in all sectors of intellectual endeavor than any other small group in all history. Their glory and volatility stemmed from the same root.

Despite Schnitzler's hopeful description, the road was not open. As Wassermann, Lessing, and Rabbi Bloch put it in almost identical terms, there was no escape, no behavior able to forestall the conflict brought by assimilation in those societies. "To whom, then," asked Scholem many years later, "did the Jews speak in that much-talked-about German-Jewish dialogue? They spoke to themselves."[98] Having succeeded in escaping the Jewish community, they mistook this as a wider social revolution. Having surrendered their religion and nationhood, they assumed others were equally willing to do so. Seeing democracy, modernization, and rationalism as their interest, they thought it was others' interest as well.

Rather than being universal and inevitable—a natural phenomenon—intense alienation was a product of the assimilation process. All have a potential to feel that sensation, but it was the Jewish intellectuals' occupational disease. Their material situation made it normal for them to feel abnormal. Instead of the usual human impulse of putting one's self or own group first, their situation pressed them to embrace another's history and interests, like the students in France's African colonies whose school readers' began "Our ancestors, the Gauls..."

The European Jewish intellectuals thought this sacrifice would make them a new elite, the first people thinking in terms of altruism rather than selfishness, scientific rationality rather than supernatural superstition, and egalitarian love for the whole human race rather than nationalism. Yet this noble objective misread the circumstances of real life and human beings. It also rested on individuals' self-interest in promoting career or social status. Cowardice in the face of discrimination and surrender of one's birthright was disguised as the highest form of morality.

In contrast, the plumber Edwin Landau rose to the spiritual heroism necessary in that situation.[99] When the Nazis gained power in 1933, his German identity disintegrated. "For this nation we young Jews had once stood in the trenches in cold and rain, and spilled our blood." Friends from army days and Christian neighbors for whom one had done favors "had a smile on their faces that betrayed their malicious pleasure. This land and this people that until now I had loved and treasured had suddenly become my enemy.

"So I was not a German anymore, or I was no longer supposed to be one. . . . I was ashamed that I had once belonged to this people. I was ashamed about the trust that I had given to so many who now revealed themselves as my enemies. Suddenly the street, too, seemed alien to me; indeed, the whole town had become alien to me." Kafka's vision was coming to life throughout Europe. He visited his ancestors' graves to give up "everything German that I received from three generations" and tell them: "You were mistaken. I, too, have been misled. I now know that I am no longer a German. And what will my children be?"

One evening, he went to a Zionist meeting.

> Had I been asleep all that time, half of my life? Had we not once become a nation and a religious community at Sinai? . . . What if one could . . . inwardly transform the infamy aimed at us into national pride, the abusive word Jew into a name of honor? Would that not show the way out of the inner devastation and despair? Would one not be able again to hold one's head high as before, in spite of everything?
>
> I thought about my school days. Our teacher, standing by the large map, said: "This is the Holy Land, the land of our fathers." And now it was once more to become the land of our children! Perhaps even our land! At the end, "Hatikvah," our national hymn, was sung. I stood up as I once did [for Germany's anthem. Walking home] I felt inwardly freer. . . . Even late in the night there was a throbbing within me: Palestine. . . . Herzl. . . . Think of the children.

Asked to lecture the group, he spoke on Hugo Zuckermann, a Jewish poet killed for his German fatherland in World War I, highlighting the paradox of that unrequited loyalty. As he spoke to the crowded room,

> I saw all the faces turned toward me, with a spellbound look. Yes, within me there began a singing, a glowing, and I saw tears in many young eyes. In a vision I saw the land of which the poet had sung. . . . I was as though in a dream, transported, and the words just flowed from me until I was finished. . . . It was a spiritual elevation. I became calmer and began living anew.

In 1934, he emigrated with his family to the land of Israel.

As antisemitism grew and Hitler seized power, however, assimilating Jews were least prepared to deal with the crisis. At least religious and Zionist Jews had a way to explain persecution and preserve self-esteem. But most Jews were used to judging themselves through neighbors' eyes. "Emigration is easy, but to leave Munich is difficult," said a law professor who committed suicide instead.[100] Freud wrote Zweig in October 1935, "It is sad that we even judge world events from the Jewish point of view, but how could we do it any other way!"[101]

With their sense of personal identity shattered and history mocking their dreams and ideas, Benjamin, Toller, and Zweig found rejection by Europe tantamount to death and threw their lives away. Freud, made of tougher stuff, answered his daughter's talk about the option of suicide, "Why? Because they want us to?" "What progress we are making," he remarked bitterly in 1933. "In the Middle Ages they would have burnt me; now they are content with burning [my] books." But as Freud sighed on reaching safety in London in 1938, "The triumphant feeling of liberation is mingled too strongly with mourning, for one still very much loved the prison from which one has been released."[102]

3

America's Founding Immigrants

These are days when it is bad for Jews who stay at home and bad for those who go elsewhere. In the past, when a man changed his place he changed his luck; now, wherever a Jew goes, his bad luck goes with him. Nevertheless, you find some consolation in moving, because you move yourself from the realm of "certainly" to the realm of "perhaps." . . . For you are certain that the place where you live is hard; perhaps your salvation will come from somewhere else.

—*S. Y. Agnon*, A Guest for the Night, *1939*

"THIS IS NO pile of ruins / Of fossilized wigs and symbols / Or stale and musty Tradition!"[1] Thus Heinrich Heine celebrated America. On the one hand, the New World had no aristocratic or anti-Jewish tradition to impede democracy and tolerance. As a nineteenth-century joke had it, a Polish Jew tells a friend he is going to America. The friend says, "But that's so far away!" The emigrant replies, "From what?" When the poet Emma Lazarus called America "Mother of Exiles," she was hinting that immigration would end the Jews' long suffering and alienation from any homeland.

On the other hand, Jews were quick to conclude that gaining this prize required them to abandon their tradition and identity. Among the arriving ethnic groups, only Jews were so eager to break away from their roots. Catholic or Protestant newcomers rarely abandoned their religion. Being Irish, Italian, or Polish as well gave them a secular self-image, too. But Jewish leaders insisted their people must choose between the past and making America their new Holy Land of milk and honey. "To pray for a return to Jerusalem or remain Hebrews in garb, customs, views or language," wrote Reform Rabbi Kaufmann Kohler, was impossible. Reform Rabbi Isaac Mayer Wise told American Jews to draw a line between themselves and those conserving tradition: "We are Americans and they are not."[2]

So America offered, simultaneously, a blessing and a curse, unlimited hope and nagging fear. At best, it seemed a new Garden of Eden. But if Jews ate from the tree of knowledge about their past and peoplehood, they feared expulsion from this garden. Forgetting or ignoring things Jews had so long conveyed from generation to generation—now associated with the Old Country rather than with an identity transcending time or place— seemed the way to salvation. If the immigrants could not so easily change themselves, their native-born or transplanted children nevertheless rushed to escape a world that meant to them, at worst, a stigma setting them apart and, at best, a sentimental memory that had no future.

In both Europe and America, Jews were willing to flee tradition and assimilate, but the New World's structure made for some important differences. In America, Jews were not alone in being distinct from the majority but were merely one group among many. In Vienna, Berlin, or St. Petersburg, Jews faced a dominant cultural tradition and national identity excluding them; in America a culture and nation still in formation was far more malleable. Earlier arrivals decried newer ones, but the new immigrants soon had the same chance to patronize those coming later. In this American society President Franklin Roosevelt could aptly address the snobbish Daughters of the American Revolution with the provocative salutation: "Fellow immigrants!" Jews did not merely adjust to an existing society; they played a big role in shaping it.

At a time when Jewish communities in continental Europe had been largely murdered, American Jews were enjoying power and success accompanied by relatively little hatred. In the United States, race, not antisemitism, was the great social divide. Equally important, American Jews found allies in a broad liberal and immigrant coalition challenging the status quo. Given America's openness to change, Jews were seen as doing more to create than subvert norms. But if far gentler than Europe, American assimilation also subverted identity and created psychological dislocations.

The relatively few early Sephardic Jewish migrants to America disappeared quietly into the Christian majority. The largest community of Sephardim, that of Newport, Rhode Island, had vanished entirely by 1850.[3] A second wave of Jews came from Germany, fleeing the reactionary aftermath of Napoleon's defeat and failed democratic revolutions, and this group prospered. But when financially ready to enter upper-class institutions, they were rejected, as in the famous 1877 incident when an upstate New York resort hotel denied a room to a Jewish banker's family. Massachusetts General Hospital would not let Jewish doctors perform surgery, as they were allegedly too nervous; quotas limited admissions to the best colleges. Banned from law firms, hospitals, and country clubs, Jews began creating their own. "The only profession I know that does not bar Jews," commented Rabbi Stephen Wise, "is the rabbinical profession."[4]

Discrimination bred fear, not pride or resistance. The elite became more imitative to prove its fitness for total assimilation. Louis Kirstein, the best-known Jewish figure in Boston, ate a lobster omelet for lunch each day and desperately sought the approval of the WASP elite. Despite his wealth, Kirstein never owned real estate, renting a house for forty years until his death in 1942. His son George called this attitude "The diamonds-sewn-in-the-hem-of-your-coat-for-a-quick-flight-in-the-night mentality."[5] Julius Rosenwald, owner of Sears, so feared charges of dual loyalty that he was said to give to any charity except an explicitly Jewish one. While employing as his chief executive from 1928 to 1954 an antisemite who refused to put Jews in high positions, he opposed sending relief to Europe earmarked for Jews as likely to increase antisemitism.[6]

Calling Jewish customs and identity "un-American" meant that Americanization required changing or abandoning them. Thus, in a classic assimilationist response, many of the Jewish elite did not use the new freedom to be Jews but thought gaining it meant they must stop being Jews. Bent on its own liquidation, this group held Christmas celebrations with trees, cards, and caroling; celebrated Easter with bunnies and colored eggs; ate bacon, ham, and shellfish; and founded clubs, resorts, and even houses of worship imitating those of Christian counterparts. The children drew the obvious lesson: Jewish ways were inferior and they were being prepared for intermarriage as soon as the Christian elite was ready to permit it. The effect was a set of contradictory impulses: dignity and shame at being Jews, smugness and insecurity in their social status.[7]

A similar mix of motives governed the elite's attempt to invent a version of Judaism appropriate for this endeavor. Their spiritual leader, the German-born Rabbi Isaac Mayer Wise, who came to America in 1846, told them to drop any law or belief contrasting with American—i.e., Christian—practice, removing "whatever makes us ridiculous before the world [and altering Judaism] to correspond with the spirit and tastes of this age and this country." When the first rabbinical class graduated from his Hebrew Union College in 1883, it celebrated with a banquet of oysters, shrimp, and crab, deliberately flaunting Jewish laws and customs.[8]

Israel's mission, said a 1909 Reform resolution sounding like a definition of Christianity, was to reject a narrow national creed and instead promote "among the whole human race . . . the broad and universalist religion first proclaimed by the Jewish prophets." Identifying with the whole world while staking a claim to lead it was among the most appealing ideas assimilation could offer.[9] Bent on persuading "Americans" that Jews were not a people, the New York German-Jewish elite's Temple Emanu-El declared it a "mistake for Jews to act together for social and political purposes." By the time James Seligman died in 1964, his grandfather's years as president of the temple's board of trustees had produced an heir whose funeral was held at Christ Church Methodist.[10] Felix Adler, son of Temple Emanu-El's rabbi, asked logically why that congregation did not "go all the way and declare themselves to be Unitarians?" In 1876, he founded the Ethical Culture movement, a non-Jewish religion with mostly Jewish members.

Yet those most eager to disappear were unlikely to become Jewish leaders. The German-Jewish figures leading the American Jewish community between the 1880s and 1945 had some traditional training and a sense of aristocratic obligation. Foremost among them were Jacob Schiff, German-born head of the powerful Kuhn, Loeb investment firm, who came to America in 1865; Oscar Straus, owner of New York's Macy's department store and the first Jewish cabinet member when he became President Theodore Roosevelt's secretary of commerce and labor in 1906; and Louis Marshall, a successful lawyer. In 1912, Straus had the memorable task of leading Roosevelt's Progressive Party convention in an impassioned version of "Onward Christian Soldiers."[11]

As demands grew for establishing a national Jewish group, Marshall invited fellow elite members to form the American Jewish Committee in 1906. Its first president was Mayer Sulzberger, owner of *The New York Times*. Marshall defended this group's self-appointed leadership role as necessary to avoid "indiscreet, hot-headed, and ill-considered oratory [which] might find its way into the headlines of the daily newspapers inflicting untold injury upon the Jewish cause."[12]

This step was in fact motivated by the entry onto the scene of a group the elite regarded as "indiscreet," "hot-headed," and too openly Jewish: more than three million East European Jews arrived between 1880 and 1921, tripling the community's size, before tight immigration laws closed the door. German Jews looked down on the poor newcomers, sometimes preferring that they be kept out of the country or at least sent away from eastern cities. "The continued residence among us . . . of these wretches" would only disgrace and make unpopular already resident Jews, claimed one leader. The *Hebrew Standard* said, "The thoroughly acclimated American Jew ... has no religious, social, or intellectual sympathies with them. He is closer to the Christian sentiment around him than to the Judaism of these miserable, darkened Hebrews."[13]

Yet at the same time the elite felt impelled to help the new arrivals, for reasons ranging from fraternal feeling to an urgent need to Americanize them lest their "alienness" produce a general anti-Jewish reaction jeopardizing its own status. Antagonism was mitigated, however, by the fact that earlier arrivals knew from their own experience that change was possible and would eventually bring acceptance. Dorothy Schiff, granddaughter of Jacob, would explain, "As to being Jewish ... once you reach a certain financial level, people don't think of you as anything but rich."[14]

Eastern European immigrants, still relatively untouched by Western society or secularizing tendencies but eager to escape persecution and poverty, soon grasped this idea. The contrast between the two cultures, and the immigrant experience itself, corroded Jewish identity. The mere act of crossing the ocean was like being reborn, losing track of days and being unable to keep the Sabbath or ensure that food was kosher. Even if parents still thought their customs corresponded to the divine will, their children thought the Old World shtetl or New World tenements were places and lifestyles they wished to escape as soon as possible.[15]

In America, aggressiveness and economic status counted far more than did piety or scholarship. Those most respected in the Old World and the main carriers of Jewish wisdom and practices—whether rabbis or modernizing intellectuals—were now at the bottom of the social pyramid. Children's diminishing respect for parents included doubt about what they saw as an impractical religion that neither put food on the table nor won them anything but ridicule. They deemed religion a distraction rather than a way of life. The public school and the street had more influence than had parents and quickly won over the child's loyalty to the English language and American customs.[16] The young generation's better understanding of the new sources of prestige and livelihood widened the generation gap. The new generation saw anything ethnic as low status. Novelist Henry Roth wrote of a son rejecting his mother's offer to bake a cake for his friends: "Aw, you bake Jewish cakes." "And what kind of cakes are not Jewish cakes?" "Oh, you know. Like in the store."[17]

The melodramatic works of Israel Zangwill, himself the son of Jewish immigrants in London, dramatized this transition and invented the phrase "the melting pot." The children flee a religion which seems an "endless coil of laws," unmoved by the ghetto's "illogical happiness" where a "dirty, shiftless peddler becomes the pious inheritor of a glorious tradition as he presides over the Seder table." Instead, they come home from school refusing to speak Yiddish, ashamed at their parents' appearance and accents. In one memorable—and not totally apocryphal—scene from a Zangwell play, the father of Leonard James—formerly Levi Shemuel—goes to invite his son to the family's Seder and finds him leaving the theater with an actress: "For one awful instant, that seemed an eternity, the old man and the young faced each other across the chasm which divided their lives." Then Levi turns away, telling the actress the man was "only an old Jew who supplies me with cash."[18]

Shame over one's parents warred with affection for them. As one journalist explained, the child's "youthful ardor and ambition lead him to prefer the progressive, if chaotic and uncentered, American life; but his conscience does not allow him entire peace in a situation which involves a chasm between him and his parents and their ideals."[19] Children were often embarrassed to bring friends home to see the parents' tiny apartment and hear the foreign accents. "I knew that my mother would look out of place and feel uncomfortable in such a strange environment," visiting him at college, one man wrote. "Yet I am sure I blamed mother much more than she deserved for her failure to become completely Americanized."[20]

Every new immigrant "was embarrassed and humiliated fifty times a day through an ignorance that was not his fault," wrote Isaac Asimov of his youth. "All self-respect was gone, all feeling of intelligence. . . . My parents went from top to bottom in the space of time it took them to go from Petrovich to Brooklyn." Having no religious training, "I was spared the great need of breaking with an Orthodox past and, after having done so, of playing the hypocrite for the benefit of pious parents, as so many of my generation had to." But he did have to see Yiddish plays dealing with long-suffering, noble immigrant parents and their ungrateful Americanized children.[21]

The flourishing of such Yiddish culture on New York's Lower East Side was clearly a transitory phenomenon. Moving out of Jewish neighborhoods uptown and, in the next generation, to the suburbs, often took them far from these influences. "Continuity was destroyed," wrote Henry Roth, when his family "moved from snug, orthodox Ninth Street, from the homogeneous East Side to rowdy, heterogeneous Harlem. . . . There would always be a sense of loss afterward, an insecurity—even though he might ultimately say good riddance to all that was so abruptly terminated."[22] The "Russian" element in the immigrants' background influenced them toward socialism, which also decried ethnic identity and religion. An immigrant wrote in 1909 that each Yom Kippur, "a longing gnaws at my breast." But if he went to synagogue, friends made fun of him because they would not understand that for some people "memories of their childhood are sometimes stronger than their convictions."[23]

The young people's inability to forget their origins entirely or totally spurn historic and religious influences shaping them, however, created turmoil in their souls. A powerful emotional force pushed them toward success in American society and away from Jewish identity. But equally ashamed of abandoning it, they often retained a strong sentimental attachment for that background. "The whole idea of escaping from Jewishness," Irving Howe pointed out, "is itself a crucial aspect of Jewish experience." Songwriter Yip Harburg explained that Americanization occurred "in a special ghetto way." Despite their poverty, the immigrant parents' respect for intellect made their children's lives diverge, recalled union leader Gus Tyler, between a "gentility" of home and "the gangsterism of the street."[24]

Nathan Birnbaum, better known by his non-Jewish stage name, George Burns, was a typical example of that generation. Growing up in a tenement with eleven siblings, Burns knew that, for his father, "religion was the most important thing in his life." He also understood that this fact caused his mother's disdain and family's impoverishment. Not only was "Jewish knowledge" worthless, but it seemed actually to drag people down, making them less fit to survive. Once, when his father was in a good mood, as his angry mother watered down "a stew to the point where it would feed a bunch of kids who hadn't eaten in twenty-four hours," she asked him, "What are you so happy about, that synagogue is paying you nothing" for being a cantor. Burns's father gave a big smile and replied, "I know, but they asked me to come back again next year."[25]

In contrast to this experience, when Burns was seven, a Presbyterian minister asked him and three other Jewish kids to represent the church at a contest, singing, "When Irish Eyes Are Smiling" and "Mother Machree." They won first prize. The church got a velvet altar cloth; each kid received a cheap watch. Burns was so excited he ran home to tell his mother, "Mama, I don't want to be a Jew anymore!"

When she calmly asked why, he explained, "Well, I've been a Jew for seven years and never got anything. I was a Presbyterian for one day and I got a watch." She glanced at it and said, "First help me hang up the wash, then you can be a Presbyterian." While he was working, the watch became wet and stopped running. "So I became a Jew again."[26] Burns seems to have psychologically repressed the fact that this event happened about the time his father died.

The contrast between unpleasant Jewish childhoods and high American aspirations characterized the life of most Jews growing up between the 1890s and 1930s. Benjamin Kubelsky—better known as Jack Benny—remembered that his father hit him with a prayer book for coming late to a Yom Kippur service. Al Jolson sneaked out of his cantor father's choir to sing at burlesque houses, later running away from home to end up in the St. Mary's Home for Boys. Jolson's stage debut, appropriately enough, was in the classic story of the Jewish generation gap, Zangwill's *Children of the Ghetto.*[27]

Nor did ethnic solidarity prove to be of much value. On St. Patrick's Day, Burns and his friends, wearing green, sang Irish songs in the saloons. A gang of tough Irish kids chased them until the smaller Jewish kids found refuge in a Jewish Boys' Club, asking some older boys shooting pool to protect them: "The biggest one in the group patted me on the head and said, 'You boys are lucky you came here, we'll take care of this.' They went outside with their pool cues and chased the Irish kids away, then came back, took all the money, and chased us home."[28]

The response to oppression and feelings of inferiority as Jews was not self-assertion but concealment and flight. Asked his father's name when applying for a library card, the future playwright Arthur Miller ran out of the library. "I could not bring to voice my father's so Jewish name, Isidore. I was paralyzed. . . . I had always been programmed to choose something other than pride in my origins." Only later did he realize himself to be "a character in an epic I did not know existed, an undissolved lump floating on the surface of the mythical American melting pot." Having been taught nothing about the history or beliefs lying behind this drama, however, he felt its manifestations to be either menaces or superstitions.[29]

"I learned camouflage. 'If you can't fight them, join them,' " wrote the journalist Michael Elkins about his childhood in a poor, tough New York neighborhood. On Christmas Eve 1925, when he was nine, he walked fifty-three blocks to the Straus's Macy's department store wearing newspapers under his sweater for warmth and cardboard in his shoes. When his turn finally came to meet Santa Claus, he stepped up and began to list the gifts he wanted for Christmas.

Santa whispered, "This ain't for you, Jewboy; go to your rabbi!"

"I spat at him; and he knocked me off the platform." The store guards threw Elkins out. "I couldn't become a Christian, but I could become less Jewish." He quit religious studies, stopped going to synagogue, boycotted the family's Friday candle-lighting, refused to speak Yiddish and screamed at his parents for doing so, "Be American!" Elkins distanced himself from any Jewish association and celebrated Christmas—symbol of his rejection by American society—until the April 1945 day he helped liberate the Dachau concentration camp as a U.S. soldier. When a barely living survivor addressed him in Yiddish, Elkins lied, saying he spoke only English, only to break down when the surprised man asked in Yiddish, "Aren't you a Jew?"[30]

For his family, wrote Paul Cowan, Judaism had gone from being an all-embracing civilization, "a source of comfort and continuity," to become "a psychological and social burden." His uncle was called a "dirty Jew" on his first day at school in 1911, while his father had been appalled to see his own Orthodox family fight and gossip the moment Yom Kippur services ended. "That wasn't religion, that was hypocrisy," he recounted. Consequently, they ran from their identity but could not escape being disturbed by the secret selves they purported to ignore. At the same time that fear of persecution drove them toward apparent assimilation; the specific routes they followed only underlined their distinctiveness.[31]

Cowan's father changed his name from Cohen when he was twenty-one, invited no relatives to his wedding, and would not let his children meet them. In his new role, he read his children Charles Dickens's *A Christmas Carol* and celebrated that holiday, ate a ham dinner for Easter, and sent his son to a WASP prep school. Yet, in retirement, the man who had hidden his own history would collect oral histories of Jews. As usual in the assimilation process, his life was a series of choices, with each rejected one leaving traces. "Was he Louis Cohen, a Jew who knew how to daven, who fasted on Yom Kippur, who didn't eat pork, or Louis G. Cowan, a cosmopolitan intellectual, a Jewish WASP, who shared the disdain his wife and children felt for those customs?"[32]

Cowan's mother came from a wealthy German-Jewish family embracing Christian Scientist beliefs, so antagonistic to Eastern European Jews that her father said of her future husband, "I don't want that kike in my house." Her worldview reflected the self-abnegating Reform philosophy: "We were chosen to suffer; chosen to achieve brilliance; chosen to wage a ceaseless war for social justice."[33] So she worked for civil rights and leftist causes while avoiding Jewish ones, though her motive was a response to discrimination against Jews; ate pork but did not enjoy it; told her son she was glad his nose was not large; urged him to learn a trade lest he have to flee from America some day; and became upset at his marriage to a Protestant though never mentioning it. Despite her assertive humanism, she believed that Christians "will kill all the Jews. Israel will be abandoned."[34]

The immigrants' children had no incentive to pass their feelings or attributes to their own offspring, who they wanted to be so fully assimilated as to lack their insecurity and psychic conflicts. The more their birthright influenced their character and work, the more they denied and belied it. Yet, many decades later, without any of these issues ever being openly discussed, Cowan and many other Jews in America and Europe found these still echoed "in our psyches throughout our lives."[35]

The choices available to native-born Jews of that earlier generation appeared in the sharply disparate perspectives of Louis Brandeis and Walter Lippmann, who respectively advocated embracing or totally rejecting Jewish identity. Brandeis, a lawyer from a highly assimilated family in Kentucky, only became involved with Jewish causes after mediating a New York garment industry case in 1911 brought him into close contact with immigrants. In 1916, he became the first Jew named to the U.S. Supreme Court.

While the Jewish elite had argued that being a good American meant abandoning or at least minimizing one's Jewish identity, Brandeis insisted that the direct opposite was true. "To be good Americans we must be better Jews, and to be better Jews we must become Zionists," he said in a 1916 speech. "Every Jewish-American must stand up and be counted, counted with us, or prove himself wittingly or unwittingly one of the few who are against their own people." Democracy "means that every Jew in this land . . . has a right to be heard, what is more, he has also a duty to be heard."[36]

He developed these themes of pluralism, democracy, and Jewish nationalism into a new doctrine totally redefining successful assimilation in terms of ethnic assertiveness. In contrast to the common assumption that Jews must change to fit in to the United States, Brandeis insisted that the real American idea was that "each race or people, like each individual, has the right and duty to develop, and that only through such differentiated development will high civilization be attained." The Jewish question

would be solved not when Jews disappeared but when they were free to
exist as Jews, shaking off the "false shame" that led them "to assume so
many alien disguises. . . . Jews should realize that few things do more to
foster antisemitic feeling than this very tendency to sail under false colors
and conceal their true identity."

To abandon a Jewish identity would be un-American; for a Jew to be
loyal to his people just as he should be loyal to city, family, or profession,
made him a better American citizen. Rather than being inferior, "The Jewish spirit, the product of our religion and experiences, is essentially modern
and essentially American." Brandeis's Jewish identity was so naïve yet confident that he actually ended one talk by quoting Chaucer on a priest as a
role model for assertiveness: "Christ's lore, and his Apostles twelve, he
taught, but first he followed it himself."[37]

Ironically, Brandeis's own high degree of Americanization made him
secure enough to suggest such a strategy, but this approach was the German Jewish elite's worst nightmare. By openly asserting that Jews were a
nation and urging them to demonstrate group loyalty, these leaders feared,
Brandeis would stir antisemitism. They hoped, in vain, that he would stop
Jewish activity once on the Supreme Court. Yet while Brandeis persevered,
the Jewish ideology he advocated had far less influence at the time than did
his legal philosophy. The new immigrants and their children usually concluded that acceptance as Americans required recasting their identity just
as it entailed shedding Yiddish language and accents or Jewish religious
practices.

This view fit more closely the dominant opinion of the era. Theodore
Roosevelt had commented, "We can have no fifty-fifty allegiance in this
country. Either a man is American and nothing else, or he is not an
American at all." Woodrow Wilson told a group of immigrants, "You
cannot become thorough Americans if you think of yourself in groups.
America does not consist of groups. A man who thinks of himself as belonging to a particular national group in America has not yet become an
American."[38] So for a variety of reasons, the great majority among the
growing group of intellectuals from Jewish backgrounds outwardly, often
passionately, rejected any Jewish identity while still being, inwardly,
heavily influenced by it.

Walter Lippmann, America's leading newspaper columnist and political theorist between the 1920s and 1950s, fit this pattern. Born to wealthy
German-Jewish parents in New York in 1889, he began political life as a

socialist but moved toward a conservative standpoint. He would have been horrified by the intimation that his philosophy's main points paralleled Jewish assimilationist themes by advocating internationalism, the superiority of informed reason, and abandoning smaller for larger groups.

There was, of course, ample justification for Lippmann urging a more active American role in the world or arguing that growing global interdependence was pulling people into a wider world beyond their local communities. Still, as a Jew, Lippmann was more detached from the American status quo and more open to a cosmopolitan, internationalist philosophy, as a biographer put it, "unconstrained by the preoccupations and prejudices of his homeland [and more] receptive to diverse currents of opinion from abroad."[39] Yet his ideas' very character made them vulnerable if Lippmann was categorized as a Jew. He had to emphasize his patriotic and impartial credentials, lest isolationists charge him with dragging America into global involvements to serve alien interests. After all, the leading antisemitic book in America then was Henry Ford's *The International Jew.*

In his liberal mistrust of the masses, Lippmann followed a Jewish variant that feared the ability of czarist, Nazi, clerical, or chauvinist demagogues to stir popular reactionary, antisemitic tendencies. Lippmann's critique of democracy was different from that of conservatives, since he worried that the majority might be too traditionalist.* The elite he championed was, like the Jewish nobility, one of intellect rather than of pedigree. His lament at American antiintellectualism was in the same vein.

Lippmann's call for Americans to break with parochial interests and abandon stale custom followed his example in leaving a smaller community behind. Yet, like European counterparts, Lippmann contradicted himself by claiming internationalism did not hinder patriotic love of country while fearing the charge of dual loyalty to his origin. As a young man he wrote, "I do not regard the Jews as innocent victims. They hand on unconsciously and uncritically from one generation to another many distressing personal and social habits which were selected by bitter history and intensified by a pharisaical theology."[40] Thus, it was a positive step to break this chain of tradition and abandon such a backward, even reprehensible, group. Lippmann's use of a traditional Christian anti-Jewish term, *pharisaical,* shows how far he accepted that standpoint toward a heritage of which he was igno-

---

*Disraeli took a parallel stance, and this issue also affected Jewish Marxists (see chapter 6) and the Jewish critique of totalitarianism by Arendt, Raymond Aron, and others.

rant. Such intellectuals either never mentioned Jewish concerns—a strenuous endeavor during the Hitler era—or spoke negatively of them.

The German-Jewish elite's view (shared by many Eastern European
Jewish immigrants) that being a true American required forsaking Jewish
identity, and Lippmann's idea (shared by many European Jewish intellectuals) that being modern required a humanism for which they must set an
example by rejecting their own group, had far more influence on American
Jewish attitudes in those years than did Brandeis's formula of pluralism and
ethnic self-assertion.

Bernard Berenson was both an extreme case and a logical product of
that position. He was an art critic who introduced America's monied elite
to collecting European painting. Like Lippmann, he disparaged Jews in
order to dissociate himself from them.* "We" can never really comprehend,
he wrote in 1888, "the puzzling character of the Jews. . . . Their character and
interests are too vitally opposed to our own to permit the existence of that
intelligent sympathy between us and them which is necessary for compre-
hension."[41]

One would hardly think that the author of these words was born Bernhard Valvrojenski in a Lithuanian shtetl. His father, like many contemporaries, broke with Orthodoxy, preferring the study of Darwin, Marx, or
Voltaire to the Talmud, and German to Yiddish. Arriving in Boston at age
ten, Bernard saw his father shattered by his diminished status in the New
World, and he resolved to go much farther toward self-transformation. Beginning his studies in the public library, Berenson advanced to the Boston
Latin School and then Harvard. Although he decided to dedicate his life to
learning—a step quite in line with Jewish tradition—his subject was
Europe's classic Christian-based art. A self-made snob who authenticated
paintings of madonnas and saints could hardly be a Jew, he reasoned. To
enter European culture, one must accept its spiritual premises. Berenson
first converted to Protestantism and then, in 1891, joined the Catholic
church.

"How glad I am to take sides, to give up the fancied freedom," he
wrote, portraying his conversion as a chance to join the aristocracy and
high society whose "larger, more intense, as well as freer life, its manners,
its customs, its habitations . . . seemed more beautiful intrinsically than
ours."[42] Berenson was more opportunist than self-hating Jew. "A Jew from

*For more on Berenson's view of the Jews, see chapter 9.

the ghetto" became his phrase to condemn the ones he disliked, though his wife wrote of a rich contact: "Mr. Loeb came to lunch, a handsome, fat, prosperous, philistine Jew, [but] as he may be very useful to us financially, [Bernard] and I listened politely while he expounded on these views. It is astonishing how interesting and unboring society becomes when you have something to get out of it."[43]

There was no end to the irony in Berenson's situation. He was the outsider who became cultural arbiter; the poor European immigrant who returned to Europe—sanitized by America—as honorary aristocrat living in his own Italian palace. What could be more appropriate than his career as the authority separating the counterfeit from genuine for rich American patrons depending on his good taste to elevate them to the social elect? Berenson's own pose as a genteel aesthete was based on an unbounded chutzpah that let him pass as an Anglo-Saxon and speak of "our Puritan forebears." Of this conceit, art historian Meyer Shapiro remarked, "His ancestors were rabbis on the *Mayflower*."[44]

Berenson's inner tragedy, however, was knowing he had forged himself. This made him attribute any social slight to antisemitism and complain, "I have not yet learned to like myself as I am. I still . . . look for flashes of hope that I am not so worthless as I often feel." His sister remarked, "What food for thought in this whole situation. Culture almost over-acquired, great wealth amassed, exquisite beauty enhaloing their lives, yet the flavor of dust and ashes."[45]

The Shoah intensified Berenson's bitter introspection. In Italy, he was shielded by State Department protection arranged, suitably enough, by Lippmann. But guilt suffused his diary: "At times I seem to myself to be a typical 'Talmud Jew'. . . . A day scarcely passes without my feeling deeply penitential about my life. . . . So what I really am—is there such an animal? What should I have been, left to myself—but what self was mine?" He confessed joy at dropping "the mask of being goyim and return to Yiddish reminiscences, and Yiddish stories and witticisms! After all, it has been an effort . . . to act as if one were a mere Englishman or Frenchman or American." He admitted his lifelong feeling of being a rootless exile, an outsider, a Jew always hoping to "attain complete assimilation" and yet feeling perpetually an alien.[46]

"Don't these converts give you a pain?" he asked a startled Jewish friend once. "That's a strange statement, coming from you," she replied. Berenson answered disingenuously, "They got me to the door of the

Church several times, but they never booted me in." Like Heine, he could fantasize away his apostasy when it suited him, claiming independence from all allegiances.

In this mind-set, Berenson could not refrain from lecturing those who remained Jews to follow his example. In a 1944 "Letter to American Jewry," which friends wisely persuaded him not to publish, Berenson warned that envious Christians would persecute them, "Even if you were as innocent as the angels . . . and you are far from that." Jews "cannot be too modest, too unassuming, too discreet."[47] Like other assimilationists, Berenson chose his object of imitation, played the role, took the reward and still—when he wished—called it a pretense.

Berenson's high culture was only one of many options available in an increasingly secular society. Many Jewish leftists of the era chose the fantasy of merging with the proletariat.* The writer Nelson Algren, originally Nelson Abraham, liked to be called "Swede" by the Irish and Polish kids he hung out with in pool halls and speakeasies. He forged himself an image as a tough guy, though he was not very good at it.[48] But whether it be aristocracy, street gangs, or bohemians, the underlying idea was that it was more prestigious or exciting to be something other than a Jew. The Jewish heritage so romantic for Disraeli—who saw himself as the scion of prophets, scholars, and Oriental princes—now seemed the essence of banality for American Jews, who felt themselves to be the offspring of rag merchants.

Such was the case of Emmanuel Radnitsky, son of tailors, who went to Paris in 1921 and renamed himself Man Ray. He was a dramatically innovative photographer and designer who combined the ordinary and the startling, skills he had used to design his own persona. The diminutive, manic Man Ray, in black clothes and beret, hung around with Picasso and other famous friends, drove fast cars, and chased beautiful women. He refused to talk of his family or origins—"I thought of myself as a Thoreau," he wrote, "breaking free of all ties and duties to society"—but never lost a Brooklyn Jewish accent.[49]

More tragic was the private life of Dorothy Rothschild—best known as wit and writer Dorothy Parker. She was the daughter of a rich New York German-Jewish merchant and a Catholic mother. At Catholic school she was, not surprisingly, an outsider who funneled her alienation into humor. In later years she would disdain her relatives, hate her own name, and cul-

*See chapter 6.

tivate an elegant accent. Changing her name involved marrying Eddie Parker, a drunkard and drug addict from a good family, with a famous Connecticut minister as grandfather. In a scene whose like would later be repeatedly immortalized in film and literature, she met his parents for the first time, aware that they saw her, in her biographer's words, as "a New York Jew on the make."[50]

When her marriage broke up, she ignored her husband's vices to blame herself for being so foolish as to have wed a gentile, especially one above her station. Dorothy's dilemma was sometimes a subject of repartee at the famous Algonquin Round Table. When Alexander Woollcott hissed at George Kaufman, "Shut up, you Christ killer," Kaufman stood up, threw down his napkin, and said he would leave rather than tolerate slurs on his race "and I hope that Mrs. Parker will walk out with me—halfway." She expressed her own feelings less comically in the antisemitic, self-loathing "Dark Girl's Rhyme," depicting Jews as dark, "devil-gotten sinners" who Christians saw as fools.[51]

But in the 1930s, if the gentile world laughed at Jews it was most often as audiences for the country's most commercially successful entertainments. The Hollywood studio heads—Louis Mayer, Adolph Zukor, Jack and Harry Warner, Harry Cohn, and Carl Laemmle—most of the writers and comedians, and many of the actors, were Jewish immigrants or children of immigrants. In general, the tycoons and their creative employees were trying to assimilate in different ways, reproducing the split between Jewish businessmen and intellectuals in Europe. The leftist utopianism of some Jewish screenwriters and actors paralleled the rightist utopianism of the Jewish studio heads. The former romanticized a working class, multiethnic society, America as they wanted it to be; the moguls sought to be patrician, idealizing the upper crust and the small-town America they thought already existed. The writer Clifford Odets, who penned the archetypal immigrant populist plays *Awake and Sing* and *Golden Boy* in New York before "selling out" in Hollywood, bridged the gap by wanting to be a revolutionary while also driving a Rolls-Royce.[52]

The clash between the Hollywood tycoons' limited education and boundless social ambition was an easy target for satire, but in many ways they were merely extremely colorful, ham-handed versions of the East Coast German-Jewish elite. Shmuel Gelbfisz, known as Samuel Goldwyn, came from a poor, Yiddish-speaking Orthodox family in Russia. In America he was a glovemaker before entering the new motion picture business in

1913. Given his own rapid rise, he loved Benjamin Franklin's comment that in America, "People do not inquire of a stranger, 'What is he?' but 'What can he do?' " Yet like many immigrants who professed such sentiments, his fearfulness and eagerness to rewrite his past showed that he didn't believe a word of it.[53]

"They were men who made all that money and realized they were still a bunch of Goddamned Jews," said Hollywood Rabbi Edgar Magnin. "So they looked for other ways to cover it up." To render this problem invisible, they believed, was to omit Jewish names or themes from their movies and lives. "Sleeping with a pretty gentile girl made them feel, if only for a few minutes, 'I'm half gentile,' " explained Magnin. "No wonder they made idols out of shiksa goddesses." They also married them, exchanging a Jewish first wife for a non-Jewish second one. Goldwyn's second wife, actress Frances Howard, insisted on bringing up Samuel Goldwyn, Jr., as a Catholic and baptized him when Sam Sr. was out of town.[54]

They rarely converted religiously—America did not require it—but they did "convert" ethnically to try to prove themselves purely American. Louis B. Mayer, MGM's chief, went so far as to change his birthday to July 4. They raised Thoroughbred horses—"from Poland to polo in one generation," as one joke put it—and taught their children to see themselves as upper class, then suffered from their inevitable rejection.* Perhaps it was inevitable that they would equate Jewishness with being poor, persecuted, and unfashionable. Their close personal friends, of course, were all Jews of similar background who understood them.

By putting their vision of America on film, the moviemakers made it more real by encouraging fellow citizens to see it as typical. They did not so much challenge as preempt antisemitism with a version of America based on a preimmigrant myth of small-town virtue and Anglophile culture. Even when dealing with gritty urban life, they airbrushed it into respectability. Ordering a cleanup of carefully strewn garbage for a film set in New York, Goldwyn said, "There won't be any dirty slums—not in *my* picture."[55]

Contrary to Brandeis's pluralist view, even populist Jews strove for ethnic invisibility. The left-leaning producer Harold Clurman asked a film director why a strike leader was supposed to have a Jewish accent. The

---

*Another joke was that they came from the *Almanac de Ghetto,* a play on the *Almanac de Gotha,* the register of German aristocracy.

director replied, "I wanted him to be somebody who was not quite American." Clurman blew up: "I'm ten times more American than you are! What the hell do you know about America? . . . You're no more American than I! You're far less! Talk about American history, let's talk about American politics."[56]

Even the moguls who privately contributed to Jewish charities were horrified by any public sign of identity. As screenwriter Ben Hecht noted, they felt guilty over abandoning Judaism and sought to counter this feeling by secretly giving some help to Jews in distress. But this also meant that they refused to use their great social power for that purpose. The producer David Selznick insisted, "I am not interested in Jewish political problems. I'm an American and not a Jew." If Jews acted by themselves, movie moguls said, antisemitism would increase. "As Americans," noted Hecht, "they could boast and swagger, apparently, but as Jews they must be as invisible as possible." These individuals "were men loud with ego, but the Jew in them was a cringing fellow almost as frightened of the world as the Jew in a German-policed ghetto."[57]

This logical trap dogged Jewish assimilation in many countries and for decades. If Selznick really felt himself to be an equal American, he would exert his right of free speech. Underneath a veneer of cosmopolitanism, bohemianism, or patriotic Americanism, successful Jews of the 1920s and 1930s were governed by fear. As Brandeis warned, such behavior entrenched their shame and made non-Jews suspicious that they had something to hide. Ironically, a Jew could show himself an American or humanitarian only by ignoring Jewish causes; the higher his social position, the more quiet he was to protect it. This attitude explained the community's passivity amidst the Shoah. Success, wonderful personally and as American as bagels and cream cheese came to be, was scary in Jewish terms. Goldwyn told one actress she must change her name because "there's so much antisemitism in the world. Why play into their hands?"

And so while ritually pronouncing faith in America, performers transformed themselves from Milton Berlinger to Milton Berle; Fanny Borach to Fanny Brice; Issure Danielovitch to Kirk Douglas; Julius Garfinkel to John Garfield; Emanuel Goldberg to Edward G. Robinson; Sophia Kossow to Sylvia Sydney; Joseph Levitch to Jerry Lewis; Judith Tuvim to Judy Holliday; Asa Yoelson to Al Jolson; Theodosia Goodman to Theda Bara; Sonia Kalish to Sophie Tucker; Isidor Iskowitch to Eddie Cantor; and Irving Lahrheim to Bert Lahr. Lahr's son later recalled his mother rebuking him for allowing friends to call him by his real name—Lahrheim. "Your father wasn't Jewish," she said. "He was a star."[58]

Commercial considerations also inspired camouflage. Israel Baline, better known as Irving Berlin, was a cantor's son who rose from poverty to become the most successful American composer. His colleague Jerome Kern said, "Irving Berlin has no place in American music. He *is* American music."[59] But the author of "Easter Parade" and "White Christmas"—as well as "God Bless America"—believed that being American and successful were synonymous, while being American and a Jew were not. He only mentioned Jews in such songs as "Business Is Business Rosie Cohen" or "Cohen Owes Me Ninety-Seven Dollars" to ridicule them. When putting on "This Is the Army," he complained that there were "too many Jews in the show." He told the *Saturday Evening Post* magazine of his "nostalgic memories of childhood Christmas on the Lower East Side," married the daughter of an antisemitic Catholic millionaire, and raised his children as Protestants.[60]

Comedy was most dominated by Jews, not only given the traditional Jewish use of humor to ward off affliction but also because it could safely deal with themes too dangerous to confront openly. The Jewish comedians, all products of Orthodox, Yiddish-speaking immigrant homes, retained none of these characteristics themselves. They saw such traits as transient, largely undesirable, and associated with poverty and low social status, elements of their past they wanted to escape.

Still, Jolson, George Jessel, Brice, Eddie Cantor, Ed Wynn, the Ritz Brothers, Phil Silvers, and many others gave America something from Jewish experience. Many, like Burns and Benny, created non-Jewish characters and homogenized themselves further by marrying their Christian partners. In contrast, the Marx Brothers took a different direction, acting out society's worst fear of Jews and other immigrants as loud, obnoxious, irreverent anarchists who twisted the English language and stole or wrecked everything in sight. Groucho Marx began his career as a soprano in an Episcopal church but was fired for deflating the organ bellows with a hatpin. Instead of gentrifying Jewish names into WASP monikers, they changed their real gentlemanly assimilationist names into ones far more ridiculous than anything brought from Eastern Europe: Leonard to Chico, Julius to Groucho, Adolph to Harpo, Milton to Gummo, and Herbert to Zeppo.

Danny Kaye, a big hit with Jewish audiences in the Catskills resorts, dropped his ethnic material when he began playing New York nightclubs.

Goldwyn signed him for movie work in 1942 but worried, "He looks too—too—" unable to say *Jewish.* "Well," his wife said, "he is Jewish." "But let's face it," Goldwyn replied, "Jews are funny-looking." Kaye refused to change his nose but, after much thought, Goldwyn gave him a chance on condition that he dye his hair blond. Assured by editors and publishers—especially Jewish ones—that readers preferred books on "real Americans," Jewish writers revised their characters. Even in Hecht's own hit film *The Front Page,* a leading figure's name changed from Irving Pincus in the 1931 version to Joe Pettibone in the 1940 version.[61]

The virtual sole exception to the absence of explicitly Jewish life from Broadway and film was *The Jazz Singer,* the classic immigrant generational tale of a cantor's son who enters show business against his father's wishes. Just before Yom Kippur, the father dies and the son gives up show business, goes to the synagogue, and takes his father's place. As the finale, he sings the Kol Nidre, one of the most hallowed Hebrew melodies.

But a less sentimental, more genuine finale took place after George Burns saw George Jessel starring in *The Jazz Singer* on stage and was deeply touched. "When the curtain came down," he later recounted, "I was crying like a baby. I felt I had seen my own life, because my father was a cantor. I ran backstage to congratulate Jessel on his marvelous performance, but Jessel's manager was standing at the dressing room door and told me I couldn't go in. 'Why not?' I asked. 'I want to tell him how much I enjoyed his performance.'

" 'I'm sorry, you can't go in, he's in there naked.'

" 'So what?' I said. 'I've seen a naked Jew before. I want to tell him how great he was.'

" 'Mr. Burns,' he insisted, 'he's got a girl in there.' So I left. I was really shocked. I didn't think anything could follow 'Kol Nidre.' "[62]

In real life, as Zangwill had warned, sons never really returned to sing the Kol Nidre, especially when they were busy shtupping the chorus girls. But show business was a great career for immigrants unhappy with the role assigned them at birth, letting them pretend to be someone else. Actors, artists, and writers reveled in individuality and often glorified an equal-opportunity alienation. Indeed, when Groucho declared his refusal to be a member of any club that would have him, the organization in question was the Jewish Hillcrest Country Club.[63]

Nonetheless, while they claimed to be self-made, their progress was often mediated through Jewish institutions or traits. "A great many traits that once struck me as being wholly personal I now see as the marks of a distinct culture," wrote Alfred Kazin.[64] Actors often began, at least as spectators, in the Yiddish theater. Composers Harold Arlen (son of a cantor) and George Gershwin used Jewish melodies, as did Irving Berlin, Moss Hart, and Oscar Hammerstein. The same point was true for writers and intellectuals, for whom the Jewish cerebral heritage was a valuable resource while the Jewish spiritual inheritance made them certain they did not belong in the lower depths but were destined for better things.

The "outsider" status of American Jewish intellectuals in that era was intensified by academia's reluctance to admit them. Those finally sanctioned, starting in the late 1930s, had undergone an especially rigorous socialization away from their roots. If they were going to engage in scholarship—that centerpiece of Eastern European Jewish culture—they were forced to do so on terms requiring secularism, humanism, and identity with non-Jewish aspects of Western civilization. Thus, Lionel Trilling, the first Jew in Columbia University's English department, merged so deeply and finely into the British cultural tradition, a critic wrote, as to incorporate it into "the poise and cadences of his prose, in all the minute calibrations of his intellectual life." City College of New York philosophy professor Morris Cohen denied there was any Jewish problem or future for the Jews until Hitler's attempt to fulfill the latter prediction led him to organize a Jewish studies association.[65]

By their own choice and the presumed requirements of their trade, these Jewish intellectuals were outside the community; by dint of their background they were not fully part of the American mainstream. "The pretense," commented Ben Hecht, "lies in the delusion that, having ceased to be a Jew, you have become something else." Artist Richard Stern would later attribute his creative "disposition to the slight displacement from ordinary life which being a Jew allowed me. . . . I liked being a bit of an outsider, not a penalized outsider but a glamorous one."[66] This was a revealing dichotomy: to be perceived as a Jewish outsider had been a drawback, being a nonconformist one was glamorous.

Indeed, among artists and intellectuals being something of an outsider was becoming the best way to be an insider. New York intellectual life from the 1930s onward was Jewish in everything but name. When Ben Hecht arrived there, he was amazed at how Jewish cultural and literary celebrities outnumbered Christians by such a large margin. Yet they had discarded three thousand years of identity overnight, believing that as Jews they would be snubbed while as Americans and talented individuals, "They could step forth as superiors and even as snobs."[67] Hecht shrewdly suggested, "They feel their importance as their only identity." A willingness to reshape themselves according to the demands of audience or market promoted success, while an inner void and inferiority complex made them fanatically seek accomplishment to prove their own worth. Songwriter Harburg put the same theme succinctly: "I'm a chameleon—I love putting myself into everyone's shoes."[68]

Up to a point, Hecht's own evolution was typical: "I was an apostle of human reason. . . . The reading of history and the observing of my fellows had convinced me that the presence of God in the human head induced lunacy and outrage, and dammed the progress of reason. I believed that the secret of human salvation lay in people's changing from the disordered worship of the unknowable to the reasonable study of the known."[69] This was hardly an exclusively Jewish view, but it was easier for Jewish intellectuals to think this way given their tradition's relative acceptance of criticizing God; a detached, skeptical view of Christianity as a tool of persecution; and equating (Jewish) history with suffering. When Hecht comments, "I could no more think of going into a church and praying and singing than of running around in an Indian war bonnet," such an allergy to churchgoing was more a Jewish than an atheist perspective.[70]

Even more than his compatriots, Hecht had no Jewish education. His cultural referents were suffused with Christian-based words *(catechism)* and Greek myths. His autobiography's very title, *A Child of the Century,* cut him off from history, a common assimilationist view of the self as blank slate. To Hecht, however, his immigrant family—large, warm, colorful, and very Jewish—was an anchoring loyalty overcoming these factors. "Although I never lived 'as a Jew' or even among Jews, my family remained like a homeland in my heart." Perhaps, like Brandeis, his very distance from Judaism made him feel more secure as unassailably American.[71] In addition, he had a true rebel disposition like that of Max Nordau and others in Europe.* Whereas many waited trembling in expectation of a snub, Hecht reveled in the fight such challenges entailed.[72]

Hecht became exceptionally outspoken on behalf of imperiled European Jews and Zionism during World War II. But many American Jewish

---

*The same provocative nature made Hecht's remarkable 1931 book, *A Jew in Love,* echoing antisemitic language in its biting criticism, a forerunner to the postwar era's Jewish novels.

leaders and virtually all the intellectuals and public figures remained silent. A wealthy American Jew, shaken by a visit to Germany in 1938, soon forgot his pledge to aid refugees, giving his money instead to a local art museum. "At the moment when the gathering Holocaust was a reality and not a memory to be consecrated in a museum," wrote the American Jewish activist Ludwig Lewisohn, such a choice made one despair.[73] But the gift to the museum—unlike aid to Jewish refugees in Europe—would consolidate his prestige and integration into American society.

The American Jewish Committee's leader, Joseph Proskauer, commented, "For Jews in America, [as] Jews, to demand any kind of political action is a negation of the fundamentals of American liberty and equality."[74] The isolationist Joseph Kennedy, back from his post as U.S. ambassador to London, persuaded film and business leaders at secret meetings in New York and Hollywood not to protest events in Germany or be too visible as Jews—to avoid more antisemitism. "You're going to have to get those Jewish names off the screen," he said.[75] Jesse Strauss,* U.S. ambassador to France from 1933 to 1936, complained that any American Jewish effort to organize against Germany's Nazi regime was "stirring up trouble" on an issue that was "none of" their business and hurting Jews by showing them as "a race apart, with a group solidarity that prevents them from becoming a sincere and patriotic part of the country in which they live."[76]

American Jewish intellectuals refused even to address the issue. Hecht assembled thirty famous Jewish writers at George S. Kaufman's house in 1943 and declared that two million Jews had been killed in Europe with no protest in America. He urged them to speak out, warning Germans they would be severely punished if massacres continued and urging the British to admit Jewish refugees to Palestine. At the end of his talk, no one applauded. A half dozen people walked out. "Who is paying you to do this wretched propaganda," heckled the popular novelist Edna Ferber. "Mister Hitler? Or is it Mister Goebbels?" One friend commented, "I didn't expect anything much different. You asked them to throw away the most valuable thing they own—the fact that they are Americans." But the guests, wrote Hecht, "had not behaved like Americans but like scared Jews. And what in God's name were they frightened of? Of people realizing they were Jews? But people knew that already.... Or did they think they would be mistaken for 'real' Americans if they proved they had no hearts at all?"[77]

---

*Strauss's daughter's obituary read: "A memorial service for Mrs. Levy will be held . . . at St. James Episcopal Church."

Having already sacrificed their religion and people for their own interests, successful American Jews were also willing to let other Jews die rather than risk inconvenience. When asked by anti-Nazi Germans if American Jews would fund an uprising, a German Jew responded, "Charitable contributions after the catastrophe: Yes! Political assistance before the catastrophe: No!"[78]

True, Jews were acting as nonconformists and rebels in the left, trade unions, and the New Deal. But this was often so in order to disappear as Jews. Even if their ideas drew on Jewish visions of social justice, these activists were comfortable only when acting ostensibly on behalf of others. Franklin Roosevelt may have been swept into power by an immigrant rebellion guided intellectually and culturally by Jews, but the cultural and psychological ramifications would not be felt until the 1950s.

The ultimate Jewish toll in Europe would have been even higher, however, if the highest-ranking Jew in the U.S. government, Secretary of the Treasury Henry Morgenthau, Jr., had not behaved courageously. Grandson of a poor Bavarian cantor and son of a wealthy real estate magnate and ambassador, Morgenthau had no illusions about the problem. "Let's call a spade a spade," he told his staff in 1943. "I am secretary of the treasury for 135 million people, see? That is the way I think of myself; I represent all of them." But he would be attacked for appearing to "have done something for the Jews because I am a Jew." Nonetheless, he complained to Roosevelt about State Department indifference to saving Jewish refugees and pressed for action. The creation of the War Refugee Board helped save thousands of lives, though far fewer than if there had been more protest earlier about restrictive U.S. immigration policies or international indifference.[79]

The assimilationist struggle to escape Jewish society in America culminated at the same time that community was being destroyed in its European core. The flight of American Jews from poverty and foreignness had resulted in an Americanization largely defined as the removal of any Jewish stigma. To become accepted, wealthy, famous, and successful was to stand astride the stage as "American" and "humanist," shorn of any other label. But American Jews were also fleeing the main source of their intellectual and creative energy. Like Samson, they were losing the source of their uniqueness and power.

Both their recent arrival and the extent of their success made these immigrants and their children feel insecure. At most, being Jews was an inevitably declining, nostalgic link to the immigrant past. To use their voices and power on behalf of other groups and for liberal or patriotic causes was meritorious; to use it as Jews was thought to court antisemitism. Again, as in Europe, a conservative wealthy elite, upwardly mobile immigrants, and radical society-changing thinkers all embraced a form of assimilation in which liberty was used to escape oneself, rather than to be oneself. As the American Jewish writer Alfred Kazin wrote autobiographically, "We were . . . in a terrible rush to get away from everything we had grown up with."[80]

Before 1941, wrote Arthur Hertzberg, "Almost no Jew could make a free, personal decision about his education and career. At every turn, the fact of his Jewishness meant that many, if not most, options were simply not available to him." Most American Jewish leaders responded by "trying to finesse the differences between Jews and all other Americans by insisting that there was no difference." But knowing this was untrue, concluded Hertzberg, they needed to "persuade the gentile majority of some definition of American society that would obscure this line of cleavage."[81]

Thus, the Jewish elements in their characters and work were defining the new American culture and thought even as they tried to keep it from defining themselves. This situation set the stage for a new, very different, era after World War II. For if the German Jews had learned German culture almost as well as the Germans, American Jews had learned American culture far better than anyone else.

4

Self-Invention,
American Style

The innocent child asks: "What is this?" As for the child who does not even know
how to ask a question, you must begin for him.

—The Passover Haggadah

I N A VERY FUNNY scene from Woody Allen's film *Stardust Memories*, two
trains stand on parallel tracks. The passengers on one are anguished,
funny-looking swarthy people—including Allen himself; on the other
train, happy, well-dressed, taller, light-haired people are partying. One
need not be Freud to read the symbols. Tempted by a beautiful blond,
played by Sharon Stone, Allen desperately and unsuccessfully tries to jump
onto the second train.[1] This parable makes assimilation seem quite sensible,
especially given the destination of trains filled with Jews not long ago. Yet
Allen owes his fabulous success to being aboard the Jewish train.

Comedian Roseanne Barr seemed railroaded toward being a national
pariah after verbally mangling the "Star-Spangled Banner" at a 1990 baseball game, then responding to boos by grabbing her crotch and spitting at
fans. President Bush said, "It's disgraceful." Barr refused to apologize and
retained her popularity. The fact that she was Jewish was never mentioned
in accusing her of unpatriotic behavior.[2] The conviction of Jonathan Pollard of spying for Israel and of Jewish brokers for manipulating Wall Street
deals in the 1980s had similarly little effect.

Equally, even those who might not like Jews had to accept their power
and win their favor. In June 1991, the Simon Weisenthal Center held a fifty-
thousand-dollar-a-table dinner to honor movie star Arnold Schwarzeneg-

ger, who reportedly contributed five million dollars to build its Museum of Tolerance. Present were Jewish executives heading virtually every movie studio including Disney, whose late founder refused even to hire Jews. The Austrian-born actor's father may have been a Nazi Party member and the actor himself a friend of Kurt Waldheim, Austria's ex-Nazi president, but Schwarzenegger also needed the favor of these powerful men.[3] Still, when Neal Gabler wrote his book on the old moguls—subtitled *How the Jews Invented Hollywood*—some Hollywood Jews were insecure enough to warn that the book would encourage antisemitism.

In short, American Jews gained tremendous cultural and political power while evincing toward their own identity a mixture of self-assertion and fear comparable to that of earlier European Jews. In contrast to Europe, there was no Holocaust at their rainbow's end but, rather, a Hollywood-style happy ending offering total assimilation. Having habitually prepared themselves for hostility, Jews now faced indifference. They had a network of all kinds of organizations and programs, raised remarkable amounts of money, supported Israel, and mourned the Shoah. But at last free to define themselves, those most successful and Americanized had lost the knowledge or spiritual orientation that could let them do so.

As late as 1939, the American Jewish literary critic Ludwig Lewisohn could write, "For our numbers we have contributed singularly little to American literature."[4] But after 1945 came a torrent of creativity and success from a native-born generation. It was torn between sentimental memory and fierce rejection of a Jewishness it equated with the petit-bourgeois banality that its parents had embraced as quintessentially American. Jews played a major role in the cultural/political revolution overthrowing WASP ascendancy during the New Deal, acting as vanguard for a liberal coalition that comprised outcasts of every variety.

Nevertheless, despite the Jews' omnipresence in writing, filmmaking, book publishing, journalism, television, universities, and many other institutions, there was no backlash. American society was different from Europe in three critical ways: First, racial antagonism generally took the place of antisemitism. Second, in much of Europe, Jews had been virtually the sole minority, alone in undergoing assimilation; in America they were one of many groups which together formed a majority of the population. Ethnic identity increasingly meant charming variations in cuisine, not repugnant aliens subverting the nation's cultural integrity. Third, in America, Jews were not dealing with an old, highly structured culture to which they must clone themselves but a civilization still in formation, which they could help create.

In short, the Jewish elite was much like German Jews in its approach to assimilation, but Americans were very unlike the Germans. American society thus came to embody the antisemite's worst nightmare—a country much influenced by the Jewish standpoint and experience—largely because many non-Jews saw their own problems with assimilation and modern society in similar terms. As Lenny Bruce described it: "If you live in New York or any major city, you are Jewish." In this same category he included Italians, African American culture, a more adventurous taste in food, and anything seeming to indicate a triumph of passion over civility, experimentation over bland custom.[5]

In this new context, Jewish authors writing about Jews won every award and repeatedly topped best-seller lists. Jewish comedians made America laugh by projecting an ethnicity quite visible even when only implied. As in Europe, Jews had characteristics well-suited for an era of rapid change and heightened skepticism. Striving for advancement, they were not afraid to seem aggressive; having overthrown their own tradition, they were irreverent. They punctured romanticism, because the world wasn't beautiful, and pretense, since antisemitism made high moral or cultural values hypocritical. "The disputatious stance, the aggressively marginal sensibility, the disavowal of community ties, the taste for scrutinizing a social event as though it were a dream or a work of art . . . this was the very mark of the intellectual Jews," wrote Philip Roth.[6]

Jewish scholars and writers excelled at describing this new American society in nonfiction works, among them: David Riesman, *The Lonely Crowd*; Lionel Trilling, *The Liberal Imagination*; Daniel Bell, *The End of Ideology*; Nathan Glazer and Daniel Moynihan, *Beyond the Melting Pot*; and Leslie Fiedler, *The End of Innocence*. Jewish novelists were self-confident enough to show Jews in a negative light, starting with the obnoxious, lustful entrepreneurs of Ben Hecht's *A Jew in Love*, Jerome Weidman's *I Can Get It for You Wholesale*, and Budd Schulberg's *What Makes Sammy Run?* Jews might even be shown hurting Christians, as in Saul Bellow's *The Victim*, or flaunting new wealth, as in Philip Roth's *Goodbye, Columbus*.

The connotation of Jewishness also changed with the new generation. George Burns, Jack Benny, and Milton Berle were quite different from Philip Roth, Woody Allen, and Lenny Bruce, but all were very Jewish. The immigrants' children, obsessed with being American, raised their own kids to be so thoroughly American that they had less fear of expressing an ethnic identity, if they still had one. As Hecht wrote, those who had fought to elude ethnic labels now entered an elite where "only the individual counted" and could afford to incorporate a bit of Jewishness "as a character side line," like a millionaire once ashamed of his lowly origin but who now boasted of it to prove himself a self-made man.[7]

These changes were related, but only secondarily, to the Shoah and Israel's creation, events that took many years to register with American Jewish intellectuals. "We might scorn our origins . . . crush America with discoveries of ardor; we might change our name," wrote Irving Howe. "But we knew that but for an accident of geography we might also now be bars of soap. At least some of us could not help feeling that in our earlier claims to have shaken off all ethnic distinctiveness there had been something false, something shaming. . . . Jews we were, like it or not."[8]

The Shoah fell in a familiar pattern of Jews as victims, allowing American Jews to see the lesson as one more indication of the importance of tolerance, though the magnitude of this massacre challenged all Jewish worldviews.[9] Nonetheless, developments at home were more important to a new generation that neither looked back across the ocean to an old country nor was awed with gratitude at America's acceptance. Rather, it rebelled both against parents' enduring Jewishness, which seemed to serve no purpose, and their concealing it, which appeared to be a shameful abasement. This new group's anger arose from attempts to resolve the paradox of their legacy. They were told to succeed in the same gentile world, wrote literary critic Rachel Brenner, which they were also taught was an enemy wishing to destroy them. Mistrust blocked complete assimilation; fear of persecution inhibited accepting their ethnic heritage. Psychologist Bruno Bettelheim's comment on Philip Roth's Portnoy clearly expresses the contradiction: "He can neither let go of nor enjoy the specific Jewishness of his background."[10]

The new generation combined fear, anger, and self-assertion by trying simultaneously to become privileged insiders while remaining cynical outsiders, pretending to besiege a city to which they held the keys.[11] Old customs had lingering effects, even submerged beneath the surface of consciousness. They relentlessly examined their consciences, whether or not observing Yom Kippur; they were obsessed with ethics and justice, even if they did not know how a page of Talmud looked. Given the past of assimilation, it is not surprising they felt both arrogantly angry and insecurely inferior, willing to do anything to succeed yet refusing to join a club that wanted them as members, thinking themselves pariahs while certain that they were the vanguard.[12]

This generation's triumph could be said to have begun with the publication of Saul Bellow's *The Adventures of Augie March* in 1953, which flaunted, up to a point, the hero's immigrant background and Jewish milieu. It begins, "I am an American, Chicago born," in effect, saying, literary critic Robert Alter wrote, "I, a Jew grown up in a Yiddish-speaking milieu, born in Chicago, am an American like all other kinds of Americans. This is one legitimate variant of the American experience."[13] But at the same time, Bellow's hero is legitimatized by being exclusively American: defined by birthplace, not ethnicity, the factor that still dared not speak its name. The Jewish milieu was not mentioned explicitly or examined in *Augie March*, being a mere launching pad from which the hero will travel ever further. This experience had already happened for the writers themselves and for many others, too.

Just as Jewishness was the Old Country shtetl for immigrants, and the Yiddish Lower East Side for their children, the fully native-born grandchildren similarly consigned it to childhood past, a place now gone, a background now escaped, contrasting an assimilationist present with a nostalgic but well-rid-of past.

No story more astutely showed this point than Philip Roth's "Eli, the Fanatic." Eli Peck is a lawyer pressed to represent his neighbors, recent Jewish migrants to the hitherto-Protestant suburb of Woodenton, who wish to evict a Hasidic yeshiva opened by Holocaust survivors. These residents just want "to get things back to normal," meaning to ensure their physical and psychic distance from anything recognizably Jewish. "When I left the city," explains one, "I didn't plan the city should come to me." But the yeshiva refuses to go. When Eli complains about the funny clothes worn by the ultra-Orthodox Jews, the headmaster explains, "The suit the gentleman wears is all he's got." Eli and his friends may change their appearance, but these people will not do so. When Eli talks of the tree-lined suburb as the wrong place for a yeshiva, the director answers, "You talk about leaves and branches. I'm dealing with [the roots] under the dirt."

Eli understandably loves Woodenton:

What incredible peace. Have children ever been so safe in their beds? Parents . . . so full in their stomachs? Water so warm in its boilers? Never.

Never in Rome, never in Greece. . . . No wonder then they would keep things just as they were. Here, after all, were peace and safety—what civilization had been working toward for centuries. . . . It was what his parents had asked for in the Bronx and his grandparents in Poland, and theirs in Russia or Austria.

This was the best way to live. Why should one continue

studying a language no one understood. Practicing customs with origins long forgotten. Suffering sufferings already suffered once too often. . . . Why keep it up! However, if a man chose to be stubborn, then he couldn't expect to survive.

Nonetheless, while Eli feels assimilation as a modern American in Woodenton is history's best outcome, he trades clothes, for reasons he does not understand, with a yeshiva worker. "Then Eli had the strange notion that he was two people. . . . To think that he'd *chosen* to be crazy! But if you chose to be crazy, then you weren't crazy. It's when you didn't choose." His wife has him hospitalized and anesthetized, "The drug calmed his soul, but did not touch it down where the blackness had reached."[14]

The "blackness" refers to his new garment, and the story ends as Eli waits to see his newborn son, not knowing what to teach him. Doubleness and choice were popular themes for American Jewish intellectuals, now free to be anything other than what lay at their own root. The play *Fiddler on the Roof* sentimentalized that past while also asking God to keep such a world—paraphrasing its humorous blessing for the czar—"far away from us."

The journalist Eugene Meyer may be a good stand-in for what Eli's son would have become. Growing up in the 1950s in a suburb not unlike Woodenton, he thought his ancestors, "Remote, alien, manifestly un-American. . . . At home, an American flag flew from the garage, but no mezuza adorned our front door." The family had changed its name. "In college, I joined a non-Jewish fraternity. I even took offense once when, as an adult, a Swedish Jew in Stockholm called me a landsman; I am a person, not an ethnic group, I thought." Only after many years did he come to consider himself, "An American and a Jew as well. . . . In this knowledge there is comfort, and also a small knot of fear."[15]

Comfort, fear, and, perhaps, some embarrassment. One generation had escaped from too exotically colorful religious, Yiddish-speaking immigrant parents in big-city Jewish neighborhoods to suburbs like Woodenton, whose "principal endeavor," Stephen Birmingham wrote of a similar town, "seemed to be the erasure of memory."[16] Their offspring rebelled against the bland pseudonormality of middle-class suburban life—clean, spacious, and safe but also isolated, artificial, and sterile—in search of some philosophy or meaning beyond material well-being.

Mia Farrow once said of her then boyfriend Woody Allen, "His whole family strikes me as exotic because their world is so alien to me." But Allen responded in a short story: "Exotic? She should only know the Greenblatts. . . . I mean they're nice but hardly exotic with their endless bickering over the best way to combat indigestion or how far back to sit from the television set." In seeing their own people as terminally banal, assimilating Jews forgot how, a century earlier, Disraeli had built his career by playing the exotic Jewish Oriental prince. Allen joked that his parents' interests were "God and carpeting," of religious belief and materialism, both rejected by intellectuals. Roth's characters find prosaic America exotic. Portnoy went into sexual ecstasy over the fact that his girlfriend grew up in Iowa and her home's street was "not Xanadu, no, better even than that . . . Elm!"[17]

The usual generational conflicts were intensified and interpreted through clashing degrees of assimilation. Lenny Bruce complained that the WASP mothers he saw in the movies made his own "sweating and Jewish and hollering" one seem intolerable. Another Bruce routine was a Yiddish play come to life:

> Now we take you to a young boy who's returning home from Fort Loeb. But first we dissolve to the interior of the home, on Second Avenue. Jewish Mother: "Soon, he'll be home. Our boy's comink home from military school. I saved every penny vot ve had to bring him der success dot der outside vorld vud neffer gif him. Ah, soon our boy vill be home, from overseas in Delaware."
>
> Meanwhile the kid is saying: [Ivy League voice]: "I don't wanna be there with those Mockies! I don't wanna look at them anymore, with their onion-roll breaths. I found something new at Fort Loeb, and a girl who doesn't know anything about the Lower East Side."[18]

It is strange to remember that Jews were once renowned for having strong families. As upward mobility pushed immigrants' children to the suburbs, their parents were linked to memories of dark stairways, stale smells, cramped apartments, loud voices, and barbarous accents.[19] In comparison, blending into a bland mainstream was a big step forward. With so much discarded, little remained to give their distinctiveness purpose except sentimental leftovers fed by kitsch, Broadway shows, and self-righteousness. Roth called this mélange, "The boring, bloodless faith of the prospering new suburbs [based on] worship at the shrine of the delicatessen."[20]

This mix of ethnic remnants and carbon-copy assimilation left such parents little to pass on. Philip Roth's father literally threw away "everything 'useless' to which any of us might have been thought to have a sentimental attachment," a symbolic disposal of the past. He left his tefillin in a YMHA locker instead of giving them to the author, who admits his father probably thought he did not want them, while Roth's own young nephews in the next generation would not even know what they were.[21]

Lenny Bruce's effort to spruce up his nonconformist credentials made him step backward in time to claim that his parents were "devout Orthodox Jews" who drilled him daily in the Talmud and felt disgraced and humiliated by his wild behavior. In fact, Bruce grew up in semirural Long Island in a house with a picket fence, rosebushes, and maple furniture—described as looking like Richard Nixon's birthplace—far away from any Jewish neighborhood. Rather than being deprived, Lenny was spoiled. But this was scarcely a romantic origin.[22]

Bob Dylan also craved a more romantic identity than being the son of the local appliance store owner. Born Zimmerman in Minnesota, his grandparents were Orthodox, his parents marginal Jews, and he had a bar mitzvah. He traded in that background for one seemingly more fitting for someone reinventing folk music, fantasizing being an orphan from Oklahoma or New Mexico, the progeny of carnival workers or Las Vegas gamblers. He took as model the folksinger Woody Guthrie, a naïve Jewish kid's image of a man of the people. When a girlfriend's mother challenged his lies and said she thought Zimmerman was his real name, he called her an antisemite, as if a mere description of the truth was bigotry.[23]

That generation resented what they saw as their well-meaning but smothering parents' superficial, middle-brow lives. But their parents' fears and memories had made them overprotective, portraying the outside world as so frighteningly hostile as to be tinglingly exciting to the naïve children. As a critic noted, " 'America' was what you wanted, but it only seemed to exist away from home, out there where things could be uncomfortable or dangerous for Jews."[24] Nice Jewish boys and girls could play at being bad, masking their real—essentially conservative, self-seeking—goal of success as radical, vindicating their compliant step into assimilation as rebellion. They took what the novelist Isaac Rosenfeld called a "homelessness in the world" for granted, though still wondering "why I should feel an inner difference when outwardly I was the same as other men."[25]

Being so Americanized, why did they still feel uncomfortable? Part of the problem was that inexplicable, seemingly senseless "inner difference," which could no longer be understood as membership in a separate people or religion. Henry Roth had earlier described well this feeling and its creative potential: "He had felt snugly ensconced in his milieu, estranged from it, but spying on it, exploiting it, and yet without the least sense of obligation to it." Such polarization was the foundation of art.[26]

Many thought themselves original in refusing to belong to any group, not realizing this was a typical Jewish assimilationist attitude. Others, like the literary critic Leslie Fiedler, self-consciously stressed the importance of group perspectives and conflicts—ethnicity, race, and gender—in American history. At the last moment before full assimilation, they might explore or even flaunt their differences, shock both the culture they criticized and the forebears who preached silence, becoming more "Jewish" while no longer being Jewish.

This intergenerational and psychic battle was often the new literature's subject matter, just as the young peoples' breakout into American life furnished its plots. "To be raised as a postimmigrant Jew in America," wrote Philip Roth, was to have "a ticket out of the ghetto into a wholly unconstrained world of thought.... Without an Old Country link and a strangling church ... without generations of American forebears to bind you to American life, or blind you by your loyalty to its deformities, you could read whatever you wanted and write however and whatever you pleased. Alienated? Just another way to say 'Set free!' A Jew set free even from Jews—yet only by steadily maintaining self-consciousness as a Jew. That was the thrillingly paradoxical kicker."[27]

Unlike Heine's ticket of conversion, this one had no apparent cost, as intellectuals gloried in a critical detachment that would last at least until one more generation reached total immersion. Ironically, by reverting to an intellectual orientation, such people were coming closer to Jewish history, as well as replicating, with several decades' delay, the path followed by their European counterparts.

The things learned in college came largely from the non-Jewish elements of Western civilization including, as Roth catalogued them: European films, German philosophers, and Greek dramas; jazz, marijuana, blacks, beats, and string quartets. Manischewitz and Velveeta were replaced by French wine and cheese:

> He thought "This is real life," though nothing in life had ever seemed stranger.... He phoned home that night in ecstasy from all the erudition, but nobody in New Jersey knew who Thomas Mann was, or even Nelson Algren. "Sorry," he said aloud, after hanging up, "sorry it wasn't Sam Levenson."

The previous generation had rebelled against an outmoded culture, but this one rebelled against what they saw as no culture at all.[28]

Of course, not everything about the wider society was so attractive, or else total assimilation would have been an easy choice. Assimilating Jews might see the goyim, as Philip Roth portrayed it, as people who ate indiscriminately and voraciously, drank liquor copiously, swaggered, shot deer, and made a dead Jew their God while persecuting living ones. Yet they also seemed "engaging, good-natured, confident, clean, swift and powerful" boys; fascinating shiksas whose love was the epitome of belonging; fathers "with white hair and deep voices"; and courteous mothers with kindly smiles. They were "the Americans. . . . Children from the coloring books come to life. . . . The kids whose neighbors aren't the Silversteins and the Landaus, but Fibber McGee and Molly, and Ozzie and Harriet. . . . So don't tell me we're just as good as anybody else, don't tell me we're Americans just like they are. No, no, these blond-haired Christians are the legitimate residents and owners of this place."[29]

Given a chance to jump on either train, Roth was fascinated by the alternative lives offered by varying degrees of assimilation. He lets his characters consider the option of being a very assimilated, gentlemanly Jewish author in *The Ghost Writer;* an outrageous, antisocial rebel in *The Anatomy Lesson;* a West Bank settler in *The Counter-Life;* and even splits himself in two in *The Shylock Scenario.* He created a fable that the author was a pariah to the Jewish community; his characters often deliberately sought this status in the eyes of non-Jews and Jews alike.

For the hero of Roth's *Goodbye, Columbus,* the prospect of Jews too totally Americanized—and hence doltishly stupefied by material goods—is both alluring and repellent. The character makes fun of his girlfriend's middle-class suburban, affluent family. Her mother keeps kosher, is active in Temple and Hadassah—an uncle is the "Kosher Hot-Dog king"—but religion is just a social activity. When the hero asks his girlfriend's mother about Martin Buber, she looks at her Hadassah membership list. Told he is a philosopher, she wonders whether Buber wore a hat to services or kept kosher. Religion is passionless, bloodless, even Godless; American Jews are cut off from history.

While the narrator's parents are still "throwing off" the old ways, these people are "gathering in" America's bounty. "Since when," asks his family, "do Jewish people live in Short Hills? They couldn't be real Jews." The hero can't decide whether to sneer at their lack of culture or envy their wealth and security. He prays—inside a church, no less—asking God, "Where do I turn now . . . ? Where do we meet? Which prize is You?" When he steps outside to Fifth Avenue he sees the answer, "Which prize do you think, schmuck? Gold dinnerware, sporting-goods trees, nectarines, garbage disposals, bumpless noses." America is safe, fun, and prosperous. But is life's meaning, history's end, to sell one's birthright not for porridge but for filet mignon?

From this position, Jews could be simultaneously criticized for being too assimilated and insufficiently assimilated. There was now every kind of synagogue, Bruce joked, including an A-frame shule with a statue of Mary because "it's contemporary." Reform rabbis were "so reformed they're ashamed they're Jewish" and sound like British gentlemen, "Do you know, someone had the chutz-pah to ask me, 'Is there a god, or not?' What cheek! To ask this in a temple! We're not here to talk of God—we're here to sell bonds for Israel!" But off the pulpit, his sophistication is a sham and he has a Yiddish accent, "Ya like dot? Vat de hell, tossetoff de top mine head."[30]

In Roth's story "The Conversion of the Jews," a boy's mother hits him for asking too many questions—a hypocrisy intensified by its happening just after she lit the Sabbath candles—and a rabbi hits the child for accusing him of knowing nothing about God. Judaism had little to offer and its credibility was eroded by the surrounding sea of Christianity. "Ozzie suspected [the rabbi] had memorized the prayers and forgotten all about God." He insisted the boy read Hebrew faster although he understood nothing. The Jews' narrow provincialism made them put everything in two categories: good-for-the-Jews, no-good-for-the-Jews.[31]

"I was unmoved by the synagogue," recounts Woody Allen, "I was not interested in the Seder, I was not interested in the Hebrew school, I was not interested in being Jewish. It just didn't mean a thing to me. I was not ashamed of it nor was I proud of it. It was a nonfactor to me. I didn't care about it. . . . I cared about baseball, I cared about movies."[32] In his movie *Zelig,* when the twelve-year-old boy asks the rabbi the meaning of life, "He tells me the meaning of life . . . but he tells it to me in Hebrew. . . . I don't understand Hebrew. . . . Then he wants to charge me six hundred dollars for Hebrew lessons."[33] Tradition has no answers for him, it only wants to exploit him, and he is unwilling to pay the price. If it was such a matter of indifference to him, then why did he build his whole public persona and career on this image? Probably because having to act the stereotype of a Jew, he was at pains to divorce himself from that guise in his own life.

Yet starting in the 1950s, Jews themselves came to seem fascinating in a society no longer fearing diversity but, on the contrary, worrying that homogeneity was destroying individuality. In contrast, as Robert Alter explained, "The Jew has a special language, a unique system of gestures, a different kind of history which goes much further back than that of other Americans, a different cuisine, a kind of humor and irony that other Americans don't have, the colorfulness and pathos which other Americans aren't supposed to possess any more." So deeply did this idea penetrate American culture that in 1960 the very non-Jewish novelist Robert Penn Warren put Yiddish words into a novel set in very non-Jewish Tennessee.[34]

Still, caution was advisable. Despite this trend, relatively few Jews played openly on their background. For most, the market's dictate did more than any prejudice to make it preferable not to seem too Jewish lest this cut one off from the best opportunities and widest audience. In Miami Beach, Jewish club owners asked Jewish performers to tone down their Jewishness in playing to largely Jewish audiences. For his play *Don't Drink the Water,* Allen preferred Lou Jacobi in the lead, but producer David Merrick wanted someone else "to Anglicize it," said Allen. "He has an aversion to anything too Jewish." American Jewish writers regularly produced works self-consciously designed to prove their versatility. Bellow's *Henderson the Rain King* features a good-old-boy millionaire who wallows with pigs in the opening chapter. Roth's *When She Was Good* was so calculatedly "American" as to be set in Libertyville in middle America where everyone is a blue-eyed, flaxen-haired, Nordic Protestant.[35]

In a similar vein, Allen himself joked that when an advertising agency hired him as a token, he tried to look more Jewish—even reading memos from right to left—but was fired for taking off too many Jewish holidays.[36]

It was a wry comment on his own style: ethnic but not too ethnic. Commercial needs as well as personal ignorance limited his Jewish references to the most superficial satire. Beyond some proven laugh words—*rabbi, kosher*—Allen's films are surprisingly devoid of Jewish ideas, despite being immersed in a Jewish style. His most ethically oriented work, *Crimes and Misdemeanors*—including a brave Reform rabbi and a satirized seder scene—contains no real Jewish precept in its moral debates. If anything, the theological tone is closer to Catholicism. A vignette in *Husbands and Wives* shows a couple named Rifkin coming out of their church wedding.

Many more films dealt openly with Jews in the 1980s and 1990s than ever before, and Jews not only remained numerous on stage, screen, and television but also became far more visible. The very extent of assimilation made them feel less threatened personally and professionally, though also uncertain as to what message they wished to convey. The safest thing was to continue to homogenize characters and situations in the traditional bargain of conformity in exchange for tolerance. Barry Levinson's assimilating gangster "Bugsy," who teaches himself to speak and dress in a gentlemanly fashion, preaches, "Everybody deserves a fresh start now and then."[37] In Levinson's film *Avalon,* a seemingly Jewish immigrant family is made generically ethnic, lacking specific customs or religion. Perhaps its title—the name of the mythic Anglo-Saxon utopia—reflects a vision of America. The Yiddish accents of Feivel Mousekewitz's animated family in *An American Tale* were no barrier to using them in Christmas promotions.

Intermarriage was the ultimate theme, appearing with startling frequency in film—*Prince of Tides, When Harry Met Sally, The Way We Were, White Palace, Used People*—and on television from such series as *Bridget Loves Bernie* to *thirtysomething, Mad About You, Sisters,* and *Homefront.* The film *Chariots of Fire* approvingly showed a Jewish track star's date convincing him to eat ham while portraying as heroic a Christian fundamentalist runner making personal sacrifices to uphold his religious principles.[38]

Marshall Herskovitz, creator of *thirtysomething,* said Hollywood believed "People in America are not interested in Jews. They feel we must be careful and circumspect." But *careful* and *circumspect* seem words more associated with an expectation of prejudice than with a yawning disinterest. The solution was to show Jews as blending away harmlessly. Thus, an *LA Law* character overcomes an antisemitic mother-in-law to be married by a justice of the peace on a Saturday afternoon; a *thirtysomething* couple shares Christmas tree and Hanukkah candle-lighting. "Now, we're allowing ourselves to be who we are, and not to be ashamed of exposing it," says *Seinfeld* producer Larry David.[39]

It was a dramatic change from Hollywood's old era. And if the characters find being Jewish a marginal, declining factor in their lives, it is a fair, accurate representation of their creators and many—though not all—of the Jewish viewers. There should be no doubt, though, that the story being told and implicitly advocated is that of a Jewish assimilationist meltdown.* The virtual absence of Jewish female characters or families is a revealing attribute showing the absence of a Jewish community in the future.

The most remarkable film dealing with assimilation is Woody Allen's *Zelig.* Leonard Zelig compulsively mimics others, as does an assimilating Jew. He transforms himself into gangster, baseball player, African American jazz musician, or Chinese, believing he is these persons and coming to resemble them. As a boy, Leonard was disillusioned with Judaism, bullied by antisemites, and found no solidarity among Jews. When antisemites beat him up, "His parents . . . side with the antisemites." His dying father has no heritage to pass on except to say that "life is a meaningless nightmare of suffering, and the only advice he gives him is to save string." A doctor diagnoses Zelig's condition as quickly fatal but, like many predicting the Jews' extinction, dies himself. Zelig suffers not from a physiological (i.e., racial) but psychological disorder. He is a human chameleon because, he says, "It's safe . . . to be like the others." Communists, the Ku Klux Klan, and Christian fundamentalists each attack him as something different. He becomes fashionable for a while but just before marriage to his WASP psychiatrist (the final act of assimilation that may "cure" him) is persecuted, held "responsible for the behavior of each of the personalities he assumed." In the end, he simply "longs desperately to be liked once again—to be accepted to fit in."[40]

Despite the humorous problems caused by Zelig's attempts to fit in, assimilation seems his sole option, albeit better pursued with more restraint. This view is echoed by David Mamet's film *Homicide,* concerning a highly assimilated policeman who, upset by an antisemitic remark, becomes involved with an absurdly unlikely Israeli and American Jewish secret group fighting neo-Nazis. In the end, the group uses him, makes him break the law he is sworn to uphold, which betrays his loyalty to America, causes the death of his Irish partner (who, despite ethnic differences, is his true

---

*The heroes are usually lone, last Jews. See chapter 7.

friend), and almost causes his own demise. Jewish identity thus appears as a disastrous error, based on magnifying antisemitism and leading to the betrayal of American pluralism. A measure of how strongly this assumption holds American Jewish intellectuals was its triumph over Mamet's ostensible goal in writing the film as an assertion of Jewish identity.

Having declared independence from Jewish family and milieu, intellectuals now claimed that isolation was the essence of being a Jew. This concept inverted antisemitic stereotypes and made the Jew an American culture hero: the paragon of alienation, escaped from the ghetto and trying to elude being thrust back there, who pointed the way toward universal freedom, cerebral individualism, and atheistic humanism. To avoid membership in a seemingly insecure group, they fled from themselves to become neurotic individuals, fearing—perhaps correctly so—that their disorder was the font of creativity. To portray positive Jewish experiences would risk being sentimental and apologetic, surrendering to parents, curbing aspirations, and courting commercial disaster. Ironically, the new interpretation paralleled a Christian view of Jews as perpetual aliens lacking a valid culture or history of their own and destined to suffer. It was an American counterpart of the European Jewish assimilationist claim that the Jews' mission was to serve humanity.

Of course, weakening religious passion and ethnic roots characterized American and modern society as well as Jewish assimilation. Yet in the nonintellectual or antiintellectual 1950s, with political radicalism discredited and change seemingly stifled, alienation appeared the ultimate moral stance and source of creativity. Woody Allen told a joke about a family that decides not to dissuade a relative from thinking himself a chicken because, "We need the eggs." Abnormality was not a burden but a golden egg that total assimilation would destroy, just as eighteenth-century philosophers warned that civilizing noble savages would take away their unique gifts.

For assimilating Jews, the situation could appear like that of a man who, having just escaped from a collapsing building, questioned the soundness of any architecture and preferred to camp in the open ground. Their own belief system had fallen in on them, and events in Europe had shown that the assurances offered by their new abode were none so secure either. In this context, alienation was an alternative to both assimilation and to being a Jew. The key was to be a professional outsider. In Bellow's novel *Dangling Man*, the main character, an ex-Communist named Joseph, was torn between the desire to find a group to join and a desire to be autonomous.

Arthur Miller wrote of his wish to identify himself with humanity rather than one small tribal fraction of it. His 1949 play, *Death of a Salesman*, presented a prime example of a generic American family that was Jewish in everything but name.

To achieve real freedom, then, one had to live without religion, history, or family. Loyalty should instead go to truth, humanity, and—in practice—personal interests. The only thing sacred was the fearless critique of everything. "To you everything is disposable! Everything is exposable! Jewish morality, Jewish endurance, Jewish wisdom, Jewish families—everything is grist for your fun-machine," complains the brother of Philip Roth's Zuckerman.[41] The community wanted apologists, Canadian novelist Mordecai Richler complained, maintaining the artist's duty was to be a critic, as he savaged Canadians and Canadian Jews alike.[42]

Often the flight from being Jewish was rationalized as a rejection of any identity whatsoever outside individualism; in practice, it often meant simply exchanging the community into which they were born for another one. Mailer described the ideal as "to exist without roots . . . to explore the domain of experience where security is boredom and therefore sickness."[43] Mailer announced in the 1950s a rebellious philosophy glorifying both nonassimilation and anomie: "The liberal premise—that Negroes and Jews are like everybody else once they are given the same rights—can only obscure the complexity, the intensity, and the psychotic brilliance of a minority's inner life." The mainstream takes its place for granted, he wrote. The eagerness to join them reaches "its lowest form as 'the Jew-in-the-suburb. . . .' To the degree each American Jew . . . is assimilated he is colorless." To be exceptional requires brutal self-criticism, forsaking the complacency or fixed patterns of one's ancestors, creating oneself continually with each act, living "exposed to the raw living nerve of anxiety" and turning self-hatred into art.[44]

Mailer's view, though idiosyncratic, expressed an important basic concept among American, especially American Jewish, intellectuals central in the social upheavals of the 1960s and 1970s. Having been most bound by tradition, the Jew can now become most free of history. Mailer insists that removing "every social restraint" would enhance creativity.[45] Standing outside tradition and above group loyalty was supposed to confer a unique perspective for grasping truth. Yet such independence was a chimera. Mailer and other Jewish intellectuals—like earlier counterparts in Europe—were merely choosing whom they would imitate from a wider assortment of possibilities.

In the 1950s and early 1960s, the involuntary models were black jazz musicians; in the later 1960s and early 1970s, Third World revolutionaries. Black Americans were seen as fellow outcasts and—less flatteringly—as unrestrained people moved by natural rhythms rather than intellectual imperatives.[46] As Albert Goldman said of this naïve mimicry: "They thought that if you said 'Man' and 'dig' and 'hep' you were coming on like a Bopper. You were coming on—to tell the truth—like a kikey little fart who would have fainted if a real Bopper hit on him for two cents!"[47]

If being a Jew made Mailer feel like an outsider, it was also an identity that seemed associated with a sense of insecurity and lack of manhood. In battling society's alleged effort to take away his essence and domesticate him, Mailer conformed to the dominant order's definition of romantic hero. As with assimilationist Viennese Jews, a hypersensitive defensiveness showed the persona to be a pose. He eagerly jettisoned part of that personal essence as an overprotected Brooklyn Jewboy. When some friends spoke of their own wild youth—including a "gang bang" and a "penis-measuring contest"—Mailer blurted out, "Christ . . . I was going to Hebrew School every afternoon."[48]

Since no one can be so totally individualistic in thought, behavior, and identity, "alienation" was just a pose concealing adherence to the dominant society, or at least the sector of it where one lives. Moreover, psyche abhors a vacuum. If religion seemed a desirable way to cope with personal problems or to find meaning, Jewish intellectuals in America, as in Europe, so ignorant or at odds with their own faith, were more likely to seek emotional or spiritual encounters elsewhere. They flocked to every fringe group, cult, ideology, guru, drug, Marxist sect, Eastern religion, or self-improvement system. If poet Allen Ginsberg or Harvard psychology professor Richard Alpert, son of a Brandeis University founder, considered the family religion hypocritical and sterile, they could become Buddhists or Hindus. Ginsberg said on a visit to Israel, "Your great ideal is to build a new Bronx here. All my life I've been running away from the Bronx." So they became something different in an effort to become someone different.[49]

At times, Philip Roth's character Zuckerman—and his real-life counterparts—found being a dangling man frightening, saying to himself, "You are no longer any man's son, you are no longer some good woman's husband, you are no longer your brother's brother, and you don't come from anywhere anymore either."[50] Yet as Bob Dylan put it in one of his born-again-Christian songs, "gotta serve somebody." Like their European counterparts who had tried the same path, they—or their children—would not stay suspended long. At Dylan's moment of crisis in 1978—suffering from a divorce, heavy drinking, and drug abuse—with no direction home, he joined a cult and became a Christian fundamentalist, then brought this doctrine into his music and life, something he had never done with Judaism.[51]

This new paradigm reduced Jews from a people with their own particular culture and history to mere empty vessels, symbols of victimization and alienation. Those producing such ideas were simply ignorant that their ancestors had a world of their own in which they were unalienated, only becoming outsiders when they cut these ties. Implicitly, the celebration of alienation defined Jewish civilization as an obstacle that the imagination must escape to reach a higher stage of consciousness, where one saw clearly for the first time.

Rejecting the idea that the abnormality of their situation sprang from having a dual identity or no bond with a community, assimilating Jews could easily conclude that society or the nature of life itself was the source of their unease. In this way, Jewish intellectual history, religious or secular, did not count as a legitimate source of sustenance. As a substitute, Woody Allen sought to be European, neglecting the huge Jewish role in that culture. Semiofficial biographer Eric Lax noted that Allen's ancestors came from Königsberg, hometown of the philosopher Immanuel Kant. None of Allen's relatives studied with Kant, wrote Lax, "But his European and Russian lineage is an integral part of Woody Allen's psyche and creativity. It is the clearest sign of where he comes from as well as of where he is coming from."[52]

Woody Allen's preoccupations with God, morality, and justice are, of course, issues raised by his Jewish background. But Jews, unlike "European" or "Russian" antecedents, seem to have been uncultured village idiots, precursors of his carpet-obsessed parents. In fact, they were among Kant's best disciples. While Dostoevski, Camus, and Søren Kierkegaard figure in Allen's canon, the great Jewish thinkers, religious or secular, are absent. To Allen, Jews told jokes; Greek and Christian thinkers were serious. *Interiors* is a "serious" film because there are no Jews in it. As one of his plays put it in a scene set in classical Greece: "She doesn't belong. She's a philosophy student. But she's got no real answers. . . . Typical product of the Brooklyn College cafeteria."[53]

When still Alan Konigsberg, himself of Brooklyn, Allen's world split in two. Like the trains of *Stardust Memories,* the attractive fantasy of WASP and European society was far superior to grim Jewish middle-class reality. He understandably preferred the world of movies and felt returning home after such splendid escape to be "The worst experience in the world." "You would . . . leave the world of beautiful women and music and . . . bravery or penthouses or things like that. And suddenly you would be out on Coney Island Avenue in Brooklyn and the trolleys would be passing and the sun would be blinding and there was no more air conditioning."[54]

"He is a Jew, as people are quick to point out and as if it mattered more than it does," Lax writes in a phrase both startling and revealing. If Woody Allen's being Jewish is irrelevant, for whom else could it possibly matter? "Under different circumstances of birth," Lax continues, his comic references "could just as easily have been those of a lower-middle-class Irish Catholic in Boston who saw prettier women and a more interesting life across the river and set out to get there." His humor is not about Jews as outsiders but a purely individualistic anxiety from "wanting what he doesn't have and by the discomfort the world inflicts on him for being the things he is."[55]

But this discomfort is his motive for escaping what he is. To be funny, he must play the Jew; to be serious, he becomes a Jewish intellectual by using European ideas dissociated from anything Jewish. This is nonsense. Of course, many people see their own dilemmas paralleled in his characters, but this makes Allen no less the caricature Jew, brilliant but neurotic, ethical but cowardly, lustful but romantically inept, both ridiculing and envying the shallow—yet athletic, beautiful, and secure—people who live for the moment. He concurrently embodies and disarms every antisemitic stereotype. What is more likely, as Lax also writes, is Allen's desire to appeal to "any person with cultural and intellectual ambitions and pretensions who wanted to move from his figurative Brooklyn to a figurative Manhattan."[56]

In *Shadows and Fog,* his takeoff on Kafka, Allen says, "My people pray in another language. I don't understand it. Maybe they're calling troubles down on themselves." Unlike Kafka, he never tries to penetrate this language or the origins of those troubles. Disliking school, Woody likened the student monitors to concentration camp kapos. The Shoah did not seem to enter his philosophical ruminations. He merely expanded his own sufferings to cosmic proportion. History begins and ends with self. The character who takes Annie Hall to see *The Sorrow and the Pity* is obsessed with doom and death generally, not the Holocaust depicted in the film.

Nonetheless, his work is full of the dilemmas of assimilation. *Sleeper,* like *Zelig,* deals with the choices facing a man with no identity, thrown two thousand years into the future—where he is superior by being a disengaged alien though inferior for being maladjusted—who must be brainwashed and taught how to act anew. Interethnic romance is always a central theme for him, as in a short story that reads like an antisemite's nightmare: "That Connie Chasen returned my fatal attraction toward her at first sight was a miracle." She was tall, blond, high-cheekboned, witty, sexy, and intelligent, "That she would settle on me, Harold Cohen, scrawny, long-nosed, twenty-four-year-old budding dramatist and whiner, was a non sequitur on a par with octuplets."[57]

In a television special spoofing *Pygmalion,* Allen played a rabbi to Candice Bergen's dim-witted WASP beauty who wants to be one of the "smart, cultured people who always have something to say." He promises in three months to pass her off as "one of the country's leading pseudointellectuals." On succeeding, he throws off his disguise to show he isn't old and ugly—or a rabbi.[58] Consequently they marry and live "in mutual harmony—until the divorce." In his real life, something along these lines happened with Diane Keaton and Mia Farrow. Allen's trick in winning real or fictional beauties was by becoming guide to their own Western civilization, which he knew better than they did.

Despite such mastery, the last remnant of Jewish consciousness was often insecurity and a bitter sense of persecution. Adrenaline is the Jewish enzyme. Yet while the threat for Jewish intellectuals in America came from within, not from oppression, they felt impelled to challenge the society to show its true, exclusionary, hypocritical face or to lavish praise when finding that it was not so horrid after all. Jews won success but felt ambivalent about it: outraged by past abuse of Jews, angry that others ducked confrontation with injustice, and quick in taking disputes to extremes. Self-assertion was a way to prove to themselves they were neither cowardly nor collaborating.

Seeing Jewishness as a likely source of discrimination, commercial failure, or even a ticket to a concentration camp made it seem a potentially mortal condition. After all, this fright had been the factor driving many European Jews into conversion, concealment, or emigration. Being quiet—as a Jew—seemed sensible; speaking out under other guises seemed courageous yet safe, setting the tone for much of the fatuous type of leftism emanating from the American intellectual and entertainment elite. The

Jewish female celebrity, from Dorothy Parker to Joan Rivers, Sandra Bern-hard, or Bette Midler, was known for a witty form of sarcastic ridicule; the male Jewish rebel was more angry than romantic, more intellect than ac-tion: Lenny Bruce not James Dean; Woody Allen not Che Guevara.

Having the option to reveal or conceal Jewish identity gave more free-dom but was also a demeaning choice generating guilt at gaining privileges in exchange for deserting people, class, or justice. Thus, one's Judaism could be displayed at times as an assertion of superior suffering. In a Richler novel, a Jewish refugee asks another character, "What's the worst thing that ever happened to you? Wait. I'll guess. Your dog was run over by a car. No, you were naughty and your mummy made you go to bed without your supper. Have you ever eaten the flesh of sewer rats?"[59] Allen's charac-ter punctures the non-Jewish Annie Hall by asking how she would stand up to torture, claiming she would tell all if her Bloomingdale's credit card was taken away. In *Bananas, Sleeper,* and *Love and Death,* he becomes an unwilling freedom fighter.

As if their wealth and success might be taken away, they saw them-selves as downtrodden even when part of the elite. Thus, Bette Midler, one of Hollywood's most powerful actresses, commented in discussing AIDS, "If it had been 129,000 little white children [who died], you can bet they would have raised a stink. You say to yourself, 'Is that how the govern-ment's going to treat me if I don't fall into the category they cherish?'" An actor's life requires a multitude of personas. In her case, this meant a career starting with a first-grade prize for singing the Christmas carol "Silent Night" to a three-year run in *Fiddler on the Roof.* Her father was an atheist, her husband is a German Christian, and she was raising her children to "talk about all the gods."[60]

For those still retaining some Jewish identity, it was likely to revolve around antisemitism, a phenomenon uncommon enough in America that it must be searched out or provoked to show its face. The need to find anti-semites derives from the unimaginability of life without gentiles and a self-definition dependent on rejection. If, unlike Groucho, assimilating Jews do join the club, they might insist against the evidence that it was an uphill battle. Lenny Bruce provoked conflict "because he liked the feeling of panic, having to scramble," one of his friends said.[61] Richler wrote, "I've never been sent to a concentration camp. But no Gentile is expected to give thanks to the government that does not intern him. So why should [it] be expected of me?"[62]

Yet what is all this chutzpah for? Such an identity, which exists only when jostled and drowses when not being insulted, is satirized by Woody Allen's character in *Annie Hall* who aurally transmutes the polite question, "Did you eat?" into the insult, "Did Jew eat?"

Mailer has more luck, finding an American Nazi on whom to vent his angst:

> "You Jew bastard," he shouted. "Dirty Jew with kinky hair."
> "You filthy Kraut."
> "Dirty Jew."
> "Kraut pig."[63]

Mailer had the last word in complete safety. His interlocutor was not, of course, a "Kraut," a powerful German Nazi, but a member of a tiny, despised band of imitators. The confrontation exhibited Mailer's neurosis, not heroism. Nevertheless, the post–1950s Jewish intellectuals sensed a change their parents' generation missed: that a bad image no longer brought anti-Jewish persecution. Making themselves hate figures or apparently dangerous iconoclasts could be a good career move. They rebelled against being paragons who, wrote Philip Roth, "would never do . . . or be anything that couldn't be written up in the *Jewish News* under your graduation picture."[64]

Indeed, this rebellion was the malady Roth described as "Portnoy's Complaint": "A disorder in which strongly felt ethical and altruistic impulses are perpetually warring with extreme sexual longings often of a perverse nature." Doing what one wants brought "overriding feelings of shame and the dread of retribution." Many in Roth's generation were torn between a desire to assimilate and a wish to provoke rejection so as to return to being an outsider, even outcast, ricocheting like a pinball from being attracted to their own community and falling into the high-scoring place open to them in American society. Portnoy cannot settle down with a shiksa but obsessively fools around with them temporarily; masturbation is a replacement for real commitment; hedonism alternates with a compulsion to act ethically. In Roth's phrase, the game is to put the *id* back in *yid* and, by disturbing the dominant society's composure, putting the *oy* into *goy.*[65]

American culture from the 1960s onward was full of such restless figures who acted out a discomfort with American society, justified as a struggle to make it better. "I can't stand rejection," said Bruce. But he deliberately provoked anger, posing as a prophet inviting his own crucifixion, a scapegoat offering himself up for society's sins. "He seemed," said a biographer, "to get a kick out of rubbing salt in the wounds he made in many people's sensibilities," in love with the idea of being persecuted for the sake of healing a sick world.[66]

Playing with defused dynamite allowed one to speak the unspeakable, ridiculing antisemitism, Christianity, and Judaism alike: "A lot of people say to me," joked Bruce, " 'Why did you kill Christ?' I dunno.... It was one of those parties, got out of hand.... All right. I'll ... confess. Yes, we did it. I did it, my family.... Maybe it would shock some people ... to say that we killed him at his own request, because he knew that people would exploit him.... Boy, the things they've done in his name!"[67]

But he was far from the last of a breed that included such diverse types as Howard Stern, the provocatively profane talk show host; Roseanne Barr, the sometimes abusive television actress; Roy Cohn, right-wing, self-consciously sleazy lawyer; Abbie Hoffman, left-wing anarchist clown; Howard Cosell, straight-talking sports commentator ("Pro football has become a stagnant bore." "I am tired of the hypocrisy and sleaziness of the boxing scene."). They cheerfully offered themselves up as public hate figures, smashing idols or running roughshod over public civility. Stern justified his style by claiming that Jews had responded to mistreatment in America and succeeded by saying, "Screw you, WASPs." Hoffman said that "modesty was invented by the gentiles to keep Jews out of real estate, banks, and country clubs."[68] This attitude, though now expressed far more openly, paralleled what some Jewish intellectuals had done in Berlin or Vienna. But acts that once risked provoking a pogrom during insecure centuries past now became a relatively no-risk flaunting of freedom.

The urge to shock Jews or goyim extended across a wide range, depending on personal style. Mailer, in "The Time of Her Life," has a playboy seduce a Jewish girl, make her unwillingly plead for more, and then finally make her climax by saying, "You dirty little Jew." Woody Allen joked that his rabbi told him to refuse a lucrative vodka ad, saying it would be immoral, only to take the job himself. By showing a lack of reverence for Jews or fear of gentiles, jests about self-hatred or money-grubbing hypocrisy were assertions of independence from both groups.

Of course, this generation had far less to fear on either count, being removed enough in space and time from real persecution to joke, as Allen did, of a rabbi so Reform that he was a Nazi.[69] In "The Conversion of the

Jews," Roth runs through Jewish children's reactions to such painful questions as their views of Christianity as a bizarre religion and their questioning
of how Jews could be the Chosen People if the Declaration of Independence
claimed everyone was created equal. The story ends with a boy forcing a
rabbi to profess belief in Jesus to stop him from jumping off a roof. Mel
Brooks's film *History of the World, Part I* portrays two-thirds of that saga as
centering on antisemitism, including a fun romp through the Spanish Inquisition. Brooks's movie *The Producers* is the phenomenon's perfect symbol: the
more two Jewish impresarios set out to offend people, the more successful
they become, through a Broadway play featuring a song entitled "Spring-
time for Hitler."

Although Lenny Bruce's material and personality were extreme, they
express important themes. In addition to unmasking Jewish fears and
Christian prejudices, he ridiculed assimilation itself. Bruce went beyond
the old staple reminder that Jesus was a Jew to make the Pope and Lone
Ranger Jewish, too. Almost everyone was really Jewish, meaning different,
oppressed, alienated. Gentiles were hypocrites, secret antisemites. Jews
were ridiculous in their efforts to pass as gentiles. Bruce joked that it was
"important to the Christian people" to know that the actor Tony Curtis's
real name "is Bernie Schwartz! . . . He is obviously not a Curtis. A Curtis is
never a Schwartz."

Such open questioning of assimilation as such was new, but the omnidi-
rectional cynicism devaluing all beliefs and the anger at being forced to
conform to another group's creed paralleled an important strain of thought
in European Jewish intellectuals. A biographer summarized Bruce's comedy as saying, "What if all the great people in this world—heroes of legend,
leaders of nations, powers, potentates, principalities . . . God Himself—are
simply . . . crude, cynical shyster businessmen and degenerate hustlers?" Or,
as Bob Dylan put it in a song, "It's easy to see without looking too far/That
not much is really sacred. . . . Propaganda, all is phony."[70]

Simultaneously having an inherited identity and a preferred self-made
one impelled Jewish intellectuals to the imagery—and practice—of double
roles. Discontented by the part assigned by history, they redesigned themselves. Allen joked that on first seeing *The Maltese Falcon,* he identified with
Peter Lorre (in real life also a Jew): "The impulse to be a sniveling, effeminate, greasy little weasel appealed to me enormously." But Allen really
wanted to be like Bogart, as in his 1969 *Life* cover story, "How Bogart Made
Me the Superb Lover I Am Today" and film, *Play It Again, Sam.* His article

ends, "The only safe thing is to identify with the actual falcon itself. After all, it's the stuff dreams are made of."[71] Jewish writers' daydreams, and plot ideas, often began with the gap between their self-image and how they wished to be.

Whatever one's abilities, acting is a field where physiognomy is destiny, a fact that typecast most—but not all—Jews. "Like other Hollywood anomalies such as Bette Midler or Barbra Streisand," wrote one reporter failing to note what these people have in common, "[Dustin] Hoffman is a testament to how talent and drive can overcome any physical differences nature may have doled out." Hoffman generally played "an outsider of some kind" and that is how he saw himself.[72] Coming from backgrounds that made many Jewish actors feel like nouveau-cultured schlemiels, they understandably wanted to be something else: suave intellectual, tough greaser, glamorous sex goddess, or securely powerful member of the establishment. Intellectuals dressed as workers, thinkers posed as men of action to escape the stereotype of passive ghetto or fatuous suburban Jews. Ben Hecht's alter ego was a heroic pirate; the left had its proletarians or Third World revolutionaries. Nelson Algren hung out with street gangs; Bob Dylan with real folks; and Mailer fantasized being a blond beast.

A friend teased Lenny Bruce about mutating his name from Leonard Schneider, "All you guys who try to get away from being Jewish by changing your last name always give the secret away by forgetting to change your *first* name. What kinda goy has a first name Lenny?"[73] But this contradiction made sense. Keeping the first name retained one's individuality; dropping the family name jettisoned one's background. Bruce was not trying to keep a secret. Rather, like the strippers he spent so much time with, he was revealing and concealing at the same time.

Mailer, boasting of affirming the barbarian in himself, sounds as though he were trying to scare his grandmother by dressing up as a Cossack. True, he stabbed his wife to test his fitness to play superman but he admitted, "It was phony. . . . It wasn't me." In his novel *An American Dream*, however, Mailer's character actually does murder his wife, Deborah.* He looks in the mirror, feeling alive, his eyes blue as a German's, "I looked deeper into the eyes in the mirror as if they were keyholes to a gate which gave on a palace, and asked myself, 'Am I now good? Am I evil for ever?' " Then he embarked on a sexual marathon with Deborah's German maid, Ruta.[74]

---

*A Jewish name. Mailer's real-life spouse/victim was Adele Morales.

An easier way out was to merge oneself into a created character, as Jack Benny, George Burns, and Groucho Marx had done. Comedian Pee-wee Herman (Paul Reubens, originally Reubenfeld) appeared only in character. The actors Leslie Howard and Laurence Harvey, both Jews, were each the model of an Englishman for two generations of American moviegoers. Similarly, the personification of the good and bad "greasers" were, respectively, Henry Winkler ("the Fonz") and Andrew Silverman.

Silverman was better known as the ferociously macho Andrew Dice Clay, whose insults to women and ethnic groups were so nasty as to be dubbed "Brownshirt humor." Stumbling onstage as nerdish "Eugene Moscowitz," he became a tough, foul-mouthed hood in a black leather jacket. In his original Silverman/Moscowitz persona, he nearly cried confessing his past failures but then, turning into his tough-guy character, gave his formula for becoming "the hottest comic in the world": "You believe in yourself, and you don't listen to nobody."[75] Or, more accurately, by not believing in yourself you can become somebody else and thus important and powerful.

The comedian Sandra Bernhard was his female opposite and equivalent, a tough crust over a molten core. Clay conceals vulnerability with macho toughness; she flaunted feminine fragility overlaying strength, a posture revealed in her show's ironic yet revealing title, "Without You I'm Nothing." In fact, she had created her own persona: "Though there was really something great about growing up in a liberal, intellectual, Jewish household," she dreamed of being a gentile with Laura Ashley dresses and glazed ham with cloves at Christmas. She confesses discomfort at not being blond, willowy, or small-nosed. "What we see when we watch Bernhard onstage," writes a critic, is the spectacle of a woman turning herself into "something she dreams of being, into something she's not."[76]

In Bruce's Jewish/goyish dichotomy, assimilation had already gone so far that Clay, Bernhard, and Dylan fell into the latter category. Bernhard called home "the cold flat badlands of the American Midwest." A neighbor to Annie Hall, all her best friends were gentiles. She had enough of a Jewish background to shape her thinking and enough American dreams to direct her yearning. Born in 1955, her experience was a blend of aluminum Christmas trees and Hanukkah candles, religious studies and coming home to "a big bowl of Campbells' bean-with-bacon soup and a bologna sandwich with Miracle Whip."[77]

The most successful Jews had imbibed, duplicated, and improved on the more sophisticated versions of culture they had borrowed. Helena Rubinstein and Sam Bronfman had become wealthy selling the European mystique of beauty and royalty, the latter adorning his scotch with crowns, scepters, and endorsements from bluebloods, none of whom were Jewish. Patrons of the avant garde like Edward Warburg and Lincoln Kirstein, financiers of George Balanchine's American ballet, or Paul Sachs, of the influential Society for Contemporary Art, created new elite tastes.

Ralph Lifshitz went a step further, transforming not only himself but millions of others into their dream persona. As Ralph Lauren, he sold them a wealthy WASP's outer appearance. Paul Goldberger of *The New York Times* was impressed by his "authenticity of conviction." But Michael Thomas, a real member of that elite, saw it as totally counterfeit: "Imagine you are a former stroke for the Harvard crew sitting on the beach at, oh, Lyford Cay." Suddenly, you notice a vile, socially inferior fellow "wearing a crew shirt beribboned at the neck with the same colors you puked your guts out to win at Henley twenty years earlier," but carrying Lauren's polo pony logo.* "Your likely reaction is to become apoplectic."[78]

Lauren once examined the clothes of the late philo-Nazi, the Duke of Windsor, and was enchanted by his style. "Which is to say," a journalist jeered, "he liked only what he saw." But that was precisely the point: the visible mattered most to him because it was the easiest way to remake one's image. Despite the quality of his goods, Lauren provoked more anger and contempt than any other designer because of his success in subverting the snobs' marginal advantages and distinctions. In the tradition of Hollywood moguls who shaped an American paradigm of small-town values and Anglophilia, he created—or rather re-created—England and the old American West in products ranging from napkin rings to clothes.[79]

Asked about his Brooklyn origins, Lauren defensively pointed out that Bill Blass was from Indiana, Halston from Iowa. "We were all born somewhere else." But the point was that he was born someone else. When receiving an award from the hands of Audrey Hepburn, he hugged her and crowed: "You want to know what the lifetime achievement is? . . . We went to the movies in the Bronx thirty years ago. Remember the princess? I got her."[80]

In a nation where Jews could get the princess, Steven Spielberg's Holo-

---

*Lauren, like Hollywood moguls and Jewish immigrant writer Jerzy Kosinski, was fascinated by polo as a symbol of aristocracy.

caust epic *Schindler's List* was a smash hit, and Charles Silberman could start a *New York Times* lead article with a Yiddish proverb, the promise of assimilation seemed fulfilled.[81] Many Jews could find some balance between identities; numerous others—especially in the intellectual and creative sectors—were dissolving into American society. If Jews were increasingly less distinct, there was genuinely less to say. As Gershom Scholem put it, "They may have been aware of their past, but they no longer wanted to have anything to do with the future of the Jews."[82]

One of Woody Allen's most famous bits involves a party where a moose loses the best costume award to a Jewish couple dressed as a moose. So well do the latter impersonate a moose that they are shot, stuffed, and displayed at the New York Athletic Club. But the joke is on the club: it does not admit Jews.[83] Jews became imitations better than the originals, outsmarting antisemites by becoming something else. They could enter any club and play any role—but the price might be forfeiting the identity and background that begat their talent and adaptability in the first place.

5

The Mystery People

Nothing can help the Jew. He will never give satisfaction no matter what he does. If he spends too much, he is ostentatious, a spendthrift; if he spends too little, he is called stingy, a miser. If he keeps aloof from public life, he is lacking in public spirit; if he takes part in political life, he is an impertinent intruder.

—*Rabbi Joseph Bloch, to Austro-Hungarian Parliament, 1890*[1]

THE PROBLEM of Jewish assimilation, wrote the Viennese Jewish playwright Arthur Schnitzler in 1908, might perhaps be solved in a thousand years: "In our time there won't be any solution, that's absolutely positive. No universal solution at any rate. It will rather be a case of a million different solutions. . . . Every one must manage to find an escape for himself out of his vexation or out of his despair or out of his loathing, to some place or other where he can breathe again in freedom. Perhaps there are really people who would like to go as far as Jerusalem to find it."[2]

During the two centuries after the French Revolution began their emancipation in 1799, roughly half the world's Jews either totally assimilated or were murdered. Previously, Jews had been a national community having distinct customs, culture, and language, as well as religion. Assimilationists wanted them to jettison this civilization to become identical with the majority except for a few theological details, an orientation that would inevitably bring disintegration. Those choosing to remain Jews—many of whom were no longer religious or traditional—rallied around ideas learned from the dominant society: they would be a people in the secular sense as well. This decision could seem frightening, a challenge to total identification with the country where they lived or all humanity. But Zionism, even if watered-down—presented, for example, as ethnicity—became the basis of a modern, secular reason for Jewish existence.

Joseph Heller's hero in the novel *Catch-22*, refusing to fly World War II missions, is asked what would happen if everyone thought the same way. In that event, he responds, he would be a fool to think anything else, a reply both endorsing and mocking conformism. In the assimilationist dilemma, how could one continue to believe that one's own minority view was true? As Ahad Ha-Am summarized the issue: if the Jews were obsolete, a mere monument to past religious progress, "Why, then, this life of trouble?"[3]

That question was the centerpiece of an era typified by massive defection. "The readiness of many Jews to invent a theory that would justify the sacrifice of their Jewish existence," wrote Gershom Scholem, "is a shocking phenomenon."[4] But it was not a very surprising one. As one of the first modern Jewish intellectuals wrote in the eighteenth century, those "delivered from the bondage of superstition, suddenly catch a gleam in the light of reason and set themselves free from their chains." Like a starving man at a full table, he "will attack the food with violent greed, and fill himself to surfeit."[5]

Even the beloved Yiddish writer I. L. Peretz, noted a biographer, "had spasms of desire to get away from the stifling disciplines of a people out of touch with the contemporaneous European world, away from the taboos and superstitions, the mumbo-jumbo, and the insularity."[6] Elias Canetti wrote of a Jewish character that he defined "Jew" as a "genus of criminal that carries its punishment with it."[7] To be Jewish, philosopher Albert Memmi recalled thinking, was "a narrow and constricted fate. Why, when my life was just beginning, should I accept this limitation? Why should I forsake so many splendid adventures to remain vanquished among the vanquished? I wanted to taste every food, enjoy every pleasure; I would be proud of my body and sure of my mind; I would practice every sport and understand every philosophy."[8]

In contemporary times, rebels are idealized and the oppressed made noble—attitudes Jews helped to create—but even in the recent past the former were seen as marginal, the latter as inferior. Suffering might be later sentimentalized, but victims prefer to escape; most people simply want survival and security, then the comforts of luxury and success. The bourgeoisie, yearning for peace and stability, usually favored silence about the ordeals of assimilation. It was left to intellectuals, who thrived on words, to justify their defection and turn it into a philosophical system.

Many assimilating Jews received great rewards for fleeing their old identity. The majority often took pride in these compatriots' success but were even more demoralized at seeing, in Ahad Ha-Am's words, "Our people . . . scattering the sparks of its spiritual fire in all directions to augment the wealth and the fame of its enemies and its persecutors," while gaining nothing for itself from such gifted offspring's work. In this unique phenomenon of a people cheering its own destruction, Jews took pride in claiming those who sought "to forget and bury the relationship [or] treat us with a lofty contempt." It was no sign of true greatness to abandon one's own people—the source of "special aptitude" and "fundamental ideas and feelings"—in order to serve a society demanding one tear "himself into two disparate halves" and to always feel deprived of "harmony and wholeness."⁹ Yet this very dissonance and its attendant pain and insecurity would be one of the main earmarks and sources of vitality for assimilating Jewish culture and ideas.

The Jewish condition was simultaneously deeply compelling and difficult to conserve, fairly easy to escape but hard to erase entirely. It was a situation, recounted Zionist leader David Ben-Gurion, affecting "every limb and nerve of the body, every conscious and subconscious act." Hannah Arendt wrote that the issue "haunted their private lives and influenced their personal decisions all the more tyrannically."¹⁰ It not only affected millions of Jews but also influenced much of Western cultural, intellectual, and political life. Like atoms shattered in a nuclear reactor, this rending and reformation of identities generated gigantic bursts of energy from a tiny mass of people. While such a result has often been attributed to marginality, other groups facing such a situation have produced different, far less spectacular effects.

Of course, Jews were inevitably influenced by those among whom they lived. Each individual had to decide how to define himself in a non-Jewish, often anti-Jewish, society. While overtly a matter of free will, these responses were bullied by demands to conform to a worldview whose omnipresence made it seem both superior and normal, even as it judged Jews as inferior, tempted them to change sides, and undermined their sense of self-worth. By requiring Jews to change—whether for material gain, survival, genuine belief that the new way was superior, or merely taking it for granted—assimilation made them concede that they were previously inadequate.

Those who accepted negative stereotypes of their people tried to dissociate themselves or disprove this image through personal achievement, patriotism, conformity, and selflessness. Each choice entailed taking on a different set of ideas, actions, and even personalities. If one was no longer seen as a Jew—as a target of hate and prejudice—it seemed feasible to achieve everything, to be anyone. The British Jewish philosopher Isaiah Berlin put the dilemma humorously, comparing Jews to hunchbacks: some denied they had a hump; others said they were proud to have one; or insisted it was shrinking and would vanish if everyone ignored it; or that it would fall off if they went to Israel.[11] For some, changing the world and creating a society where they had no hump—even if that required a universal plastic surgery to make all humanity beautiful—was the most attractive solution of all.

In whatever fashion they aimed to transform themselves, Jews faced three special dilemmas. First, they might use the new freedom and knowledge they were gaining either to abandon or to enhance the community into which they were born. The former way meant selecting another nation, doctrine, or religion; the latter option meant reforming Judaism in religious, nationalist, or ethnic terms.

Second, they had to select what route to take in order to live in that new world. In contrast to their neighbors—who could simply conform to their own way of life—Jews had to make decisions. They could even "change" their ancestors to Christians (by conversion) or Greeks (by intellectual assimilation). The very fact that they had choices fostered creativity—making everything that existed seem arbitrary rather than destined—and made them ready to bring systematic thought to bear on it. Moreover, as assimilating Jews became better at role-playing they generally retained an alternative, Jewish, identity, a potential that novelist Philip Roth called the "counter-life." Having two points of view within one head gave them the advantages of a clearer, stereoscopic vision even as it also brought the drawbacks of a split personality.

Third, Jews adapted everything they adopted. Assimilation did not so much dissolve old traits as create a new synthesis, Jewish variants built from a historic heritage and contemporary situation. As the critic Harold Bloom noted, "the various paths of modern exile are circumscribed by the world of Jewish memory."[12] Assimilating Jews became advocates of specific ideas and institutions since their background determined which of their new culture's aspects and ideas most appealed to them, playing a part—however silent—in setting their intellectual and political agendas or platforms. Even when Jews took opposite sides in debates, they drew from a common pool of concepts and used parallel arguments on behalf of competing causes. As Arendt wrote of Rachel Levy, "She had walked down all the roads that could lead her into the alien world, and upon all these roads she had left her track, had converted them into Jewish roads."[13] The very fact that they were engaged in assimilation was a distinguishing mark. "The louder he protested his emancipation from Jewishness," as was said of Heine, "the more his Jewishness seemed to be evident and protruding." Equally, among those trying to conceal their Jewish aspects, wrote Ahad Ha-Am, these became apparent "in all that they attempt, and gives their work a special and distinctive character."[14]

The only point on which most Jews' intellectual fearlessness failed them was in understanding themselves. Still, even the most conscious, strenuous attempt to escape the Jewish condition brought along pieces of it. The very act of trying to forget and transform themselves kept them different, creating ideas, movements, or behaviors that might be called "Jewish Variants": very Jewish in origin and content despite an ostensibly non-Jewish, even anti-Jewish nature. Thus, Gershom Scholem called the Marxist Frankfurt school a "Jewish sect"; a Jew invented Esperanto to be a universal language, though it remained a marginal curiosity; and traditional British names—like Milton, Irving, or Morris—became identifiably Jewish since so many Jews used them to masquerade as Anglo-Saxons.

Their highest creation was a subculture of assimilating—but not yet totally assimilated—Jews with its own literature and ideas, at the center of intellectual and creative activity. In this partly separate, highly creative subculture of their own, assimilating Jews associated mainly with each other. But even as its remarkable productivity deeply influenced the world's transformation to modernity, these Jews rejected intimations of any special Jewish "angle" toward Western civilization as seeming to confirm antisemitic propaganda. Yet even as they broke away from anything Jewish, their new ideas and creations were highly influenced by that background.

This distinct perspective began with differences in the religion's content and its attitude toward political structure. In contrast to Christian churches, whose hierarchies reflected their theology and social function, Judaism was more democratically structured, mirroring a rejection of distinctions among people in their status before God and certainly in their absence of divinity. After all, its patriarch, Abraham, was the original iconoclast—literally a breaker of idols.

While Jews practiced relentless self-criticism and debate, Christian doctrine was more akin to modern propaganda, proclaiming itself always in the right and condemning those thinking otherwise. "The instinct of a people leads them to believe in justice," wrote the French Jewish politician Léon Blum, expressing an idea most typical of Jews. "When they have been injured, they need to believe that they have not been wrongly injured, and they examine their own hearts to discover the guilt within them."[15] This attribute, though, was used against them by Christians and antisemites as proof of the Jews' sinfulness. As a Jewish scholar noted, "For the nations among which they sojourned, not given to much self-criticism, and having a lower moral standard than the Jews, naturally thought: 'If they call themselves bad, what extraordinary villains they must be!' "[16]

Christian dogma accepted a conservative idea of human limits stemming from Original Sin and the innate carnality of earthly life; for Jews, the law was set in stone but obeying it was open to ingenuity. In Judaism, social behavior was the measure of piety. The physical and spiritual were collaborative, not inevitably opposed. The duality of assimilation was prefigured by a Jewish sense of a doubleness, of being caught between the memory of Jerusalem and the reality of exile, in the need to fence off their lives from a largely alien world. In Judaism, too, God's obligations to man gave humanity grounds for complaint about an unacceptable reality.

Differences in historical experience widened the gap. To believe, as the Jewish situation suggested, that those oppressed were right and the enthroned ones wrong was an idea that would turn society on its head. Jewish tradition never accepted a divine right of kings, who often acted wrongly and turned God against them.[17] Persecution only confirmed a sense of the dominant system's illegitimacy. But for Christianity as a state religion—as for the aristocrats and bourgeoisie accepting its teachings—success was often equated with virtue. Those whose worldview had governed for two thousand years found it easy to assume that the existing authority and order were just.

Jews took so successfully to modern thought—and gave it their own interpretation—because they already possessed its essential method and style. Jewish learning built on its own internally consistent order and—within those confines—applied rigorous logic. In the Jewish framework, it was precisely by following a system that one became free; "Turn it over, and turn it over again, for everything is in it," in a rabbi's view of the Talmud.[18] In a constant process of reexamination and implementation, Judaism used a critical analytic system of thought, albeit restricted to a single subject matter: the sacred writings and texts derived from them. Even when

God had been stricken from the equation and a Jewish religious viewpoint explicitly expunged, its heirs went on seeking the purpose and the plan.

Once detached from the traditional object, this method was applied elsewhere as a remarkably effective intellectual or artistic tool. Having left the Garden of Eden of their own tradition, which resolved all questions and gave them a place in the universe, they felt impelled to seek—and expected to find—another system of all-explaining answers constructed on intellectual principles. Without realizing it, assimilating Jews duplicated these and many other premises from their background in the secular sphere.

Coming from a small, slandered people inclined one to believe that a little group might possess the truth while the rest of society was wrong. If the majority rejected the assimilating Jewish thinkers and their ideas, that was not novel. The result was the strange blend of intellectualism and romanticism found in Marx, Einstein, Disraeli, Freud, Trotsky, Kafka, Herzl, and so many others. But while Jewish intellectuals might benefit by remaining in transition, that was a state far less pleasant or satisfactory for ordinary Jews.

For those assuming Christianity's obvious correctness—as more than a few assimilating Jews also did—perseverance of the Jews was hard to understand or justify. Much of this confusion came from regarding them as solely a religion—an insufficient explanation of that history and an inadequate basis for survival in a secular age—rather than as a nation and civilization closely melding people and religion, government and culture.[19] Judaism did not continue only because of inertia. New debates and thinkers renewed it in each generation. Even the most pious evolved, borrowing many of their supposedly ancient ways from Eastern Europe.

The hardship of human life, Moses Hess wrote, made religion all the more necessary. Nothing could be more cruel than to demand that "utterly desperate" people renounce faith and hope. "Religion can turn the miserable consciousness of enslavement into a bearable one," lessening the pain, "just as opium does serve painful maladies."[20] Hess compared religion to opium as a type of medicine; Marx—totally alien to any such positive content—could approach it only with the utmost cynicism, revising the metaphor to denounce it as a harmful drug.

Thus, the revolt against tradition's constricting dictatorship went to the opposite extreme, denying any value at all to a wisdom and community assembled from sage individuals and the experience of many generations.

As a result, most Jewish intellectuals were uniquely prejudiced against their own civilization, thinking it devoid of interesting art and literature, viewing the West as a product of Greek and Christian ideas, and Judaism as a religion either surpassed by Christianity or obsolete in secular times.

"Those who laugh at these regulations and deride them," wrote Ahad Ha-Am, are ignorant of "their deep patriotic meaning. . . . What would have become of . . . the Jews if they would not have wrapped themselves up, until the day of national rebirth, like a cocoon in their Talmudic learning in order to appear again, at the end of a fully attained spiritual regeneration, as a butterfly next to all other liberated nations." To improve on this past was sensible; to discard it entirely was wasteful and illusory. No person or generation can really draw a dividing line between self and inheritance. "In every generation there are those who say that no belief can hold its ground in the face of logical deduction or scientific evidence," he added. But most people, "even educated ones, ignore these proofs, so influenced are they by what has gone before," and so reluctant to believe their ancestors were fools.[21]

But that point applied even more to non-Jews, who were less ready to break sharply with the past or denounce their traditions. Above all others, Jews were in a position to see that other ways existed, with each group thinking its own customs most natural and in tune with God. Christians felt far less need for a systematic new tradition, despite such iconoclastic thinkers as Darwin and Nietzsche. But the secular assimilationist needed to believe that humanity could shape and change the world according to its will. After all, knowing he was in a transitional state made him seek completeness or normality through either full assimilation or trying to maintain that in-between state of tension.

The Jews' behavior in regard to assimilation made them even more mystifying—a strange people with obscure goals whose multiple identities could be interpreted as so many false masks. Suspicious about the assimilationists' professed altruism, the majority naturally assumed Jews wanted power to advance themselves as a group. Consequently the Jews were viewed in sinister terms, as enemies of Christianity, the state, and order; economic parasites; or racial inferiors. While Jews were unconcerned about other's faith, Christianity and Islam—generally considering nonbelievers as inferiors to be hated, conquered, or converted—expected them to have similar beliefs and a desire to rule or subjugate. In their tradition, Jews had behaved on the highest, nonviolent moral plane. Their refusal to fight, however, even against insults and oppression, was not admired but seen as a symptom of their strange inferiority or a hint that their aggression and ambition took another channel like ritual murder or conspiratorial plotting.

Antisemites now decried the Jews' entry into the dominant culture as a danger, fearing they would not accept the status quo but revise it to suit themselves. Those most sharply breaking with Judaism in order to assimilate inspired as much antisemitism as did those steadfast in faith and customs. Jewishness hidden behind emulation seemed more menacing than when Jews had worn distinctive clothes and kept to themselves. Those non-Jews fearing change would subvert their own cherished identity associated a threat from liberalism, atheism, secularism, internationalism, or modernism with Jews as a group, since most assimilating Jews favored such ideas. Jews, claimed the antisemite Brentano, despised "old festivals . . . sagas of the people" and everything traditional.[22]

Thus, antisemites either denied that assimilation was possible or demanded that Jews go further in relinquishing any independent character. Conservatives maligned secular Jews; liberals reproached traditional ones, arguing that an appearance of assimilation concealed a refusal to do so, a secret agenda to seize power. Aware of these suspicions, many Jews became even more defensive and eager to integrate to the vanishing point. The very things of which Jews had been most proud now became dangerous. Since antisemitism and discrimination rested on the idea that Jews were different, they wanted to disprove this charge by extinguishing any deviations themselves.[23] Disappearing was the best way of all to show that the critics were wrong, and assimilationists were often merely requesting a bit more patience until total invisibility could be achieved.

Overwhelmed by Christian society's prizes, power, and influence, many Jews felt their own beliefs becoming the frailest of all doctrines, eroded like soapstone by surrounding granite. The more they asserted how fully integrated they were, the more everyone was reminded of the remaining gap. No matter how they praised or tried to imitate the majority society, they felt neither completely integrated nor totally accepted by it. Ostentatiously ignoring one's background was merely another proof of its importance. Acceding to this demand to abolish their own heritage, assimilating Jews might conceal their origins, revise customs to resemble those of Christians, or minimize links to other Jews or their ancestral land. Yet ceasing to practice the religion, they often retained some sense of identity that made them uncomfortable or at least ambiguous about behaving that way.

As long as imitation was self-conscious or Jews existed as a separate group, the process of assimilation would remain incomplete. Full member-ship in society would be granted only at the end of the process, after Jews proved themselves by forfeiting all distinction. Consequently, Jews highly visible as such—Orthodox, recent immigrants, Zionists—provoked anger from those more assimilated. Calling attention to Jewishness—much less promoting it—was seen as holding back progress and even endangering those who sought to assimilate. Each Jew knew he could be judged by—and held responsible for—the behavior of other Jews, whether loud and boor-ish, criminal or saintly, capitalist or revolutionary, in their ability to obey what one called "the strict rules of the civilization game."[24] This emphasis on perception and its variability fostered a Jewish fascination with media, culture, and public relations as they were transmuted from the world's most inward-oriented community to that most obsessed with its image in the eyes of non-Jewish rulers and neighbors.[25]

In the first stage of evolution, assimilating Jews still had a full knowl-edge of tradition, but being Jewish seemed incompatible with modern life. The result was a loss of belief, reduction in observance, immersion in a non-Jewish milieu, and aspiration for social or professional advancement, leading to schisms with traditionalist forebears. In the second generation, familiarity with Jewish civilization declined sharply, coming mostly from the parents' remaining practices rather than from any serious direct educa-tion. Jewishness was now a minor factor in daily life but, by the same token, an empty symbol not worth saving or conveying to children. The process was consummated by a rift or rebellion from partly assimilated parents leading to total assimilation of some sort. This entire cycle usually took three generations, occasionally interrupted when individuals rediscovered a Jewish identity, often as a response to oppression.

Of course, there was no such thing as generic assimilation, it was always a matter of which nation, class, religion, and political philosophy would be the model for imitation. Picking cosmopolitan humanism over patriotism implied disloyalty to the country of residence, while choosing any one group to join or support might anger others. For example, many Jews be-came advocates of German culture, alienating Czechs, Poles, and Hungari-ans among whom they lived. Assimilating Jews were unable to follow the wise, traditional path encompassed in the tale of a yeshiva student who re-fused to say anything as the couple with whom he lodged argued over whether the soup was too salty. "Whoever I side with," he thought, "the other one will throw me out."

Enlisting in a social class was also a dilemma. Jews seeking to enter the elite were rebuffed or pressed to convert, disdained as plutocrats by radicals and as usurpers by the bigoted right. Trying to join the masses by gravitating to the left brought hatred from rulers, conservatives, and often from the common people they presumed to champion. Entering the middle class as professionals and liberal reformers bred rivals who accused the Jews of snatching jobs and redirecting society to suit their own preferences.

This struggle against so many pressures, and often under lonely conditions, built strong egos, a useful trait for becoming an innovator. "Because I was a Jew," Freud wrote, "I found myself free of many prejudices which restrict others in the use of the intellect; as a Jew I was prepared to be in the opposition and to renounce agreement with the . . . majority."[26]

The rejection of conventional wisdom and search for the root factor, so evident in Freud, Marx, Einstein, and many others, was the bane and glory of Jewish assimilationist intellectualism. A greater willingness to break with the status quo to make something better might at times create something worse. Freedom from one tradition was often gained at the cost of subjection to another, despite an illusion of total independence from such influences. The novelist Herman Wouk described this as "sweeping the dust of orthodoxy out the front door, and never seeing it drift in again at the back door, settling down in somewhat different patterns."[27]

Living in a society ruled by principles alien to one's own heritage was a recipe for disaffection. Surrounded by assumptions they did not accept, assimilating Jews were less tied to the majority's myths, symbols, or sanctioned opinions. Philip Roth recalled how his college's Christian milieu let him more easily ignore its strictures and oppose its tenets "without feeling bedeviled by long-standing loyalties." For Jews, historic events held different meanings, and the majority's heroes were often their tyrants.[28] Assimilating Jews rejecting their own civilization, religion, and nation with such relentless energy exaggerated the likelihood that non-Jewish counterparts would do the same.

Being such thoroughgoing rebels against their own people's traditions and customs made some assimilating Jews become iconoclasts toward others' convictions and a society they saw as hypocritically breaking its promise of equality. Their own vacuum of beliefs made them seek a new way to understand the world's workings, inventing an assimilationist version of the Chosen People concept: that the Jews' very anomie—a term invented by the French Jewish sociologist Emile Durkheim—was their glory. They thus became the most passionate critics of a society whose religion vilified them and whose nationalism attacked them. By advocating daring ideas, they were ready, like Samson, to bring down the idolatrous temple of persecutors who taunted them. Freed from the web of loyalties to nation, society, or religion, they would pave the way for humanity's unity, rationalism, and progress. Jewish intellectuals often saw themselves as prophets of cultural misogyny, standing above all parties and peoples, transcending rather than imitating the divisions among others.

Another theme common to assimilating Jewish thought was the world's malleability. In Arendt's words: "Perhaps reality consists only in the agreement of everybody," a mere social phenomenon that might "collapse as soon as someone had the courage forthrightly and consistently to deny its existence."[29] In a sense, Freud's main innovation was his assumption that individual psychology—like Marx's view on society—derived from life rather than being an inalterable fact of nature. The problem with using "reason" as a map revealing the truth, however, was that not everyone agreed on its definition or were capable of using it.

For example, Léon Blum wrote in the 1890s, "Among ordinary people, religion is only a collection of family superstitions, to be obeyed without conviction and only out of respect toward one's ancestors who have conformed to them for twenty centuries; for enlightened people, it no longer means anything."[30] But far more assimilating Jews than Christians thought in such terms, especially at that time. Non-Jews were generally less willing to surrender their identity or attack their own religious faith, nation, or culture.

More actively and often than others who still dwelt amidst a framework of comforting answers, assimilating Jews were dissatisfied with the roles assigned them at birth. They had to choose, comprehend, justify, and change course, throwing themselves into some solution with that extra energy bestowed by newness and a passion engendered by free choice. Creating alternative worlds of the mind—a characteristic Bloom called "extreme interiority"[31]—removed them more from the material constraints of a status quo they doubted, since its principles were alien to them and its institutions discriminated against them.

While the transition from an age of reverence to one of iconoclasm was far less a Jewish cause than antisemites claimed, assimilating Jews wounded over exclusion often saw themselves as "destroyer of human illusions," in the historian Peter Gay's phrase.[32] George Bernard Shaw called Max Nordau "One of those remarkable cosmopolitan Jews who go forth against modern civilization as David went against the Philistines . . . smiting it hip and thigh without any sense of common humanity with it [but] trumped up an indictment of its men of genius as depraved lunatics."[33] "He broke all the set rules, all accepted canons of taste and style," wrote a biographer of sculptor Jacob Epstein. His works brought—and were designed to provoke—an "eruption of furious criticism from the self-appointed arbiters of good taste and guardians of moral values."[34]

Another common theme was a politics learned in battle for fair treatment. Jews generally favored equality and opposed prejudice against weaker groups as a dangerous precedent for themselves, often seeing such oppressed people as potential allies. The appealing promise of justice, equality, and protection from persecution was why liberalism—in the broadest sense, including socialism—attracted them. An open society was more resistant to antisemitism and tolerant of assimilation. Dictatorship and demagoguery, seeking scapegoats and enforcing homogeneity, inevitably menaced Jews. Truth was the best tool against libel or superstition. There were also some notions—conservatism, patriotic chauvinism, or fascism—few would accept, and then only as protective coloration, seeing the political right as the domain of antisemites.[35]

As a result, Jews formed a relatively high proportion of liberal or left movements and, to some extent, that involvement flavored each of them, creating Jewish variants in socialism, liberalism, modernism, humanism, and even various nationalisms. Antisemites played up this idea of a dominant Jewish role in such causes. But these movements did not necessarily serve particularistic Jewish interests and sometimes actually hurt them.

Despite all obstacles, Jews proved so adaptive that they came to embody almost every social trend and fill every field of innovative human endeavor, appearing in art, finance, and politics in such profusion that one might easily believe them ten or even a hundred times more numerous than they were. Consciously or otherwise, these roles were infused with Jewish and assimilating Jewish features. They insisted that all perspectives were arbitrary and tried, less successfully, to impose their own set of laws onto this relativism. This pattern recurred in many diverse forms. The Jews, that stone once rejected by the builders of Western civilization, became the cornerstone of its progress.

Nonetheless, the Jewish assimilationist subculture's glory was inevitably transitory, built on a delicate balance between separateness and total incorporation. "The unending Jewish demand for a home," explained Scholem, "was soon transformed into the ecstatic illusion of being at home."[36] In much of Europe, this wishful thinking collapsed in tragedy; in America, a very high level of integration was eventually reached, allowing a far more realistic option of total assimilation or some balance between integration and alienation.

The era that threatened Jews with assimilation also made possible a secular Jewish identity in which Israel became a surrogate homeland. Those choosing to remain Jews had to decide that they had not only a shared—if dead—past but a living present and future as well. Partly assimilated Jews appreciated their own civilization's values, adapted ideas from Western thought, and questioned assimilation when it appeared not to be working or succeeding so well that the Jews would disappear. Given their dispersion among so many nations and cultures, survival required a place—Israel—claiming some allegiance from all: "Each section," wrote Ahad Ha-Am, "will develop its own individuality along lines determined by imitation of its own surroundings; but all will find in this center at once a purifying fire and a connecting link."[37]

Rather than Jews melting away as individuals until they disappeared, the Jews as a group would adapt to the modern world by becoming a nation reentering history. Their extraordinarily unique situation required unprecedented solutions. The fundamental Jewish dilemma was a choice between rending oneself or becoming whole. Arthur Koestler extolled the first condition, proclaiming "that the restless traveller has only one goal: to escape from himself." Philip Roth had the opposite interpretation: one must understand that in trying to flee things at home for "the deep emancipating world . . . he had taken them all with him."[38]

6

In Dubious Battles: The Revolutionary Left

Leon Trotsky [born Lev Davidovich Bronstein] told a village rabbi that the Revolution would give the Jews equality, justice, and prosperity. "All I know," said the rabbi, "is that the Trotskys may get the power, but the Bronsteins will get the blame."

—Apocryphal story

HERSCHEL LEVI, son of Trier's chief rabbi, had little time to enjoy the emancipation brought by Napoleon's conquest of the Rhineland. The returning Prussians soon revoked the emancipation decree and again barred Jews, including Levi, from being lawyers. To keep his livelihood, he converted in 1817. Under his new Christian name, Heinrich Marx passionately supported that same oppressive regime. The hypocrisy, insignificance of religious and nationalist labels, and primacy of social class and economic factors suggested by his father's life surely shaped the worldview of Heinrich's son, Karl, who was born in 1818.

Exactly a century later, on the night of November 8, 1918, sixteen-year-old Werner Cahnman went out to see what was happening in Munich's anarchic streets. Imperial Germany had collapsed and Kurt Eisner had proclaimed a socialist republic the previous day. When Werner heard a man complain that now the Jews were in power, he was shocked. What did his ultrarespectable, promonarchist, middle-class family have to do with revolutionaries? Nonetheless, many Germans considered the ill-fated rebellion Cahnman witnessed, led by such anti-Jewish Jews as Eisner and Rosa Luxemburg, as a "Jewish republic." The idea that Jews were antipatriotic and pro-Communist was to play an important role in the antisemitic propaganda that would recruit mass support for the Nazis.[1]

In fact, the link between Jews and leftism in Europe did have a basis in reality. Jews played a disproportionate role in the Russian revolution, Communist parties, and left-wing intellectual circles. Yet Marxist groups were indifferent to Jewish concerns and were supported by only a minority of Jews. The left's inability to deal with the Jewish question and Jewish radicals' failure to cope with their own Jewishness was a key element in the movement's ultimate failure and inhumanity. In the end, well-intentioned Jewish leftists helped build repressive regimes persecuting other Jews and often themselves. Since Christianity venerated a dead Jew while persecuting Jews, why should not Marxists do the same thing? Of course, many non-Jews joined the same movements but the ideas had a special appeal to assimilating Jews who saw them as confirmation of their own lives and attitudes.

"Under a dogmatic and assured exterior," wrote the philosopher Albert Memmi, Jews on the left were "determinedly logical, but blind to the obvious, a mixture of desperate intellectual severity and annoying naive sentimentalism; stubbornly insisting on seeing as friends people who would watch [a leftist Jew] being tortured with indifference." Above all, "on no condition can anyone suspect him for a moment of thinking of himself or his people."[2]

This last point especially betrayed the enterprise's delusion: Jewish leftists claimed their comrades and the masses accepted Jews as equals while knowing this was not really true. Their basic view was identical to that of the Reform Jew expecting self-sacrifice to humanity to win humanity's love, or the patriot hoping devotion to country would gain the country's favor. Communism, explained Koestler, "again promised a magic cure—not only for a small ethnic group, but for the whole of mankind."[3]

In contrast to Marxist theory, it was not economic suffering leading so many Jews toward leftism but rather their cultural inheritance, oppression as a people, and the assimilation process itself. "Since I had failed in my self-transformation," wrote Memmi, "I undertook to transform the world." Jews leaned to the left because one had to "want a new arrangement of a society which is so continuously hostile to him." Even when hatred seemed to be waning, Jews were always aware of its potential menace.[4]

The religious Jew had thought himself to be among a chosen people; the radical Jew transmuted this feeling into a desire to be part of an intellectual vanguard, a counterelite. Even those socialists or impassioned social critics who most denied it carried Jewish heritage in their enthusiasm for social justice, casting themselves as heirs to the Jewish prophets of old. Being ambitious outsiders with few prospects of climbing in existing cultural or political institutions, they were quick to join or establish new ones. Insisting the world could be a paradise if others just opened their eyes to reject old beliefs and loyalties, as they had done, Jewish radicals were baffled as concepts so logical in their own minds did not persuade or transform people different from them, people who had less incentive to abandon nationalism and religion, reject the social order, or combat antisemitism.[5]

Wishful thinking made them assume that everyone had learned the lesson of universalism taught by their own situation. The belief that an alternative way was possible arose from both Judaism's religious content and tradition. Judaism focused on life in this world, wrote Hess, while Christianity looked to heaven, assuming human misery as "the normal condition of the world" to be set right in the next one.[6] Jewish doctrine saw the highest task as studying, comprehending, and implementing God's decrees. It was a small step for secular Jewish intellectuals to turn this quest into a search for laws explaining society and making possible its improvement. God, wrote Koestler, "was replaced by Utopias of one kind or another."[7]

Such a system, once discovered, merited the utmost devotion by those who could insist, like the American poet Emma Lazarus in 1883, that socialism was rooted in Jewish law, while her colleague David Edelstadt hailed socialism's "new prophets" who would "deliver us from exile."[8] But it was usually forgotten that the biblical prophets scourged contemporary assimilationist trends, beseeching Jews to return to their own nation and tradition. Moreover, as always happened, most of the new prophets were false.

While elements in this pattern of belief and behavior can be found in any modern intelligentsia, such attributes were unusually salient—and this type of intellectual more numerous—among Jews. "Utopia," wrote Lewisohn in 1939, "is the opiate of great sections of the Jewish people."[9] Breaking with their own people's beliefs but still reluctant to accept their old persecutor's tenets impelled them to seek new systems of wisdom and identity.

A century earlier, the socialist Moses Hess began his spiritual journey by discarding Judaism, only to find other religions deficient: "Nothing remained. I was the most miserable person in the world. I became an atheist. The world became a burden and a curse to me.... Nature appeared to me as chaos without order.... I could not stand this situation.... I had to have a God." In socialism, he found "a moral world order, which satisfied me."[10] Will Herberg, a Russian-born immigrant to America who became a Communist in the 1920s, wrote in similar terms: "Marxism was to me, and to others like me, a religion, an ethic, and an ideology; a vast all-embracing doctrine of man and the universe, a passionate faith endowing life with meaning."[11]

Marxism was also a substitute loyalty for those whose spiritual and intellectual vacuum was empty of all nationalism, communal loyalty, religion, or even immersion in the local society. This mind-set caused serious dilemmas in Marxist outlook and strategy, since it claimed worldviews were conditioned by their creators' material circumstances yet never applied this theory to itself, as a perspective shaped by special interests and experiences. Jewish intellectuals were covered with the writing of earlier generations though thinking of themselves as being clean slates.

Jewish religious concepts of social justice, future utopia, and a disciplined cadre of believers were secularized into equivalent socialist ones: an intricate intellectual dogma interpreting the universe; a complex set of writings to be studied and debated; a stress on ethical justice; and a special sense of mission, albeit transforming the world by socialism rather than teaching it monotheism. Of course, this was only part of the story. Judaism also urged balance—opposing asceticism, encouraging the use of reason to circumvent rules, insisting that judgment embody justice rather than bend either for the rich or poor. Only the weakening of tradition allowed an unfettered, abstract reason—hitherto bound by authority, custom, and law—to follow its inductive process to such radical ends.

Most important, the emotionally intoxicating notion of socialism sanctified assimilation: Jews would not have to subordinate themselves to Christian society, they could enlist to struggle for a better society where all contrasts among peoples would be obliterated, with both Jews and Christians fusing into something higher and better. "Perhaps in this new world everyone would be welcome," Arendt said. "Belonging . . . was promised precisely to the person who had 'annihilated' himself [as an individual with] a particular origin and a particular situation."[12]

Signs that this was not happening only intensified anger and rebellion. Germany, the flagship society for Jewish assimilation, was beset by murderous fascism. In America immigrants were disappointed when denied its abundance and outraged at low status and lingering discrimination. The poet Muriel Rukeyser wrote, "We wanted something different for our people: not to find ourselves an old, reactionary republic, full of ghost-fears, the fears of death and the fears of birth. We want something else."[13] Instead of surrendering their identity merely for individual material gain—selling their birthright cheaply—the Jews' integration into society was supposed to precipitate history's turning point, utopia's creation, the secular Messiah's arrival.

Nonetheless, this process still required the Jews to disappear. They could not survive as a religion because the atheist left saw that as reactionary; they could not be a people since that would disregard class divisions and divide them from the masses. Thus, religious or nationalist Jews and even communal institutions endangered the potential earthly paradise as well as the leftists' personal status in the movement. The radicals wanted these distinctive interests sacrificed for humanity's alleged well-being, an interpretation paralleling the Christian view of Jews as suffering servants, whose misery was retribution for sin. A classic assertion of this doctrine was the Marxist writer Isaac Deutscher's concept of the non-Jewish Jew, who fought for others while giving up his own identity.

Leftist ideas also emerged from the Jewish situation, as the revolutionary test of emancipation built impatient expectations of an historic leap forward. Given their Jewish and intellectual orientation, radicals put excessive faith in ideas as capable of sparking this change. When the semi-Marxist literary critic Walter Benjamin said the Marxist philosopher Ernst Bloch could warm himself with his thoughts, he pointed to an unworldly naïveté. The fact that the cynical, iconoclastic Viennese essayist Karl Kraus could proclaim, "Nothing is true, and it is possible that something else will happen," expressed the wishful thinking infecting even the most sardonic Jewish radicals.[14]

Jewish history also confirmed a view of the rich, powerful, or aristocratic as not society's cream but dregs, thugs, and parasites. They had never acted nobly toward the Jews and no divine right of such kings came from that divinity the Jews worshiped. In contrast to this false elite, the truly virtuous were the excluded, despised, and downtrodden. Though Christian thinkers were also exploring history's meaning and society's roots, the Jews' experience of past oppression and current exclusion predisposed them toward a radical critique of society as a web of lies and hypocrisies. Emancipation and assimilation challenged their thinking far more than modernity did for the reigning Christians. Jews becoming atheists did so more thoroughly than those whose world was saturated by their own Christian belief and custom; when they became rebellious they were more completely so since they had less stake in the society.

Radicalism was especially attractive for the children of wealthy, partly or newly assimilated families, more willing to "betray" a class for which they were qualified but which denied them full membership. Thus, from the apparently unpromising tinder of such otherwise privileged people, radical firebrands emerged. Other Jews, pushed below the level of their economic and educational attainments, were natural recruits for a doctrine of social change that exalted the lower classes. The intellectuals among them, the most alienated group of all, were cut off from both old ways and new environment. Such tiny groups knew they required a larger, stronger ally to achieve change. To argue that the working class, too, wanted and needed to overthrow the system suited them, as did a radical doctrine proposing these alienated intellectuals themselves as the best leaders of a revolution and new society.

Non-Jews or Jews still faithful to tradition had less craving for a new ideology; assimilating Jews were more open to a radical view of the existing social order as neither eternal nor natural but wrong and outdated. They granted that society less legitimacy both because they doubted its assumptions—having their own history and worldview—and because they knew its sordid persecution and exclusion of them belied its claim to morality and justice.

Still, while radical Jews rejected their own community, non-Jews saw the assault on their loyalties and beliefs as typically Jewish. Activism won more hatred than esteem as Jews were accused of usurping any cause a few of them supported and subverting any institution some of them opposed. The French novelist Romain Rolland wrote, "Unfortunately, the past does not exist for the Jews." As a general statement this was ridiculous, for there was no group for whom the past was more potent. Such accusations were only true of those Jews who had abandoned the Jews, but by their ideas and acts the community would be judged and stigmatized.[15]

Radicals, though, did not see this as their problem or responsibility. A revolutionary, wrote psychologist/philosopher Erich Fromm, "is one who is identified with humanity and therefore transcends the narrow limits of his own society, and who is able, therefore, to criticize his or any other society. . . . He is not caught in the parochial culture which he happens to be born in, which is nothing but an accident of time and geography. He is able to look at this environment with the open eyes of a man who is awake and who finds his criteria of judging the accidental in that which is not accidental (reason), in the norms which are in and for the human race."[16]

This passage is a virtual inventory of assimilating Jewish attributes: identifying with humanity and rejecting any parochial identity, yet concurrently acting from that smaller group's atypical standpoint; employing a "reason" transcending what actually exists; and seeing reality as arbitrary and irrational. In contrast, the majority saw their culture as essential, not accidental; judged the world precisely from their society's "narrow limits"; and were patriotic or pious, not "identifying with humanity" as a whole.

But Fromm's analysis perfectly fit such figures as Marx, Trotsky, and Rosa Luxemburg. Their Jewish Variant of radicalism included a passionate antinationalist stance and utopian expectations, sweeping aside the status quo and human limitations. In their philosophy, humanity replaced God as the ordering principle. Any concern for the Jews was equated with personal selfishness. Before the veteran Bolshevik Adolph Joffe committed suicide in 1927 to protest the course of the Russian revolution, he revealed his credo to Trotsky: "Human life has meaning only to the degree that, and so long as, it is lived in the service of something infinite. For us humanity is infinite. The rest is finite, and to work for the rest is therefore meaningless."[17]

This escape from one's self as Jew became a flight from self. Just as the Jews were to give up their beliefs and autonomy, the individual was to remold himself into a member of the working class, a revolutionary cadre subordinate to the party and willing to sacrifice himself for humanity. Marx's doctrine was an exercise in self-hatred of one's identity as Jew, bourgeois, intellectual, or citizen of a country. In the 1960s, the New Left and its ideological successors would extend this list to include being white or male.

Yet despite this self-abnegating style, the left's approach was saturated with the Jewish experience as victims. When the Jewish radical gazed at the proletariat or Third World, he implicitly saw oppressed Jews; perusing the ruling class, he saw antisemites. The American writer Kim Chernin recalled that when her mother, a Communist leader, spoke of the Ku Klux Klan and lynchings it "reminded me of the pogrom." When New York police charged an unemployed march in the 1930s, "To me it seemed we were standing in a village and the Cossacks were riding down." In contrast, the USSR's power and progress "made you feel that even to a worker, to a poor Jew, even to a woman . . . the whole future belonged." Chernin found out otherwise on first visiting the Soviet Union in the 1950s, however, when relatives told her, "To be a Jew in the Soviet Union I wouldn't wish on my worst enemy."[18]

Karl Marx's career and ideas showed clearly the Jewish and assimilationist basis of anti-Jewish radical theory. While describing Jews as individuals, people, and religion in antisemitic terms, he never mentioned his own Jewish background. As Isaiah Berlin wrote, "His origin was evidently a personal stigma which he was unable to avoid pointing out in others; his denial of the importance of racial categories, his emphasis upon the international character of the proletariat, takes on a peculiar sharpness of tone, directed as it is against misconception of which he himself had been a conspicuous victim."[19] Weakly rooted in society, Marx mocked the appeal of nationalism and religion, a personal attitude he then attributed to history's laws and humanity's interests.

By arguing that the Jewish question was not a real problem, Marx was insisting that it was not his problem. Thus, he had to portray the Jews as nothing in themselves, neither creed nor civilization, as Berlin explained, "not a race, or a nation, or even a religion to be saved by conversion to some other faith or way of life, but a collection of parasites, a gang of money-lenders" produced by an unjust society and fated to disappear along with that society. He used antisemitic taunts against rival radicals, called Judaism "repugnant," and wrote, "Money is the zealous God of Israel, before whom no other god may be." He rejected an idea as a "dirty Jewish manifestation," called the Paris bourse the "stock exchange synagogue," and commented, "Every tyrant is backed by a Jew."[20]

Despite Marx's denial, many of his concepts sprang from the Jewish condition. Alienation from society came from a feeling of apartness far more profound than nonownership of the means of production. Marx's analysis of the group destined to liberate German society matches the Jews better than the proletariat: "A class with radical chains, a class of civil society which is not a class of civil society . . . a sphere which has a universal character by its universal suffering and claims no particular right because no particular wrong but wrong generally is perpetrated against it; which can no longer invoke a historical but only a human title."[21] Marx identified this working class with the future—his future—and Judaism with capitalism and the past—his past.

In short, he transferred bitterness from family history and personal predicaments to identify them with grievances of insulted and oppressed people everywhere. He demanded and prophesied justice and revenge, making the common assumption that others thought or acted as he did. Marx's seemingly irrational hostility toward Jews arose from the fact that their existence threatened to unmask him personally and subvert his "scientific" system by revealing the subjective factors behind it. The Jews also embodied a living challenge to his theory of history and society. So he turned Judaism into a sterile category—worthless, even evil. These mistakes subverted Marxism's ability to comprehend the world and contributed to its eventual downfall.

Just as Marx underrated the durability of the Jews and religion in general, he equally misunderstood nationalism since it meant nothing to him. He claimed, "Proletarians have no homeland" and capitalism was erasing national contrasts. Rather than discerning the appeal of patriotism, tradition, culture, or identity, he thought them mere ideological structures a ruling class used to hold power, illusions others would reject as readily as he did. Ignorant of real workers, Marx dehumanized them as his own tools to eliminate the rulers persecuting humanity's champions and avengers: revolutionary Jewish intellectuals like himself.[22]

Marx was by no means alone in these opinions. His main contemporary socialist rival and target of his antisemitic jibes was Ferdinand Lassalle, founder of the German Social Democratic Party. Despite his parents' wealth, being a Jew exposed Lassalle to humiliation. In 1840, when fourteen years old, Lassalle wrote in his diary: "I think I am one of the best Jews in existence, although I disregard the Ceremonial Law. I could ... risk my life to deliver the Jews from their present crushing condition. I would not even shrink from the scaffold could I but once more make of them a respected people." His favorite fantasy was to lead the Jews to liberation. But he also wrote at the same time, "A people that bears this is hideous; let them suffer or avenge this treatment. . . . Even the Christians marvel at our sluggish blood, that we do not rise. . . . Cowardly people, thou dost merit no better lot."[23]

To dispel that stigma, Lassalle looked for another identity, but was as conflicted in his solution as in his assessment of the problem: "Had I been born prince or ruler I should have been an aristocrat, body and soul. But now ... I shall be a democrat." His first step in shaking off Jewishness was refusing to study medicine or law, since "the doctor and the lawyer are both tradesmen who traffic with their knowledge." He would study for knowledge's sake alone, though, ironically, this nominally anti-Jewish attitude was closer to Jewish tradition in exalting study as its own reward.[24]

Lassalle saw being a leader of German workers or a nobleman as equally attractive escapes from Jewish inferiority. His life's finale was consistent with that ambiguity. Although a socialist leader, Lassalle fell in love with an aristocrat whose parents scorned him. In contrast to the theory of materialist primacy—but incarnating chutzpah—Lassalle was certain that his vibrant personality would charm them. He recruited the reactionary Prussian regime, the antisemitic composer Richard Wagner, and even a Catholic bishop to win over the family, promising to convert if successful. When all else failed, he fought a duel with a rival over the woman and was killed.

Of these Jewish socialist theorists, only the obscure Moses Hess took a positive attitude toward Judaism. Like Marx, Hess was exiled from Germany in the 1840s; unlike Marx, he had a traditional Jewish education. While Marx was denigrating the Jews, Hess wrote that their social role was especially progressive, "The element of fermentation in Western humanity . . . destined, from earliest times, to force upon it the element of movement and change."[25]

By rejecting the dominant Christian religion, Hess wrote, Jews became the model for a future society beyond religion. Judaism was also essentially social democratic and more advanced than Christianity, claimed Hess, because Jewish laws "referred to the inner as well as to the outer man. Religion and politics, Church and State were internally interwoven, possessed one root, bore one fruit. The Jews did not know the difference between religious and political commands, between the duty to God and the duty to Caesar." In contrast, "The Christians never possessed a social order based on God; they never had a holy state or a divine law." Christianity thus abandoned law to faith, earthly life for the hope of future life.[26]

But Marx and Lassalle had far more influence on Jewish and non-Jewish radicals than did Hess. The dominant model of socialism was as an assimilationist alliance with the masses in which Jews would dissolve themselves. The first step would be for Jewish intellectuals to renounce religion and community. But strangely enough the same strictures did not apply to Christian comrades, since if they were too openly atheist it would isolate the party from the masses. Rather than freeing Jews to be Jews, the revolution—like other assimilationist programs—would free them from being Jews.

As socialist movements developed in Europe, they followed this line laid down by Jewish theorists. On a practical level, neither Jewish leadership nor fighting antisemitism was allowed to become too prominent since this might alienate the proletariat. Jewish radicals supported this orientation, ignoring its contradictions.[27] As Herzl pointed out in 1897, the last thing the Socialists "want to be is an army for the protection of the Jews; they would rather not be reminded that there are Jews in the world." But since no one could ignore the many Jews in their ranks, the Jewish members themselves "must be afraid of a simple statement pointing out their growing numbers and disproportionate power in the party. There is something tragic about this, for many of them have invested their good will and their best talents, even their very lives in this cause."[28]

Rosa Luxemburg was a case in point. She was born in Russian Poland in 1871, descendant of several rabbis but to parents with few remaining ties to the community. As heir to no apparent identity of her own, she adopted humanity as her constituency and self-sacrifice as her method. "I constantly had to look after the urgent business of humanity and make the world a happier place. . . . I never did 'have time' for . . . myself." Attending an elite high school with few Jews or even many Poles, she became involved in radical politics and came to oppose nationalism without understanding it. National self-determination, she argued, had nothing to do with the working class, "The [Socialist] International is the fatherland of the proletariat."[29]

Actually the Polish Social Democratic Party's antagonism to Polish nationalism was not unrelated to the fact that three of its four founders, including Luxemburg, were Jews. In rejecting Polish nationalism, these radicals were extrapolating from their own rejection of Jewish nationalism or identity. In essence, the radicals were telling Poles that they should copy the behavior patterns of assimilationist Jews.* But the party's opposition to Poland's independence did not endear it to the Polish people, whose dislike of both Marxists and Jews intensified.

The Social Democrats praised Polish workers for not participating in pogroms by saying, "You have shown the whole world that for you a Jew or a German does not exist, that you know your enemies well, the capitalists of all faiths and nationalities," while all workers, including Jewish ones, were their comrades. This approach did not define ethnic groups as equal but argued they were nonexistent. Thus, Jewish workers should ignore their identity since, "The yoke which they perpetually bear as Jews could conceal from them the yoke which they suffer as workers. . . . They could fall into a trap and perceive their chief enemies as foreign nationalities rather than the capitalist class and the Czarist regime."[30]

Luxemburg herself changed nations again to become a revolutionary in

---

*More moderate assimilating Jews supported the Polish nationalist party, which turned against them when it held power in the 1920s and 1930s. The Jewish Marxists' opposition to Polish nationalism then and later objectively favored Russian imperialism.

Germany, where she was killed in the ill-fated 1919 revolt. Jewish, Polish, Russian, German, these things meant nothing to her. Her universalist credo was that of many Marxist and liberal humanist Jews: "I feel equally close to the wretched victims of the rubber plantations in Putumayo or to the Negroes in Africa with whose bodies the Europeans are playing catch-ball. . . . I have no separate corner in my heart for the ghetto: I feel at home in the entire world wherever there are clouds and birds and human tears."[31] But to most people—including those of Putumayo and Africa—religious and national designations meant a great deal. Moreover, they would proba-bly reject her socialist solutions and denial of community, and would not reciprocate her sympathy.

Karl Kautsky, the Jewish theoretician of German Marxism, took a simi-lar tack. In 1903, he responded to Russian pogroms by blaming antisemitism on Jewish distinctiveness, whose survival he attributed to czarist compul-sion rather than to Jewish culture. Still, if the Jews' "alien" characteristics made them scapegoats, these must be melted in the pot of common revolu-tionary struggle and anything retarding such fusion was wicked. This atti-tude and Kautsky's definition of nationalism so as to exclude Jews was the one adopted by Lenin, Stalin, and most other Marxists. In other words, the problem was that the Jews had been forcibly kept from disappearing, not that they wanted to survive as a group or had something legitimate to pre-serve. Any Jews wishing to exist as a separate community were reactionary, should be suppressed, and were responsible for their own persecution. This was a view Christian leftists, often somewhat antisemitic themselves, could easily understand and accept.[32]

Similarly, the Jewish leaders of Austria-Hungary's socialist party championed the rights of different national groups but refused any such consideration for Jews. So strong was the Austrian socialist leader Victor Adler's commitment to German culture that he named his first son Fried-rich Wolfgang, after Schiller and Goethe, and warned that young man against marrying a woman Adler deemed to be too Jewish. Before becom-ing a socialist, Adler had converted and sought assimilation by joining radi-cal German nationalist youth groups that later became antisemitic.[33]

But it was in Russia, where the first socialist revolution would take place and the most Jews lived, that the relationship between Marxism and Jews was determined. Most Russian Jews were poor and harassed by school quotas, long military service, residency restrictions, and periodic pogroms. They responded to growing antisemitic pressure by converting, emigrating, or becoming politically active. From the 1880s on, Jews bereft of Jewish culture and religion, educated at Russian schools, were won to a revolutionary version of assimilation. In 1895, the Russian Jewish orator Shmaryahu Levin warned in despair, "Jews will always follow any false prophet preaching in the name of justice and progress, who will promise [them] shamelessly and with unbridled chutzpah a better future Here and Now."[34]

When the Peoples Will populist group justified pogroms as showing the Russian people's revolutionary energy, Jewish radicals argued that to protest would alienate the masses and split the left. Typical was the retort of Pavel Axelrod, a founder of the socialist party, "What significance can the interests of a handful of Jews have, I thought, compared with the interests and the idea of a working class, with which socialism was imbued?" If socialism would liberate everyone, "How senseless then and indeed how criminal to devote oneself to the Jews who are only a small part of the vast Russian empire!" A comrade explained radical Jews as "sincere assimilationists. . . . Russian literature, which implanted in us love of culture and of the Russian people, also to some degree implanted in us a conception that Jews were not a people but a parasitic class."[35]

By 1905 the number of Jewish leftists was more than nine times higher than the proportion of Jews in the population, including about 23 percent of Menshevik and 11 percent of Bolshevik leaders.[36] This radicalization among Jews increased the rulers' and public's antagonism toward all Jews. Traditional Jews were upset by this trend and the trouble it brought them. One of them told a Russian official in 1872, "As long as we educated our children there were no nihilists among us; but as soon as you took the education of our children into your hands, behold the results!"[37]

Even worse, revolutionary agitation and assassinations triggered anti-Jewish pogroms, sometimes organized by the authorities. After a Jewish revolutionary tried to assassinate the governor of Vilna in 1902, the chief rabbi of Minsk proclaimed it dangerous for Jews to meddle in politics in such a way: "Beware, Jewish children! Look well at what you are doing! God only knows what you may bring upon our unfortunate nation, upon yourselves, and upon your families."[38]

Jewish Marxists were impervious to these problems. Despite having actually crossed over to the Russian nation, they nonetheless proclaimed themselves the most constant enemies of national identity. During a meeting in Berlin in 1890, the Russian Jewish Marxist Alexander Helphand claimed, "Today nationalism is meaningless. Even the manufacture of my coat demonstrates the international character of the world: the wool was taken from sheep pastured in [Turkey]; it was spun in England; it was woven in Lodz; the buttons came from Germany; the thread from Austria."

The Zionist Nachman Syrkin interrupted, "And the rip in your sleeve comes from the pogrom in Kiev!"[39]

As this debate showed, not all Jewish intellectuals on the left took the same stance. An individual's opinions usually corresponded with his cultural background, education, and place of origin. Those living in areas of high Jewish concentration and with some Jewish education became Zionists or—if their families were a bit more assimilated—joined the Jewish Socialist Bund. Those already part of Russian society with Russian educations became assimilationist Marxists in the Bolshevik—forerunner of the Communist Party—or Menshevik faction of the Social Democrats. For them, Jewishness had little emotional appeal because they did not know much about it.[40] The Bolshevik Lev Kamenev's father was one of the few Jews able to become an engineer. Kamenev, like most of his comrades, never saw the inside of a synagogue or Jewish school. The same was true of Trotsky. In contrast, Zalman Shazar, a socialist Zionist who later became president of Israel, had a strongly Jewish family and education.[41]

The Bund, founded in 1897, rejecting both assimilation and tradition, demanded equal rights and national autonomy for Jews in a socialist Russia. It urged a common struggle alongside the Russian proletariat but as an autonomous part of the Social Democratic Party. Along with the Zionists, it set up groups to defend Jews from Russian attackers during pogroms. As one Bund leader argued, Jews must organize independently to protect their own interests: "A working class that is content with the lot of an inferior nation will not rise up against the lot of an inferior class. The national passivity of the Jewish masses, therefore, is also a bar to the growth of its class consciousness. The growth of national and class consciousness must go hand in hand."[42]

This program, however, threatened Jewish Marxists. After all, if Jews were a separate people to be led by the Bund, their own goal of assimilation and claim to rule all Russians would be irretrievably compromised. The Russian revolutionaries' attitude derived from both Marxism and their own society's antisemitism, reinforced by assimilated Jewish cadre sharing this standpoint.

The showdown came at the Social Democrats' 1903 Congress. Refusing to recognize Jews as a nation, Lenin and Trotsky mocked the Bund for doubting the party's sincerity in fighting antisemitism and defending Jewish rights. The Bund walked out, a decision soon justified when the Social Democrats did not criticize new waves of pogroms. Any attempt to combat nationalism by ignoring "the very facts of national differences and national character," a Bund leader warned in 1909, had proven worthless.[43]

Some Russian Jewish intellectuals agreed. The future Zionist leader Chaim Weizmann wrote how the revolutionaries he met as a student "would not tolerate in the Jewish youth any expression of separate attachment to the Jewish people, or even special awareness of the Jewish problem." Lenin and Trotsky treated with contempt "any Jew who was moved by the fate of his people and animated by a love of its history and its tradition. They could not understand why a Russian Jew should want to be anything but a Russian. They stamped as unworthy, as intellectually backward, as chauvinistic and immoral, the desire of any Jew to occupy himself with the sufferings and destiny of Jewry."[44]

The historian Simon Dubnow urged his people to fight for full rights without assimilation rather than for a revolution to make them Russians, warning in 1905, "Do not put your trust in Amalek,* neither the Amalek of the government nor the Amalek of the people, for the old Russia may yet revert in the new!"[45] A once avid assimilationist, the folklorist Solomon Ansky expressed hope in 1915 that the world's workers would unite but predicted that one of the main things they would find in common was to blame the Jews for their misfortunes.[46]

The Communist seizure of power in 1917 allowed a test of the Marxist idea that the Jews survived because antisemitism persisted and that once the revolution abolished that scourge the Jews would assimilate voluntarily, following the example set by the Jewish Communists. In practice, though, since the new rulers treated Jewish culture and religion as an enemy, smacking of nationhood, the official abolition of anti-Jewish intolerance entailed new types of discrimination against them.

In their drive to be Russians—or, more properly, Soviets—Jewish Communists were more adamant than their colleagues in persecuting Jewish religious and communal life. In the 1920s, a special government office, the Jewish Commissariat, was created to implement the radical assimila-

---

*Amalek, whose treacherous attack on the Jews is told in the Bible, is a symbol for irreconcilable enemies.

tionist policy by suppressing these institutions. Support for Zionism became a crime, synagogues were closed, and use of the Yiddish language discouraged. Most members of the outlawed Bund joined the Communists as
individuals, only to be purged and killed by Stalin, along with many leading Jewish Communists, in the 1930s.

From ambition and personal antisemitism, Stalin adopted a Russian nationalist version of Communism against Trotsky's defense of the original
internationalist one. To some extent, the Jewish Marxists were defeated
because they were too idealistically committed to the revolution's higher
aims of liberation. But during Stalin's repression they were accused of the
Marxist equivalent of ritual murder or poisoning wells—sabotage and espionage—as well as the sin of cosmopolitanism, of which Marx himself could
have been convicted. After eliminating them, Stalin made a pact with Hitler in 1939. Even after the war against fascism was won, Stalin murdered
scores of leading Jewish cultural figures. Only his own death prevented a
far broader anti-Jewish pogrom.

Radical assimilation's failure in the USSR, though, was not apparent to
the many Jewish Communists or Marxist intellectuals elsewhere between
the 1920s and 1950s. Aside from the doctrine's assimilationist appeal, they
had other reasons to support Moscow. The Communists claimed to fight
antisemitism and fascism; the Soviet Union played a key role in defeating
Hitler. Being less imbued with patriotism, Jewish intellectuals were often
readier to put the USSR's interest above that of their own country, especially where it treated them unfairly or they were recent immigrants. With
nationalism unattractive and the right wing a would-be executioner, it was
natural to embrace a doctrine promising them equality and a better future
among the masses fighting for peace, justice, democracy, and universal fraternity. Ann Kriegel joined a Communist group resisting the Nazi occupation, since France had rejected her love while Communism offered an
alternate realm transcending national boundaries: "All those people who
did not want us to be French ... we had become stronger than they. We had
compatriots all the way to Vladivostok!"[47]

The link between leftism and assimilation was illustrated in the life of
Rose Pastor, daughter of poor immigrants in New York who married the
handsome heir James Graham Phelps Stokes in an Episcopalian ceremony
in 1905. As columnist for a Jewish newspaper, she had recently criticized
Israel Zangwill for intermarrying. Pastor now wrote that Judaism and
Christianity were the same religion and she accepted the latter's "addi-

tional truths" and "the teaching of Jesus unqualifiedly." By the time they divorced twenty years later, Pastor had become a socialist, then communist, leader, easily exchanging disparate routes to assimilation as socialite, Christian, and revolutionary.[48]

The Jewish Marxists' dedication to a bad cause often brought personal tragedy. They were frequently among the Soviet cadre or Communist International's agents shot by Stalin, purged, or disillusioned after giving much of their lives to serve that antisemitic dictator. Listening to his Communist brother, later murdered at Buchenwald, orate to German workers about the class struggle, Scholem heard one of them say, "The Jew makes a nice speech." He told his brother, "You're deluding yourself by imagining that you represent Germany's exploited industrial workers. That's a lie. . . . You're the son of a middle-class bourgeois Jew. That makes you furious, so you go off wandering into other fields; you don't want to be what you are."[49]

These Marxists embodied Marx's concept of alienation in their own lives, by working, fighting, even dying to serve a movement that exploited them and suppressed their identity. Margarete Buber-Neumann, daughter-in-law of Jewish theologian Martin Buber, remarried German Communist leader Heinz Neumann. Stalin shot her husband in 1937, then delivered her and other Jews to the Nazis, and she spent four years in Ravensbruck concentration camp. Julius and Ethel Rosenberg and a largely Jewish espionage ring stole nuclear secrets for Stalin at the very moment he was slaying Jews.[50]

One such American case was the tragedy of Henry Roth, only twenty-seven years old in 1934 when he published *Call It Sleep,* the vivid story of his childhood and the most brilliant novel on Jewish life written by someone of the immigrant generation. But the Communist Party, to which he belonged, condemned it as too Jewish and introspective. So he tried to write a politically correct novel, unsubtly entitled *If We Had Bacon,* intended, according to *The New York Times,* as "an attempt at a wholly American project—no Jews in sight." By definition, the proletariat could not be antisemitic, so the bigots that had persecuted the central Jewish character in *Call It Sleep* saved his life in a later short story. Instead of being that gang's victim, Roth explained, he was equally to blame.[51] Not surprisingly, Roth failed to find inner or literary fulfillment in this manner. Fleeing alienation, he intensified it in seeking self-eradication. He married a Baptist minister's daughter, had a nervous breakdown, and tried to become one with non-Jewish workers in Maine and

New Mexico, as far as possible from the New York streets he understood. He was unable to integrate into this new world. "I was no longer at home," he later wrote.

Like other leftists, Roth was determined to root out of himself every form of class, national, and religious prejudice, except for the one he held against his own people. He needed this last bias in order to be equally detached from all aspects of the world. This "alienation from my own folk," he later admitted, had "a strong antisemitic element," as when he exhorted Jews to disappear as a boon to humanity. Roth's complex showed how radicalism could be a variant of the motives that moved snobbish conservatives such as Bernard Berenson and Rachel Levy.[52]

In America and Europe, the left was often so heavily Jewish as to be virtually a communal activity in itself, especially in the 1930s. If Jewish, "one was expected, almost automatically, to join," recalled the American Jewish intellectual Lionel Abel, "and accorded very little credit for having done so." Jews had "no right not to be in a left-wing group, whereas non-Jews had such a right, and so gave greater evidence of seriousness and judgment in becoming left-wingers." Since Anglo-Saxon Christians were expected to be better able to recruit workers, their Jewish counterparts "were supposed to give up, or at least forget about, their Jewishness for the sake of the universalist . . . principles they were supposed to serve." But no matter how hard or altruistically a Jew fought, he was supposed to be invisible as such, "Even in this elite circle, composed almost entirely of Jews, one felt at a certain disadvantage in being Jewish."[53]

There was some charming innocence in the pretensions of such marginal individuals to represent the masses, regardless of their community, class, or even shame at having working-class parents. Like so many on the left, their own lives contradicted the universalism they professed. The socialist Irving Howe described how in the 1930s, radicals felt safe in Jewish neighborhoods, but trying to organize elsewhere "meant taking your life in your hands" since non-Jews "didn't like a bunch of sheeny kids coming in and telling them about politics. . . . We had large ambitions about winning over the American working class and really that wasn't going to be done by a lot of 'Jew boys,' " explained Howe, so "Jews would have to be content to play the background music."[54] But expressing such truths at the time was ideologically unacceptable.

Marxist intellectual circles in those years were heavily Jewish in composition and profoundly Jewish in their thinking. They included such alienated, romantic radical thinkers as Max Horkheimer, Ernst Bloch,

George Lukacs, Herbert Marcuse, Theodor Adorno, Jurgen Habermas, and Walter Benjamin, most of them associated with the Frankfurt Institute for Social Research. They were all born into highly assimilated, wealthy families, and were devoted to German philosophy, contemptuous of liberalism, and obsessed with finding a philosophical system to explain the world.

In 1931, even before Hitler gained power in Germany, Benjamin explained his interest in Communism by comparing himself to "a castaway who drifts on a wreck by climbing to the top of an already crumbling mast. But, from here, he has a chance to give a signal for his rescue."[55] What wreck had cast them away and who or what could rescue them? Benjamin could mean the Jewish community's decline or its assimilating intellectuals' desire to be heirs of a German culture in which they did not feel fully integrated and which indeed rejected them. In another sense, the wreck was the foundering of democratic Germany, that ship Heine had helped launch a century earlier. Equally, it was the wreck of the left itself, to which they stayed loyal though aware of the USSR's shortcomings and Marxism's failure to win over the masses.

The 1930s cruelly thwarted the hopes of Jewish radicals. The triumph of irrational sentiments and stubborn human nature shook their faith in progress; the difficulty of making a revolution, keeping it virtuous, and transforming society was painfully apparent. A proletariat so easily misled was not so clearly the motive force of history. It was hard to glorify workers when they were arresting one's family and guarding concentration camps, equally hard to explain why the people were so steeped in "false consciousness" as to reject socialist revolution, much less flocking to Hitler's swastika banners. Why did the ability to imagine a just society outrun the capacity to create one? Antisemitism's endurance posed an added difficulty. Such intellectuals could have understood that Communism would disappoint the utopian hopes of radical Jews, or acknowledged the deep contrast between their communal standpoint and personal background and that of the populace as a whole.

As self-proclaimed materialists, these thinkers should have asked why a certain group of people seemed immune to the social controls shaping the majority's thinking.* The need for obfuscation arose from a basic incongruity: Jewish intellectuals were more likely to reject the status quo—and oth-

---

*Several non-Marxist Jewish thinkers like Hannah Arendt, Raymond Aron, and Daniel Bell did use these lessons in criticizing Marxism.

ers were unlikely to heed them—because of their distinct situation. An atypical rootlessness and marginal place in society explained their aberrant thinking. Marxism, despite its claim to be scientific, was really an argument that society's direction coincided with their wishful thinking and that the underlying structure of history was very much like that of the holy books they rejected, based on proof texts and deductive reasoning.

Jewish Marxists avoided facing the mass support for fascism by misrepresenting the movement as a ruling-class conspiracy. Those claiming the working class as their savior could not admit that it might be anti-Jewish; if antisemitism was seen as a transient passion that socialism would melt, one could not acknowledge its true depth and intransigence without abandoning Marxism. Instead, these thinkers responded with an intellectuality turning in on itself and increasingly detached from reality. First, they explained how forces manipulating consciousness were so strong as to make real revolution impossible. Next they made a leap of faith to assert that it would still happen. Scholem rightly called the Frankfurt School one of the "most remarkable 'Jewish sects' that German Jewry produced."[56]

The masses' refusal to accept radical ideas, they concluded, must be because capitalism clouded minds to hide the truth. Unable to comprehend viscerally the basic values and principles dominating their societies, they cynically ascribed these core beliefs to a created, controlled system for perpetuating domination and blocking the road to utopia. "It is nothing new to find that the sublime becomes the cover for something low," wrote Adorno. "That is how potential victims are kept in line." Prevailing ideas, they asserted, merely hid "the unalleviated discrimination of societal power." Anyone courageous enough to "penetrate what hides behind the façade" would be forced to wear the "yellow star of one who squanders his intelligence in impotent speculation, reading things in where there is nothing to interpret."[57]

Despite his reference to the yellow star—a seeming equation of Jews and dissidents—Adorno and other German Jewish Marxists had no sense of this Jewish dimension, denying its existence at the very moment it underpinned their ideas. Indeed, the radicals identified the very "Jewish" concepts they rejected personally as the danger: love of one's people, religious belief, and sense of community. Adorno wrote that fascism arose from a "chosenness" claimed by those fearing change, a false and reactionary religion already "disintegrated and ... exposed as something untrue," a love of nation even when it "covers up the most atrocious deeds," and a fraudulent sense of a community caring for all its members to conceal the jungle that was capitalism.[58]

Thus, with the cynical yet sorrowful alienation that was their trademark, Marxist Jewish intellectuals who had abandoned religion and people far more than anyone else in Europe saw their own experience as proof that culture was not a living organism growing out of history but an artificial plant stuck into mud. But the great majority, no matter how critical or reform-minded, was not so ready to desert or declare their own identity and worldview kaput. Kafka correctly foresaw this problem, noting that the Jewish radicals "have always tried to push Germany into things which it might have accepted slowly and in its own fashion, but which it was bound to reject because they came from outsiders."[59]

Blinded by their own ideology, such radical Jewish thinkers saw everyone else's ideas—but not their own—as products of false consciousness originating from one's position in society. After all, only Jews—not German workers—stood as a group outside the framework of German history or culture and were those marked for sacrifice. Consequently for them society most clearly seemed a fraud, bureaucracy a mask for terror; a banal bourgeois life on stage veiling violence and death behind the curtain.[60]

Living in a society not expressing their innermost selves, assimilating Jews were more likely to think it innately alienating. Since they had been implicitly forced to join another culture, their new condition did not seem to be freedom but a form of slavery. Choice, then, was an illusion. One might join any religion, explained Horkheimer and Adorno, because all were empty. "Freedom to choose an ideology—since ideology always reflects economic coercion—everywhere proves to be freedom to choose what is always the same." People are forbidden self-expression to the point that "the idea of anything specific to themselves now persists only as an utterly abstract notion: personality scarcely signifies anything more than shining white teeth and freedom from body odor. . . . Consumers feel compelled to buy and use [the culture's] products even though they see through them."[61]

Yet despite all these parallels, Jewish Marxists could not deal with the Jewish element in their own thought and situation. Hitler threatened to exterminate them; any self-affirmation endangered their own self-image, equally compelling problems for intellectuals. Thus, they could deal with antisemitism only as a caricature, a bourgeois-engineered distraction that, Horkheimer and Adorno wrote, "has a specific economic reason; the concealment of domination in production." Marxism and assimilationism even made them deny the issue's importance, claiming the Nazis "could just as easily replace the antisemitic plank in their platform by some other just as workers can be moved from one wholly rationalized production center to another."[62]

Such banality removed not only the horror of this particular concern but any broader implication it might have. After Hitler fell, Adorno, Habermas, and Horkheimer all went back to Germany. A compatriot who remained in America remarked, "I understand a certain attraction in returning to the old predicament."[63] Indeed, such men could not exist outside that predicament. Angrily quoting the cheerful lines of a German poet writing in 1950, Adorno wrote that this was penned not long after Jews were gassed or burned alive. Yet he could not really react to the specificity of persecution since it was merely another sin of bourgeois capitalist society, thus neither any bar to returning to Germany nor any incentive for reevaluating one's own life.[64]

If the defeat of fascism did not dispel the Jewish Marxists' illusions it did free the left and the USSR to resume their ambiguous attitude toward the Jews. For instance, the French Communist Party ignored the Jewish identity of Hitler's victims and its own resistance heroes. Few Jews were made leaders; party propaganda was sometimes anti-Jewish. "We Communists have only genuine French names," one leader wrote in 1948. In the 1967 Middle East war, it suggested France must choose between national interests and those of Jewish plutocrats.[65]

In Eastern Europe, socialism disguised a new, ruling class and Soviet domination. But it was easier to attribute the party's unpopularity to the large number of Jews in its ranks. Thus, Communist regimes sought popular support by attacking the Jews, who were presumably also more liberal, and likelier suspects for treason to the fatherland. In Hungary, Romania, Czechoslovakia, and Poland, leading Jewish Communists were fired from their jobs or imprisoned. Anti-Jewish, antisemitic, and anti-Israel propaganda pervaded the Soviet bloc, while publicizing the Jewish Shoah was forbidden.[66]

At the 1952 Czech purge trial, eleven of fourteen defendants were Jews—including party secretary-general and vice-premier Rudolf Slansky, the architect of the Communist takeover—and identified as such by the prosecution. The Russians wanted them described as of "Jewish nationality," a designation they had fought all their lives to escape. One of Stalin's men preparing the Czech trial wrote, "I don't care how true [the evidence] is. . . . What do you care about some Jewish shit anyway?" The regime portrayed them as Trotskyists (i.e., followers of another Jew), Western spies, and Zionists. Having proved their devotion through struggle, suffering, and torture, these Jewish Communists now made a last sacrifice for a party that betrayed them and for peoples who hated them. Having abandoned any individual or communal identity, they lacked the inner strength to resist. Convicted of being Zionist agents, most of them were executed. Before being hanged, in December 1952, Slansky said—rather ambiguously—"I've got what I deserved."[67]

Despite this tragic history, parallel circumstances pushed many in the next generation of European and American Jewish intellectuals into the New Left during the 1960s. When Students for a Democratic Society splintered in 1970, each of its factions were led by Jews. Assimilating Jews argued among themselves whether workers or blacks, China or Cuba was the vanguard. Oblivious of being a tiny sect imperiously speaking for people incomprehensible to it, the New Left proved Marx's dictum that history occurred first as tragedy and then repeated itself as farce.

By the 1960s, the fact that Jews were now prosperous and less persecuted—and Israel's portrayal as an ally of U.S. imperialism—made Jewish identity seem more dispensable for the radicals. But a history of oppression, culminating in the Shoah, could also be cited to show Jews as the ultimate victims, outsiders, and rebels, justifying a limited Jewish identity as long as one favored its dissolution in revolutionary struggle. African National Congress spokesperson and ex-Communist Gail Marcus expressed a common sentiment, "For me the essence of being Jewish is in trying to live a life that has value. You make a contribution to others . . . on the side of humanity, against oppression." "For 5,000 years, Jews always had the opportunity to rebel against authority, because for 5,000 years there was always someone trying to break their backs," wrote Abbie Hoffman.[68]

After the leftist wave of the 1960s and 1970s passed, many abandoned political radicalism and, a decade later, European Communism collapsed.

A variety of factors would reduce greatly—though not end altogether—the attraction of political radicalism for assimilating Jews in the late twentieth century. The democratic West's freedom and high living standards coupled with the decline and fall of European Communist regimes were the key factors. From the standpoint of assimilation, however, political radicalism had already lost much of its usefulness. As a group, Jews were no longer oppressed. The successes of liberal reform and assimilation had let them shed much of their outsider status.

Some of the left's stands—especially a bitter antagonism toward Israel—as well as growing awareness of Soviet antisemitism repelled many Jews. Finally, Marxism's historic assimilationist orientation—demanding that nationalism and all such lesser distinctions be dissolved into the masses—was abandoned by a Western left increasingly obsessed with racial or social minority groups. A disproportionate number of Jews were still attracted to the left for the standard reasons, but they became increasingly marginal.

In France, this era of disenchantment with the left began in 1967 when, the political analyst Raymond Aron pointed out, "French Jews who have given their souls to all the [Third World] revolutionaries are now crying out in sorrow, while their friends" advocated Israel's destruction.[69] Jewish intellectuals began criticizing the Communist Party and the New Left for demonizing Israel while ignoring the Shoah and Soviet antisemitism. Antoine Spire, grandson of a famous Jewish poet and son of a convert, asked, "Why is the left so uninterested in Soviet Jews and other issues while obsessed with the Palestinians while ignoring refugees in other parts of the world?" The philosopher Alain Finkielkraut accused Communists and the left of portraying Israel as Nazi so as to erase the Shoah's memory. Once depicted as capitalists, Jews were now, Bernard-Henri Levy complained, ostracized and called "fascists."[70]

The same forces were at work among Jews in the USSR, where disillusion with assimilation Soviet-style produced a movement demanding the right to emigrate to Israel.* The endeavor of some Jews to liberate their societies through socialism ended with the new system victimizing them while making them even more hated as purveyors of a system seen as antinational and antireligious by its subjects. In some places, Jews became prominent in the struggle to overturn Communist regimes.

The great experiment had ended leaving many Jews still unassimilated. Marxism's failure was shown by the reemergence of both antisemitism and of many thousands of Jews who had fearfully hidden their identity for decades. The descendants of Communist luminaries emigrated to Israel, including the heirs of Lazar Moiseyevich Kaganovich, Stalin's lieutenant; Yakov Sverdlov, the USSR's first president; Samuel Agursky, founder of the Party's Jewish Commissariat, which repressed Jewish institutions; and

---

*See chapter 8.

even of Trotsky. Andrei Reznitsky, whose four great-uncles were early Communists shot by Stalin in 1935, said of his forebears, "They made stupid choices and they paid for them with their lives."[71]

This was an unsympathetic epitaph for Jewish leftism, yet one more accurate than the hero worship of failed revolutionaries and wrong theories so common in Western intellectual life. Koestler noted, "The social origin of parents and grandparents is as decisive under a Communist regime as racial origin was under the Nazi regime," finding "a distinct parallel here with the Nazis' contempt for 'destructive Jewish cleverness' as opposed to the 'healthy and natural instinct of the race.' "[72] Despite having chosen a new allegiance, revolutionary Jews were handicapped by their background, threatened by comrades' antisemitism and by the surviving separate identity of those Jews who did not join them. That the Soviet Communist regime's most closely guarded secret was that Lenin had a Jewish grandfather amply illustrates this point.

No matter how much they apparently evaded their background, Jewish leftists and their outlook were products of it. They founded or joined intellectual and political sects reproducing the Jewish community's patterns: a small group bound together by common ideas, a derided minority loyal to its doctrine and viewing apostasy with contempt. Their utopianism sprang from expecting Western society to reflect themselves. Devotion to assimilation made them overestimate the masses' ability to overcome all distinctions in order to unite, just as they underestimated the ability of incumbent regimes to woo people through church, tradition, and nationalism.

The intellectuals' quest to overcome their caste's isolation from society was especially intense for those further separated by being assimilating Jews. The intrinsic rebelliousness of writers or artists was also intensified by a special Jewish alienation. Certain events, such as the overthrow of the czar and the rise of fascism, had a heightened resonance for Jews. Having "outgrown" nationalism, they expected everyone else to do so. The same reduced commitment applied to their class. If rich, that entry into the elite was so recent, insecure, and under discriminatory conditions as to make them an oppressed subclass far more conscious of other's oppression. If poor themselves, they were more likely to consider that status as artificial, temporary, unhallowed by habitual resignation. As people geographically, religiously, and culturally in transition they saw change as more inevitable and positive. In short, they could see the existing order as transient, unnatural, and unsatisfactory rather than ordained by God, nature, or human temperament.

Assimilation was a learning process about the society they were joining, and fascination with the left and revolution was a passing stage in that evolution, just as it often was in the lives of individuals. With Israel, upward mobility, and enhanced opportunities for total assimilation, the radical impulse was greatly reduced, though there remained a pattern of activity that almost made radicalism seem to be a Jewish tradition in itself.

Yet it was a dead end. Those in rebellion against themselves were manipulated by ideas playing on their feelings of guilt, doubt, and confusion. Having banished historical continuity, their sense of reality was fragile. Trying, in Marx's phrase, to storm the heavens, they had forgotten the existence of gravity. Many radical concepts "stood no chance of realization," as Scholem noted, being "messianic vision[s] to which the transition is not possible with the forces functioning in history."[73] But from where, then, to ask a properly Marxist question, did a belief to the contrary arise? People did not behave as Jewish radicals expected because the would-be vanguard was dispossessed of what others willingly embraced. Offsprings of a different tradition, assimilating Jews were unfettered only as a temporary stage between two sets of social beliefs. Leftist Jews congratulated themselves on universalism but their behavior and ideas were conditioned by particularity—a singular process of assimilation; a special variety of alienation.

By the same token, Jews often saw injustice more clearly than others and also embraced many righteous causes. Some particular factors helped Jewish intellectuals avoid or outgrow radical ideas. The force of reason attracting them to Western civilization and driving them away from tradition equally made them suspect irrationality and dogma. Their embrace of individual freedom made them reluctant to accept ideological servitude. The antisemitism of some movements underscored the paradox of an alleged universalism built on self-denial.

But those with a revolutionary vision were jilted by humanity. They suffered from the idiocy of geniuses: the inability of those with exceptional minds to understand the consensus of common sense, blaming society for an uneasy isolation actually rooted in their personal situation. Those whose identity put them at odds to the state thought this meant it could be remade; those artificially held down concluded that all class division was artificial; those rejecting their own people thought everyone wished to emulate them.

In the end, the radicals were tragicomic figures claiming the right to direct humanity's future when they lacked the most basic understanding of themselves. Their good intentions often led people to disaster; they were heroic on behalf of bad causes. Walter Benjamin imagined himself trying to escape a shipwreck by clinging to the lifeline of radicalism. But for Jews, revolutionary assimilationism was a hidden reef, seemingly a course that pointed to a safe harbor but instead brought their vessel to grief.

7

The Last Jew

Everything had been prepared beforehand; a thin crust of earth had been constructed only for [appearances]; immediately beneath it a great hole opened out,
with steep sides, into which K. sank, wafted onto his back by a gentle current. And
while he was already being received into impenetrable depths, his head still strain-
ing upwards on his neck, his own name raced across the stone above him in great
flourishes. Enchanted by the sight, he woke up.

—Franz Kafka, "The Dream"

D URING THE 1880s, a wealthy Russian Jew took his daughter to visit
the well-known novelist and editor Peretz Smolenskin, hoping
Smolenskin could persuade the young woman to drop out of the revolutionary movement. The meeting was unsuccessful and, instead, the daughter ran away to join her radical comrades. When the father bitterly blamed
Smolenskin, he retorted that it was parents, not children, who needed to
learn since those seemingly rebellious offspring were really acting as their
parents had conditioned them:

> How did you bring up your daughter? You had governesses and tutors,
> teaching her foreign languages. You sent her to high school, where she
> learned about other peoples. Did you teach her about our own people?
> Did you teach her our own language? Did you interest her in our own
> history? Did you want her to know about our own people and our own
> national aspirations? To whom, then, should you bring your complaints, if
> not to yourself?[1]

When Philip Roth's fictional Alexander Portnoy rejected his religion,
his father told him this alienation arose from ignorance: "Do you know
Talmud, my educated son? Do you know history?" A bar mitzvah "was the
end of your religious education. . . . Do you know a single thing about the

wonderful history and heritage . . . of your people?"[2] Yet this precondition-ing had come from adults' decisions, not the fourteen-year-old boy being rebuked.

"It is a law of nature that however much one may grieve over the death of a dear one, at the end of a year consolation finds its way into the heart of the mourner," says rabbinic tradition. "But the disappearance of a living man can never be wiped out of one's memory."[3] The passage refers to Jo-seph, who vanished from his family into Egypt. He returned to the Jewish people, as did Moses, Hess and Herzl, Nordau, Schoenberg, and a pitifully small remnant of others. But the number of those leaving the community forever to convert or assimilate totally was very many times larger. Each Jew in every generation, wrote Arendt, had to choose between remaining to some degree outside society or conforming to its demands, including be-traying one's people by abandoning them.[4]

Aside from the Shoah, Jews vanished far more often in the nineteenth and twentieth centuries due to voluntary assimilation than to antisemitic persecution. This factor of choice was Kafka's theme in his story "A Hun-ger Artist," about a circus performer whose act was to starve himself for long periods of time. "Why stop fasting . . . after forty days of it? He had held out for a long time. . . . Why stop now. . . . Why should he be cheated of the fame he would get for fasting longer?" Jews were thought to remain faithful to their God and way of life from stubborn inertia. But the hunger artist explained his abstinence as knowing no food tasty enough to tempt him. "If I had found it, believe me, I should have made no fuss and stuffed myself like you or anyone else."[5]

Kafka knew that his family's abandonment of Judaism shaped his own fate. His father conveyed little Jewish heritage to him, Kafka wrote, "it all dribbled away while you were passing it on." But he read Jewish history and like many in his era found in it a substitute for Jewish religion. De-prived of the necessary knowledge, the young Kafka "yawned and dozed" in synagogue, frightened that he might be called to read the Torah and make a fool of himself. His bar mitzvah was "ridiculous memorizing"; the Passover Seder "more and more developed into a farce." Franz could not understand the significance of a few gestures performed "with an indiffer-ence in keeping with their flimsiness. . . . For you they had meaning as little souvenirs of earlier times . . . that was why you wanted to pass them on to me, but since they no longer had any intrinsic value even for you, you could do this only through persuasion or threat."[6]

Most Jews clung to their little souvenirs and some customs until, soon enough, many came upon another religion, ideology, or nation offering them spiritual sustenance and material benefits. A large portion of each generation became more distant from its ancestral and parental traditions or loyalties until reaching a point where total departure was an easy step. Every day, scores of people chose to become the last Jew in a line stretching perhaps three thousand years, turning their energy to other causes, deciding not to reproduce someone like themselves, taking as role models those who had been their persecutors.

Gerson Bleichroder came from an Orthodox background and so built up the family banking business that on his death in 1893 he was Berlin's richest man. Despite Bleichroder's generous help to persecuted Jews, his sons all became Protestants, married non-Jews, and were wastrels in the nobility's dissipated style. His grandsons would be active rightists who claimed to be loyal Nazis but were instead classified as Jews and died in concentration camps.[7]

The son of Sam Lapowski, a Jewish storekeeper in Texas, declared his family's name to be Dillon at the Worcester Academy and Harvard, becoming a Presbyterian. His son, C. Douglas Dillon, switched to the posher Episcopalian faith at Groton, and became ambassador to France, secretary of the treasury, president of the Metropolitan Museum, and even joined the notoriously discriminatory Chevy Chase Club after members were assured that he was only 25 percent Jewish.[8] In the Debré family, grandfather Simon had come from Alsace to serve as Paris's chief rabbi; his son Robert was a doctor and freethinker; and grandson Michel was a Catholic and the prime minister of France responsible for carrying out its anti-Israel policy in the late 1960s.[9]

If such people—along with Heine, Disraeli, Marx, or Woody Allen—showed a robust Jewish creativity, they also embodied its disintegration.[10] Even Einstein, despite his Jewish loyalties, was indifferent to his children growing up as Catholics. Humanist parents produced Christian children; cosmopolitan parents produced nationalistic children. When Jews were excluded from society, they assimilated from fear; when permitted entry, they assimilated out of indifference to any remaining distinction. As the historian Todd Endelman wrote, Jews ceased "to be Jewish in England because resistance to their incorporation into society was weak; in Germany, their ties to Judaism were being sundered because the resistance was strong."[11]

Thus, assimilating Jews demoted their own culture from being their life's treasure to an obsolete item whose greatest virtue was the apparent ease of jettisoning it. Koestler remembered walks in Vienna when his grandfather bought the boy, but not himself, a ham sandwich, saying, "It would be wrong for me to eat ham but it is not wrong for you. I was brought up in prejudice." Koestler commented in his autobiography, "It was an attitude which combined respect for tradition with enlightened tolerance." But this was hardly true: equating tradition with prejudice was hardly tolerant. Respecting others' rights was quite different from accepting their beliefs as superior to one's own and teaching your offspring to imitate them.[12]

Everywhere in exile, Jews lived amidst confident peoples preaching other values, traditions, and ideas. As Lenny Bruce expressed this social pressure: "The Jews lost their god. . . . Because to have a god you have to know something about him. . . . Our god has . . . no manger in the five and ten, on cereal boxes and on television. . . . . Your god, the Christian god, is all over . . . on bank buildings—he's been in three films. He's on crucifixes all over. It's a story you can follow. Constant identification."[13]

In any free competition, Judaism was at an extreme disadvantage since to side with the majority brought subjective and material advantage while to stand apart was to be alienated and stigmatized. Charles de Rothschild, a Jewish student at Britain's elite Harrow school in the 1890s, pledged, "If I ever have a son he will be instructed in boxing and [judo] before he enters school, as Jew hunts such as I experienced are a very one-sided amusement."[14] Those far advanced in assimilation, however, might choose whether to be among the hunters, hunted, or onlookers.

A few, on their way out the door, tried to help the community or at least—like Rachel Levy, Heine, and Disraeli—expressed some pride in their former selves.[15] Daniel Chwolson converted in 1855 to obtain a Russian university post. Asked if he had changed religion out of belief, Chwolson replied, "Yes, I was convinced it is better to be a professor in St. Petersburg than a [humble Hebrew teacher] in Eyshishok." He fought antisemitism, but inevitably his children were indifferent and became fully Christianized.[16] The Russian financier and scholar Jan Bloch, though baptized when young, could say, "I was my whole life a Jew and I die as a Jew," but all five of his children were Christians. The Zionist leader Nahum Sokolow wrote on Bloch's death in 1901, "Thus are we bereft of strength. So, without leaving a trace behind, vanishes what the potential energy of the Jewish race accumulated through a thousand years, what Jewish industry has built up."[17]

Sometimes, wisps of Jewish distinctiveness remained visible for a while. Converts, as Marcel Proust showed in his character Swann, were still considered Jews even two generations after becoming Catholics. A French writer proclaimed in 1917, "It takes a lot of water to baptize a Jew!"[18] Francis Cohen converted to become Francis Palgrave in the early 1800s. Abandoning his own history, he wrote that of England, burying his background but specializing in legal studies because, he wrote with a hint of Jewish orientation, "The character of the People mainly depends on their Laws." Three of his sons became pillars of the British establishment; the fourth traveled to Arabia and—searching for some identity—became a Catholic priest, then a Protestant, and took the name Cohen. What began in the wholeness of one community could only end with membership in another or in a general restlessness, neurosis, and anomie.[19]

For most, there was a slow decline in observance and identity, with rituals first being stripped of any meaning or enthusiasm, so undercutting any motive to continue them. In contrast to a human urge so strong as to seem instinctive, many Jewish parents strove to ensure their offspring did not follow in their footsteps. Added to other pressures of modern life on the family, assimilation accelerated and deepened that institution's decline. Continuity was disrupted as each generation had different cultural and religious values or loyalties, scorning its precursor's lesser degree of assimilation. Philipp Landau describes his German Jewish family's typical devolution between the 1870s and 1914. At first, his parents still observed the main holidays, fasting on Yom Kippur and attending services, "not so much from an inner need, but . . . from custom and habit" and to avoid criticism by Jewish neighbors. "Lacking were the prerequisites that allowed things to become truly alive and necessary: true belief and genuine piety." The remaining formal observances—such as keeping kosher or going to synagogue—were like "a structure from which almost all the supports have been removed . . . only barely holds together in its old form as long as no one touches it. A fresh wind, isolation from the old companions that used to surround it, knocks it over."[20]

On occasional visits to the synagogue as a child he remembered feeling "sacredness and solemnity . . . strangely purified and lifted up into another, noble world. . . . Is this perhaps the dormant memory of the feelings of departed generations?"[21] More likely, it was a living memory of experience. Yet there also came a Yom Kippur when his father did not fast.* "On this

*"To break the law, all you have to do is—just go ahead and break it! All you have to do is stop trembling . . . and finding it unimaginable and beyond you." Roth, *Portnoy's Complaint*, op. cit., pp. 78–79.

memorable day I witness lunch being served. . . . Contrary to all custom, father is at home and not at the synagogue. . . . He hesitates to sit down at the table, and I sense the importance of the moment and the tension as to what will happen next. . . . My mother urges him on and ridicules him. But only after she, laughing and joking all the while, has securely drawn the curtains and windowshades so that no eyes of the surrounding neighborhood can see the outrage, does he sit down to eat." Having made this difficult decision and suffering no divine punishment, "My father, too, parted for good from the old strict customs, to which he had been bound, not by a true heartfelt need but rather only by fear, habit, and piety."[22]

Freedom from Judaism's customs left a gap that might be filled by Christianity, nationalism, socialism, or some combination of such elements. Clara Geissmar, another German Jew, wrote, "My unsatisfied religious need was fulfilled by the firm belief in a moral world order" embodied in German philosophy and history. She and her husband "agreed that our life in the Judaism of our childhood had left something within us, an extract upon which we could draw for the rest of our lives." But what would their children have? One alternative was to keep some customs, as her husband preferred, especially celebrating the Sabbath, "But if Saturday is not also celebrated by other friends and acquaintances, and especially if the children see their father carrying on his weekday activities on Saturday and that he has his holiday on Sunday like everyone else all around us, then Saturday can hardly be maintained as a day of rest."[23]

The pressure of peers, society, and their own habits made it impossible to maintain this effort. With some stones removed, "The wall with which [Judaism] surrounded its God . . . shakes and finally collapses." She wanted the children to be raised as Protestants, though her husband was reluctant lest this shame his father. That religion's attraction was more cultural than religious for her. Political and intellectual success made it seem loftier, more civilized, the creed of Lessing, Schiller, and Goethe. Protestant friends urged her to baptize the children. "A tender soul once had tearful eyes at the thought of how our little Leopold would someday fare in the world, at all that he would have to suffer if he were to grow up a Jew." Geissmar's relatives reacted angrily to the idea of such a conversion. Her brother said that a person could only live properly by doing "justice to a whole series of claims."[24]

At last, Geissmar attended a church service. When it began, "In the name of the Father, the Son, and the Holy Ghost," she recalled the Hebrew words "that introduced Jewish prayers: 'Hear, oh Israel, the Eternal, your God, is one, a single, eternal Being.' When the service ended with the words 'May the Lord bless you and keep you' . . . I thought of my father, who, when I went to meet him at the door on his return from prayers on Friday evening, laid his hands on my head and in the original Hebrew said the words that the Protestant clergyman bestowed upon his congregants on their way home. I did not go to a Protestant church again."[25]

In the end, only sentimentality and family loyalty proved a last barrier to total assimilation—at least for one more generation. Similarly, the Russian revolutionary author Isaac Babel, who had written that "when a Jew gets on a horse he stops being a Jew," did not change so easily. On Friday, wrote the cavalryman Babel, he dreamed of "a Jewish glass of tea, and a little of that pensioned-off God in a glass of tea."[26] For the atheist, religion lives on as custom and community, but a custom not taught and explained no longer exists after a generation or two, especially when it runs counter to the prevailing practices.

Geissmar's brother discouraged her from baptism by raising the claims of family, community, society, nation, and memory. But for many, there came a time when all these factors waned, on whom no family pressure or communal loyalty still made a claim or a memory. Nothing was left to stand against the benefits promised to those willing to be a last Jew and the threat against those who refused. Sensing on some level that they acted wrongly, those crossing the line might be angry at the society forcing them, feeling guilty at surrendering, eager to minimize the deed or make it seem virtuous by doing something useful with their assimilation. A few turned cynical, loyal only to themselves and unbound by belief in any moral system. Such fiscal or political adventurers fed a common antisemitic stereotype that hurt other Jews.

It was unlikely that Jan Hoch, born in 1923 to a poor Orthodox family in Czechoslovakia, would someday become a world-famous tycoon, but it was even more unlikely that his entire family would be murdered by antisemites in a death camp. Hoch reached England in 1940, joined the British army, and became an officer decorated for bravery. To succeed, he systematically changed identity and shed his past, also dispensing with its ethics. What system could he accept except the glorification of that most good for himself?

Thus, Robert Maxwell, Englishman, was born. "All of us here are Englishmen together," he liked to tell audiences. "The difference is that you are Englishmen by accident. I am an Englishman by choice." He insisted that he was not a Jew but "a member of the Church of England," by another such decision. True, the newspapers—at least ones he did not own—made fun of his social pushiness. Wrote Anthony Delano, a biographer, he "loved England but never learned to understand what it meant to be an Englishman [or] why England did not love him as much as he loved it."[27] Yet perhaps he was so flamboyant, egotistical, ruthless, and protean because however much he acted the part, Maxwell did not credit his own metamorphosis as anything more than disguise. A man whose origin had proved fatal to his family might well believe that to feign transformation was to escape extinction.

Only in 1988, age sixty-five and near the peak of his power, did Maxwell decide to reestablish a Jewish connection—helping Jews leave the USSR, financing memorials to the Shoah, and making investments in Israel. According to his son Philip, "He wanted to close the circle of his life and return in death to his origins."[28] But like many of his generation, he sought only to close the circle, not extend it into the future. After his death in 1991 and burial in Jerusalem, Maxwell's massive thefts and impending bankruptcy emerged. His newfound Jewish pathos was a case of patriotism as a scoundrel's last refuge or, at best, a memorial to a dead past.

Those whose background equipped them for the greatest achievements were also most often deserters, further reinforcing the association between abandoning identity and gaining security, success, and power. Only seemingly senseless stubbornness stood in the way, though hesitation might still deter the final, irreversible step. Even such avid assimilationists as Scholem's father called baptism "an unprincipled and servile act." Rathenau, who formally withdrew from the German Jewish community in 1895, rejected conversion as a degrading surrender to discrimination. German Jewish groups condemned converts as "renegades who sacrifice their honor and conviction to win recognition." Such people measured success, a British rabbi wrote, by their distance "from all Jewish associations."[29]

But those really wishing to leave the community were indifferent to its opinion, especially if their parents had begun the process. The wealthy American Straus family was a case in point. One son of Percy Straus changed his name progressively from Percy Solomon Straus to Percy Selden Straus to Percy Selden, and withdrew from the family. Another son, Donald, later wrote, "Jewishness was like sex. It was absolutely taboo as a subject for discussion with either of my parents. By example rather than by word they raised the three of us to be antisemitic." Children absorbed their lessons well. Socially, the goal was be accepted into non-Jewish institutions. Being taught to view Judaism as inferior, they joined St. James's Episcopal Church. "It was just as clearly preferable to meet and take out Christian girls and of course we all married Christians." Instructed, "Don't make yourself conspicuous," they erased any characteristic—even name—standing in the way of conformity.[30]

Having trained children to seek social success and fame away from the ghetto, parents watched them follow this blueprint. A generation that had known the humiliations of poverty, immigration, or discrimination chased children away from the apparent source of this pain for their own good. "The parents have eaten bitter grapes," as the Bible put it, "the children's teeth are set on edge."[31] The situation was encapsulated in a story by Bernard Malamud, "The Jewbird." A Yiddish-speaking bird flew in the Cohen family's dinner window and tried to tutor the son. But the father threw the bird out. On that day, the boy's grandmother, his link to the past, died.[32]

With no understanding or sense of belonging, people were profoundly, usually irreversibly, alienated. Paul Muhsam, a German Jew, wrote of the synagogue, "There was such a lack of discipline, such a babble of voices, conversations, whispering, looking around, and letting oneself go, and the service was so far removed from any solemnity of atmosphere and ceremony that it could only be called an utter and complete chaos. . . . I asked myself what all of these repulsive carryings-on had to do with God and religion, and since my schooldays, except for special occasions, I have never again attended services."[33] Yet his ancestors who had been taught to understand and participate fully had seen this not as chaos but as freedom. Eventually assimilating Jews began seeing their own background through the eyes of the Christians and countrymen they were imitating.

Muhsam's parents neither taught him holiday customs nor held "the family celebrations, which at all times have contributed most to the bond among Jews through living tradition and reverent cultivation of the heritage of the past." Inevitably business required that stores owned by Jews be closed on Christian holidays and open on Jewish ones. The only Jewish custom left his parents was commemorating the day of their parents' death, a symbolically appropriate look backward into a deceased past. "At Christmas no tree was set up, but we did exchange presents. The religious holidays, Shabbat, the Haggadah . . . remained mere names for me, and I did know when Christmas was, but not Hanukkah. To be sure, every Friday evening I saw my mother quietly praying to herself from her prayer book, conscientiously rising up at the prescribed places, but I myself did not have the urge to do the same."[34]

The inner contradiction of these tenets was, to be sure, often painfully realized by the children, although not by their parents. Philipp Lowenfeld, a contemporary of Muhsam, noted that Jews often "imagined that they were more refined if they socialized with Christians than if they were in the company of members of their own religion." Many, including his mother, "found a child to be prettier if it 'did not look Jewish.' " Why should it be a question of character to remain within a group if it was more refined to associate with the others? And why, conversely, should the others be better than us if, in our opinion, we had a true religion, and, according to our religion teachers, the only true one?" But defection or conversion angered these same people. "My father used to express this by saying that 'one does not abandon a besieged fortress.' "[35]

One of a besieged fortress's main attributes, however, is that those trapped inside want to get out if possible. And when sieges finally end, the fortress is often an empty ruin. It was only natural that for assimilating Jews surrounded by Christian society, Christianity became the measure of all things. Many Jews now thought their own religion and group inferior because it differed from dominant views they shared or had less power and prestige. They defected or at least revised customs to bring them into line with the ruling majority. Paradoxically they extolled these societies as superior while their actions proved they doubted that doctrine of freedom and equality, or at least knew conformity was the price for simultaneously gaining and subverting these treasures.

But glittering prizes beckoned them across the line. Bernard Berenson said he refused to be held back by an anachronistic, squalid religion. "I had ears, but could not hear because of my ear locks; I had eyes and could not see because they were closed in prayer." Yet his father refused to let his wife go to the synagogue and encouraged his children to ignore Jewish customs. Berenson remodeled himself from Yiddish-speaking shtetl Jew to German-speaking Lithuanian to polished Bostonian who concealed his past and never invited Harvard classmates to his parents' home. His father once fled a house where he was peddling on seeing his son was a guest there. Berenson and his sisters pitied a less ambitious sibling who refused to hide his origin or eliminate his accent. Bernard may have had some doubts—he wrote a story about a boy who died a horrible death after discarding Judaism—but his family and society supported his decision.[36]

Fear was another factor encouraging conversion or concealment, and not just in Europe. A powerful rancher in the American West, haunted by the antisemitic bullies of his youth in the East, kept his Jewish birth a secret from everyone, showing, said his therapist, that the Nazi view "of an evil Jewish identity is no worse than that harbored by many a Jew."[37] The writer Mary Morris was so named by parents living in the American Midwest when she was born in 1947, "so no one would know by my name that I was a Jew." This did not, however, make her as secure as being given a real identity. "I am orphaned, disenfranchised, removed," she wrote. "A Jew, a lost one, searching for my clan. I have not been able to find my mate, my place. Like most Americans I dwell far removed from the source—in deserts where no one knows where we've come from, in cities where no one cares. Like the ghost of a restless soul, it seems I must search until I find what I am looking for—community, family, the place to belong."[38] At his life's end, Berenson, who had donned so many masks, no longer knew "who is the real I, where does he hide from me?"[39]

The German-born immigrant father of Alfred Melchett, founder of Britain's giant Imperial Chemical Industries, still felt after twenty years in England, despite his own riches and power, "a stranger in a foreign country," whose relations with British people remained "formal and can never create true bonds of friendship." But like most immigrants, the Melchetts wanted their children to belong to the new country. In theory that meant being modern, cosmopolitan people; in practice it called for conforming to Christian and British customs. At Christmas, the family exchanged presents and sang carols around the tree. Alfred's parents gave him no religious instruction but sent him to a boarding school where Christian chapel was mandatory. Feeling like an outsider, he chose a wife who seemed to personify English womanhood as he had been taught to appreciate it. He was an atheist; she was a devout Christian. So naturally, in 1892 this scion of rationalists married her at St. Mark's Church and later agreed to raise their children, Henry and Eva, as Christians, merely telling his wife, "If you want to believe that stuff, go ahead."[40]

Though seeing no reason to pass it on, Alfred did not personally abandon his Jewish heritage. He became a Zionist after the 1917 Balfour Declaration and told his son: "Next time anyone calls you 'A dirty Jew,' hit him on the nose and if he does it again hit him harder." But British civility was not so easily transgressed. When one of Alfred's speeches to the House of Commons was interrupted by a member shouting, "Silence in the ghetto," he ignored it.[41] Alfred's admirers, too, recalled his background. Showing the strange contradictions implicit in assimilation, a friend proclaimed, "It required a great Jew, with the divine fire burning brightly in his spirit, to express and to embody in action the somewhat vague hopes and aspirations of the British race."[42]

In 1914, Alfred's daughter, Eva, a baptized Christian, was to marry her lapsed Jewish fiancé, Gerald Isaacs, in Holy Trinity Church but the archbishop of Canterbury refused to authorize a religious wedding involving a non-Christian. Gerald wrote Eva, "The natural religion for me to follow was that of the Jews. Strive though I might (and please God I never will) I could not rid myself of the mantle of the old race even though the shackles of the old faith have fallen by the way. You know I am obstinately proud of my people for bad as are the worst of them, so good are the best of them!" But this was no barrier to intermarriage or raising children without such shackles. After a civil ceremony, the couple went to church for a special blessing.[43]

The Melchett family's steady march to the altar was interrupted by one thing. After Hitler came to power in 1933, Henry attended a secret meeting of Jewish members of Parliament to discuss the plight of the German Jews. Impressed on a recent trip with Jewish achievements in Palestine and wishing to identify himself with their oppressed German counterparts, he decided to convert to Judaism. Unknown to him, Eva was doing the same thing.[44] Henry later became the Jewish Agency's chairman and led other Jewish organizations; Eva headed the Reform movement's and World Jewish Congress's British sections.

But Henry's baptized children laughed at his efforts to make them Jewish. In 1947, his son Julian was married at St. Paul's Church and, on his death, had a memorial service in Westminster Abbey. Not only did the family become Christian but Imperial Chemical Industries—founded by the admirable Jew Melchett—became the most faithful executor of the Arab economic boycott against Israel and sent no Jewish employees to Arab countries to avoid offending those customers.[45]

Just as Alfred Melchett was said to embody British virtues, the writer Donald Katz picked a Jewish clan as subject of his book, *Home Fires,* on a typical American family. This choice seemed to show the success of Jewish assimilation. But each aspect of the Goldenberg family's story instead proved how distinctive was the experience of assimilating Jews and how profoundly they were shaped by a spiritual, intellectual, and communal vacuum. In four generations, their names evolved from Yosef and Yetta

Goldenberg, to Samuel and Eve Gordon; to movie star appellations like Susan [Hayward] and Lorraine [Laraine Day], and finally to such pseudo-cosmopolitan ones as Shiva and Magdalena, signaling adherence to other groups.

As a soldier in World War II, Sam Goldenberg attributed the survival of Europeans to family continuity. But for American Jews of his generation, the highest precept was to free one's children from such shackles. Identity was rejected by such tendencies as his own mother's preference for blond, blue-eyed, non-Jewish-looking grandchildren over darker ones. Neither his mother's observance of Jewish dietary laws, nor bias encountered in the army, nor news of the Holocaust or Israel's creation made him hesitate to shed old customs in order to be American.[46]

Details intended to prove the Gordons' alleged typicality as Americans actually demonstrated their distinctiveness as Jews. After seeing a film on the Nuremberg Trials, the Goldenbergs' daughter had nightmares of Nazis taking her away, later wondering which fellow students might have hidden her. The family's decision to change its name, Sam hoped, would win him more Christian clients. This step was rationalized as "an American tradition," Katz wrote, since "many of the Americans Eve admired most had smoothed and celebrated their emergence from the past by shedding Kaminsky for Kaye (Danny), Levitch for Lewis (Jerry), and Berlinger for Berle." Remarkably, Katz did not notice that this trio had something in common beyond altered names. Sam's favorite movie star was the "mysterious" Paulette Goddard, whose exotic appeal might owe something to her originally being Pauline Levy. The Gordons were also distressed when mostly Jewish performers were blacklisted and their favorite show, *The Goldbergs,* was canceled. Senator Joe McCarthy's anticommunism and the Rosenbergs' execution, Katz claimed, "terrified and infuriated urban children of the Depression years," a factor applying less, say, to Irish or Italians, who were more likely to be anti-Communist themselves.[47]

In their upward mobility and drive for assimilation, the Gordons moved to a suburb of New York with the arcadian name of Harbor Isle. Since most of the families there were Jewish, however, the neighboring town's people dubbed it "Hebrew Isle." Sam had a vestigial belief that Jews were better people who drank less, worked harder, and treated women with more respect. He wanted his daughters to marry Jews and was sorry that they made few Jewish friends. "We bring them to a place full of Jewish kids, and they go out to find goyim. . . . How is it possible that we have two antisemites for daughters?"[48]

Yet like the father Smolenskin rebuked, Sam could look to himself as an answer. Having given them no background in Jewish history or religion, he could not expect them to become magically like himself later in life. Without a meaningful identity, his professions of Jewish superiority or uniqueness could only strike his children as empty of content or expressions of racism. Like Philip Roth's fictional Portnoy, they could well respond, "I am sick and tired of goyische this and goyische that! If it's bad it's the goyim, if it's good it's the Jews! . . . Stick your suffering heritage up your suffering ass—I happen also to be a human being!"[49]

Hurt by his children's attitude, Sam asked his wife, "How much farther from a ghetto could we have taken them?" This was precisely the problem. When a daughter referred to Harbor Isle as a "ghetto" she meant not that it had a high concentration of Jews but that it was an island of privilege isolated from the American mainstream. To enter into real life was to find a group offering a meaningful worldview and integral sense of community, human needs unanswered by a Jewishness lacking any apparent meaning or by an upbringing equipping them with no ostensible convictions. When the inevitable happened, Sam was astonished at his daughters' mixed marriages, saying, "For a thousand years not one member of my immediate family has ever married outside [our] religion."[50]

Yet Sam's notions no longer appeared heroic or worthwhile to his children, merely biased and obsolete. Bob Dylan justified a generation's rebellion by saying, "Our parents were in a sad situation. They were probably just into no down payments and aluminum cans. I don't know what kind of knowledge they could have really passed on."[51] Materialism was typical of modern life and American culture, but despiritualization, abandonment of any search for transcendence, and shrugging off of history went further among assimilating Jews than in other groups. So children were programmed to rebel as much by what their parents had discarded as against what they had chosen. The vacuum of values, ideology, and identity—less typical of, say, Catholics or evangelical Protestants—did not make them cosmopolitan humanists so much as eager adherents to other religious, political, or even ethnic groups offering the very things they lacked.

Many paths competed for their attention, alternatives which might contradict each other but were consistent in their rejection of Jewish identity. Thus, Sam and Eve Gordon's eldest daughter, Susan, who later became a leftist, first became a snob. On visits home from Vassar, she put on a phony accent and tried to act in an upper-class manner. Her mother understood that Susan was treating her as she had her own parents when leaving the Bronx for the suburbs: "Vassar is her Harbor Isle. I am a source of shame." Another daughter, Lorraine, named her offspring Magdalena, inspired by Nikos Kazantzakis's novel *The Last Temptation of Christ.* A third daughter ardently studied exotic cultures and creeds, mainly Buddhism, concluding that she should have been born Japanese.[52]

Young people decrying Judaism as hypocritical and superficial suspended such a critical stance as they joined cults. At a transcendental meditation ashram, one daughter played Mary in a Christmas play. The Indian fakir who ran the place had a keen sense of his followers' motives: "Where do you go if your institutions don't offer you anything? To a tepee in Vermont, that's where. . . . They are all searching for the necklace that's around their necks." But that family heirloom was held in low esteem by the more than half of his apostles who were Jewish. Jews could even become gurus in their own right. Jack Rosenberg took the German name Werner Erhard to make himself feel powerful, teaching at his expensive *est* seminars that every individual could create his own universe through personal willpower, a common assimilationist theme.[53]

All the Gordons' children end up in various groups purveying an alternate identity, ranging from Alcoholics Anonymous, to Oriental religions, to cultlike self-help programs, to New Age superstitions, as a way to dissolve alienation by finding a system of knowledge and membership in some sort of community. The oldest daughter finally became a junkie, living in a different sort of ghetto and affecting a black street accent. Katz wrote, "To Susan's ear the street idiom sounded like real Americans talking."[54] One might well ask, however, why she did not consider her own American-born parents as legitimately American or whether average Americans would so deprecate their claim to that status.

The Gordon's son had a bar mitzvah but it was richly symbolic that he did not understand the words he spoke, having only mastered their pronunciation. Being Jewish to him only meant being excused from school for extra holidays. Seeing *Fiddler on the Roof,* he thought his own grandmother's faith "to be largely compounded of superstition and fear." His dreams of Nazis from *The Diary of Anne Frank* made him associate being Jewish with "loss and terror . . . like being haunted." When, after years of therapy he concluded, "There has to be more to existence than the history of me" and that his emotional foundation "seems like it's a thousand years old," he did not turn to the long history actually behind him, but connected to that chain of being by embracing New Age mysticism.[55]

Only Jews had deliberately held back their identity to foster assimilation, were adverse to their own history and worldview as illegitimate, and programmed themselves into a deliberately bequeathed cultural vacuum. To fill this hole with an enduring new identity required finding another creed and community. Clara Geissmar had written that even her love for German culture and Shakespeare left her spiritually unfulfilled. "I missed belonging to a religion." Paul Muhsam admitted that his rejection of an increasingly watered-down Jewish background "was an expression of the wish to live in a community, which was possible only by getting rid of every trace of otherness." There was no path back for him: "I knew nothing about Judaism. It offered me nothing whatever. For me it was only an empty shell, and I saw in it nothing but a burdensome fetter." He rejected baptism only because it would hurt his parents and make him feel "cowardly, characterless, and contemptible to abandon the oppressed and join the side of the oppressors, embracing a religion for which, despite the most radiant genius from whom it took its name, almost two thousand years had not sufficed to fill its followers with a humanity that would have made such oppression impossible."[56]

It was inevitable, though, that many Jews would reject being perpetually on the losing side. To justify the seemingly shameful decision to join the persecutors, the new group could be proclaimed spiritually superior. Leaving the Jewish community might best be rationalized as departing a small, narrow cause for a larger, better one.

When the poet Osip Mandelstam was growing up in Russia before the revolution, his parents gave him no Jewish education or sympathy. Having been educated not to think of himself as a Jew, he resented being one and was determined to correct this accident of birth. Visiting grandparents as a child, he felt as if "being taken to the native country of my father's incomprehensible philosophy." When his Orthodox grandfather "wanted to take me in his arms I almost burst into tears. . . . Suddenly my grandfather drew from a drawer of a chest a black and yellow silk cloth, put it around my shoulders, and made me repeat after him words composed of unknown sounds; but, dissatisfied with my babble, he grew angry and shook his head in disapproval. I felt stifled and afraid."[57]

Thinking he was defying his parents, he merely conformed to their rebellion. Having been socialized not to understand or identify with Jews, he naturally neither comprehended nor identified with them. Thinking Judaism "crude," he did not see all religions as vulgar but rather embraced the

Russian Orthodox church as sublime. This was no objective, disinterested judgment but one inspired by his upbringing and surroundings. On his father's bookshelf, "The books relating to Jews occupied a despised position [where they] lay like ruins . . . the Judaic chaos thrown into the dust." When his parents, "in a fit of national contrition," hired a Hebrew teacher, "his refusal to remove his cap made me feel awkward" and Mandelstam ridiculed his bad Russian. Feeling he had nothing to do with the little boy pictured in the Hebrew primer, Mandelstam, "with all my being revolted against the book and the subject." Even the teacher's self-respect as a Jew was fraudulent: "I knew that he hid his pride when he went out into the street, and therefore did not believe him."[58] If everyone else was ashamed to be a Jew, why should Mandelstam be one?

How could this shadow identity stand against the surrounding world's splendor and power? "The strong, ruddy, Russian year rolled through the calendar with decorated eggs, Christmas trees, steel skates from Finland, December, gaily bedecked Finnish cabdrivers, and the villa. But mixed up with all this there was a phantom—the New Year in September—and the strange, cheerless holidays, grating upon the ear with their harsh names: Rosh Hashanah and Yom Kippur."[59] Lacking a religion or people of his own, he naturally sought another one.*

A sense of displacement often spurs creativity by forcing individuals to explore or explain what is usually taken for granted. After passing through a dozen philosophical systems, the Jewish thinker Solomon Maimon concluded, "I was always devoted to that system which for the time I regarded as alone true."[60] In the longer term, systematic alienation or serial loyalties were inevitably transient. The ideal of nonidentity marked the apogee of an orbit away from group identity's gravitational pull, usually resolved in the following generation by a fall into the majority group's domain, less often by a return to one's starting point.

Paradoxically, as rebellious intellectuals became the cultural establishment this condition came to be seen as essential for creativity. Mark Gertler, a British Jewish artist born to a poor immigrant family in 1891, thought, "By my ambitions I am cut off from my own family and class and by them I

---

*Despite this rejection, his work retained enough of an implicitly Jewish character for later Russian Jews to draw on it. For the dissident Petr Kriksunov in the 1960s, "The poet's symbolism, images, and ways of viewing the world seemed essentially Jewish. He found a remarkable correspondence between them and the figurative structure of the Bible. Through this interest he came to identify personally with Jewishness." Y. Roi and A. Becker, *Jewish Culture and Identity in the Soviet Union* (New York, 1991), pp. 59–60.

have been raised to be equal to a class I hate! . . . I am an outcast." Though his best work was done in Jewish east London, he felt stifled there and moved to gentile Hampstead in 1915, declaring, "I shall belong to no class."[61] In 1930, he married a Christian—their son was named Luke—and, in poor health, committed suicide in 1939.

There also comes a point when for many persons their very existence becomes a rebellion against tradition, a genetic statement, an institutionalized nonidentity. Thus Denise Levertov, a half-Protestant, half-Jewish poet, spoke of being, "Split at the root, neither Gentile nor Jew, Yankee nor Rebel, born in the face of two ancient cults, I'm a good reader of histories." And the similarly situated Adrienne Rich, raised in the Episcopal church, concluded in typical assimilationist fashion that identity is a foolish form of servitude, in "By No Means Native":

> Yet man will have his bondage to some place;
> If not, he seeks an Order, or a race.
> Some join the Masons, some embrace the Church,
> And if they do, it does not matter much.[62]

But Rich searched out the bondage of identities with great diligence, becoming quite radical and dedicating her work, as one critic writes, "on behalf of the deprived and disesteemed, lesbians, gays, African-Americans, Latin Americans, the poor, the unemployed and the ill-employed, the undervalued."[63] Given such a background, rebellion was a more banal than innovative response.

Glorifying the addictive tension of life on the edge may delay the dissolution of a deliberately chosen nonidentity into the mainstream for a generation. The novelist Mordecai Richler, whose work was based on the principal of such a comprehensive rejectionism, has one intermarried character say, "All the same I've managed to remain an alienated Jew. . . . His forebears hadn't fled the shtetl, surviving the Czar, so that the windows of the second generation should glitter on Christmas Eve" like those of the antisemites who persecuted them.[64]

Yet surely his offspring would identify these lights not with Russian pogromists but with kindly neighbors and joyous celebration. The American Jewish writer Ludwig Lewisohn said of Christmas, "Either you let yourself slide and betray the souls of your children by letting them love something in their most impressionable years which they *must* not love if ever their lives are to be integrated . . . or else, carefully, you abstain and withdraw and feel, despite your better knowledge, that there is something sullen and unfriendly in that withdrawal."[65] Having to waste so much energy on resistance leaves little for substance. It is unnatural to wish oneself into a cold, lonely place altogether, equidistant from all communion. Every society and civilization has demonstrated that individual human beings need some sense of faith, belief, and belonging.

The assimilating Jew's need to find a community was often more important than the specific character of that community, which was why so many jumped around so often like Maimon and Koestler. Marvin Liebman, born in 1923, first became a Communist, then an anticommunist convert to Catholicism and conservative fund-raiser. Disillusioned by the right's racism, antisemitism, and homophobia, Liebman said he felt "like a Jew in Germany in 1934 who had chosen to remain silent, hoping to be able to stay invisible as he watched the beginnings of the Holocaust." He proclaimed his homosexuality and declared, "I have moved from place to place, from idea to idea, from person to person, from left to right, from Jew to Catholic . . . looking for a family, a place, a home where I could be me."[66]

Many assimilating Jews saw no contradiction in trying to build a philosophy of truth or a moral society by first creating a bogus self. When Erik Homburger fled the Aryan supremacists in his native Germany, he changed his name in the New World to Erikson, presenting himself as an expert on identity without openly confronting his own personal transformation. He had taken a very Nordic name and, equally revealing, one saying he was his own ancestor, a blank slate: Erik son of Erik. This idea was also signified in a common assimilationist habit of breaking Jewish custom by naming sons after fathers—as well as adjusting first or last names to local usage—as if a new dynasty was beginning.

Despite expectations, the notion of agnostic humanism proved very fragile. Just as Jewish slaves built Pharaoh's cities, assimilation provided many examples of how the subjugated constructed the edifice of their own oppression. By joining the dominant group, former Jews freed themselves while undermining those they left behind and causes they ostensibly favored. This pattern recurred with political parties, intellectual movements, Marxism, and Christianity.

The alternative to belief is belief, and to a people is another people. The French Jewish Nobelist philosopher Henri Bergson thought Catholicism superior because intellect was insufficient to comprehend truth and intuition was necessary. Since the Judaism he knew no longer had confidence in its own beliefs, his intuition led him elsewhere. When the baptized German Jewish financier Sir Ernest Cassel was to be sworn in as a privy councilor in England in the early 1900s, a skullcap and Jewish Bible were supplied for the ceremony. After he refused these items, the presiding official immediately asked for a contribution to Westminster Cathedral.*

Similarly, many Jewish immigrants to England or America rejected both their own and all other religion, but especially their own. The British industrialist Jacob Behrens said, "All forms of service conducted on lines strictly laid down and according to dogma find no response in me, even if they do not repel me. When either Christian minister or Jewish rabbi calls on the inscrutable God with the audacity and familiarity of an old acquaintance, I can see nothing but a hollow lie or an unfathomable depth of stupidity." Thus, he gave his children no religious training, convinced it was hypocritical to educate them in a faith to which one did not hold. Surrounded by the British elite and eager to become part of it, his descendants and those of his two brothers became Anglicans.[67]

Marcel Dassault, France's leading manufacturer of military aircraft, converted after being freed from Buchenwald concentration camp and ordered employees never to mention in his presence that he was born Marcel Bloch. During his imprisonment, he was said to have criticized other Jews for putting their mutual ties ahead of solidarity with other French prisoners. But he did not criticize the French for betraying solidarity with their own Jews. He gave generously to the church and his company obeyed France's embargo of arms sales to Israel after 1967, while still selling warplanes to Libya and Iraq.[68]

E. A. Filene, a liberal Boston Jewish philanthropist, founded a local, then national, then international Chamber of Commerce to make business more humane and democratic. Instead, these groups became strongholds of reactionary forces. His children were raised as Protestants and one of them married a right-wing congressman. His lawyer, the liberal and Zionist Louis Brandeis, declared, "Filene is forever making weapons for the enemy."[69]

Intermarriage is the ultimate form of continuing the human line while ending a family's Jewish affiliation. Samuel Montagu, one of England's richest Jews, was, from the 1870s until his death in 1911, Orthodoxy's leading

---

*His granddaughter was Edwina, wife of Earl Mountbatten, the last viceroy of Britain's Indian empire.

champion in that country. His son Edwin, a Cambridge graduate elected to Parliament at age twenty-six in 1906, clashed repeatedly with his father. Edwin wanted to escape being a Jew to revel in being an Englishman. He even criticized his sister's charity work among Jewish girls as "sectarian" acts strengthening "barriers" among people. Edwin was angry at being dependent on his father to finance his political career and humiliated by a clause in Samuel's will letting him inherit only if he remained a Jew and did not intermarry. Instead, Edwin married the aristocrat Venetia Stanley, who converted explicitly for the couple's mercenary purpose. Although he loved her, she treated him badly and spent his money lavishly.[70]

Meanwhile, Edwin's career prospered. He became minister of munitions, then secretary of state for India. Many of his friends were antisemites, as were his patrons, Liberal prime ministers Lloyd George and Henry Asquith, who became Venetia's lover. These politicians—who Edwin saw as fellow outsiders and reformers—thought Jews arrogant or obsequious cowards, looked down on him as a foreigner, and made fun of him. At the moment Edwin was decrying Zionism as threatening the status of the Jewish elite, Asquith was calling him "the Assyrian" and "Shylock, the merchant of Venetia." "I never think of myself as [a Jew]," wrote Edwin. "If people never thought of us as Jews, Jews like myself would forget all about it." It was this bitter man—bent on being a last Jew but technically barred from doing so—who became the most important Jewish opponent of Zionism and of the Balfour Declaration.[71]

Leonard Woolf, Edwin's contemporary and fellow reformer, a mainstay of the Bloomsbury literary set and publisher to the modernists, made fun of his own ethnicity. To him, religion was a superstitious relic and none of his best friends were Jewish. His wife was the writer Virginia Woolf, whose antisemitic remarks were sometimes directed toward her own husband. In his novel *The Wise Virgins,* a character's self-conscious Jewishness leads to the breakdown of his relationship with a character based on Virginia.

Ettore Schmitz chose the pseudonym Italo Svevo to show his loyalty to the neighboring Italian and Swabian peoples. Svevo, a friend of James Joyce, served as the model for Leopold Bloom in Joyce's novel *Ulysses.* When Svevo's Catholic wife became ill in 1897, she worried at her sin of marrying a Jew and persuaded him to be baptized and undergo a church wedding. Another such union was that between the Austrian Jewish writer Franz Werfel and Gustav Mahler's antisemitic widow, Alma, who described her spouse as "a small hateful corpulent Jew." Werfel did not keep his promise to convert but praised Catholicism as "more universal than anything else on earth." Even as an exile from Nazi Germany, his portraits of Jews were negative, including a line that might well have been applied to himself, "An infernally cunning fellow, this Jew. He managed to get onto the right side in good time." Marriage to an antisemite—or more often into a family with such sentiments—might be called the ultimate assimilationist predicament.[72]

Philipp Lowenfeld, a German Jewish lawyer, became betrothed around 1900 to a Christian woman whose family found intermarriage so alien that, she said, "One could just as soon marry a Negro as a Jew." Her father, a right-wing Krupp company official, received Lowenfeld icily and refused to approve. But once convinced resistance was futile, Lowenfeld recalled, "His shock that I was a Jew was somewhat neutralized by the fact that I was a professor's son, that in my career until then there was nothing bizarre."[73]

Montagu's elite intermarriage, consolidating the Jewish partner's social standing and the Christian spouse's financial position; Woolf's bohemian/radical one, as a sign of being cosmopolitan; and Lowenfeld's pairing, absolved by worldly success, were common types. For social and psychological reasons, people may seek mates like themselves or hunt for ones as different as possible. As much as opportunity and romantic chemistry are prime ingredients in marriage, they are also to some degree responsive to social factors. Montagu had said self-righteously, "It is not only that I don't as a rule like Jewesses. It is also that I firmly believe to look for a wife in one set of people is as wrong as it would be to say you must look for a wife among blue-eyed women." But his choosing an eminent aristocrat showed the limits of his supposed free choice.[74] Ethnic difference or even conflict could also be an aphrodisiac. Ben Hecht wrote of such a fictional romance, "His Jewishness had become for her an exotic mask, mysterious and Oriental." This admiration made him feel transformed in her eyes "from an antisemitic cartoon to a glamorous illustration out of the Arabian Nights."[75]

As religion has waned on both sides of the Jewish/Christian divide, intermarriage has replaced conversion as a way to be the last Jew, far less sharp or painful than converting oneself or baptizing one's children. Jews demanded intermarriage as a right, a victory over antisemitism proving their acceptance as individuals though it meant they dwindled as a group. But this gesture's motive also changed over time from an ideological or philosophical one to a byproduct of romance, in which a spouse's beauty and status did not so much further assimilation as prove it already complete. Moses Hess married a poor Christian seamstress as a way of redressing social injustice and to preach love among different classes and creeds. Over a century later, Arthur Miller wed Marilyn Monroe, Eddie Fisher became husband to Debbie Reynolds, and singer Billy Joel married model Christie Brinkley.

Like many of his fellows, Paul Cowan, the American Jewish essayist, came to see Jewish women as banal and materialistic: "I wanted to use my romance with a blond woman who played the harp beautifully, sang American folk songs, and had a father who was in the State Department, as a way of proving that I could gain the approval of the society that had spurned me." But, feeling equivocal, he invited a girlfriend with all the right credentials—Episcopalian, Smith College—home for dinner and tested her by saying he might change his name to the more Jewish equivalent Saul Cohen. She responded, he thought, with a hint of bigotry: "That's not you. You don't want to go back to the ghetto." The scene ended with the woman in tears. "For years I remembered her as a latent antisemite. She remembered me as one of the chosen people, who secretly believed that everyone else was inferior." In the end, Cowan married another woman of his dreams, who not only converted but became a rabbi.[76]

Such a solution was unique. Most often, the Jewish spouse abandoned identity or at least kept it in silence. In theory, the two sides maintained equality; in practice, the surrounding society's influence prevailed and the next generation's connection with any Jewish identity was reduced by far more than half. Philip Roth has a character say, "A Jew who marries a Jew is able at home to forget he's a Jew. A Jew who marries an Aryan like my mother has her face there always to remind him."[77]

But this also means that preserving the marriage requires silencing or subordinating the issue. "Mixed marriage," wrote Albert Memmi from personal experience, "doesn't even satisfy the Jew's great desire for reconciliation with the world. . . . Henceforth, the marriage partner will embody the non-Jewish presence which thus becomes continuous, daily and obligatory, even in their intimacy."[78] Such tension—even warfare—may enhance the craft of those who turn it into stories but it also creates unbridgeable gaps in other people's lives. Alfred Mond after visiting the Jews of British Palestine rhapsodized in his diary, "I have learned much . . . which, possibly, no one who is not a Jew will ever be able to understand, for it can only be felt." The point was proven by his non-Jewish wife's diary entry about the trip: "Visited our property at Migdal and planted banana trees."[79]

In his semiautobiographical book *The Facts,* Philip Roth describes his marriage to a psychologically disturbed woman who was also blond, Midwestern, and a seeming embodiment of the American dream. The story parallel's the scene in *Annie Hall* where Woody Allen's character visits Annie's seemingly ideal Midwestern family only to find it shot through with insanity. In his own case, Roth had ignored the warning signs of his wife's difficult personality and troubled family, perhaps hoping to prove his worth by rescuing her from such large dragons or subconsciously knowing the romance would explode, leaving him free again and punishing his lust for her. At any rate, as a critic wrote, "He needed her to be *different.*"[80] The resulting relationship was so awful that Roth announced himself resolute never to remarry or have offspring.

These were, of course, personal and highly complex decisions. Perhaps ethnic differences increase the strain of sustaining a marriage, an enterprise difficult enough in modern times under the best conditions. Sometimes special circumstances intervened. Gershom Scholem's aunt married a fellow doctor and they lived a cosmopolitan life until, after twenty years of marriage, her husband divorced her in 1933 so he could marry a fellow Aryan. Scholem's aunt died in a concentration camp.[81] In America, a convert told a Christian prayer meeting how after losing her Wall Street job, she turned to Jesus, who also answered her prayer for a "Jewish man who'd found the Lord." This left unexplained why her Christian husband's origin should matter at all.[82] An eminent American Jewish businessman, in a television interview celebrating his triumphs, sat beside his Christian wife and blond daughter recounting the moving story of how he started his firm. A woman he barely knew gave him money to atone for what the Germans had done to the Jews. That was why, he explained, he now gave so generously to the Metropolitan Museum, Metropolitan Opera, and New York City Ballet.

Affluent and famous Jews deeply immersed in mainstream society were most often plagued by self-doubt since personal success did not fully resolve a sense of communal inferiority. Leading Jews tended most often to become last Jews. The intellectual Max Nordau refused to convert in his youth because he neither believed in Christianity nor wished to make his mother unhappy and disgrace his father's memory. After lacking contact with anything Jewish for a quarter century, he became a leading Zionist but then still married a Christian and rejected her offer to convert.[83]

When the daughter of Arthur Cohen, British Jewry's highest official for fifteen years, intermarried in 1895, he resigned his post. A colleague asked to do the same after participating in his own daughter's church wedding was so angry that he, too, converted.[84] In later years, intermarriage became so accepted, however, that any such strictures on Jewish leaders became impossible to enforce and unthinkable to advocate. Jews were even impeded from criticism lest they seem intolerant or offend the growing portion of their fellows involved in this process directly or through relatives. In America, intermarriage symbolized pluralism and was depicted as a heartwarming tale of progress, freedom, and love triumphing over narrow-minded prejudice. Thus, George Burns joked of the deal his brother and sister-in-law made: she stayed Italian; he stayed Jewish. For dinner they ate spaghetti on a bagel. When Groucho's daughter was refused entrance to a pool at a country club barring Jews, he wrote its management, "Since my daughter is only half Jewish, can she go into the pool up to her waist?"[85]

To reject intermarriage was made to seem hypocritical and biased, as in one Lenny Bruce routine: "As beautifully liberal as any Jewish mother is— she'll march in every parade—yet, let the daughter bring home a nice, respectable Filipino son-in-law, with a nice, long, black foreskin and a gold tooth."[86] But this was duplicity or racial prejudice only if the same mother would have welcomed a WASP Christian. In the 1992 presidential election, some controversy arose from a report that billionaire populist H. Ross Perot tried to discourage his daughter from marrying a Jew. It was not easy for Jews to act in a similar manner.

What remained most Jewish in popular entertainment was a continual propaganda for intermarriage. Scores of films, novels, and television shows defined Christian women (and occasionally men) as more attractive and desirable, with elements of this theme not far from traditional antisemitic stereotypes, albeit defused by humor.* Herman Wouk gave a classic version of this negative image of Jewish women in *Marjorie Morningstar*. While pretending to have career or intellectual ambitions she exhibits a terrible "solid dullness" and really wants a "big diamond engagement ring, house in

---

*See chapter 5. In *The Heartbreak Kid*, a Jewish groom deserts his neurotic, dark Jewish bride for a blonde. The jilted bride was played by the daughter of the film's writer, Elaine May.

a good neighborhood, furniture, children, well-made clothes, furs." What made such attitudes more ridiculous—showing them to be a product of assimilation and not just the free, random choice of romance—was the implication that Jewish women were banal, ugly, or materialistic at the very same time that Christian men were attracted to them by perceptions of exotic beauty, adventurousness, professional success, and intellectuality.[87]

To celebrate the extinction of one's line reflects both self-abnegation and the egoism of desiring the world end with oneself. Erik Erikson commented, "The pride of gaining a strong [individual] identity may signify an inner emancipation from a more dominant group identity."[88] As if to illustrate that point, Arthur Koestler wrote with apparent pride, "I am the last of the short line of Koestlers . . . and with the present writer's death, the Koestler . . . saga will come to a fitting end."[89] Woody Allen, archetype and parody of the American Jewish intellectual, gave away his only begotten son to be raised by Mia Farrow. Allen had named the child Satchel, after an African American baseball player. Following her successful custody suit, Farrow changed the boy's name to a traditional Irish one, Sheamus. Allen had already plunged into an affair with his "adopted" Korean daughter. His behavior was said to border on incest, as loving someone too proximate. Yet given her background, the young woman could not have been more distant from him. His undoing seemed to stem more from an embrace of otherness than from a perverted obsession with sameness.

Some became professional Last Jews, unable to stop talking about the subject. "They couldn't stand the ignorance, the feuds, the boredom, the righteousness, the bigotry, the repetitious narrow-minded types," explained Philip Roth, "they couldn't endure the smallness; and then they spent the rest of their lives thinking about nothing else. Of all the tens of thousands who flee, those setting the pace for the exodus are the exiles who fail to get away. Not getting away becomes their job."[90] A few self-conscious iconoclasts threw more fuel on the blaze, making it flare brightly before being extinguished forever. Some were confused by feelings they could not explain, shreds of identity still remaining, while others left quietly. In the end, the struggle to escape being a Jew almost invariably succeeded since it was a voluntary act. Kafka's character Joseph K. was not eradicated by others. When taken to the place of execution, he finally understood "that he was supposed to seize the knife himself . . . and plunge it into his own breast."[91]

The parents' disregard for forms made the next generation ignorant about content and the one thereafter forgetful of everything. The meaning of being a Jew was defined ever downwards: from people to religion, from religion to ethnicity, and then to merely being an outsider, a meaningless model for those now fully integrated into society. Even if it took a generation or two more, what began with some alternative system like Marxism, atheism, or humanism usually culminated as total assimilation into the mainstream. Trying to bring up world citizens—unfettered by identity, loyalty, or superstition; declaring themselves in rebellion against any remaining shreds of identity—produced people not quite at home anywhere. The obsession robbed them of things whose existence they often did not fathom. Such imbalances sometimes made for great art or interesting—often disastrous—politics but also for diminished lives.

In a story by Israeli author Shai Agnon, children find a buried building that first seems a castle, then a church, and finally proves to be an ancient synagogue. The door resists every locksmith, then swings open itself. All was still in place, ready for use. The Jewish civilization that had created so much, both in itself and when blended with Western culture, was still available for those desiring it. As the writer Stuart Schoffman suggested, it is like a rare violin passed down as an heirloom that not every descendent wants to play but which should be available for those who do.[92]

8

Other People's Nations

As Gregor Samsa awoke one morning from uneasy dreams he found himself transformed in his bed into . . .

—*Franz Kafka, "The Metamorphosis"*

FTER THE 1881 pogroms in Russia, Moses Lilienblum, an advocate of assimilation, changed his mind. "Why," he asked, "should we Jews relinquish our nationality and assimilate with the people we live among? We will not be merging with all humankind, but only with one people. The name of Israel will be erased but the division of nations will remain and humanity will gain nothing from this."[1] Almost thirty years later, one of Arthur Schnitzler's Viennese characters commented, "A Jew who loves his country . . . with a real feeling of solidarity, with real enthusiasm . . . is without the slightest question a tragic-comic figure."[2]

As in other areas, the Jewish response to nationalism had a special character requiring such decisions as whether to become patriots of any individual state; if so, which one to choose; how to prove their allegiance; and whether to take that nation as it was or try to improve it by reform or revolution. In the last case, Jews often endorsed one of two competing national visions, trying to delegitimize a less congenial, conservative tradition by backing a progressive liberal alternative. Where treated well, Jews were grateful and eager to reciprocate; when suffering discrimination, they strove to win acceptance or induce change. In either case, they responded to any hint they were not proper citizens by asserting all the more loudly their country's merit and denying any communal loyalty interfered with that allegiance.

Everywhere they were tossed between what Schnitzler called "the inner consciousness of being at home in the country where they lived and worked, and their indignation at finding themselves persecuted and insulted in that very place." Einstein said he felt toward Germany like "a man who is lying in a beautiful bed tortured by bedbugs." Alfred Kazin's socialist father, oppressed as a Jew in Russia, would still downgrade any American sight by sneering, "Nice! But you should have seen the Czar's summer palace."[3]

The majority group often doubted Jews could be absorbed, demanding they totally abandon any distinctiveness and constantly prove their devotion in order to earn equal citizenship. Later, Jews were suspected of assimilating too well, gaining excessive power and influence. It was hard to believe that any group would be so altruistic as to give up its own identity and customs on demand. Antisemites claimed that Jews conspired together to serve a self-interest different from that of patriotic Frenchmen, Germans, or Poles.

Hence, denying Jewish nationhood and downplaying distinctive customs served as the basis of assimilationist ideology. Knowing they were on trial made Jews nervous and defensive, often evincing, Moses Hess suggested, "A much more vociferous patriotism than [that of] their Christian colleagues," at the expense of solidarity with Jewish brethren in other countries. "The Jews' patriotism has something sick about it; it is much tenser and more demonstrative than that of the Christians, who possess a nonartificial and natural patriotism."[4]

The Anglo-Jewish writer Israel Zangwill tried to handle this problem by insisting that the country itself was responsible for successful assimilation. But in fact the burden of proof was always on the Jews to prove their loyalty.[5] They found it hard to resist the state's demand for sole domain over its subjects' fealty and pressure to drop any other attachment, including the idea that Jews were a people in their own right. Count Clermont-Tonnere told the assembly of the French Revolution in 1799, "It is intolerable that the Jews should become a separate political formation or class in the country. . . . The existence of a nation within a nation is unacceptable to our country."[6]

Thus, even when the one-sidedness of this romance with other nations did not doom it to frustration, the peculiar situation of Jewish distinctiveness and assimilation made it a very unusual relationship. "The problem is far too complicated to be really solved," Schnitzler had written. "At times one might believe that things are not so bad. Sometimes one really is at home in spite of everything, feels one is as much at home [in Vienna]—yes, even more at home—than any of your so-called natives can ever feel. It is quite clear that the feeling of strangeness is to some extent cured by the consciousness of understanding."[7]

This conflict over how to feel and what to believe took place on an individual level. An example of these psychological and identity problems can be seen in Charles Hannam's autobiographical account of a young German Jewish refugee in England during World War II. Being persecuted had made him "hate the Jewish part of himself." Lacking any pride in his heritage, he felt Jews were being punished for having done something wrong and believed that "if only he had not been a Jew all would have been well." Among Jews, "he felt a stranger. He detested their bad English. . . . Karl wanted to be like his teachers and friends at school whom he admired, whose manners and attitudes he was learning to respect and adopt; most of all he wanted to be accepted, and if the price was the rejection of the people to whom he had once belonged, it seemed well worth paying at that time."[8]

When a sympathetic teacher professed admiration for Jews and asked him about them, Karl was pleased at the attention but also felt his aspiration to be English threatened, thinking, "I am not fascinated by the religion at all. It is meaningless to me. It destroyed our family." He wished to distinguish himself as an individual who had none of the "Jewish traits" imputed by the Nazis. "More than anything he wanted to become an Englishman, to disappear forever into a new identity, a new language, and clothes that in no way distinguished him from other boys."[9]

A second round of battle over identity came with Karl's induction into the British army. Asked what religion should be put on his record, Karl thought, "This is the moment to shed my religion. . . . I am sick and tired of being asked about and labeled with a religion I do not believe in. . . . So he answered 'Leave it blank, please, no religion.' " But in trying to shed his Jewishness he acknowledged it, since virtually no real Englishman would have made such a request. When the clerk refused and suggested writing Episcopalian, "That was too much for Karl, leaving it blank was one thing," but to declare himself a Christian—even a member of the Church of England, the ultimate identification with the nation—was too much. "What's the matter with you?" asked the annoyed corporal. "Don't you even know what your religion is?"* Trying to blend in, he only drew attention to himself.[10]

After the war, he was confronted with still another critical contradiction. On his first day at his new teaching job, he met a colleague just back from serving in the British Palestine Police. Karl had heard about their antisemitism and mistreatment of concentration camp survivors. The man lived up to his reputation, angrily saying, " 'Those blasted Yids. . . . I know what I would have done if I'd had my way. . . . Hitler had the right idea, should have gassed the lot.'

"Karl wanted to say, 'Look here, I am a Jew, you can't say things like that.' But then he felt it was too late. He had concealed his origins, and now he would either have to leave or [fight]. He felt utterly depressed. 'Is it ever going to stop?' he wondered."[11] The answer, of course, was no, and Karl's unending challenge was to deal with the dual stress of his own inner feelings and his adopted country's attitudes. To ignore slights and taunts, one must surrender even more completely or rebel.

A few decades earlier, a British official had described Jewish immigrants as being like a drop of acid able to poison a whole glass of water.[12] But while some newcomers were radical, the majority, as a London teacher noted, were "very proud to believe that they will become English. . . . They mean to try and be English in everything." And they succeeded—as did counterparts elsewhere—to the point where they could say, like Sir Robert Waley-Cohen, managing director of Shell Oil company, that British Jews were "entirely British in thought, aspirations, interest and zeal."[13] Yet a fellow mogul expressed an equally common thought among evidently assimilated, wealthy Jews: "Deep down, I have always had the feeling that something could be stirred up again; that somebody may start screaming and shouting and that we may have to take our bundle and run." Israel's existence was "an insurance policy," a potential refuge.[14]

Another challenge to Jews as patriots was that their dispersion among many states made them suspected of foreign loyalties as well as Jewish ones. A French Jewish newspaper in the 1930s insisted their history was "a progressive denationalization." Where Jews "live, there is their father-

---

*This was a common problem. Arrested as a revolutionary after World War I in Germany, Ernst Toller told interrogators that he had no religion. Without hesitation the police officer told the stenographer, "Put down 'Jew, non-professing.' " Frederic Grunfeld, *Prophets Without Honor* (New York, 1979), p. 135. When the novelist J. D. Salinger's Jewish father, an importer of hams married to a Christian, filled in his son's school form, he marked the space for religion "with irritated horizontal scratchings of the pen." Ian Hamilton, *In Search of J. D. Salinger* (New York, 1989), p. 19.

land."[15] But to be a German patriot in the early 1800s was to side with an anti-Jewish state against the liberator of the Jews, France. German nationalists accused Heine, who lived in Paris, of allegiance to France. "I am a friend of the French," he replied, "as I am the friend of all men who are sensible and good."[16] Yet this was not good enough. Fifty years later Dreyfus was accused of spying for Germany against France. A half century after that, Jews in Communist states were accused of being agents of the capitalist West and vice versa.

As if all these barriers were not enough, assimilating Jews faced three additional problems. First, it was not always clear which nation they were supposed to join among their often warring neighbors. Borders moved, leaving Jews in different countries, or Jews migrated themselves. Often they lived among various peoples, each with their own nationalism, and had to choose among them. At different times, they tended to side with Germans against Czechs or Poles; Russians against Poles and Ukrainians; as well as a variety of other combinations. The fact that Transylvanian Jews were Hungarian patriots even under Romanian rule did not stop Hungary from sending them to German concentration camps in World War II.

Second, a large part of the Jewish intelligentsia saw itself as universalist rather than patriotic. Having weaker national roots, they denounced nationalism as antiquated or threatening the higher unity of humanity. Such opinions enraged patriots in every country and alarmed many Jews as making them appear to be disloyal citizens by association. The French Jewish writer Julien Benda penned a famous critique in the 1920s accusing intellectuals of abandoning universalism and neutrality for nationalism or Zionism, as putting support for the state ahead of justice.[17]

Third, Jews became champions of states torn apart by their constituent peoples or warring ideologies. In short, even being nationalistic could make Jews unpopular. "Jews everywhere became fervent patriots," a German Jewish historian noted, "because they knew that they owed their emancipation to governmental fiat in the face of popular reluctance." But when an anti-Jewish party or policy won control, the Jews' role as "patriotic citizens" availed them not.[18] In 1848, Vienna's leading rabbi wrote that the Jews demanded emancipation as an integral part of the German people, since German nationalism was liberal, humanist, and had a cosmopolitan spiritual mission while Slavic and Czech nationalisms were fanatical.[19] An Italian Jew wrote, "In a sense, [Jews] are the only true Italians."[20]

Such problems continued into the twentieth century's last decade. In disintegrating Yugoslavia, a Jewish relief worker said his local counterparts "tell us they are the only real Yugoslavs left."[21] A reporter visiting the republic of Georgia was told, "We have never been persecuted. These Georgians are not like Russians or Germans, you know. Georgians are civilized people with culture!" In Azerbaijan, Jews died fighting for that Muslim state in a war with Armenia.[22] Albie Sachs, a leader of the South African Communist Party and African National Congress—one of five Jews on the latter's National Executive Committee—coined the slogan, "For the nation to live the tribe must die," arguing that popular rule must override all ethnic divisions, implicitly using his own Jewish assimilation as a model for all South Africans.[23]

And so in contrast to the majority group's members, for whom it was natural, patriotism for assimilating Jews was a matter of choice and, consequently, uncertainty. The antisemite's denial of the Jews' right to be part of the country only made the Jews all the more insistent that the country was theirs, too. Yet not only were the obstacles sometimes too great to overcome, but their own situation made assimilating Jews all the more sensitive and defensive. They also had difficulty in finessing some points of Jewish doctrine: their peoplehood; special relationship with God; exile from their land to which they would one day return; need for their own schools, holidays, and marriage laws; duty to help fellow Jews in other countries; and an entwining of nation and Christianity which often discomfited them.

A small minority of Jewish thinkers suggested that the assimilationist strategy was badly flawed. Showing disloyalty to their own people, they argued, made Jews seem more suspect in proclaiming other patriotisms. European nations, wrote Hess, would never "respect us so long as we deny our great historical tradition and so long as we make the maxim, 'Where it is good for me, there is my homeland' into our credo. . . . It is not the old, orthodox Jew, who would rather have his tongue cut out than betray his nationality—but the modern Jew, who denies his nationality, who is being despised." This pluralist idea was taken up by Louis Brandeis in America, too.[24]

But before the Shoah, and even after, the majority accepted their host nations' view that loyalty was a zero-sum game. A Bundist leader charged, "The Jew, trembling and humiliated, accustomed to have other people spit in his face, found no other way to make his rights secure than by himself spitting at his own nation and renouncing his own national identity. In order to become a citizen of the world, he was forced to become a Frenchman, a German, etc."²⁵ The French Jewish intellectual Bernard Lazare, al-most alone in the community as an active defender of Dreyfus, called com-patriots, "not content with being more jingoist than the native Frenchmen; like all emancipated Jews everywhere, they have also of their own volition broken all ties of solidarity" with foreign-born brethren.²⁶

Some were ready to collaborate in destroying Jewish institutions to modernize the community and prove their own patriotism. In 1841 a group of middle-class Jewish reformers wrote Russian officials, urging that they force Jews to study Russian history and language to bind them to "the dominant nation" and "thwart the harmful influence of the Talmud." The government should approve an official religious textbook to teach "in accordance with the accepted principles regarding civic responsibilities to the Czar and the motherland." Any unapproved educational activity should be severely pun-ished: "The Jews must be ordered to change their dress" to conform with the common fashion.²⁷

While not going so far, most assimilating Jewish intellectuals passion-ately urged that the idea of Jewish nationhood be buried. Although many ethical and other arguments were adduced, the underlying motive was to make credible the claim of joining without reservation those they lived among. Yet arguments used against Jewish nationalism were often aban-doned when it came to embracing the patriotism of the state ruling them. The early twentieth-century German Jewish theologian Hermann Cohen opposed Zionism by saying that the prophets' universalism and humanism precluded loyalty to a state—even a "Jewish" one. Yet at the same time he advocated assimilation into German culture and support for the German state.²⁸ Nobel-winning chemist Fritz Haber claimed that he converted in the 1890s in order to show cultural allegiance to the German people yet saw no discrepancy in praising a society that was so intolerant.²⁹ Jewish leftists coupled an internationalist creed with an ideology amounting to patriotic allegiance to the Soviet Union.

Among the most systematic thinkers on these issues was Ludwig Gum-plowicz, a sociologist advocating national states—except for the Jews themselves—as preferable to such multinational empires as Austria-Hun-gary and czarist Russia. "We are, sorry to say," he wrote in 1861, "still a na-tionality," but this was a regrettable survival of the past that "keeps creeping after us like a vampire, sucks our blood and destroys our vitality." Jews had to discard this relic by merging with the Polish people in identity, language, and nationalism as a way to win their sympathy. Despite this

strategy's failures, Gumplowicz was enraged by Zionism as one more example of the "unnatural stubbornness" making Jews prefer "to keep alive
an eternal race struggle against themselves rather than sacrifice their out-
lived and mummified nationality to the rejuvenated and vital culture of
other countries and ages."[30]

Such ideas determined how European Jews lived and often died, as
adopted children trying to earn a fatherland and motherland whose esteem
could not be taken for granted. To justify their country as worthy of their
devotion, assimilating Jews extolled it as the most cultured and virtuous of
all. They reconciled patriotism with internationalism by saying their state
served humanity's interests best, reassigning the Jews' national mission to
Germany, France, Britain, or Soviet Russia. Rabbi Abraham Bloch emotionally declared in an 1889 sermon that Jews worked hard to succeed "to
show how they cherish their new homeland to make themselves more worthy of her love and protection."[31] He showed his sincerity by dying for
France on a World War I battlefield.

If, however, their country refused to grant Jews equality, they advocated reforms to make it better and more democratic. Jews were less sus-
ceptible to conservative arguments against change since one of the main
reforms being opposed was Jewish equality. "Yes," the nineteenth-century
liberal Ludwig Börne told Germans, "because I was born a slave, I love
freedom more than you. Yes, because I have experienced slavery, I understand freedom better than you. Yes, because I was born without a fatherland, I yearn for a fatherland more passionately than you."[32]

But if the Jewish vision of the nation was arguably better, it was also
different from that held by many or most non-Jews. The local majority
might oppose assimilating Jewish patriotism as insincere or object to the
specific political or cultural effects they thought Jews were having on the
country. Moreover, insistence on earning the homeland's "love and protection" implied acceptance of the antisemitic argument that the country did
not belong to Jewish citizens as a right. Finally, the Jews' love for the nation—like that for the proletariat—was often unreciprocated. As Scholem
wrote, "No German stood forth to recognize the genius of Kafka, Simmel,
Freud, or Walter Benjamin—to say nothing of recognizing them as Jews."[33]
Moreover, though those assimilating might shun any mention of the fact
they were Jews in noting their achievements, those disparaging them
evinced no such restraint about raising the subject.

Not all states or peoples, of course, responded in the same way. Some countries—like Poland, Germany, and Russia—rejected real Jewish equality; others—like England and France—set high standards but did embrace those meeting them, on condition that virtually every Jewish feature be left behind. At first, the United States was in the latter category, but eventually its Jews became architects of a consensus culture and political order. In Europe, only the Shoah snapped nationalism's appeal for Jews in German-speaking lands and undermined it in France; in the USSR it was eroded by the experience of Communist rule; and in Poland by both.

The widest chasm between Jews and the majority nationality was in Poland, with its strong romantic nationalism so closely linked to Catholicism. The great Polish writers Tadeusz Konwicki and Adam Miskiewicz were of Jewish descent, but Poles forgot that fact in honoring them. While many Jews followed Gumplowicz's advice, the main Polish nationalist party implemented antisemitic policies in the 1920s and 1930s, and most Poles were indifferent to, if not supportive of, the ensuing Nazi massacre of Jews. Up to the end, some Jews tried to earn that nation's approbation by self-sacrifice. Henryk Goldzmit, a third-generation assimilationist and son of a Polish nationalist, changed his name to the Polish Janusz Korczak and fought for Poland in two wars. He became a best-selling childrens' writer and headed a Jewish orphanage. But since an exclusively Jewish institution clashed with his creed, Goldzmit also started a nondenominational one until forced out by Poles who did not want a Jew to be guiding Catholic orphans. Under the Nazi occupation, he and his Jewish children were all put to death.[34]

Proclaiming himself as both a Pole and a Jew in a passionate 1944 essay, the poet Julian Tuwim wrote: "I am a Pole because I like being a Pole. . . . I do not divide the Poles into those with a pedigree and those without. . . . I divide Poles, as I do Jews, and men of any nationality, into intelligent and stupid ones, honest and dishonest." At the same time he proclaimed his Jewishness because "We, Shloims, Sruls, Moishkes, dirty, garlicky, we with our endless insulting nicknames, we have proved ourselves the peers of Achilles, of Richard the Lion-Hearted and other heroes. In the catacombs and bunkers of Warsaw, in the stinking sewers. . . . We arose as soldiers of freedom and honor."[35]

But even all this did not make them Poles. Too much blood had been spilled, too many hopes betrayed. During the war, the father of Yitzhak Shamir, later Israel's prime minister, begged his Polish business partner to hide his family, but the man surrendered them to the Germans. Shamir's father later escaped on the way to a death camp only to be murdered by Polish neighbors.[36] As Isaac Bashevis Singer put it after *The New York Times* called him a Polish writer, "The Poles never thought of us as Poles and we didn't either."[37]

Communist Poland was no better than republican Poland. The few Jews who tried to return there after 1945 faced new persecutions by the Poles. Those who had joined the Communist Party to liberate Poland provoked antisemitism by associating Jews with that hated regime, which itself unleashed antisemitic purges in the 1960s. Jerzy Panski, a Communist who fled Poland for Sweden, remarked, "I try not to think of the years I wasted in that pitiful love affair [with Poland and Communism]. It was all one way. . . . After the 1973 war, I began attending a synagogue for the first time since my Bar Mitzvah. Just to show that I'm part of the Jewish people. . . . There has to be at least one identity no one can ever take from you."[38]

By the 1990s, the last two Jews publicly active in Poland embodied the traditional dilemma. Jerzy Urban, "the most despised person in Poland," the Communist regime's spokesman who, after it fell, became an iconoclastic magazine publisher, symbolized the Jew as seditious to Poland's deepest beliefs.[39] Adam Michnik, in contrast, tried to play the role of Jewish saint. He had grown up a staunch Communist unaware that "normal people knew that Communism meant terror, lies, imprisonment. . . . We thought it meant liberty and truth." But his parents and other Jews became Communists because they were not "normal" Polish people. To them, Polish nationalism and the Catholic church were oppressive. As a founder of the Solidarity movement, Michnik merely chose another form of political assimilation. "The situation is different," he said, oblivious to the ethnic implication in that remark, "when you have ten million people behind you than if you have a few thousand." His detachment from past Polish reality, urge to merge with the masses, and drive to improve the homeland were old assimilationist themes. But, despite Michnik's efforts, a deep Polish suspicion of him was equally typical. Even when good intentions prevailed, the lines of nation and creed were so entangled that a Polish nationalist pope showed his regard for Michnik by presenting him with a Christian Bible.[40]

In Germany, too, assimilationists strove sincerely—if not always to the majority population's liking—to encourage progress and tolerance. In response to the antisemitism of German nationalists, Jews created their own alternative patriotism for a democratic humanist Germany. But this Germany existed largely among the assimilated German Jews themselves. "When we restore dignity to the poor people who are deprived of happiness, and to genius condemned to scorn and to desecrated beauty," proclaimed Heine, "all of Europe; yes, all the world will become German."[41] One historian wrote of such enthusiasm, "The imagined 'real Germany' was the only Germany to which the Jews could reasonably hope to be admitted." Of that country, allegedly hidden inside the place they actually lived "and struggling to get out, they were genuine, ardent and passionate patriots."[42]

Some tirelessly protested their loyalty. Gabriel Riesser, a hero of the 1848 revolt, said German Jews wanted no "national existence of their own, such as had formerly been imposed upon them by their enemies, but . . . [to] think and feel as Germans."[43] Others, like Arnold Schoenberg, who bragged that his work ensured "the supremacy of German music . . . for the next hundred years," strove to win full citizenship by proving their value to the motherland.[44] Yet German nationalists continued to regard cultural figures of Jewish origin—even converts—as alien partly because these people put their own "spin" on German culture, partly because their very success gave them so much prestige, prominence, and power. "It did not help" the composer Giacomo Meyerbeer, wrote Hess, "that he was always most careful not to include Jewish themes in his operas; still, he became the victim of German Jew-hatred." German newspapers pointed out that his real name was Jacob Meyer Lippman Beer. The German liberal patriot Börne complained, "Whenever my opponents are at a loss of an argument against Börne, they always bring up Baruch," his original, Jewish, name.[45]

Even personal contacts often failed to convince Germans of the Jews' patriotism. Heinrich von Treitschke, a leading historian, criticized Jews for inadequate national fervor. Playing on a phrase of Heine's—who had called Jewish heritage "a misfortune"—von Treitschke declared the Jews to be "our misfortune" and justified Jew-baiting as a "natural reaction of German folk-feeling against an alien element," even though his own mentor had been the Jewish professor Jacob Bernays.[46]

As in Poland, one could find acceptance only in anonymity or total self-abnegation. The Nazis put "Author Unknown" on Heine's "Die Lorelei," turning a poem by a Jew into a piece of Germany's folk tradition. Some have deemed this a great honor for Heine, the consummation of his goal to be one of modern Germany's ancestors. Yet never was it clearer that the price of acceptance was a loss of identity. Kathe Leichter, a leftist Viennese sociologist, claimed none of her schoolmates or colleagues in the 1930s thought of her as Jewish. But such a complex itself was uniquely Jewish, a boast coupling a claim of universalism with snobbish pride in feeling superior and separate from other Jews.[47]

Of course, it was only natural that Jews living in Germany wanted to be part of that society, a feeling augmented by their doubt that there was any other choice. "Who would want to go back in time to Palestine, that hole in the old Ottoman Empire, and leave behind the culture of 20th-century Europe," wrote the novelist Aharon Appelfeld about his family's attitude. But under the Nazis, his parents were killed and he was lucky to survive, wandering the forests alone as an eight-year-old until eventual rescue and migration to Israel.[48]

"I feel at home here. I feel part of the place and of the very air they breathe, in a way that only those who have not been completely naturalized and thoroughly assimilated can understand," wrote the French writer Romain Gary in a satire on this kind of thinking. Gary was talking not about his love of France but about a German Jewish ghost haunting a Nazi after the Holocaust. Gary, himself of Russian Jewish background, became a French patriot, World War II pilot, and highly honored diplomat. But he hinted at his own sense of dual identity by later writing under the North African Jewish pen name of Emile Ajar.[49]

Although Russia had been the most oppressive European country for Jews, many of their most intellectual, affluent elements were eager to join its society by either changing themselves or transforming the state. Hundreds of thousands emigrated, but large numbers also joined the Russian Orthodox church to gain material benefits and try to become fully Russian, seeing religion as an integral part of that culture. Two of the country's greatest poets just before the Revolution—Boris Pasternak and Osip Mandelstam—were converts.[50]

Mandelstam's life reflected the yearning of Jews to assimilate even into what was then the world's most antisemitic society. His father was an ex-yeshiva student who, like many Jews, transferred scholarly allegiance from the Talmud to Spinoza, Rousseau, and Schiller. Mandelstam portrayed this man as fluent in no language, belonging nowhere, though in fact he spoke Russian and German well. In contrast, he wrote glowingly of his more assimilated mother's speech as "clear and sonorous without the least foreign admixture . . . the literary Great Russian language." He yearned to be a real

Russian rather than a lowly, homeless Jew.[51] Cut off from both Jewish community and Hebrew, he viewed these things as totally alien. Being a Jew, he had learned, was obsolete and shameful; being a Russian was colorful and glorious. Sent to secular schools, he converted in 1911, desiring to join Russian society as well as to circumvent the university quota on Jewish students.

This was not, of course, the sole option or interpretation of life experience, especially for those more closely linked to a Jewish community. Vladimir Jabotinsky, born in 1880, had a Russian education but grew up in multinational Odessa, where one-third of his classmates were Jews and ethnic Russians were a minority. Jewish students socialized mostly with each other. When pogroms broke out, Jabotinsky identified with the Jewish community and became a Zionist leader.[52] Marc Chagall came from a more traditional family than did Mandelstam. When he was discriminated against in applying to art school or exhibiting his paintings, other Jews helped him study in Paris instead. He blamed Russia rather than Jewishness for his problems. "I thought: it must be because I'm a Jew and have no country of my own. . . . Neither Imperial Russia nor Soviet Russia needs me. I am a mystery, a stranger, to them." Instead Chagall took his inspiration from Jewish themes.[53]

Since many Jews saw mother Russia as inherently antisemitic, a Communist fatherland promising them equality offered a far more appealing national identity. The enemies of the USSR and of Jews seemed identical. The Soviet system encouraged intermarriage and let Jews easily abandon any ethnic bond. While German and Polish Jews suffered for having failed to transform their countries, Russian Jews were beset partly because some of them succeeded in doing so. They took part in the revolution hoping it would ally them with the people and create a better society for all. Assimilating Jews associated so much with each other as to be insulated from Russian antisemitism. But many Russians continued to hate Jews partly because of their role in the revolution, which itself murdered its own Jewish supporters in the 1930s and 1940s.[54] In World War II, idealistic Jews tried to show their patriotism by seeking dangerous duty. Pavel Kogan, a talented, almost blind poet, volunteered for combat and was soon killed. A friend attributed his rashness to "the feeling which I knew so well—what if someone will think that a Jew is a coward, that a Jew is sitting in the rear."[55]

The Soviet government's later anti-Jewish campaigns—including discrimination, persecution, and anti-Israel propaganda—undermined faith in

the regime. Some Soviet Jews became active in dissident and Zionist movements and many emigrated. Others found their strong link to the Russian
nation and culture reinforced by Communism's fall. Said the daughter of
party members who returned to Russia after a brief stay in Israel: "We felt
we betrayed those democrats, just so we could go to a country where there
is enough food."[56]

But despite hope that assimilation would work the third time around,
there were ample signs to the contrary, including the continuing popularity
of antisemitic parties and movements in Russia. Ilya Roitman, a leader of
the center-right Democratic Party, explained he could never head it because "having a Jew in the top position would cost the party votes. . . . One
should remember that nationalism remains a serious force in our society."[57]
Ironically, the exception was the most important ultranationalist antisemitic leader, the half-Jewish Vladimir Zhirinovsky.*

In Romania, Walther Neulander, a founder of the Communist Party,
had changed his family name from Neulander to the more patriotic Roman
and intermarried. Nonetheless his son, Petre, had to resign his top post in
post-Communist Romania in 1992 after accusations that he was one of those
Jews "hiding under Romanian names." Roman defended his nationalist credentials by appearing on television standing in front of a Christian icon.[58]

In France, where Christianity and national identity were also entwined,
Jews placed their faith in the counterimages of revolution and republic.
This proved a more successful strategy there than it had in Germany or
Russia. French Jews emancipated by the revolution assimilated, to be replaced and imitated by arrivals from Alsace-Lorraine. Next came post-1918
immigrants from Eastern Europe, many of them later killed in the Shoah,
with survivors reinforced by newcomers from North Africa in the 1950s and
1960s. Each wave gradually transformed itself into patriotic, culturally
cloned French citizens. France's image as liberator made its betrayal in the
Dreyfus case, the Shoah, and President Charles de Gaulle's November 1967
accusation that Jews were an "elite people, sure of itself and domineering"
equally disappointing.

The ideas of the French Jewish leader Theodore Reinach in 1887 were
typical of assimilationist thinking in many countries: "Being as we are,
the smallest religious sect; being, as we are, strangers newly arrived in the
French household, we are especially subject to jealousy and criticism." The

*See chapter 9.

only way to avoid stirring up antisemitism was that "our merchants must all be honest, our rich men all unassuming and charitable, our scholars all modest, our writers all disinterested patriots."[59]

"Then, naturally," responded a skeptical Ahad Ha-Am, "such angels will please even the French." No matter how bad things became, assimilationists would continue to speak optimistically. "And yet, if you listen carefully to their quavering voices, when all their talk is of belief and hope, you will hear the stifled sigh, and the voice of a secret doubt, which would make themselves heard, but that they are forced back and buried under a heap of high-sounding phrases."[60]

Nonetheless, French Jews could participate far more easily in the life of the country than could German or Russian Jews. Despite real antisemitism, schools and jobs were generally open to Jews on an equal basis. France, like all European countries, rejected cultural pluralism and demanded conformity. Nonetheless, its national tradition did esteem a liberal democratic society and cerebral activity. Moreover, since its intellectuals were generally patriotic, Jewish thinkers were less tempted to take radical, antistate views than they were in Russia or Germany.

Antagonism toward Jews in France was often linked to their alien origin. Catholic and chauvinist forces pointed out that wealthy French Jewish families were recent arrivals from Germany while Jewish workers came from Eastern Europe. Jacques Offenbach, whose music was later deemed quintessentially French, was often criticized as un-French and pro-German. Nordau reflected in 1878, "Poor Offenbach!" If he had remained at home Offenbach "would probably be today a Jewish cantor in an obscure synagogue and not a world famous composer," but at least the meanest Frenchman could not snub him.[61]

By basing themselves on France's historic progressive role and state interests, French Jews found it easier to portray aiding compatriots abroad as a patriotic act. They established the Alliance Israelite Universelle in 1860 to help persecuted Jews and raise them to the eminence of French culture. Adolphe Cremieux was the first political figure in Europe to show how one could be both a Jewish leader defending his people's rights and a national leader. As minister of justice in the revolutionary regimes of 1848 and 1871, he fought to abolish slavery and to grant citizenship to Algerian Jews.[62] Jews justified their patriotism in World War I by claiming France's enemy Germany was the font of modern antisemitism, though many of that ideology's founders were French.[63]

At home, French Jewish leaders were eager to transform immigrants into Frenchmen to show the French that Jews were good citizens. "These new arrivals," Baron Edmond de Rothschild complained in 1913, "do not understand French customs." They kept together and used Yiddish, "their primitive language." Baron Robert de Rothschild, president of the Paris Consistory, warned in 1935 that the immigrants must assimilate as soon as possible. Until then, "One does not discuss the regime of a country whose hospitality one seeks."[64]

But however patronizing native-born French Jews might be, they also tried to persuade immigrants that becoming French did not require conversion. In a 1937 sermon, Jacob Kaplan, future chief rabbi of France, even declared that French Jews must support Zionism without fear since, "We have given sufficient proof of our patriotism." At that moment, though, the growth of the antisemitic right undercut this apparent security. The election of a Jew, Léon Blum, as prime minister heading a left-liberal front gave fuel to this reaction, which Blum charged the French Jewish elite wrongly thought might be turned aside by "their cowardly neutrality."[65]

Despite the right's effort to impugn Blum's patriotism, he strongly believed his country superior to all others. Using a common Jewish assimilationist technique, he sought to bridge the apparently irreconcilable gap between nationalism and universalism by arguing that nations thrived in an atmosphere of international peace and solidarity. The French became the new chosen people, and France had a sacred mission to save the world: "This harmonizing of humanism and patriotism comes more naturally and easily to a Frenchman than to the citizens of any other nation, for it is a French characteristic . . . to think and act for universal causes."[66]

In another Jewish Variant, Blum first presented socialism as an outgrowth of moral values, then claimed this idea corresponded "to the peculiar genius of France, whose people have, throughout their history, from the Crusades to the French Revolution, held that human solidarity and a desire for universalism constituted the highest form of patriotism. This is what men and nations must teach—I am almost tempted to say preach—if they are to be worthy of their historic mission." Blum conveniently overlooked the Crusades' antisemitic massacres and the revolution's demand that the Jewish community dissolve.[67]

Such apologetics were poor preparation for large-scale French collaboration during the Nazi occupation. Jews like sociologist Georges Friedmann who felt themselves totally integrated into France now discovered "the shattering importance" of being labeled Jewish. Deprived of full citizenship, Friedmann was determined to prove himself a true Frenchman by joining the Resistance under a French name and finding there "a community in which all discrimination was swept away." In short, France was not antisemitic because the Resistance represented its true face.[68]

The historian Marc Bloch also embodied this crisis in French Jewish assimilationist patriotism. His ideas, which revolutionized the study of history in France, drew implicitly on assimilationist experience: highlighting the common people, interconnectedness of all aspects of society, and transnational comparisons. It was also not accidental that he said that a society's treatment of its outcasts showed its true nature. His own family followed the typical pattern: great-grandfather, a rabbi; grandfather, rector of a Jewish school; father, a professor of Roman history. Bloch had no religious instruction and, though he had a Jewish wedding, was an atheist. He went to France's finest schools and fought in World War I. When his academic appointment at the Collège de France was blocked by antisemitism, he went to the Sorbonne.

While calling himself "A stranger to all credal dogmas as to all alleged racial solidarity," Bloch simultaneously accepted the superiority of French patriotism over other allegiances: "Attached to my country by a long family tradition, nourished by its spiritual heritage and its history, and, indeed, incapable of conceiving another land whose air I could breathe with such ease, I have loved it very much and served it with all my strength. I have never felt that my being a Jew has at all hindered these sentiments." Putting precedence on being a Frenchman while continuing to be a Jew made for strange contortions. On one hand, he requested and was granted by the Vichy collaborationist regime special permission to teach given his "exceptional services" to France; on the other hand, he died fighting in the Resistance, a way of reconciling his two identities.[69]

The trauma of the war and mass murder strengthened some in their adherence to Judaism but made others determined to shed it by changing names, intermarrying, or—in about fifteen thousand cases—converting. Some accused France of betraying its principles; others saw the antisemitic campaign as waged by people betraying French traditions. These tough issues were largely buried, like Paris's Holocaust monument located—practically hidden—beneath Notre Dame's splendor. Saying nothing about the victims' identity, it was a more fitting memorial for France's offer of equality on the basis of anonymity than for the slain Jews themselves.

Like Bloch, the political philosopher Raymond Aron personified these contradictions. He denied that his Jewish background set him apart from other Frenchman but recalled how he felt inhibited from warning about Hitler in the 1930s lest his objectivity be questioned. "If one wished to be French, if one is French like all one's compatriots," Aron asked himself, "why should one refrain from comment on any matter of interest?" So he stated in a 1936 paper, "How could I honestly assert my impartiality, when Hitlerism has always been antisemitic and while it is now multiplying the risks of war."[70]

In the spirit of liberal nationalism, following an assimilationist tradition, Aron proclaimed himself patriot and citizen of Europe at the same time, citing as predecessor the Danish intellectual Georg Brandes, neglecting to mention that Brandes, too, was Jewish. Aron argued that as a good Frenchman, liberal, and humanitarian—not as a Jew—he must have sympathy for Jews and support Israel's survival.[71]

On this basis, Aron denounced de Gaulle's disparaging, antisemitic 1967 statement about Jews and Israel. This was an especially painful situation since de Gaulle had been commander of the Resistance, embodiment of the good France. Aron claimed to be simply exercising his citizen's right to express his view on the Middle East from the standpoint of French interests. He insisted that a French Jewish general must be willing to fight Israel; a French Jewish writer should be French above all. Yet "to believe oneself obliged to maintain one's reserve, whatever the occasion, is to accept discrimination between oneself and the others."[72] But this line of reasoning did not explain why other Frenchmen, who were not Jews, remained silent or took an opposite stance.

Only totalitarians force one to abandon traditions as the price of citizenship, Aron concluded. Nonetheless, like many—perhaps most—Jews he was ready to do so voluntarily. Aron attributed his willingness to speak about his Jewish background because he felt securely French, unlike his parents' generation. But he only did so to claim its irrelevance for him: "One cannot betray or desert a community unless one has belonged or wanted to belong to it." Other French Jews had the right to make a choice, as long as they clearly selected one loyalty or the other: "If they have not forgiven France, it is no longer their nation, but only the country where they live pleasantly."[73] Blum had spoken in similar terms: "In the free democracies . . . those who have acquired a country and who cherish it do not seek any other." In effect, Israel was for those who had been betrayed by their countries despite loyalty to them, "for all Jews who have not had, like myself, the good fortune to find [a homeland] in their native country."[74]

The next generation of totally integrated Jews is well represented by France's leading filmmaker, Claude Berri. "I am more French than the French," he declares. "If you are a Jew, you must know where you come from. If your family is Jewish, you are a Jew, no question. But my culture is French and I am an atheist. My religion is art." His father was a Polish immigrant and Communist, his mother from Romania, his father's father was Orthodox. A "real" Frenchman would not have to make such disclaimers, nor change his name from Claude Langmann to that of a French province, nor have foreign-born parents who also joined a party subversive of the existing French order. But Berri's claim was not mere bravado. Many assimilating Jews felt exactly as he did in so blending patriotism, self-consciousness, an adopted culture, worship at the shrine of the intellect, and a more balanced view of what had come before.[75]

Roughly similar compromises were worked out by Italy's Jews, a tiny but remarkably productive community. By 1894, eleven Jewish deputies sat in the Italian parliament. Between the 1890s and 1910, Jews served as prime minister, ministers of war and finance, and as mayor of Rome. Only 0.1 percent of the population in 1930, Jews furnished 8 percent of Italy's university professors. Between 1930 and 1940, 30 percent of Jews intermarried. While many Jews joined the anti-Fascist opposition, others backed the regime, some trying to show their loyalty by fire-bombing a Zionist newspaper in Florence. Even Italian dictator Benito Mussolini had a Jewish mistress. Italy adopted antisemitic laws in 1938, albeit with little popular enthusiasm. Cultural conflicts endured, too, as in 1945 when the Vatican proudly announced the conversion of Rome's chief rabbi. "We would not be erased that easily," said one Roman Jew.[76] But the very tininess protecting the community ensured its gradual decline.

In England, too, relative tolerance brought personal success, communal liberty, and a high rate of conversion. London clubs were so willing to admit Jews that it was unnecessary to found separate Jewish ones.[77] In exchange, British Jews did everything possible to imitate Englishmen, which led to their acceptance while perhaps limiting their creativity. As a critic noted in regard to a British Jewish poet, his verse seemed to say, "Pray don't imagine that because I'm a Jew, I'm given to any passion or excess; I'm just an English gentleman who writes verse."[78]

Alfred Mond, who founded the huge Imperial Chemical Industries, passionately longed to be accepted as British and thought he had succeeded until greeted by taunts of "German Jewish traitor" during World War I. To prove himself, he worked tirelessly running the Ministry of Works, while his sixteen-year-old son, Henry, lied about his age to join the army and fight. But once he took on a Jewish role, Alfred found himself quickly reclassified by his peers. In 1929, as a former cabinet minister, he asked British authorities to protect his house in Palestine during anti-Jewish riots there but, to his anger and bewilderment, they refused. When he asked the colonial secretary to investigate the disorders, that official's wife commented, "I can't understand why the Jews make such a fuss over a few dozen of their people killed in Palestine. As many are killed every week in London in traffic accidents and no one pays any attention."[79]

Everywhere the same patterns recurred with differing levels of acceptance or oppression. One might well conclude, as Einstein wrote, "The assimilation of the Jews to the European nations among whom they lived . . . could not eradicate the feeling of a lack of kinship between them and those among whom they lived. . . . Nationalities do not want to be fused: they want to go each its own way."[80] Nonetheless, Jews pledged patriotism and swore each country was their true promised land, insisting its institutions and culture were the best. The Jews of every country blended its history and character with their own, adapting so well as to produce cultural artifacts exemplifying the national spirit of any society they joined. In music, they furnished archetypes like Irving Berlin and George Gershwin in America; Mahler and Mendelssohn in Germany and Austria; or Offenbach in France. In literature, there was Proust in France, Heine in Germany, Italo Svevo and Alberto Moravia in Italy, Bellow and Mailer in America.

Partly from hunger for a national allegiance, radical Jews sought groups of struggling underdogs—implicitly comparable to their own people—to become vicarious patriots for other peoples' causes. A leading Arab-American intellectual even commented privately, "If not for the Jews, no one in America would care about the Palestinians." Jews have been disproportionately active in supporting Third World nationalist movements ranging from those of the Kurds to those of Nicaragua's Sandinistas. Such apparent altruism arose from the void that assimilation left in their own makeup.

Those divorcing themselves from any Jewish link—proportionately far more numerous than those disaffiliating from any other ethnic or national community—required some new home for physical, psychological, and intellectual security. The fact that American Jews believed American culture was the greatest in the world, the British Jews so designated the British, French Jews chose the French, and so on, suggests that the process involved was not some objective judgment but simply familiarity. In claiming to accept the best they merely copied the nearest, the very idea they claimed to reject by refusing to be Jews just because their parents were. Even the greatest professional advocates of alienation followed this pattern—Koestler rhapsodized over England, the revolutionaries had the USSR, and so on. In declaring German, French, Russian, British, or American culture superior to Jewish civilization, assimilationist ideology made debatable assertions but ones perfectly fitting its goals.

Yet over time Western states became more tolerant and pluralist, better able to accept an assertive Jewish minority. Patriotism itself became more moderate as historical experience showed how it could be misused to foment war and hatred. Jews emigrated away from the most chauvinist lands. In other places, new generations of Jews felt themselves fully native, and gentile compatriots increasingly agreed.

After the Shoah and Israel's creation, Jews might focus communal sentiments on that far-off land, while keeping such an emotional engagement intangible enough so as to keep their place in the society where they lived. This approach was not so different from the Jewish attitude before the onset of assimilation. As the American rabbi Isaac Lesser explained in 1840, "We have a tie yet holier than a fatherland, a patriotism stronger than the community of one government, our tie is a sincere brotherly love, our patriotism is the affection which united the Israelite of one land to that of another. As citizens we belong to the country we live in, but as believers in one God, the inheritors of the Law, the Jews of England, Russia and Sweden are no aliens among us, and we hail the Israelite as a brother."[81]

While distinctions within each country diminished, Jews still had to decide whether to dissolve them entirely by disappearing into total assimilation. Like Berri, they might remember where they came from but were now in a completely different place. But in the 1930s Alfred Mond's son Henry had an ingenious solution to the problem of dual identity: "There are plenty of people to look after the English; there are so few to look after the Jews."[82]

9

The Contrary Children

The contrary child asks: "What is the meaning of this service to you?" Saying *you*, he excludes himself.

—*The Passover Haggadah*

THE TRAIN ROLLS ALONG. A Jew, somewhat shabbily dressed, is alone in a compartment. An elegantly clothed gentleman enters, sits opposite him, pulls out a notebook, and does some calculations. The original occupant sits stiffly trying to look respectable. Finally, the rich man looks up at his fellow passenger and asks, "Excuse me, but do you know on what date Yom Kippur falls this year?" The other fellow smiles, relaxes, and stretches out his legs nonchalantly. He realizes the newcomer is another Jew and that changes everything.

Freud told that story as a joke showing the special fellowship among Jews, but an assimilationist character in Arthur Schnitzler's novel used the same anecdote to demonstrate that the Jewish condition was hopeless, "that no Jew has any real respect for his fellow Jew, never."[1] Such contrary responses cannot easily be explained. Why did a student at Cornell University in 1917, shocked to find that her sorority had mistakenly admitted her since it barred Jews, become a Zionist and move to Israel, while a contemporary at Columbia University, refused entry to a fraternity because he was Jewish, suppress every element of his identity and blame that background for every future disappointment?[2]

Such mortifying experiences for assimilating Jews—Koestler called them "things to forget"—elicited drastically different reactions. The Jew, wrote Berenson, is most assaulted by "his own gnawing frustration and inferiority complex."[3] Depending on one's self-image and psychology, rituals may seem deeply moving or ridiculous; solidarity can feel exalting or foolish; being part of a community, natural or horrifying; persecution can spark rebellion or surrender. To condemn society for fostering oppression implied a need to change or defy it. But to blame Jewishness itself as the problem could make the victim see it as his adversary.

Nothing could be more typical of assimilating Jews than to rail against that fate, strenuously deny that fact, denounce Judaism as narrow and obsolete, or declare adherence to some other group. As the Jewish scholar Maurice Samuel described such a personage: "For the sake of 'intellectual honesty' he is not there in the beleaguered citadel. . . . He is on the outside, living [safely] . . . among the armies of the besiegers."[4] Isaac Bashevis Singer thought such behavior rooted in the ghetto Jew's sense of helplessness, making him "hide from danger, avoid showdowns [and creep] into a cellar or attic while armies clashed in the streets outside."[5] Yet in the new era, flight was no longer a case of dodging someone else's war but of changing sides altogether; not of hiding oneself from physical harm, but from exposure and ridicule.

"You may don a thousand masks, change your name and your religion and your mode of life, creep through the world incognito so that nobody notices that you are a Jew," wrote Hess. "Yet every insult to the Jewish name will wound you more than a man of honor who remains loyal to his family and defends his good name."[6] A man wearing no mask does not tremble lest his face be seen. But an individual morbidly self-conscious of this alleged flaw may accuse or condemn himself even if no one else cares to do so. Many assimilating Jews, of course, merely kept silent about their former status, preferring it—and the existence of the Jews in general—be overlooked. As King Edward VII's official biographer in the 1920s, Sir Sydney Lee omitted many of the monarch's Jewish friends or at least any mention of their background, perhaps influenced by he himself having been born Solomon Lazarus Levi.

The pressures and contradictions of assimilation could also, however, prompt a kind of structural or ideological madness, creating anti-Jewish Jews whose animosity made them obsessed with that subject. For a Jew, then, accepting essentially antisemitic notions could be construed as a progressive, courageous, humanitarian step. By denouncing Jews, their religion, or their actions in some disproportionate way, such individuals could turn their powerlessness into a sense of might, their handicap into an asset. Baiting Jews gave them a share in the superiority of their betters and oppressors; by turning against their own origins, they could also be the ultimate iconoclasts. The anti-Jewish Jew acted with the moral authority of some new creed, proclaiming himself an incarnation of the ancient prophets. Instead of being an object of disdain, he decided who was acceptable and who was beyond the pale, as Berenson did in absolving patrons like the Rothschilds from "scarcely any trace of the ordinary Jewish vices."[7]

This was not an entirely new phenomenon. In medieval times converts became powerful and wealthy by denouncing Jews as anti-Christian. In 1584 Pope Gregory XIII, prompted by one of them, forced Rome's Jews to attend weekly sermons given by apostates, a practice that endured for three centuries. In a sense, Jewish Communist officials or modern Jewish intellectuals, couching their denunciation of the community and religion in currently fashionable terms, followed the same pattern.[8]

Such antagonism contained varying portions of calculating opportunism or fervent obsession to the point of psychological breakdown or even suicide. Standing outside the Jewish community, such people were indifferent to its reproaches, less sympathetic to its hopes or afflictions, and often ignorant of its beliefs or views. In emulating a society, antisemitism might be one feature imitated. Apparent moral courage in criticizing Jews as backward and narrow could win applause from one's new audience. A cowardly eagerness to please peers often marked intellectuals, whose very isolation from other groups makes them all the more dependent on their fellows.

If efforts to escape or adjust were hindered, such anxiety intensified. As families suppressed their Jewish knowledge and identity, generations were raised as outsiders to that heritage. Instead of fostering inclusion in the community, customs now heightened a sense of exclusion from it. No longer deriving any comfort from belonging, assimilated Jews might see communal claims as the efforts of a primitive tribe to kidnap them. To that intrusion, many reacted with angry resentment, proud superiority, insistence on personal autonomy, and a resolve to disprove the assertion that they were somehow Jews.

A first step toward being an anti-Jewish Jew was anger at those whose visibility—by calling attention to Jewish distinctiveness—negated the safety of one's own silence or painfully built camouflage. Those appearing less evolved than oneself by being "too Jewish" held one back or exposed one's most embarrassing secret. In 1943, Laurence Steinhardt, the first

American Jewish career ambassador, complained, "A single individual can frequently draw attention . . . by his conduct just as the diners in a restaurant are made conscious of the presence of a Jew by his loud or rowdy conduct or bad manners, whereas prior to his entry there may have been a dozen well-behaved Jews . . . of whose identity . . . the other diners were not conscious."[9]

"If a Jew has bad form in my presence, or behaves in a ridiculous manner," says Schnitzler's archetypal assimilationist, "I have often so painful a sensation that I should like to sink into the earth. One gets embittered at being always made responsible for other people's faults, and always being made to pay the penalty for every crime, for every lapse from good taste, for every indiscretion for which every Jew is responsible throughout the whole world."[10] "Every Berlin Jew felt like a Grand Sultan in contrast to his poor backward co-religionists," wrote Arendt.[11] Disraeli described a relative as having "that dislike for her race which the vain are too apt to adopt when they find that they are born to public contempt."[12]

Yet the problem was less public contempt than the assimilationists' private bitterness. As Arendt wrote of Varnhagen, "The world became peopled with evil demons who shouted from every corner, at every opportunity, the thing she wished she could conceal forever."[13] But when traditional Jews or Zionists were held in contempt they never felt contemptible. It was the assimilating Jew who was insecure, partly accepting the arguments that condemned him. To agree that Jewish distinctiveness fostered hostility meant that Jews, by continuing to exist, were responsible for their own problems and causing the anti-Jewish Jew's personal difficulties as well. Such people viewed traditional or Zionist Jews much as would a southern planter finding black half-brothers on his doorstep. A contemporary journalist writes that among most of his New York Jewish friends, the mere mention of Hasidim usually sparks a strongly negative reaction reminiscent of "classic antisemitism. . . . Their eyes would narrow, their noses would bunch up, and their mouths would curl at the corners in disgust."[14]

Assimilating Jews offset any sense of guilt by explaining that Judaism deserved to be abandoned and they were abjuring a reactionary doctrine based on superstition to join a more advanced country, civilization, religion, or ideology. As humanity advanced, Henry Roth wrote in 1963, Jews in America might add one "last and greatest boon" to previous achievements by "ceasing to be Jews."[15] If departure was a moral act, remaining a Jew would be an immoral one.

"I really dislike Judaism," said the American writer Isaac Asimov, son of Jewish immigrants. "It's a form of particularly pernicious nationalism. I don't want humanity divided into these little groups that are firmly convinced, each one, that it is better than the others. . . . Every once in a while when I'm not careful, I think that the reason Jews have been persecuted as much as they have has been to punish them for having invented this pernicious doctrine."[16] Ironically making this assertion, Asimov was also claiming to belong to a small set "better than the others," that of cosmopolitan intellectuals. This basic idea was a common assimilationist response, since most non-Jews continued to accept the value of their own "little"—or, more likely, big—groups.

Asimov claimed to be sure "that everyone knows I'm a Jew, so while I'm deprived of the benefits of being part of the group, I am sure that I don't lose any of the disadvantages, because no one should think I am denying my Judaism in order to gain certain advantages."[17] But Asimov lived in a time and place where a Jewish background brought prestige and shedding it, if anything, even greater credit. By concurrently announcing lapsed membership and critical independence, an anti-Jewish Jew was simply claiming to be effectively assimilated, mentioning a Jewish past for the sole purpose of demonstrating that he had risen above it.[18]

Asimov's invention of moral laws for robots was an amusing example of a Jewish Variation, and he even wrote a science fiction novel—*Pebble in the Sky* (1950)—advocating his view of assimilation. Joseph Schwartz lives on a future, decadent Earth ruled by humans from other planets who have forgotten that it was their race's birthplace and who dislike its inhabitants for being obsessed with ritual and obeying "it with such masochistic fury." The authorities demand they "abandon their cliquishness, their outdated and offensive customs: Let them be men and they will be considered men. Let them be Earthmen and they will be considered only as such." A moderate Earthman replies that ending oppression would ensure full assimilation: "We are no different from you . . . [but] as long as we . . . are treated as pariahs, you are going to find in us the characteristics to which you object." Hating they hate, being pushed they are pushy. Fanatic Earth nationalists want to regain independence by unleashing germs to wipe out everyone else. But the moderate Earthman betrays his "people," and successfully appeals for compromise: "Give us but the chance, and a new generation of Earthmen would grow to maturity lacking insularity and believing wholeheartedly in the oneness of Man."[19]

In some cases, the assimilationist's desire to battle insularity and self-interest made him a self-styled scourge of those remaining Jews, betraying them for their own good by warring on their distinctiveness. When Jewish students objected to the University of Pennsylvania's scheduling registration on Rosh Hashanah, an official of Jewish origin rejected the complaint, calling them "sensitive" and "pushy." Since he ignored such holidays, Jews observing them trespassed on his own self-image, embarrassing him by seeking special treatment and calling attention to what he preferred be forgotten. The university's non-Jewish president, in contrast, quickly accommodated the students since he had nothing to lose by practicing a true, even-handed tolerance.[20]

An individual feeling trapped in a despised class may hate himself as its inevitably inferior product. It is far easier, though, to denigrate the group while exempting oneself from its bad attributes. "I do not love my people. I rather dislike them," wrote Koestler. "Self-hatred is the Jew's patriotism." He was attracted by their intensity and brains, "but their achievements were spoiled for me by their ostentation. I hated their acid analytical faculty, their inability to relax, their shortcuts from courtesy to familiarity, their mixture of arrogance."[21] Koestler certainly did not feel that any of this applied to himself, a man who could—and often did—take a new identity at will.

By forcing changes in beliefs, loyalties, tastes, and even personality, assimilation was bound to be accompanied by confusion and discomfort, possibly a creatively productive neurosis and sometimes a serious psychological dislocation. "Hunted, always insecure," wrote Berenson, "our ancestors must have developed unusual gifts of inner as well as outer observation, which nowadays turns us into psychologists, scientists, novelists, critics."[22]

Extreme self-consciousness was inevitable for someone creating a new persona at every moment in every act and choice. "The normal man," wrote Ludwig Lewisohn, "lives in a state of instinctive self-affirmation in respect of his race, his religion, and his nationality." He may doubt himself but is sure of the value of his ancestors, faith, and nation. The worst view others as inferior; the best are quietly confident of their own group's worth. This is an essential element of psychological health, ethical balance, and normal relations with disparate cultures.[23]

But assimilation, Lewisohn wrote, was based on a self-denial that did not really transform the self. The result was a set of people "living and dying as Jews and with Jews [but acting] as unJewishly as possible." These pressures exacted a high cost on individuals, especially if they believed the charges made against Jews had some merit. Seeking something better, some identity, made many "succumb to all kinds of silly and false propaganda . . . the willing victims of every shallow notion and untenable doctrine, if only it is not a Jewish notion and a Jewish doctrine."[24]

From their dilemma, the assimilationist intelligentsia made a new ideology that proclaimed separating from tradition as a first step in their transfiguration as the first people rising above partisan interest, a vanguard serving humanity and advancing it toward a higher level of rationality, internationalism, peace, and happiness. Claiming to stand above society reflected their origin in a group outside society. To say they had no community was in their community's material interest, the seemingly disinterested standpoint inspired by feeling trapped between rejected and coveted affiliations. Their statements of devotion to the oppressed were partly motivated by the desire to be among them no longer. Hess saw how often such "fine words about humanity and enlightenment [were] intended only to disguise disloyalty to his brothers."[25]

The assimilating Jew's yearning to be judged as an individual is understandable, since the alternative was to be scorned as one of a group for which he felt no kinship. It was better to be an aristocrat of the spirit than an outcast or martyr for a cause in which one did not believe. "I am most often rather annoyed than flattered to be told that I am the best or foremost Jewish artist," said the sculptor Jacob Epstein. "Surely to be an artist is enough."[26] "How loathsome it is always having to establish one's [own] identity first," wrote Rachel Levy. "That alone is enough to make it so repulsive to be a Jew." It was a uniquely Jewish assimilationist theme to say, as did a Schnitzler character, "Every race as such is naturally repulsive, only the individual manages at times to reconcile himself to the repulsive elements in his race by reason of his own personal qualities." For Jews to preserve their singularity ran against progress, the French Jewish intellectual Julian Benda wrote in the 1920s, adding "one more arrogance to those which set men against each other."[27]

But shame, not arrogance, was the root of this problem. As Schnitzler put it, young Jews were "systematically educated . . . to look upon Jewish peculiarities as particularly grotesque or repulsive."[28] They were trained to avoid attributes identified as Jewish and to imitate others deemed superior or, at least, customs more likely to bring them security and success. Being virtually the only group that took such an attitude toward itself, its members became all the more distinctive.

When accused of being ashamed to be a Jew, Hecht's character Boshere replied: "You might as well have accused me of being a kangaroo. I'm no more Jew than kangaroo. I'm Boshere." Being a Jew subtracted from a person's uniqueness, threatening to limit or take over one's character, though the same people seldom worried about being typecast as American, German, or any other nationality. "Being ashamed of one's parents, birth, class, religion is the first symptom that we're superior to them," explained Boshere. "It's only natural for any one who feels himself a prince to be shocked at first over the fact that he comes from moujiks."[29]

Shame, Hecht wrote, makes one conscious "of not being a normal social human being." That awareness accounted for much of the character and creative ability of many assimilating Jews. For such people, to be "natural" was abnormal and trying to do so anyway was a source of their maladjustment. Having alternative Jewish and assimilated personas gave them the power to decide—which their "normal" neighbors did not have—who they wanted to be. Roth's Portnoy was only one of many engaged in this internal argument: "But I don't want to escape! Well, that's nice too—because you can't. Oh, but yes I can—if I should want to! But you said you don't want to. But if I did!"[30]

The psychologist Kurt Lewin defined a self-hating person as one feeling endangered and penalized by association with a group where he remains only because outsiders force him to do so.[31] In contrast, most anti-Jewish Jews acted from self-love, pursuing personal advantage or egotistical satisfaction. Only a minority hated themselves, either being unable or fearing it impossible to discard a subordinate Jewish status. The Harvard Jewish professor Harry Wolfson told students in 1922 that being Jewish was a handicap "like being born blind . . . deaf, [or] lame." They could only "submit to fate" rather than "foolishly struggle against it," because there was no solution for this problem.[32]

Since Levy "had not wanted to accept herself," wrote Arendt, "the central desire of her life had been escape from Jewishness, and this desire proved unfulfillable because of the antisemitism of her milieu." Rather than condemning the oppressors, Levy internalized the blame: "I do not forget this shame for a single second. I drink it in water, I drink it in wine, I drink it with the air; in every breath. . . . The Jew must be extirpated from us . . . and it must be done even if life were uprooted in the process." This goal forced her, in Arendt's view, "to sacrifice every natural impulse, to conceal all truth, to misuse all love, not only to suppress all passion, but worse still, to convert it into a means for social climbing."[33]

Thus, self-hatred was most often a conservative impulse: the victim had to accept the legitimacy of a system treating Jews as inferior and doubt that things could be different. Rachel Levy, explained Arendt, detested "the grinning caricature of herself that . . . others had fashioned."[34] But this meant that Levy accorded this description some validity. In contrast, Marxists or liberals believed change was possible, attacked the status quo's legitimacy, and expected Jewish assimilation to succeed.

But Levy did achieve her goal by a conversion that ended social discrimination and greatly reduced the psychological trauma. The same can be said for Heine, who wrote—but did not publish—a poem in 1825 after hearing of the baptism of his friend Gans, president of the Society for the Culture and Science of the Jews:

> O for youth's sacred courage!
> How speedily you are tamed! . . .
> You have humbled yourself before the cross
> the very cross that you despised. . . .
> the man who but yesterday was still a hero
> has turned into a knave today.[35]

Heine, who had only recently had himself baptized, thought Gans's crime in defecting "all the more revolting" because of his leading role in the Jewish community: "Traditionally it is the duty of the captain to be the last to leave his floundering ship—but Gans saved himself first."[36] The phrase "saved himself" signaled how Heine, Disraeli, Berenson, and Levy saw conversion as deliverance. Self-hatred was for them a passing phase. Conversion furnished a certificate of immunity even if others still saw them as Jews. Even the Nazis conceded that Jews could become Aryans if enough generations had passed since conversion or intermarriage. Such solutions did rescue many Jews from self-hatred.

Once safely out of the Jewish camp, those leaving could even take some nostalgic pride in what they now saw as positive Jewish qualities or achievements. Once outspoken about Jewish inferiority, Berenson could comment in later life that Jews were resented because they were more "intelligent, quicker, abler. . . . Where is there another people who has produced unceasingly for 3,000 years individuals of genius, creators in every field requiring use of mind, as Jews have?" He professed himself, "more and more amazed to discover how seldom I meet an interesting thinker, scholar, or writer who does not turn out to be a Jew, half-Jew, or quarter-Jew." Visiting the Vatican, he wrote, "What a triumph for the Jewish race that a Galilean peasant should have such a grand monument." Criticizing racial bigotry, he noted, "We Jews know the horror of being looked down upon by our inferiors everywhere."[37]

Like many Jews of widely differing viewpoints, Berenson attributed his people's shortcomings to external forces. The Jew, he explained, "may be pushing, indiscreet, and a snob, but surely that is the fault of a world which persists in boycotting, ostracizing him, so that he never feels at home, is never wholly accepted."[38] This concept that bad Jewish traits were due to social conditioning acknowledged inferiority while offering a bit of hope that this condition was somehow correctable.

But when some Jews accepted inferiority while also doubting any cure was possible, the chain reaction of self-hatred could reach terrifying proportions. That phenomenon's most epidemic, psychopathic phase occurred between the 1880s and 1945, the era of a new antisemitism preaching that racially inferior Jews were unredeemable even by conversion.[39] Some Jews suffered psychological scars, internalizing anti-Jewish ideas to the point of becoming two warring people in one body. Others, who found no escape yet agreed that they were loathsome, engaged in truly bizarre behavior. Those believing themselves inescapably inferior could only be humbly grateful for any undeserved mercy received. Hermann Levi, a rabbi's son and the greatest conductor of Richard Wagner's music, agreed with Wagner's view that Jews were repulsive and un-German. Masochistically servile, he made himself that antisemitic composer's slave, even kissing his mentor's hand humbly in the midst of a concert he was conducting.[40]

This position's most consistent ideologue was the German Jew Otto Weininger, who converted in 1902 but—finding this penance inadequate—killed himself the next year at age twenty-three. His book *Sex and Character* equated Jews with women as inferior while extolling Aryan preeminence. Weininger was faithful heir to a father who despised other Jews and admired Wagner. But rejecting the easy dodge of finding Jewishness a defect in others from which he was immune forced Weininger into self-extinction. In contrast, his disciple Arthur Trebitsch sidestepped that fate by claiming to have evolved into a pure Aryan. As such, asserting he best understood the danger, Trebitsch lectured about Jewish plans for world conquest.[41]

Gilbert Frankau, a successful novelist from a British Jewish family, educated at Eton and intermarried three times, desperately tried to prove himself a right-wing aristocrat like the dashing, tough heroes he created in his books. Frankau wrote a 1933 article entitled, "As a Jew I Am Not against Hitler." His daughter rebelled against his political views by switching from the Anglican to the Catholic church. The poet E.H.W. Meyerstein, a child of converts, dismayed to discover that British anti-Jewish prejudice also applied to him, protested that he was not a Jew, did not like Jews, and was ashamed to be part of the race that crucified Jesus.[42]

Such concepts could be toyed with in Britain, but on the continent self-hatred was a deadly serious matter. Arnolt Bronnen, a Viennese half-Jew, wrote nationalist, antisemitic plays and became a literary advisor to the Nazis, while the anti-Nazi leftist Kurt Tucholsky wrote implicitly anti-semitic vignettes ridiculing bourgeois Jews. The behavior of Theodor Lessing, a convert who first described the phenomenon of self-hatred and loathed his short stature and dark features, provoked Freud to call such symptoms "an exquisite Jewish phenomenon." Lessing's childhood showed how many Jews were literally raised as antisemites. When he teased a fellow pupil by calling him "Jew," the other boy answered, "You're one yourself!" Lessing replied indignantly, "It's not true!" When he asked his mother what a Jew was, she laughed and gave an evasive answer. "But," Lessing later wrote, "the word took on a sinister meaning for me. Since I had childishly absorbed all the patriotic and religious prejudices of the school, and there was nothing to counterbalance them at home, I became convinced that being Jewish was something evil."[43] He later recanted his views, became an anti-Nazi and Zionist, and was killed by Hitler's agents in 1933. Maurice Sachs, a homosexual French Jewish convert to Catholicism, praised the Germans and even moved to Nazi Germany, where he lived until being caught and killed in 1943.

A year later, the thirty-five-year-old Simone Weil died of malnutrition in London. Born into a highly assimilated family, she trapped herself in a series of paradoxes, arguing that the Jewish question must be solved not through equal treatment but by the Jews' disappearance. Advocating universalism and individualism, she joined a specific, hierarchical group by becoming a Catholic—a religion she still disparaged as too akin to Judaism. She extolled the working class—laboring in a factory for a year, briefly visiting Spain to support the Republican cause—but also advocated appeasing Hitler and said that a fascist victory was preferable to war. She joined and was expelled from the French resistance. When the collaborationist French regime barred Jews from employment in teaching, she unsuccessfully demanded an exemption as being no longer a Jew. In the end, deciding that she had no moral right to consume more calories than the hungriest French person, she paid for the guilt of her existence by starving herself to death.[44]

Such true self-haters showed their sincerity by forfeiting their lives, genuinely convinced that it was impossible to uproot the wicked Jewishness from within themselves. These were extreme, exceptional cases but reflected smaller-scale traumas among a great many Jews. Not surprisingly, self-haters are rarer than self-worshipers: the former are victims of a terrible psychological disorder rooted in suffering; the latter are opportunists who direct their own behavior for personal advantage.

Communism, for example, needed Jews willing to combat their own religion and people. But unlike other Communist leaders, these Soviet Jewish officials had to appear openly as Jews. The more oppressive the regime, the more it required such people as apologists and tokens. In the midst of anti-Jewish purge trials, the 1952 Stalin Prize was awarded to the writer Ilya Ehrenburg, who one Soviet Jew later likened to the thief "whose job it is to distract people's attention when the robbery is taking place."[45] He said nothing when Stalin murdered Jewish cultural figures and warned Soviet Jews to denounce Israel. Yet in another of the assimilationist process's many incongruities, despite Ehrenburg's function as the regime's court Jew, his visibility also gave hope and pride to others.

In the 1970s and 1980s, a leading public Jew in the USSR was Samuel Zivs. Having once tried to change his ethnic designation from Jew to Latvian, Zivs settled for a career as a KGB operative, heading an anti-Zionism committee and insisting that Jews were well-treated in the USSR. Vladimir Pozner, a slicker apologist for Soviet policies, smoothly switched sides when the regime fell. His father had converted to Russian Orthodoxy and "always vehemently denied he was Jewish," said Pozner, "but it did him no good because the name Pozner fingers you automatically."[46] That same fact, though, first made the younger Pozner useful for the Communist regime, then helped him appeal to the West as victim and dissident to become a frequent performer on American television.

The syndrome of self-hatred was never the same after 1945. The horrible reality of antisemitic hatred culminating in the Shoah largely quelled the folly of self-hatred. European society and anti-Jewish prejudice were now supposedly dishonored, while Jews were vindicated and more self-assertive.[47] Yet the massacre also made many Jews feel even more shame and fear thereafter. When powerful or prominent individuals sought to prove themselves separate from Jewish interests, their acts of commission or omission could injure other Jews.

Bruno Kreisky returned to Austria from exile after 1945 to hold several high posts, though doubting, "because of my Jewish origin," that he might become the Socialist Party's leader or the nation's chancellor. In 1970 he won both jobs. To enjoy and exploit success, Kreisky sought to prove he had no Jewish facets and never confronted Austria's endemic antisemitism. He quickly capitulated to Palestinian terrorist demands in 1973 to close the escape route through Austria for Soviet Jewish emigrants. He cultivated close contacts with the PLO during its most extreme terrorist phase, courted ex-Nazis in Austrian politics, and attacked "Zionist racism." The election of such a Jew as leader did not show tolerance, and Austria's press constantly depicted him by such loaded phrases as "too clever," "tricky," "shrewd," or "a useful outsider in difficult times." The historian Robert Wistrich writes that Kreisky "gave a new legitimacy to antisemitic feelings in the Austrian population." His successor was ex-German army officer and participant in genocide Kurt Waldheim.[48]

The most remarkable modern case of the anti-Jewish Jew is the right-wing, antisemitic, ultra-nationalist Russian leader Vladimir Zhirinovsky. Post-Communist Russia seemed a reincarnation of the hostile societies facing assimilating Jews in pre–World War II Europe. Zhirinovsky, whose faction ranked second among parties in Russia's 1993 parliamentary elections, startled the world by denouncing a score of nations and groups in racist, aggressive terms; threatening Russia's neighbors with conquest; and making the most extreme antisemitic charges. He firmly, almost hysterically, denied any Jewish antecedents despite ample proof that his father was Jewish and that Zhirinovsky had once thought of himself as such, too.[49]

Echoing earlier assimilating Jewish—as well as anti-Jewish—concepts, Zhirinovsky claimed that Jews were responsible for antisemitism. His own personal response was to become a totally assimilated, non-Jewish Russian nationalist whose antisemitism was inspired by camouflage and psychic disorder. He consorted with neo-Nazis, threatened Russia's neighbors with war, and promised to fire Jewish television announcers and replace them with Russians having "good, kind blue eyes and fair hair."[50]

Yet Zhirinovsky acted less like a shrewd would-be Hitler than as a man bent on self-sabotage, whose internal psychological drama was more important than seizing political power. His behavior echoed that of the assimilating Jewish iconoclasts who provocatively made themselves the object of public hate in culture or politics. Intent on not being a Jewish pariah, he was eager to be a pariah of his own design, earning the dubious distinction of being the first assimilated Jew to be compared to Hitler, though not the first to become an antisemitic ideologue.

In contrast to these European models, America's pluralist cultural revolution and evolving tolerance made a Jewish background an asset. Open self-hatred was relegated to a few intellectually unbalanced or psychologically disturbed individuals like Noam Chomsky, who did not stop short of defending those denying the Shoah took place; Mark Lane, who worked with the antisemitic Liberty Lobby; or chess champion Bobby Fischer, who hated Judaism while joining a fundamentalist Christian sect that observed Jewish dietary laws and the Sabbath. Aptly, Fischer first made his mark by winning the Lessing J. Rosenwald Trophy Tournament, named for America's leading anti-Zionist Jew.[51]

The goal of such behavior, aside from self-aggrandizement, was to confess a Jewish background while striving, like Asimov, to prove that one had transcended it by an aversion for "little groups" and alleged devotion to humanity as a whole. One technique to achieve this was to maintain that the essential nature of Jews and intellectuals was to be alienated outsiders. Thus, to have a Jewish past was equivalent to being a perpetual universalist. The man who belonged nowhere—formerly an antisemitic or Communist jeer that assimilationists rejected—now became a proud claim.[52]

But presenting the Jew as archetypal victim, the idea of someone so assimilated and ignorant on the subject as to see Jews only from the gentiles' standpoint, once again robbed that people of any purpose in its own right: "Jew is only the name we give to that stranger, that agony we cannot feel.... Each man has his Jew; it is the other. And the Jews have their Jews," wrote Arthur Miller in his play *Incident at Vichy*. But it is the assimilating Jew, not the Jews, who holds such ideas and is an outsider. Indeed, if the "Jew" is always "other" and "stranger," then nobody can actually be one. This formulation also declares the writer's total neutrality, neither identifying with Jews nor attributing any moral preeminence to them. For some, an obsession with proving the "Jews have their Jews"—to show they are hypocrites and that their creed provides no solution—is the core of the psychosis of being an anti-Jewish Jew.

More common and more useful for the ambitious, however, is a milder form, the wish to escape that label by hiding or denying it. One of Washington's most powerful figures during the 1980s was Richard Darman, who held a series of high-level government jobs including director of the Office of Management and Budget. Smart, competitive, and power-hungry, he would, a former colleague noted, "do anything to advance himself." "If the cavalry is winning, he's for Custer," said another, "and if the Indians are winning, he's for Sitting Bull." Even by Washington's standards, Darman's self-manufacture was especially relentless as he quoted T. S. Eliot, referred to his blond Christian wife as having been "the most beautiful woman on the Radcliffe campus," and called his photographic album "quintessentially American."[53]

Darman bragged about a supposedly aristocratic lineage in part to divert attention from his self-made Orthodox Jewish, Russian immigrant grandfather, who was for three decades president of his synagogue; from his father, who was a founder and president of another synagogue; and from his own bar mitzvah. But now Darman was an Episcopalian. He recounted a year spent at Oxford but omitted mentioning a degree from Boston University. Similarly, he spoke of growing up in a fancy Boston suburb but not of his first thirteen years spent in Woonsocket, Rhode Island.

His anxious obsession about being normal, coupled with a self-consciousness about every such trait, revealed the artificiality of his pose, a point sensed in his WASP elite mentor Eliot Richardson's evaluation: "Non-rational factors do not distort his view of anything . . . [he does not] allow his view of a situation to fall into a pattern or a mold imposed by convention . . . [and] instinctively understands the fallacy of believing that there is a real thing behind every label."[54] These attributes may stand out for Richardson because they are less aristocratic ones than qualities coming from the assimilationist situation: extreme intellectuality, indifference to tradition, and a view of life as highly malleable.

If those in the Executive branch may be tempted to understate Jewish affinity to prove their "objectivity," legislators—supposed to be partisan and represent constituents—are pushed to overstate ethnic allegiance. Paul Wellstone was criticized in Minnesota's 1988 senatorial election by his rival Rudy Boschwitz for being distant from the Jewish community and intermarried. This effort backfired—as some Jewish voters saw Boschwitz's tactic as a violation of the rules of pluralism—and Wellstone won. He then took his first trip to Israel and claimed to be studying Jewish philosophy, stating, "I guess that I never understood the ways in which parents and family have shaped my existence. I never really understood why I think the way I think."[55]

Never having a side of one's own facilitates always being on the "right" side. Whether cynical or from deep conviction, such behavior was expedient in promoting career and reputation.[56]

It is admirable to uphold high standards of fairness, a scientific-minded openness to evidence, a fearless search for truth, no matter who is offended or affected. Yet a perceived need to prove one's credentials, especially by attacking Jewish practices or concerns, is a distortion of objectivity. Supposedly proof of total integration, it was actually a graphic demonstration of continued insecurity. As an American Jewish professor put it in a gratuitous attack on Israel for temporarily deporting leaders of radical Palestinian terrorist groups, "I feel the daily horrors of Zionist treatment of the Palestinians, perpetrated in my name and with the financial support of my community, as a personal as well as a political tragedy. My ideology is of the old-fashioned Enlightenment sort that demands freedom and justice for everyone, not just for Jews."[57]

There were many such people who, in Alan Dershowitz's words, never identified "with Israel or other Jewish causes" except when they speak out against Israel *"as Jews,"* though they would have been furious if asked to undertake any other protest on that basis. Their underlying motive was to show "the 'real' Americans [that] *they* were the good Jews, not like the ones in Israel who were doing those embarrassing things. They were identifying themselves as Jews specifically in order to *disassociate* themselves from other Jews, [to say] 'We are not part of *them.* We are part of *you.* We are the good guys. We are good guests in your home.' "[58]

Compelled by high or base motives, everyone selects affiliations. Those claiming to belong to no group may simply have shifted to one other than that of their birth, applying universalist arguments only against a Jewish identity. "The intelligence is defeated as soon as the expression of one's thoughts is preceded, explicitly or implicitly, by the little word 'we,' " said Weil.[59] Yet this standpoint loses its cogency when one remembers her constant effort to distance herself from being a Jew combined with her strenuous effort to be Catholic, leftist, European, or French patriot. It is not intrinsically more virtuous to belong to no group or change one's allegiance unless the new community is better, not merely more powerful.

Hannah Arendt herself was an example of this ailment. Her criticism of Jewish leaders for alleged collaboration with the Germans apparently issued from her equivocal feelings about Jewish identity. Having herself escaped Germany, she reduced the charges against a German intellectual tradition to which she was so attached. To blame the victims could also

pardon American Jewish intellectuals, who otherwise had to face their own
sin of inaction at the time. When Scholem, who criticized Arendt's book on
Adolf Eichmann as almost sneering at the Shoah, wrote her, "I still regard
you as a daughter of our people." Arendt replied: "I come only from the
tradition of German philosophy," a remarkable response since many elements of German philosophy—including that of her own teacher Heidegger—was implicated in sanctioning mass murder. Lionel Abel wrote, "I can
imagine voices shouting across time to those of this decade who happen to
be Jews: 'You do not come from philosophy, or from politics, of the Right or
of the Left. You come from us, from your fathers.' "[60]

Yet this was precisely Arendt's objection. Such a claim seemed to challenge her individuality and place in German intellectual history. She, of
course, had the right to choose her course. Still, since one of the assimilating Jewish intellectuals' main ideas was that society and identity were
something chosen—not the natural, sole conceivable order—one might
expect a more critical scrutiny of how such choices are made. Arendt's adherence to the German tradition was much conditioned by a family background and education that prepared her to seek its prestige and legitimacy.
The fact that considerable elements of German culture denied her right to
its heritage made Arendt's claim to membership—like that of many other
Jews—all the more insistent.

Arendt was expressing characteristics common among many assimilating Jews. The antisemite who wanted to deny them the chance to join society was far more dangerous to them. But those assertive as Jews, whose
existence contested their motives and identity, seemed to molest their
inner life, threatening to exhume what the assimilationist was eager to have
dead and buried. The German Jewish leader Gabriel Riesser was angry on
hearing that Moses Hess was writing that Jews were a nation, asking, "Who
has set you up as lord and judge over us?"[61] Fear often provoked nervous
hatred and passionate anger at those seeming so arrogant as to assert a right
to define one's life or undo a painfully constructed self-image as revolutionary, cosmopolitan, world-straddling intellectual, Christian, or ordinary
citizen.

Thus, the intellectual delegitimizes the road he rejected, just as
Christians, the British, Germans, and others sought to usurp the title of
chosen people by denigrating the Jews. To argue that Jews were a nation
undermined the assimilationists' claim to have no such loyalty. How
could those who denied Jews were a people not feel threatened by Is-

rael's existence? Those for whom total assimilation and humanity's one-ness were the highest values felt disgust at Jews advocating a continued separate existence. Each self-affirming Jew challenged those who advocated a different course—as Hess seemed threatening to Marx, as black-coated Orthodox appeared repugnant to the fashionable Jewish gentlemen, the Bund repelled Trotsky, or Zionists made would-be humanist citizens of the world feel insecure.

The opposition of Jews to the Jews arose from the nature of assimilation, a process that could cause psychological manifestations or even symptoms of derangement. Some Jewish intellectuals stood with persecutors against their own people because they sought to define themselves in a different manner. Leaving the besieged fortress, they assumed bizarre disguises to enlist in an attacking army whose victory seemed certain. In a world slandering Jews and rewarding desertion, presenting such acts as courageous was the worst perversity of the assimilation process.

IO

Philosophy Wars

Sometimes in his arrogance he has more anxiety for the world than for himself.
—Franz Kafka, "He"

LIBERALISM WAS by far the most suitable philosophy for Jews in the assimilation era since it coincided with their history and needs while being admirably flexible for the purposes of assimilation. By proclaiming citizens' equality and rights, liberalism allowed individuals to leave the group and merge into society more easily. But it also let those wishing to remain Jews enjoy the same treatment as others and freely preserve their own institutions.

The same forces that resisted Jewish rights were also sworn enemies of liberalism. As disapproving antisemitic traditionalists often noted, Jewish—or at least assimilating Jewish—attributes paralleled those of liberal or social democratic capitalism. Assimilating Jews were more inclined to internationalism than to xenophobia, toward innovation rather than convention; and to be energetically adaptable instead of conservative. They prized educated reason over convention and were eager for reform rather than accepting what already existed.

Despite the traditional religious community's social conservatism, moderate political liberalism also meshed in many ways with Judaism as a religion, with the very significant exception that the latter's laws were held to be ordained by God and thus unchangeable. But this factor was circumvented up to a point by a flexible system of continuing interpretation.

Moreover, once secularism or revised forms of religious observance removed that foundation stone, the liberal features were further enhanced. Often, the struggle for reform, democracy, socialism, and trade unions became the only "Jewish" characteristic that assimilating Jews displayed.

"Who has placed a higher premium on human dignity than the Jewish people?" asked Nordau. "Who has more profoundly grasped the equality concept . . . and recognized no nobility other than that of richer knowledge and higher virtue?" Jewish law exalted social justice, charity, and laborers' rights.[1] Their small numbers forced Jews to be always conscious that other groups and beliefs existed. Centuries of minority status made Judaism favor social pluralism. Its very exclusiveness encouraged tolerance since even the most strictly pious, who wished to impose their will on other Jews, knew the community was a small minority whose strictures did not apply for society in general. Unlike Christians or Muslims, Jews did not demand that others join them or change their beliefs.

Being powerless and mistreated kept them aware of suffering and existing social defects. Religious doctrine and historic experience made Jews obsessed with social justice. "The Jew in me," wrote Arthur Miller, "shied from private salvation as something close to sin. One's truth must add its push to the evolution of public justice and mercy."[2] The non-Jewish majority lived in a well-established national and religious setting, giving them—regardless of any economic grievance—a secure, stable foundation that was denied to assimilating Jews, who found society's basis not sheltering but alienating. Marx far better described Jews than the proletariat when he defined the vanguard favoring change as a group "with radical chains" whose "universal suffering" meant both that its claims could only be presented in humanity's name and that it could only liberate itself by freeing society in general.[3]

In contrast to Marx's doctrine, liberalism permitted a continuing Jewish religious or ethnic identity alongside equal citizenship. Many intellectuals, like Freud, derived from that predicament a willingness to doubt or oppose the dominant ideas or traditions that conservatives defended as the basis of state and civilization.[4] Thus, conservatism appealed to few Jews, regardless of economic status, since the non-Jewish right extolled a way of life identified with the majority nation of Christian believers, peasants, and aristocrats. Jews who wanted to be conservative simply remained traditional and unassimilated. Some Jews did don upper-class or super-patriotic camouflage to appear—by an exaggeration usually exposing them as impersonators—more indigenous than the natives, more royalist than the king. But this strategy was difficult, unpleasant, and usually unattractive, requiring they quickly cease to be identifiable Jews while embracing a status quo that discriminated against them.

By the time assimilating Jews achieved wealth and social acceptance it was already too late for most of them to be conservative: they remained psychological outsiders to some extent, equating gains with liberal reforms and persecution with the political right.[5] Wealthy Jews also retained a tenacious link to poorer compatriots pushing them to remember the existence of the needy while not taking for granted their own station. Having been unfairly assigned low social rank, they found it harder to take so seriously the idea that social status and virtue coincided; having risen from poverty, they could not easily forget that others could do so; rejected by snobs, it could be harder for them to make a pretense of superiority. Fear of change was often less troubling to those who had flourished from change. "Jews don't hunt," wrote an American Jewish comic writer, "Jews don't like roller coasters, Jews are never state troopers. Jews . . . do not equate danger with pleasure."[6] Perhaps this was because for them, security—not risk—was the diversion.

But liberalism also contained a sharp contradiction: it eased full assimilation but permitted partial assimilation, freeing Jews to build a new synthesis joining Jewish identity with equal citizenship. In the latter case, they could ally with, rather than join, other groups in the healthy dialectic of Rabbi Hillel two millennia earlier: "If I am not for myself who will be for me? And if I am not for others, what am I?" In a time of secular logic, Nordau rephrased this concept as mandating moral acts not from fear of Hell but as a rational identification with the human race: "Its prosperity is your prosperity and its suffering is your suffering." Zangwill spoke similarly, claiming Jews were the main advocates for "the brotherhood of humanity under [God's] common fatherhood."[7]

What did "rational identification" or "the brotherhood of humanity" mean in practical terms? One could argue with equal ease for the melting pot's uniformity, by claiming that ethnic or religious identities were divisive and obstructive, or advocate the diversity of a pluralist mosaic, by insisting that different loyalties were mutually compatible and culturally enriching. But a particular need of assimilating Jews was to find ways to persuade non-Jews not to oppress them by appealing to common goals, total similitude, moral values, self-interest, or other methods. When rumors swept a French city in the mid-1800s that the homes of rich Jews would be looted, the Jews' pleas for protection were ignored until there were reports that all rich people might be attacked. An assimilating French Jew said this story showed how mutual interest overcame prejudice. The political left had a parallel argument in its rhetoric of class solidarity and united fronts.

Such hopeful thinking inclined Jews to consider reciprocal aid as a political golden rule and to view moral action as essentially pragmatic. Sometimes this idea worked; often such hopes were disappointed. Either way, however, this approach sustained an older tactic of survival through subservience. Ahad Ha-Am angrily called "this trick of exciting sympathy with the Jews on the ground that it will benefit other people" a terrible idea, "sufficient in itself to show how far even Western Jews are from being free men at heart." A man attacked by bandits should be aided by all without having to show how saving him benefited them, "As though the human race were something apart in which I have no share, and not simply a collective name for its individual members of whom I am one!"[8]

This reliance on the kindness of strangers was a constant assimilationist literary and political theme, as in Berthold Auerbach's story of a gentile befriending a Jewish peddler and helping him when he became mortally ill, even reading him the Jewish prayers. A priest praises this act as serving God's will.[9] The dialogue of tolerance in Europe, however, was largely one-way: only Jews, not Christians, wrote this type of tale. Similarly, as Jews embraced specific ideas—democracy, liberalism, socialism, ethnic tolerance—these concepts often lost some of their attraction to non-Jews by becoming identified with Jews. To a large extent, assimilating Jews furnished the audience for their cultural output, certainly in terms of their own special exegesis of it.

Just as teenagers enter the world thinking it can be easily changed—that social arrangements are based on misunderstanding, problems are irrational, and correct ideas will easily persuade people to change their ways—so the Jews came into Western life. Assimilationists, sincerely believing that what was specific to them typified everyone, displayed tremendous chutzpah in first denying Jewish particularity, then reasserting their chosenness by claiming to be humanity's vanguard.[10] They imitated the traditional Jewish style of scholarship by accumulating their own sets of laws and authoritative prophets. Many of them almost inevitably accepted a set of ideas stressing the mutability of individuals and conditions, putting immense faith in each generation's chance to break with the past, and over-estimating the reforming power of science and systematic thought. All these concepts were in line with general modernizing trends, but assimilating Jews took them up with exceptional unanimity and zeal.

But the Jew was not a universal figure. In Europe, being in exile and living as a minority were exceptional conditions. True, Jews shared in the human condition, though this idea was strange enough for Shakespeare's merchant of Venice to have to explain that Jews, too, bled. Individuals are lonely, life falls short of one's desires, suffering occurs, anxiety and neurosis exist. Seeing that things can be different from the way they are is a spur to knowledge. To be oppressed is a condition shared by the vast majority of humans, according to the contemporary definition.[11]

Jews were not completely encompassed by these categories any more than anyone else, for they also had a very specific culture, history, and religion of their own. The categories of "human" and "oppressed," however, were especially attractive for assimilating Jewish intellectuals, who wanted to leave behind the old specifics and seek safety by enlisting in a larger group. An individual's universalism can be like a state's imperialism: a rationale for annexing the whole world to himself as a dominion.

Many major events—Jewish emancipation, wars, revolutions, new ideas and discoveries—were seen as harbingers of a breakthrough to a universalist society into which all groups would be dissolved. After all, assimilating Jews were only asking from others what they had already done themselves. Over and over they proclaimed, as Eduard Gans did in 1822, that what seemed "an age of recurrent, incomprehensible hatred and reawakened barbarism" was really the dawn of utopia.[12] Messianic expectations moved from the divine to secular spheres, as the triumph of rationality in the world, including the extinction of that ultimate irrationality—antisemitism—and the sweeping away of such superstitions as religion, nationalism, and intolerance.

In short, assimilating Jews built a parallel, semiintegrated, secular civilization, marked by what Philip Roth called "moral stubbornness" and "passionate otherness."[13] At best, it was a unique blend of sentiment and rationalism, warm spontaneity and love of learning, profound apartness and a need to belong, radical protest and yearning for tradition. But the assimilationist version of this view was employed by intellectual magicians who would make their Jewishness disappear by defining it out of existence or even defame it as an obstacle to human progress.

Erich Fromm was an exemplar of a moderate humanist position. Born in 1900 in Frankfurt to an actively Jewish family, he studied Judaism and philosophy, Freudian psychiatry, and Marxism before fleeing to the United States in 1933. Like so many Jewish intellectuals, he restlessly moved from one ideology to another, a search provoked by an empty, lonely feeling of separation from one's original community, then goaded onward by an iconoclastic creed of universal doubt. In Fromm's philosophy, this experience of repeated disaffiliation and assimilation became the model for human progress. One needed to feel "as a stranger in the world . . . in order to be able to become one again with himself, with his fellow man, and with nature."[14]

Contrary to harsher radical humanists like his Frankfurt School colleagues, though, Fromm recognized that community—a "framework of orientation and devotion," "a sense of rootedness"—was also a human need. In a 1939 article, Fromm tried to cope with the persistence of antisemitism, war, and other evils through a psychological dialectic. Individuals transcended existence's "accidentalness" and aloneness to achieve "purposefulness and freedom" through either creation or destruction, "to love or to hate." Here Fromm echoed Jewish religious/philosophical tradition in which God set before humanity both blessing and curse, life or death, urging the choice of life.[15]

But for such people, no matter how well-meaning, to isolate pure reason from other facets "in the complex of human urges," warned Scholem, was most deceptive. Many seemingly sensible ideas "stood no chance of realization . . . [given] the forces functioning in history."[16] So it was for the vision of universal human assimilation, the hope that a day would come when the fraternity of all humanity would be obvious though it appeared, as Elias Canetti wrote, "possibly in a single country at first . . . until no one can doubt any more."[17]

Assimilating Jews thought themselves to be the Prometheus who would bestow this liberation. But fate was cruel to the pioneers of Jewish humanism since they were largely alone in being so eager to replace religion, nation, and self-interest with a cult of altruism, objectivity, and humanism. Professing universalist humanism was an assimilationist strategy, a way Jews could be included without being mentioned. After all, if everyone is treated fairly Jews must be, too, which was one reason antisemites and supposedly internationalist Communist regimes made such cosmopolitan thinking a crime. To expect that logic would resolve all problems neglected the lack of consensus over what comprised the realm of reason; ideas defended by appeals to science or logic could also justify terrible deeds.

The mass murder of the Shoah was a German act, but other peoples— unconvinced, as Ahad Ha-Am had warned, that they had any interest in protecting Jews—collaborated or refused to save the victims. One-third of the world's Jews—over three-quarters of those in Europe—perished; both Jewish tradition's stronghold and assimilation's main constituency were decimated. Human deeds undermined faith in human reason, leaving each remaining Jew a survivor traumatized philosophically and psychologically. "The life of the mind was of no use unless it addressed itself to the gas," the American Jewish critic Alfred Kazin wrote. But on this subject, he added, "The left had nothing to say," while the right argued, "There is evil in all of us."[18] Antisemitism's irrationality exemplified the perversity of history and society; its stubborn refusal to perish made it appear that other problems would not so quickly fall to the forces of progress.

In ensuing decades, however, some ideas invented or favored by the assimilationist struggle did triumph. Most Western societies became far more humanist, democratic, pluralist, and hospitable to Jews. In the United States, Britain, France, and elsewhere, discrimination declined and Jews held high places in politics, culture, and business. This trend, along with awareness of Soviet antisemitism and the radical left's hostility to Israel, largely weaned assimilating Jewish intellectuals from Marxism.

Growing self-confidence permitted some in the new generations to shed assimilationist complexes. Feeling more secure and integrated, they could afford to rekindle interest or feel some sentimental attachment for their identity. Others, however, were now totally immersed in democratic societies where they lived and ignorant of Jewish sentiments, which their own successful integration made all the more backward, restrictive, and superstitious to them.

Thus, success at merging into Western, especially American, life—no less than the earlier failure in Europe—again brought to the fore the old question of how to use freedom: to be a Jew—however that might be defined—or to stop being one. The fundamental assimilationist strategy changed remarkably little from a century earlier. As long as one was conscious of past persecution and any separateness from the social mainstream, some deep-seated feeling remained—no matter how irrational—that rights might be withdrawn unless Jews put nation above people or religion in order to earn equal treatment.

America itself is blameless for this diffidence. Bias is insignificant there; government policies are friendly to both Jews as a group and to pluralism. The source of the insecurity is no longer the society itself but the precedent, psychology, and situation of assimilation within individuals. Jews have been most moved to public action by fear of antisemitism or Israel's destruction and eagerness to make neighbors see them favorably. Having so long been on the defensive, they still lived the old biblical curse in a faintness of heart so powerful that "the sound of a driven leaf shall put them to flight. Fleeing as though from the sword, they shall fall though none pursues."[19]

The many contradictions of assimilation contributed to the large number of Jews among psychiatrists and their patients. Freud's theory itself rested on a notion of the mind as the main source of reality, as interpreter of conditions open to multiple explications. Jews were more accepting of such an idea both because of their greater stress on intellect but also since assimilation loosened moorings to the status quo and allowed them wider choices.

Ironically, while assimilationists broke sharply with the ghetto past, they retained some of its style of behavior toward the larger society. No matter how outspoken as democrats, socialists or humanists, they were tempted to be meek and invisible when in danger of being seen as Jews. A part of their psyche felt powerful and talented, while another part might feel unworthy.

The civil rights and anti-Vietnam War activist Allard Lowenstein provided a good example of this liberalism so generous in fighting for the rights of others while so reactionary and psychologically crippled in its attitude toward Jewish identity. Lowenstein argued that individuals should be treated as distinctive human beings, not as members of an ethnic, racial, or religious group. Yet he also fantasized about living in a small Midwestern town full of Protestant farmers, attended church services, chased after handsome WASP men, married a patrician New England WASP, bragged that most of his friends were Protestant, and was sensitive about his big nose and Jewish appearance. This lack of self-esteem and sense of being an outcast led to a passionate quest to be accepted as a "normal American," which he defined as ridding himself of any aspect of Jewishness.[20]

The purpose of ethical behavior was no longer to please God but to dispel antagonism. This was the true subtext of the concept that Jews must behave better than everyone else, a strategy designed to prove either that one was not a Jew or that Jews were good citizens. Berenson put into words an idea guiding many assimilating Jews, a constant caution lest antagonism be stirred up. "Even if you were as innocent as the angels you could not escape its venom, and you are far from that. . . . It is the irresponsible wealth, as well as the arrogance in the high ranks of Jewry, that led to the periodical persecutions and massacres. . . . Spiritual wealth more even than material, is apt to rouse secret resentment. . . . [You] cannot be too modest, too unassuming, too discreet."[21]

Thus, assimilating Jews often engaged in what Lewisohn called "a frenzy of self-justification": "We are honest . . . and law-abiding and decent and useful. We have no special interests beyond those of our fellow citizens (a flagrant untruth, of course); we produce more than our share of intellectual and spiritual goods (which is true but beside the point) and therefore—thus runs the abominable and degrading argument—therefore we ought to be tolerated." As Paul Cowan noted, arguing that Jews had to be more ethical and altruistic was to make it seem "immoral if they organized their lives around their own self-interest."[22]

But the type of actions needed to further assimilation might be the opposite of those required to maintain a community or people. The drive for assimilation made people profess themselves individuals detached from history or ethnicity, downplay any collective goal or distinction from Christianity or Americanism, distrust nationalism and conservatism, and be very sensitive in placating neighbor's opinions. Self-preservation came to mean gradual absorption into the mainstream; urged Jews at least to be translucent if they were not to disappear entirely. Declaring independence from communal influences meant being increasingly shaped by American and Christian ones. In the name of pluralism and tolerance intermarriage was good, while opposing it was backward and prejudiced. If being part of society required repressing parochial interests, it was better to avoid being part of any such narrow group. To apply high standards to themselves meant being more harshly critical of one's own community than of others.

The conflict between self-assertiveness and timidity fostered the famous neurosis and rebelliousness associated with assimilating Jewish intellectuals. Energy, resentment, and intellectualism were the last passions to disappear in the process, sometimes—at the last moment—blocking its culmination. Assimilating Jews were bred for contradiction, inconsistently taught to take pride in differences they no longer understood yet to be ashamed at feeling superior; to sense themselves outsiders, while being permeated by the native culture.

Every act—whether flaunting or spurning one's successful assimilation, trying to win favor or provoke outrage—was done with an eye to how the majority would interpret it. Intense anticipation of discrimination—even, or especially, if never fulfilled—induced paranoia; knowing the gap between society's professed virtue and real intolerance made for cynicism; the failure of good deeds to eliminate antisemitism imparted anger; striving for achievements that might risk ethnic jealousy made for nervousness. Ambiguity between proving one's worthiness and seeing success as selling out one's own people produce radicalism, iconoclasm, or self-conscious defensiveness.[23]

Thus, championing tolerance and pluralism—especially on behalf of other minorities or underdogs—became a principal self-definition of assimilating Jews in America. In contrast to Europe, the United States was culturally and psychologically more open to diversity. The nation's motto, *e pluribus unum,* "one out of many," implied both its people's diverse origins and determination to weld them into a single entity. The original American pattern of traditions, literature, tastes, and language established by the dominant Protestant majority was assaulted by a series of movements in which Jews played a leading role. The New Deal populism of immigrants and their children, for example, glorified workers and common people. Yet this very approach, suffused with Jewish values and interests, deliberately had nothing to say about communal interests in order to emphasize the unity of the people and to assert that all could be assimilated or integrated.[24]

This ethos of pluralist populism is embodied in a *Washington Post* column by Richard Cohen, directly inspired by a hotel concierge who in uniform looked to be a servant but whose off-duty suit made him seem too urbane even to be a guest there. Appearance, Cohen concluded, was superficial and the social order at any given moment deceptive. After all, he reasoned, Jewish immigrants had been poor and dirty: "Here are my grandfather and grandmother. Leonard Bernstein and Philip Roth, Lauren Bacall and Kirk Douglas. . . . They appeared so different, so weird that they could be considered a different species, not quite human." He applied the same point to the Third World's "turbaned and burnoosed ones" whose class, culture, and behavior might seem "permanent, immutable, ageless [but] can change in a historic snap of the finger." "A proper suit. And, of course, time" would transform them, too. Preaching against prejudice, he also negated real differences of culture and worldview from which people took pride and identity, patronizingly setting a single standard while toler-antly insisting on anyone's ability to meet it.[25]

Jewish intellectuals constantly searched among subjugated groups for allies, objects of rescue, or analogues. Fighting discrimination was an indi-rect way of defending themselves while simultaneously asserting individu-alism and universalism. Jews were the only group that found it so easy to engage in such displacement, since appearing under another guise allowed them to avoid troubling questions of self-interest and identity. Depicting another massacred people, Koestler, Werfel, Mandelstam, and Joseph Heller all wrote books with Armenian heroes. By the late twentieth cen-tury, many Jewish writers, scholars, or artists focused on other races, women, and various unpopular groups as stand-ins for the Jewish situation and subjects of sympathy. A Jewish academic wrote, for example, that while antisemitic rhetoric once portrayed "the Jew as a dangerously effeminate being" spreading contamination, these same charges were now being at-tributed to gay males.[26]

A disproportionate Jewish involvement in the American feminist movement was, unlike many other such commitments, inspired by a healthy self-interest among those who were both Jews and women. Even in this case, however, assimilation's special conditions provided incentive for activism and leadership. American feminists often drew on analogies from Jewish oppression and assimilation to analyze women's problems. More-over, many Jewish women tended to conform to certain feminist ideals like high intellectual and career achievement, and less to a gentile society's tra-ditional definition of feminine beauty or social grace. Betty Friedan, a movement theorist and founder, recalled how high-school sororities and social cliques had excluded her, presumably because of her ethnic back-ground. As so often happened, the denial of the usual routes and roles led assimilating Jews to seek alternative ways toward empowerment, as well as an outsider's relative detachment to society and class.

Discussing his efforts to help post-Communist Eastern Europe, wealthy investor George Soros explained: "As I looked around me for a worthy cause, I ran into difficulties. I did not belong to any community. As a Hun-garian Jew I had never quite become an American. I had left Hungary be-hind and my Jewishness did not express itself in a sense of tribal loyalty that would have led me to support Israel. On the contrary, I took pride in being in the minority, an outsider who was capable of seeing the other point of view." So he gave $1 billion to Hungary and neighboring states to help "build a country from which I wouldn't want to emigrate."[27]

Fighting for the rights of others was virtuous since it was not a pleading for self—and was hence unselfish—despite an underlying pragmatism that each struggle indirectly benefited assimilating Jews, too. David Selznick, the film producer who made *Gone With the Wind,* said, "I feel so keenly about what is happening to the Jews of the world that I cannot help but sympathize with the Negroes and their fears." Perhaps this motivated him to tone down the book's racism, a step that also, however, understated slavery's brutality. A civil-rights volunteer leaving for Mississippi in 1964 after three others—two of them Jews—had been murdered there told his mother, "Of course I'm still going. . . . If someone in Nazi Germany had done what we're doing, your brother would still be alive today."[28]

Yet the energetic good intentions of Jews could also stir—as had happened before—the resentment of oppressed groups who sometimes thought they were being patronized or dominated. Jewish philanthropists gave much of the money for New York University's Martin Luther King Afro-American Center only to hear its director accuse Jews of practicing genocide against his people.[29] While the vast majority of African Americans were not anti-Jewish, they were averse to criticize some leaders, like Louis Farrakhan, who purveyed anti-Jewish attitudes.* Some rap songs had antisemitic lyrics, and the role of young Jewish entrepreneurs in marketing rap music induced attacks by radical black newspapers. One publicist said, "Given what I'm doing, my viewpoint has to be that whatever comes out of the black community . . . is the right thing. I know my place." He said his main concern was that the music bring the races together and teach black children about their culture and history. Asked about the antisemitism, he showed ignorance of his own history by responding, "I hadn't thought about it that way. That stuff's been around since the Thirties, hasn't it?"[30]

Social justice and individual liberty were delicately balanced. Despite the considerable power held by Jews, they were the group most reluctant to use and most eager to understate their influence. Using the power of individual Jews to achieve gains for the community risked unleashing antagonism. Although many were members of the upper or upper-middle class, Jews still thought of themselves as outsiders and rebels. The long history of rulers oppressing Jews made a strong government frightening, but equally so was one too weak to protect them.[31]

---

*But minority groups often saw themselves as having parallel interests. When a 1981 black-Jewish relations panel was interrupted by news that a young man had just shot President Reagan, a black speaker cried, "I hope he's not black"; a Jewish one said, "I hope he's not Jewish!" Minutes later it was announced: "Its all right! The president's okay and the gunman was blond!"

Fear of the majority's hatred was no mere illusion. Henry Kissinger, himself a refugee from Germany, noted that even paranoiacs have enemies. But it was also possible to exaggerate the antisemitic threat or—more likely—to incorporate it as an integral piece of one's own psyche. Nothing showed the fragility of their situation more clearly than the fact that many assimilating Jews thought themselves the freest of people—in exchange for living within the narrowest confines of assimilation. "Deep down we see ourselves as second-class citizens—as guests in another people's land," said Alan Dershowitz. "We worry about charges of dual loyalty, of being too rich, too smart, and too powerful."[32]

The more one possessed, the greater the danger that it might be lost. Superman, an ostensibly strong, anxiety-free gentile created by two American Jews in the 1930s, was really, behind that guise, an exile from a destroyed civilization. He hid his true identity and was vulnerable only to pieces of his old culture, his home planet's soil. For assimilating Jews seeking some new identity or ideology—whether that of aristocrat, average citizen, or rebel—their Jewish past was the equivalent of kryptonite.[33]

Instead, assimilationist ideology had a strong, romantic identification with those lacking power, psychologically transferring a Jewish situation to apply to other peoples or to types of behavior. Outsiders were virtuous, creativity the fruit of struggle. Ahad Ha-Am described this classic type among Jews in 1901: "He has given up his specifically Jewish character . . . but the land of his birth is denied to him. His countrymen repel him when he wishes to associate with them. He has no ground under his feet and he has no community to which he belongs as a full member."[34]

Even an anticommunist, antiassimilationist like Lewisohn could apply the lessons of Jewish history to insist, "It is always the proclaimers of unpopular truth who are in the minority and who are persecuted, and it is precisely that unpopular truth which, when mobs or majorities or dictators rage, needs to be emphasized and needs to be defended. Those who are persecuted are always the least worthy of persecution. . . . The very fact of their persecution is the supreme witness of their worth." Given the contradiction between the Jews' weakness and claim to be all-important, the traditional Jewish view was based, as Rabbi Jacob Neusner put it, on "the paradox that the weakest is strongest, the most despised the most honorable, the least important the most significant."[35]

No wonder there was such a strong preference for posing as alien and outcast. Boys and girls were taught to respect—even if not to practice—

Jewish traditions while concurrently mastering the skills needed to assimilate successfully and raise the community's reputation among others. The discrepancy entailed created a strong impulse to disdain rectitude by rebelling against both Jewishness and gentility. Torn between being a human rights' champion and a sex fiend, Roth's Portnoy defends himself by protesting that his motto is, "Don't step on the Underdog."[36] Woody Allen satirized this posture by joking that if even one person was suffering, "It puts a crimp in my evening." A Jewish reader protested an article's implication that whites were inevitably racist by asserting, "As a Jew, I am white and yet outside the majority. This is painfully evident every Christmas, every Easter."[37]

Richler called himself "the loser's advocate," achieving moral omnipotence by constantly jumping between roles as Jew, Canadian, or prophet of justice to wring the maximum personal innocence and moral outrage from any situation. He attacked Jews as parochial for mourning the Shoah without also saying "a sad word for those Germans whose cities were criminally battered beyond strategic need." Yet elsewhere he wrote, "Germans are abomination to me. I'm glad that Dresden was bombed for no useful military purpose."[38]

In his play *The Fever*, Wallace Shawn fantasized being tortured by oppressed revolutionaries who incarnate his privileged agony and guilt. A fire-breathing, scatological, cultural subversive, Wallace Shawn is the rebellious son of William Shawn, perhaps the ultimate Jew-as-WASP figure and for many years editor of the ultragenteel magazine *The New Yorker*. But even that establishment bastion was founded by the heir to Louis Fleischmann's bakery. In conquering high society, a bit of Jewish chutzpah helped. Alexander Liberman, designer of *Vogue* and similar publications, brought, a critic wrote, "an air of real-life modernity, intellectual highjinks, journalistic breeziness, and social consciousness to magazines that had ossified into showcases for Social Register gossip."[39]

Whatever zeal and protest Jewish heritage and the assimilation process implicitly inspired among intellectuals, they usually considered that experience irrelevant to the content of their ideas. The secular intellectual abandonment of Jewish thought and experience sometimes was phenomenally ironic. Professor Allan Bloom argued that the purpose of education was to allow one to make choices, not just to "propagandize acceptance of different ways, and indifference to their real content."[40] Yet his insistence in *The Closing of the American Mind* on the need to find a standpoint chose

Greek philosophy as the foundation of Western civilization. The fact that a Jewish scholar preaching ethical values, self-awareness, and a firm identity could do so with no reference to his inherited body of thought is remarkable.

"Higher education," Bloom complained, does not tell one how to conduct his life.[41] But what provides a set of values, identity, and place in life and history if not the religion, people, and set of ideas from whose seed one grew? At a time when knowledge is increasingly narrow and technical— with many experts but few intellectuals—a foundation in a broader ethical and historic vision becomes all the more important and useful even if it is secularized for that end. Moreover, their own history and orientation gives American Jews stronger links to the past, other places, and the life of the mind than has been the case with any other group in an essentially ahistorical, provincial, and obsessively practical society.

The ubiquity of this factor makes understanding it all the more vital, not merely as a residue of the past but as something valuable and powerful today. Freud observed that humanity, "Never lives entirely in the present. The past, the tradition of the race and the people, lives on in the ideologies of the super-ego, and yields only slowly to the influences of the present."[42] Original thinkers, like great chefs, use the same basic set of ingredients yet produce quite different results. Each generation of Jewish intellectuals did not fully invent themselves from external materials and their own thought's spontaneous combustion. Insisting on being incorporated "into the universal history of mankind" is no more sensible than abolishing one's national cuisine. It also impoverishes humanity by extinguishing some of its color and variety.

When accused of parochialism, the Yiddish writer I. L. Peretz had answered, "I am not talking of shutting ourselves up in a spiritual ghetto. We want to get out of the ghetto, but with our own spirit, our own spiritual treasure, and exchange—give and take, not beg. . . . If you have no God you look for idols."[43] The task that Peretz undertook but most Western Jewish intellectuals avoided was to secularize Jewish wisdom as they and others had done for a Greek and Christian thought equally imbued with religion.

Far more common, however, is the biography that the novelist Shai Agnon gave one of his characters, a university professor, who "learned neither the elements of religion nor anything related to Hebrew. . . . He didn't feel he was missing anything; he pored over the literature of Germany and all the other nations without being aware that, although he was taking in foreign wisdom, his own people's wisdom remained foreign to him."[44]

In considering a British writer's hostility in describing his relationship with Judaism, Stuart Schoffman asked, "How can a man so canny and erudite [be so] . . . fearful of feeling, so bereft of surprise?"[45] On this subject, however, erudition and empathy are abandoned and more primitive instincts of flight take over. Iciness and intellectual paralysis is a defense mechanism to protect the sophisticated image derived from one's other credentials. Like the Jewish writer speaking of a computer system as "picayune, huffy, digressive, a cross between a late-night dorm bull session and the Talmud—and worthless, if you have no interest in the subject at hand."[46] Yet this is the subject in which one is supposed to have no interest; things Jewish are most appropriately mentioned when in criticism or in jest, the key to much Jewish humor.

The answer to this problem was the unspoken codicil, the Catch-22, in the assimilationist humanist creed: nothing human is alien to me—except Jewishness, for any special link to it would make everything non-Jewish less equal in my affections. Jewish professors championing Western civilization and classical Greek philosophy battled other Jewish professors fighting for multiculturalism and more Third World material in the curriculum. Both sides saw themselves as impartial fighters for truth. Yet that pose, self-interest, and self-definition barred their studying Jewish matters or involvement in Jewish causes. Identifying with suffering or ideals was the product of impartial, unbiased judgment only if they denied themselves any vested position of their own.

Many thus squandered the new freedom that would have permitted a balance of communal civilization and successful assimilation, closing their otherwise free-ranging minds to this one subject precisely because of its intimate significance. No other group produced so many people extolling neutrality or self-criticism as proof of even-handedness. The community's decline or collapse easily coexisted with the accumulation of power and prestige by individual Jews. Assimilating Jews often took up the cause of humanity or various parts of it, but no imported replacements existed to replace those abandoning Jewish ones.*

The Russian Jewish writer Solomon Ansky met a Dr. Shapira before the revolution who was government physician in a village where there had been a pogrom. He offered her money to treat injured Jews, but she did not want to deal with specific Jewish problems. Ansky wrote, "This intelligent

---

*This predicament made it all the more remarkable that enough energy and talent remained for reviving Jewish nationalism and such a wide range of institutions and scholarship.

woman, who exhibited the most remarkable bravery in operating under
fire, didn't have the courage to declare herself a Jewess and to defend her
persecuted brothers."[47]

The same basic principle was exquisitely illustrated by Allen Ginsberg's 1974 poem "Jaweh and Allah Battle," ridiculing with careful equiva-
lence both sides in the Arab-Israeli conflict: "Both Gods Terrible! . . .
Which stronger Illusion? Which stronger Army? . . . . We shall triumph over
the Enemy! Maintain our Separate Identity! Proud/History evermore!"[48]
After African Americans rioted against Hasidic Jews in Brooklyn, the car-
toonist Art Spiegelman drew *The New Yorker* magazine cover showing a
Hasidic man and an African American woman kissing. Responding to the
ensuing controversy, he claimed to have acted in a "knowingly naïve"
manner: "It is my wish for the reconciliation of seemingly unbridgeable
differences in the form of a symbolic kiss." Actually, Spiegelman's own
marriage to a French Christian may have made romance seem a reasonable
way to conciliate intergroup conflicts. But he also showed a more iconoclastic side of the assimilationist pattern in a proposed cover for the magazine showing Santa Claus urinating on a wall in the shape of a Christmas
tree.[49]

The irony is that those craving personal freedom were willing to pay
for it by relinquishing free will, accepting a demand for a conformity, an
identity that they would reject in any other matter. Many assimilating Jews
were eager to disprove the classic antisemitic accusation that they used
their positions to benefit Jews as a community. Indeed, their caste interest
was to foster the dissolution of that group and carefully avoid any appearance of partiality. Thus, the exploits of assimilating Jews might bring honor
to the community but would deny the use of their talents to develop that
community, thus further impoverishing and marginalizing it.

Assimilating Jews powerful in culture, entertainment, or politics had
personal, professional, and historic reasons for diminishing such links and
stressing themes of pluralist liberalism, secular humanism, alienation, in-
dividualist suspicion of community, and reticence on the subject of religion. While Judaism can be shown as no worse than Christianity, it is risky
to present it as better, and most preferable to show it as not much different.

The paradox is that choice is inescapable but no choice fully offers an
escape: to neglect Jewish subjects in one's work is as conspicuous and self-
conscious as being obsessed with them. "Does Meyerbeer really think,"
asked Hess of the composer, "that anyone besides himself is deceived be-

cause he so carefully avoids biblical themes in his operas?"[50] Yet most intellectuals and artists concluded that eluding Jewish themes, characters, or situations often seemed an indispensable strategy for success and proving artistic versatility.

Ludwig Lewisohn noted sadly: "Escape, escape. Anything on any irrelevant periphery. . . . Anything but that to which one is called by nature and unperverted instinct and tradition and where one is wanted and needed and where, despite insufficiencies and inadequacies and a thousand human imperfections, one can give one's whole heart. Any place but home. Any people except one's own. Any God except the God of one's father . . . [as long as] it be not Jewish, so it be not the Jewish people, so it be not the land of Israel."[51]

Certainly, such an attitude was then—and remains—common. On one side lay a ghetto bounded not by walls but parochialism; on the other the glittering prizes, the mass audience. To defend Jews seemed selfish, to extol others appeared altruistic, evincing a higher loyalty to truth, country, or humanity over a narrow special interest. The group's faults can be counterposed to personal virtue. By pulling up anchor, the individual can sail from identity to identity, avoiding responsibility for any misdeed by country, religion, or race by always claiming to be elsewhere. He can be American, white, Jewish, affluent, liberal, or leftist—benefiting in various ways by all these attributes—while claiming to have no identity at all except a devotion to truth and justice.

Yet there is inevitably friction among these roles. Philip Roth explored this position in his controversial story "Defender of the Faith." The Jewish Sergeant Marx must cope with the obnoxious Jewish Private Grossbart, who demands religious rights purely to avoid duty and discipline. The gentile commanding officer—like most contemporary Christians—is not antisemitic, merely baffled and uninterested. The assimilation struggle is mainly fought among Jews. Marx worries that Grossbart will stir antisemitism and must draw the line between Jewish rights and citizen's obligations. By conceiving Grossbart as insincere and Marx as driven to examine his own ethnic feelings, Roth sets up the ending. When Grossbart switches his orders by deceit to avoid combat, Marx changes them back by pretending the private is courageously eager to fight the Nazis. Grossbart complains, "You call this watching out for me?" Marx answers, "No. For all of us." Communal interests require protecting the community's image among the gentiles; liberty in America requires adherence to the nation's rules.

The issue is how one handles these rules: when to advocate and when to remain silent; when to defend and when to criticize constructively; when (or whether) to put on each of one's multiple identities. When right-wing politician Pat Buchanan was accused—on rather strong grounds—of antisemitism, Michael Kinsley, his partner on the "Cross-Fire" television program, defended him as merely a man with "an eccentric passion for accused Nazis" who could not be characterized as antisemitic since he did not think of himself as such. Kinsley's only objection was Buchanan's doubt that the Holocaust happened. He asked Buchanan to take back this statement; Buchanan refused, and Kinsley stopped there. (Although the two became famous for debating each other on television, a real confrontation on such an emotional issue—rather than their presumably entertaining simulated ones on stage—might destroy their association.) Of course, Kinsley was less reticent on other issues. He did not hesitate, for example, to characterize the 1988 Bush campaign's advertisements as racist.[52] The latter matter, however, was a racial or partisan issue that allowed him to act as liberal, altruistic hero. A Jew who speaks on behalf of a community cause seems to be acting parochially, though silence may be more an act of personal self-interest.

But why should a man who defines himself as adherent to a liberal pluralist society feel anxiety or engage in self-censorship? America's lack of antisemitism makes this opportunistic approach superfluous: If non-Jews no longer looked down at Jews or bothered to hate them, why should Jews take up this burden? If one can walk away from a Jewish background amidst general indifference, why should this be a source of psychic conflict? In the early 1970s, National Security Adviser Henry Kissinger feared becoming involved in Middle East policy lest he be accused of dual loyalty. Twenty years later, much of the Bush administration's and almost all the Clinton administration's foreign-policy team on the issue were Jews. No one complained. Neither the stock manipulations of Ivan Boesky and Michael Milken nor the spying of Jonathan Pollard—events which in Europe had produced pogroms and the Dreyfus case with far less justification—had any effect.

The battle over assimilation had moved inward, becoming a problem almost solely addressed by Jews. Guilt at deserting the community competed with doubt about staying in it. During a time of advanced, but still incomplete, assimilation, concealment was easy; asserting that ethnicity or religion was irrelevant became ideologically correct, though no such claim meant that what was hidden or downplayed was necessarily inconsequential. Concealment became a centerpiece of character.

A Jew sees Jews as outsiders only if viewing the Jewish community from the outside. Of course, Jews might have been alien to the lands where they lived but were unalienated natives to their own community. Earlier assimilationists knew both societies from personal experience. A mere generation later, however, those born outside this community and body of knowledge were barely aware that either had ever existed. For example, in the familiar progression, Hannah Arendt's grandfather had been a Jewish community leader; her parents left Judaism as ardent left-wing socialists. Integrated into German intellectual life, Arendt wrote a doctoral dissertation on Augustine's concept of love. She also produced a sensitive biography of the self-hating Rachel Levy, with whose life her own had some parallels. History forced on her an interest in antisemitism and totalitarianism.

But seeing Jews as victims of an oppression that would not let them disappear peacefully, Arendt thought them empty of content themselves, a pure reflection of the assimilationist situation. "All vaunted Jewish qualities—the 'Jewish heart,' humanity, humor, disinterested intelligence—are pariah qualities," she argued. "All Jewish shortcomings—tactlessness, political stupidity, inferiority complexes and money-grubbing—are characteristics of upstarts."[53] Similarly, her discussion of the active versus the contemplative life ignored Jewish insights on this matter. But she was trained to believe, from Christian doctrine, that nothing important happened to the Jews after the "Old" Testament and that Western civilization was only a Greek/Christian synthesis.

As a critic of reactionary forces, she regarded herself at war more with Jewish tradition than with German culture. "The deceased force themselves upon us and upon the institutions that govern us and refuse to disappear into the darkness into which we try to plunge them. . . . The more we try to forget," she wrote, "the more their influence dominates us," perhaps persecuting "us into the third and fourth generations." The cause of persecution, she thought, was an illusory belief in Jewish differentness shared by Jews and antisemites. Her heroes were Heine and Börne "who, just because they were Jews, insisted on being considered men and were thus incorporated into the universal history of mankind." While those forgotten—and rightly so—insisted on remaining Jews.[54] This celebration, however, overlooked the fact that Heine and Börne were converts who chose in practice to join not "universal history" and "mankind" but a specific nation named Germany and a particular sect called Christianity to gain privileges for themselves.

For Arendt, too, some groups and systems of ideas were more equal than others. Her love for German philosophy paralleled her love for the philosopher Martin Heidegger, whom she met in 1924 when she was an eighteen-year-old student. He later joined the Nazi party, which promoted him to the position of university rector, and forbade his own teacher, Edmund Husserl, to enter the campus since he was a Jew. After the war, Heidegger refused to renounce his views and held that everyone was responsible for the wrongs done. Arendt visited him and even kept his picture on her desk while reporting on Eichmann's trial in Israel, where she took a similar tack on the matter of blame.[55]

The subject of religion or religiously derived values remains very dangerous for even the most secular Jewish intellectuals since it raises questions about their own identity. Being outspokenly atheist could make them seem to be anti-Christian Jews. To portray Christianity as superior was craven. The most honorable solution was to stress that different faiths were appropriate for different people, though they had no wish to embrace one as their own or call attention to distinctions they wished to erase. The safest approach promoting assimilation was to reject the religion into which they had been born and remain silent on the majority faith.[56]

A remarkable example of this dilemma was Hollywood producer Norman Lear. He sponsored People for the American Way, a group advocating secular humanism—and whose very name portrayed assimilating Jewish ideology as American tradition. The group played a key role in a case leading to a Supreme Court decision backing a Jewish parent's objection that a rabbi's invocation at his daughter's high-school graduation violated separation of religion and state. Aside from the American issues involved, two latent aspects involved assimilation. First, Jews have a special reason to feel threatened by religion in public life since its manifestation would be overwhelmingly Christian and implicitly anti-Jewish. Second, since an essential part of assimilating Jewish thought was demanding equality by preemptively denouncing one's own separate communal rights, how could Jews insist that Christians reject an exclusivist nationalist identity based on religion or giving a civic role to their own faith unless Jews did so first?[57]

A decade later, though, Lear turned around to advocate a revival of spiritual values. Having little apparent interest in or knowledge of Judaism but not wanting to embrace Christianity, he discussed the issue without ever even mentioning the word *religion:* "The sophisticates of our politics, our culture and the media," he complained, a category certainly including himself, "are embarrassed to talk seriously about the life of the spirit." He now voiced the need to seek "our connection with that place in each of us that honors the unquantifiable and eternal . . . to rediscover together what is truly sacred."[58] Yet by not addressing God, religion, or disparate traditions—where distinctive standpoints contested the idea that this could be done by everyone "together"— such talk was reduced to the vaguest mishmash.

Another interesting example of such incongruities was Adrienne Rich. The same poet who could claim total free choice—"As for himself, he joined the band of those/Who pick their fruit no matter where it grows,/ And learn to like it sweet or like it sour/Depending on the orchard or the hour"—could in the service of the Politically Correct proclaim the determinist nature of personal background in claiming everyone is "marked by family, gender, caste, landscape. . . . Poetry is never free of these markings even when it appears to be."[59] This is a profoundly assimilationist contradiction between the determination to define oneself as being above all groups and as self-made, to "pick their fruit no matter where it grows," coupled with a recognition—or at least a suspicion—that such independence is not really possible.

Even the design of a Holocaust museum in Washington, D.C., reflected this situation. Its purpose, in the words of project director Rabbi Michael Berenbaum, was to Americanize the Holocaust, interpreting the event through assimilationist ideology, which meant advocating pluralism and democracy. After all, to teach Americans to eschew totalitarianism, bigotry, and mass murder, it would seem more appropriate to build a museum of American racism. Equally, concentration camps are not imminent threats in the United States. In reality, the project originated in the desire of elderly survivors to tell their story and memorialize the victims—an honorable motive. But the underlying political doctrine expressed became the familiar one of defining past Jews as victims from a vanished civilization while seeking sympathy for living ones as being identical with the majority and by flattering the host country.

The archetypal victim used in the museum's publicity kit, named Haskel Kernweis, was said to have come from a religious family though his religion went unmentioned. In effect, he was presented as a convert from

Judaism to Americanism—whose fascination for the United States made him change his name to Charley and long to live there. One might conclude that the German motive for persecuting him was anti-Americanism. Asked about this, Berenbaum cynically remarked, "Clearly, when they're sending out fund-raising things they want to attract American people—to attract and interest the Americans without falsifying events."[60]

But that goal was the problem. This marketing approach meant presenting Jews as Americans, or at least potential ones. The exhibit began with U.S. soldiers liberating death camps, minimizing the U.S. government's earlier refusal to admit refugees or bomb the railway leading to Auschwitz. Just as eminent American Jews were so intent on protecting their own assimilation that they did not help European Jews, a bid to show patriotic credentials was now reflected in the museum board chairman's refusal to invite Israel's president to speak at the opening (until the resulting embarrassment forced President Clinton to request the chairman's resignation).

Rather than depicting Jewish civilization or viewing the Shoah as a part of its history, showing a need for self-reliance and self-defense, the U.S. Holocaust Museum uses Jews as a case study to serve others. Compared with projected Native American and African American museums, which would express those groups' achievements, the "Jewish" museum portrays the essential fact about that people as its death. Finally, the Holocaust museum demonstrates the limits of American pluralism: as a government institution it is open on Yom Kippur but closed on Christmas.

Insisting on one's complete integration while feeling so insecure is a curious combination. Over time, once open sentiments were buried ever deeper to become opinions unspoken, emotions unexamined, and ideas never even formulated. Thus, while unprecedented strength and security make many individual American Jews more assertive than ever, others display the same behavior and assumptions familiar from the Europe of a century ago.

The Jewish situation was rich in paradoxes. "The Jews are schizophrenic about many things," a non-Jewish British author accurately wrote: "They desire to be an integral part of Gentile society and yet they wish to remain apart; they identify passionately with Israel and yet they are undoubtedly sincere when they profess loyalty to England; they seek out Jewish achievement wherever they can find it but are frequently resentful when anybody else does so, accusing them of antisemitism. The Jews, one sometimes feels, love to be loved but hate to be noticed."[61]

As individuals, they loved the spotlight, some glorying in being pro-vocative or subversive. But notice of their Jewish aspect made them uneasy from an old sense of inferiority and a new one of consummating a campaign whose great achievement would be to sound, act, and think precisely like the majority even on matters of Jewish concern. Nonetheless, the very mar-gin of success for individual Jews often rested on an ability to view things differently. As products of marginality, the class of assimilating Jews was equally threatened by a return to religion or emigration to a Jewish state.

An easier solution was found in identifying with humanity, which usu-ally meant simply copying their peers while displaying neutrality when their own people were involved. Given a plethora of choices where others had none made it easy to assume that normality was as undesirable as it seemed impossible. Not for them was the banality of a community to which they might belong without guilt or with pride. The team of those insisting they belonged to none was most often composed of members from the group of assimilating Jews who, while claiming independence from all groups, might still become members of the Christian, French, or proletarian club. By standing aside from the struggle as neutral observers, they professed them-selves free to play any other role in the world. Considering themselves at a higher stage of evolution than others, they possessed less; thinking they were freed from historic human behavior, they conformed to old precepts in new guises.

One might be humanitarian, patriot, citizen, free-thinking intellectual, and iconoclast, but to confront the root identity making possible that multi-plicity, character, and thought was a far more dangerous enterprise. It was a question too dangerous to confront, as asked by Philip Roth: "Why shouldn't the Gentiles have suspicions? [Someone] committed to being a Jew ... believes that on the most serious questions pertaining to man's sur-vival—understanding the past, imagining the future, discovering the rela-tion between God and humanity—that he is right and the Christians are wrong," and that Christianity's record as moral order was not so successful. Instead, difference is devalued and a "deadening 'tolerance' [silences real debate]. Instead of being taken seriously as a threat, a man is effectively silenced by being made popular."[62]

More paradoxically still, assimilation has been both a total failure and a complete success. The same forces producing death, destruction, betrayal, and a flight from true self also brought creative triumphs, professional suc-cess, and wealth for many. The assimilationists' hybrid ideas gained a re-markable hegemony in the West. The old ambiguity of freedom—as escape into a new, lesser identity or liberation to take up their original one—was increasingly inescapable. By the twentieth century's end, the Jews of Europe and America were well enough integrated to choose between a painless decline or attaining what had once seemed the most unattainable luxury of all: their own identity.

II

Nationhood, Diaspora, Galut

This people's mysterious destiny . . . always expressed itself in every one who sprang from the race, not less in those who tried to escape from that origin of theirs, as though it were a disgrace, a pain or a fairy tale that did not concern them at all, than in those who obstinately pointed back to it as though to a piece of destiny, an honor or an historical fact based on an immovable foundation.

—*Arthur Schnitzler*, The Road to the Open, *1908*

"L ET US NOT forget what we know and what we have learned across the ages but let us beware of remaining behind the times," said Max Nordau. "Let us continue to learn all the good things that progressing Europe can teach us. The Hebrew mind is broad enough for this double knowledge."[1] In effect, "double knowledge" meant a concurrent affiliation to two societies, cultures, histories—a condition behind much of the Jewish creativity and innovation of modern times. This was the opposite of being an alienated outsider who belonged to no community, and different from an assimilation that demanded the abandonment of one group for the other.

To become whole again, individuals had to face their personal and familial pasts. "Self-understanding is man's highest requirement," wrote Isaiah Berlin. "To prosper spiritually," Lionel Abel's father told him, "Jews need the Jews." Lewisohn asked how one could "be a true and great poet if he begins by denying what is truest and greatest in himself as a man?"[2] "If you do not let your son grow up a Jew," Freud told a patient, "you will deprive him of those sources of energy which cannot be replaced by anything else." The added struggles Jews faced demanded extra strength but also bred it. Freud found in himself "many obscure emotional forces, which were the more powerful the less they could be expressed in words, [giving] a clear consciousness of inner identity [and, with other Jews] the safe privacy of a common mental construction."[3]

Whichever orientation Jews chose, the resulting personal exploration and struggle over self-definition begat intellectual creativity. Whether inner battles led one to denial or to affirmation, their very existence was a spur to innovation. Ignorance of those forces predating one's birth but shaping one's life intensified a sense of discontent; angry rejection was often a symptom of yearning for a place or belief of one's own. Those fleeing the familiar became lost or debilitated among strange surroundings.

The assimilation era ran from the late eighteenth to the end of the twentieth century. Through this phase, the Jews evolved from an autonomous community whose culture was filtered through religion into a national community equally or more influenced by ethnicity. As the theologian Mordecai Kaplan wrote, the defining issue was no longer "the authoritative character of the Bible and the Talmud but ... the will of the Jews to live as a people ... not how to maintain the infallibility of a tradition but how to save our people from dissolution."[4] Herzl expressed this answer to the historical riddle of the Jews as, "We are a people—one people," who would be modern but on their own terms.

During this period of upheaval and change, individual Jews denied or struggled with their sense of community, nationhood, peoplehood, and connection to the land of Israel. Setbacks temporarily intensified skepticism about the possibility of assimilation but made many Jews determined to struggle harder to succeed. Many left the fold altogether or were on the verge of doing so, unable to bear contempt and persecution or unwilling to withstand the dominant system's alluring promise of more freedom, prosperity, and knowledge. Of those staying inside the besieged fortress, some heightened the walls of religious observance to keep modernity at bay; others passed through the fire of self-doubt to achieve a proud, national self-image.

The climax of the assimilation era began with the Shoah, casting doubt on assimilation's viability; Israel's creation, offering an alternative; and antisemitism's decline, which made a voluntary Jewish disappearance or maintaining an identity easier. Although Western societies no longer demanded that Jews conceal or abandon their identity, many were still doing so. Their ranks had declined through murder and assimilation from 16.6 million in 1900 to 12.8 million in 1991. But even without persecution, the trend continued: in Britain from 450,000 in 1951 to 300,000 in 1991; in Argentina from 310,000 in 1960 to 213,000 in 1991; in the USSR from 2.2 million in 1959 to 1.8 million in 1979, before the main wave of emigration.[5] Even in America, there were only barely more Jews in 1994 than in 1918.

A large community would continue to exist in the United States and medium-size ones in France, Russia, Ukraine, Canada, Britain, and Argentina, but the rate of defection climbs higher. Of the 52 percent of American Jews intermarrying, fewer than 5 percent of their spouses converted and only 10 percent of their children would marry Jews. As an American Jewish activist put it, "Diaspora Jewry came through 1,800 years of persecution and deprivation and remained morally and spiritually intact. Now, with freedom, affluence, and social acceptance—circumstances that should enable people to thrive—Jewish identity is crumbling."[6]

Only in Israel did the Jewish population grow. Professor Daniel Elazar pointed out that there were ten times more Jews in the United States than in Israel in 1948; in 1990, the figure was 1.5 and falling. The day is in sight when Israel will be the largest single community of Jews in the world and, beyond that, Israeli Jews would become the majority—according to Professor Sergio DellaPergola, a leading Jewish demographer—in the year 2002.[7] Perhaps half of the remaining Jews in the diaspora would eventually walk away due to disinterest or defect as a result of intermarriage.

To some extent, Jewish assimilationist dilemmas prefigured the spirit of an age where humanity increasingly saw itself as a purposeless accident, doubted loyalty to community, and rejected historic tradition. The Jews' experience in deciding to abandon or revise their tradition, to affirm or abandon their own identity, and to what extent they would imitate others has been a prototype first for Western and later for Third World intellectuals and groups.

Faith in humanity and ideology had not fared so well, nor was it so evident that modern doctrine produced the most happy and stable people or the best society. Those who fled old beliefs sometimes found worse ones or discovered that being free from everything might mean possessing nothing. "In America," wrote historian Henry Feingold, "it becomes more clear daily that not all people are capable of such internalization of controls. As the extrinsic controls of government, family, church, school and the various socialization agencies are removed in the name of freedom and individualism, the index of social chaos rises. Having lost church, tribe, and family, modern man becomes his own lonely tribal chieftain and does for himself what used to be done in the context of community."[8]

But there are countertrends, too. After all, if life is so meaningless, why does Woody Allen make so many films? The twenty-first century seems still an early phase of the age of nationalism, nor does religion seem so close to extinction as it once appeared. Moreover, while it had once seemed impossible, many Jews are now assimilated enough to be fully part of the societies where they live while maintaining a sense of ethnic autonomy as well.

Those who wished to find a solution in total assimilation will do so, since being a Jew is one of the few "victim" situations—in contrast to race and gender—capable of being shed. Many Jews in Europe and America will so act. Some may view Jews sentimentally as among their ancestors; far fewer will number them among their descendants.[9] The history of assimilation itself has provided, however, some compelling arguments against the solution of total assimilation at a time when it is easier but also far less necessary:

—Total assimilation diminishes the individual. Departing from a communal or religious identity as a Jew imposes a new worldview not quite corresponding with one's life experience or psyche, like wearing a suit of clothes that do not quite fit and—despite the tailor's insistence—make one feel that something is very out of place. To ignore the unique factors shaping one's standpoint is intellectually and psychologically impoverishing. Lingering qualities, loyalties, attitudes, and sentiments restrain complete assimilation even when the individual is unaware of them or they seem otherwise irrational. To abandon these qualities is to deny part of one's own worth, to excise part of one's own being, sacrificing whole realms of possibility and denying them to descendants.

—Equally, total assimilation means the extinction of a type of individual whose worldview and standpoint has shown extraordinary social and intellectual worth. Cultural achievement may come from self-vexation, like the grit causing oysters to produce pearls. Yet, to extend the analogy, a perfectly assimilated oyster is fallow. After an explosive, exciting breakthrough into a new culture, creativity declines if assimilation is so successful that Jews merely imitate the mainstream. "Once the drama of assimilation is over (or, rather, where it is over)," wrote Zygmunt Bauman, "so is the story of a uniquely creative and original Jewish cultural role."[10] Assimilation, though, not only entailed its own demise but also offered another outcome: If individuals learn to play multiple roles so successfully, they can preserve more than one identity.

—However cloaked as altruistic or universalist, total assimilation is a desertion of comrades for basically selfish interests. The Russian Jewish intellectual Peretz Smolenskin decided not to abandon being a Jew since, "For four thousand years, we have been brothers and children of one people; how can I sin against hundreds of generations and betray this brotherhood?"[11] Albert Memmi explained, "In abandoning the group he labels it as unlivable and unredeemable. Worse still, by effectively depriving it of his own participation, he contributes to its approaching death and accelerates it," shaming, demoralizing, and impoverishing those remaining.[12] It is like, to use a Talmudic parable, a boat passenger drilling a hole who rejects protests by saying he is only digging under his own seat.

—Rejection of Jewish peoplehood for another ideology, nation, or religion does not denote progress but a descent in moral and historical consciousness. To throw away an identity containing so much worldly wisdom and ethical guidance—a link to so much of time and the globe—in exchange for conclusions formed not so much by timeless reason but from the immediate fashion and limited view of a single place at one narrow point in history, is a questionable judgment. Many good things can be said of American culture's variety, innovation, and mass appeal. But its most unattractive aspects were those augmented in individuals as they lost any Jewish consciousness: antiintellectualism, rootlessness, amoral commercialism, confusion of quantity with quality, provincialism, and triviality. Like Kafka and Disraeli, Tony Kushner, in his acclaimed play *Angels in America,* wanted to see angels break through into a banal world. The work takes its title from his line: "There are no angels in America, no spiritual past, no racial past."[13] Jews, however, do possess such a past and an alternative intellectual universe extending before and beyond America.

Western society offered huge incentives for suppressing this extra dimension. "Either the Jewish artist respects his tradition and then resigns himself to the role of a minor artist," wrote Memmi, or "liberates himself from it to become a true artist, but to do so he must renounce being a Jewish artist."[14] It was easy to reject being restricted to a small, mediocre stage. But in America, this choice is no longer necessary. Moreover, whether assimilating Jews followed inspiration or commercial forces, they brought with them some imagery, ideas, and experiences from their background. Equally, they still operated in an assimilationist situation that had a big effect on their choices among roles and priorities, subject matter, and cultural references.

Factors like these kept alive some sense of a divided identity, always making possible enormous changes at the very last moment of assimilation. The very success of the process heightened the likelihood that it would be transcended. As the scholar Robert Alter explained, "The more we become like other Americans, the more we want also to be reassured of our positive self-validating difference."[15] This is one reason why obituaries of Jewish disappearance in America have been premature. President John Adams predicted in 1819 that Jews might all "become liberal Unitarian Christians." In 1872 a young American Jew declared that in less than fifty years Jews would disappear. In 1964, *Look* magazine devoted an issue to the "Vanishing American Jew."[16]

But such predictions did prove accurate for many individuals and families, especially if Jewish identity had nothing positive to offer them. The heartfelt issues for American Jews—the Shoah, fear for Israel's survival, antisemitism—were defensive and displaced feelings to distant times and lands. Equating Jewishness with precariousness, affliction, suffering, and alienation made it extremely unattractive. The most enduring form of victimization is an obsession with defining oneself as a victim. In that situation, abandonment of the persecuted group becomes the ideal solution, recalling Lewisohn's ironic remark: "When the man is dead, his troubles are over."[17] If Jews exist merely as victims or assimilators they—like fireworks—are visible only just before they flame out.

Similarly, the popular assimilationist concept that alienation freed the mind to discover truth most often meant, in effect, yielding to another set of rules, either that of the assimilating caste itself or the majority culture's overwhelming power. Against the latter force, a vacuum of identity cannot persist, at least not more than a generation. Human life and psychology create a need for belonging in a world where the vast majority of people already have a decided standpoint. Consequently, those harshly judging Jewish identity often accepted in other doctrines precisely what they had rejected in it—self-discipline, faith, ritual, group loyalty—ignoring shortcomings and contradictions to which they had formerly been so sensitive.

The last remnant of Jewish consciousness was often a reflexive defensiveness and a recitation of past persecutions akin to saying, I am hated, therefore I am, as if only a desperate effort to prove the club refuses to accept one justifies staying outside it. The same holds true for assimilation's innately other-oriented approach, where one's self-definition rests on what non-Jews would accept, standards set by the wider society and the need to please it. This stance is obsolete in places where antisemitism is minimal, barely touching people's lives. The real challenge is to use freedom creatively, not to choose between trembling or confrontation.

The ethos that Jews did so much to create made it a sign of sophistication to criticize and transcend the interests of one's natal group. Jews had more practice than any other group in detaching preference from judgment, personal opinion from professional evaluation. But each of them still had something to prove: the journalist, fairness; the scholar, objectivity; the politician or official, that he put his country's interests first. In itself, this is quite proper. Yet it often required a new type of bias: bending over backward to prove that one is standing up straight. What was virtuous for others—self-assertion and love of one's own people—seemed dangerous for Jews. To defend one's own—even to have one's own—made one appear narrow and biased.

As a result of all these factors, the Jewish component in the thought of most Western intellectuals was declining. Those supposed to ask questions became the very ones for whom certain queries were off limits or even ceased to exist. "Most Jews," Scholem wrote, "lacked discrimination in all matters affecting themselves, yet in all other matters they mustered that faculty for reasoning, criticism, and vision which others have justifiably admired or criticized in them."[18] Geniuses bragged of ignorance about their own past, which they thought held nothing of value since a full vessel one has not peered into can easily seem to be empty. Knowing nothing, they assumed there was nothing to know; abandoning the inquisitiveness, they would focus on any other subject, wishing to remain ignorant precisely because to explore the relevance and effect of their Jewish inheritance was the only knowledge in the universe that threatened their self-image.

Of course, the enshrinement of ideas in tradition did not make them correct, coming as they did from a less enlightened or scientifically learned era. But, equally, the past's people were not fools. They found solutions for recurring problems of life based on cumulative wisdom evolved over centuries and generations. The value of religion, identity, and tradition rests not only on any theological accuracy they may have about the universe, but also in their ability to act as guides for living. What is dressed up as God's arbitrary command may be an effective way to maintain a people's cohesion and ethics. Spinoza compared that heritage to a ladder one has climbed up and does not then kick away. To jettison previous experience dooms each generation to recapitulate mistakes.

Human reason can disprove timeless claims and cancel customs. Yet it is equally remarkable how quickly and totally the best peoples' finest thinking becomes dated, how what appears so objective and obvious may soon be quaint or obsolete. The latest fad's supposedly manifest wisdom lasts only a season; apparently logical systems produce the irrationalities of communism, fascism, and many shorter-lived cults. "The mind is always a hero to its own generation and usually a clown to the [next one]," wrote Hecht. "It is well to remember that we are in the midst of a constant yesterday of folly."[19]

Humans most differ from animals in being able to test and refine systems of thought over many generations. Just as individual sensibility and judgment need the freedom to meet changing times, they also require grounding in a broader foundation to balance a person's limited experience and lifetime with some collective wisdom and perception. The thinking person most of all needs to reach toward places where one's lone thought falters, not only in pondering the cosmos but also in comprehending the broader reaches of history and human nature.[20]

Nordau came to see "the religious sentiment [as] rooted in the desire for knowledge, the need for an ideal, and the yearning for triumph over death."[21] As a child, he had been disillusioned on realizing that his father had lied in warning him not to look at those giving the priestly blessing lest he be blinded. Such episodes shaped the lives of many but were beside the point: a religion's most ludicrous excess or distortion need not reveal its essence. Superstitions always cling to symbols and real people require systematic rules as well as abstract philosophies. Even if religion was a crutch, taking it away did not necessarily let humanity stand unsupported.

Aside from religious observance, however, Jewish history and philosophy offered a worldview and ethical system equal to or greater than that of any other nation. But since it saw life, as Philip Roth wrote, as "boundaries and restrictions," intellectuals were often torn by these fetters. Roth's character Portnoy was both a sex-crazed hedonist and "the nicest little Jewish boy who ever lived": grateful to his parents, loyal to his people, devoted to justice and the downtrodden.[22] The title of Roth's trilogy, *Zuckerman Bound*, recalls both Prometheus' punishment for purveying enlightenment and Isaac's voluntary decision to let his father truss him for sacrifice.

The allergy of many secular Jewish intellectuals to explicitly Jewish concepts, defined as religious and irrelevant, did not stop them from employing ideas from other faiths. Everywhere religion was secularized into national cultures. Having fought to incorporate Jews as individuals, they were willing to restrict Jewish thought or identity to a ghetto, though it might flourish in that confined corner. Despite their use of Christian texts, Isaiah Berlin, Hannah Arendt, or Allan Bloom virtually ignored Jewish tradition or thought in studying philosophy.[23] If one can employ Greek myths or philosophy without believing in Zeus, then the Jewish tradition—and the assimilating Jewish subculture, addressed in that framework—can also be a source of ideas, images, and worldview.

Using a tradition comprised largely of religious texts for nonreligious purposes is far simpler than it appears since Judaism is so largely moral precept, social philosophy, and historical commemoration. Its works are as literary and humanist as Homer, Chaucer, or Dante, themselves infused with religion. Mention of "God" need not render irrelevant for all other purposes everything happening to Jews before, say, 1880, nor did its omission make non-Jewish the achievements of semi-assimilated Jews after 1780.

Orthodox traditionalists still doubted there could be any Jewish culture outside full observance of ritual. But for many Jews, faith—at least in its ancestral form—was no longer an alternative to assimilation. More responded to a Jewish nationalism drawing heavily—though often critically—on a blending of tradition and modern thought, and which dealt with the actual lives of contemporary Jews rather than just tenth century B.C.E. ones. The disintegration of Jewish society created a need for new ideas and institutions to take the place of what had once been unquestionably obeyed as God's word. "The Jewish tradition is for me an infinite well out of which I draw what I need," wrote Israeli professor Yosef Yerushalmi. "What we seek is not authority, what we seek is sustenance."[24]

Consequently, Jewish identity had transcended religion without necessarily abandoning it, and its great modern spiritual achievements occurred outside the theological domain. Kafka and others were only incidentally universal, depicting feelings other people might undergo, but these were experiences that Jews did actually endure. Whatever their stand on assimilation, these intellectuals shared a set of ideas, experiences, references, and attitudes. Together they produced a semi-independent culture equal to any in the world, even if many of its contributors vanished personally as Jews while leaving this legacy.

In Israel, both tradition and that modern heritage achieved a revitalizing reinterpretation that is still in its early stages. The secular Zionist leader Beryl Katznelson observed the fast that mourned the Temple's fall for national reasons, did not eat pork because Jews had died rather than do so, urged that public institutions be kosher and that kibbutzim observe the Sabbath. "A generation that is innovating, creating, does not toss the legacy of the generations onto the garbage heap. It tests and distills, rejects and embraces, sometimes seizes an existing tradition and embellishes it, sometimes even . . . digs out a forsaken piece and cleans it of rust, reviving an ancient tradition that can nourish the spirit of innovating generation." "Everyone in Israel observes Jewish holidays," wrote the poet Gershom Gorenberg. "Some people observe them by going to the beach." It is just as important knowing "what religion you don't keep and whose God you don't pray to [as] millions of Americans without a hint of Jesus in their hearts will make a similar statement when they decorate trees, buy gifts, and stay away from church on Christmas."[25]

In this regard, knowledge may be more important than gestures and is what those who are semi-assimilated can put in place of ritual. A nineteenth-century rabbi asked a Jew he saw smoking on the Sabbath, "Do you know that today is Shabbat?" "Yes," the man replied. "And are you aware that Jews are enjoined not to smoke on Shabbat?" The man nodded. "Blessed art thou, Lord," proclaimed the rabbi, "whose children do not lie." Just as Jews at Passover must act as if they were the generation of the exodus from Egypt, they can recall a tradition left behind but which still has a visceral, sustaining sense of their own culture, history, and people. Philip Roth offered a formula to this effect: Whatever Jews learned anew, "You must not forget anything."[26]

Kafka composed a complementary tale. A man seeking to learn the law is stopped at the gate by a doorkeeper who warns him that this is a long, difficult journey. Daunted, he waits many years, not daring to continue. Finally, near death, he asks why no one else came to that door during all those years. The guard explains that this path was meant for him alone and now the door would be closed forever.[27] Kafka was probably unaware that Rabbi Isaac Luria, a millennium and a half earlier, said that each of Israel's tribes had its own gate to the Temple and that every Israelite had to find his own path, though it be to the same goal.

In modern times, only voluntary choice could sustain a vision that could no longer be imposed. Still, the community's continuing solidarity across so many borders gave ample evidence of its national basis. "Who says we are not a people? Someone who doesn't know his Jews," wrote Lewisohn. "Everywhere the same characters, problems, reactions, dreams, fears, aspirations—extraordinary unity within this rich and often staggering diversity."[28] That relationship did not cut Jews off from links with neighbors and humanity at large. "Internationalism," said Isaiah Berlin, "is a movement not to abolish, but to unite, nations."[29]

Herzl's very success as a thoroughly modern European let him discover in Zionism a remedy for his own as well as the Jews' needs. His material life, income, and career were all satisfactory. The deficiency he felt was on a spiritual level.[30] Provoked by inner choice or outer pressure, many Jews would recapitulate this experience to find that what began as a reaction to oppression or a means for philanthropy became intensely fulfilling in itself. Hess expressed this spirit well: "After twenty years of alienation, in the midst of my own people, participating in its feast of joys and days of mourning, in its memories and in its hopes. . . . An idea which I thought I had stifled forever in my breast, reappears living before me: the idea of my own nationality."[31]

Zionism was intended as a solution for those wishing to live in a Jewish state. But it also gave the majority remaining outside a way to gain new courage and pride by living evidence that theirs was not a fragmented, declining, inferior, doomed people. Thus, the concept of peoplehood could reinforce the adaptations of religion and culture by those who were semi-assimilated. If Jews continued to feel the solidarity with that center sustained over so many centuries of exile, wrote Hess, and made easier to preserve given improved transport and communication, it mattered far less whether they physically lived in Israel.[32]

Ahad Ha-Am prophesied that a Jewish state's very existence would give those remaining "in exile" a new basis for prestige, energy, and idealism.[33] Alfred Mond, whose family history proved this principle, wrote in the 1930s: "The dignity and importance of our whole race will be enhanced by the existence of a national home where those of our people who have been compelled to live under less favorable conditions than we enjoy will be able to establish themselves on the soil of their ancestors."[34]

Israel re-created the basis for Jewish identity that had existed before the age of assimilation—a concentration of people, an institutionalized role for Judaism, and self-rule—adding to this political sovereignty for the first time in over two thousand years. That country's 1948 creation and 1967 victory inspired an upsurge of Jewish activism and identity throughout the world but also presented Jews remaining elsewhere with new dilemmas. If living in Israel was the highest expression of Jewish identity, what was their rationale for not being there? Even such a hitherto hostile Marxist as Henry Roth exclaimed on the latter occasion, "Sympathy flared up in the face of doctrine. . . . A miracle! The pall lifted that had so long encompassed him. . . . Here was a people reborn—*his* people—regenerated by their own will. Was he mad not to share in that regeneration?"[35]

Of course, people were tied to professions, families, and societies into which they were partly assimilated. Yet practical considerations did not altogether suffice to answer an existential question. In psychological terms, it became imperative to argue for the diaspora's superiority. Koestler resolved the contradiction for himself in 1948 by arguing that a Jewish state's establishment also enabled a guilt-free full assimilation, "with an occasional friendly glance back and a helpful gesture [while joining fully] the nation whose life and culture they share, without reservation or split loyalties." He ended the call for a liberating disappearance with a hint—including Christian imagery—that it was a final act of surrender: "The fumes of the death chambers still linger over Europe; there must be an end to every calvary."[36]

While Jews overwhelmingly supported Israel, they reacted in ways as diverse as the Seder's four children: reflexively loyal or hostile; well-informed or ignorant. Their responses reflected the character of assimilation as much or more than any event in the Middle East. "What the Israeli does or thinks has no impact on Israel-Diaspora relations," said Professor Charles Liebman. "The American Jew plays out his relations with Israel in his own mind. It has very little to do with Israel."[37] Israel was abstracted to keep it at a distance, to ward off any implications for one's own life, to protect the compromises worked out in the assimilation process. For example, American Jews considering Israel too dangerous to visit often lived near high-crime zones. But these were "their" risky areas and, if they were harmed, at least it would not be as Jews. Less than 20 percent of American Jews ever went to Israel in part because—unlike travel to London, Paris, Rome, or Beijing—this journey compelled an encounter with themselves, a potential threat to one's self-image unlike any other destination.

Moreover, Jewish nationalism itself challenged assimilation's most cherished ideas. To argue that "we ought to endeavor to strive toward a higher stage, one in which national differences have disappeared," Herzl noted, was an understandable standpoint but not a realistic one. Still, as long as "all our contemporaries actively espouse nationalism to our detriment, it would be foolish of us to reject this idea which could afford us protection."

Assimilating Jews could respond, though, that rejecting that idea gave them more protection. Claiming to belong totally to the state where they lived and the people among whom they dwelt encouraged distancing themselves from any concept that Jews were a people. As Agnon described this point, when the gentiles heard that Jews would be a nation, "They would say: 'If so, what do you want here? Be off with you and go to your own country.' "[38] Nationalism, having so often oppressed or excluded them, seemed scary even if it was their own. They had so long demanded the separation of church and state and insisted that ethnic distinctions be ignored as to be equally leery of Jewish self-assertion.

Koestler's view of Israel's new Jews asserted the diaspora's superiority: "Their parents were the most cosmopolitan race of the earth—they are provincial and chauvinistic. Their parents were sensitive bundles of nerves in awkward bodies—their nerves are whip-cords and their bodies those of a horde of Hebrew Tarzans. . . . Their parents were intense, intent, over-strung, overspiced—they are tasteless, spiceless, unleavened and tough. . . . In other words, they have ceased to be Jews and become Hebrew peasants." This might, he mused, cure the diseases of exile and "the racial inferiority complex," but at too high a cost.[39]

Agnon had a different judgment on that society's first stage, in which the pragmatism of construction had to displace exile's abstract intellectuality. The diaspora's productive tension was lost but a future was being created that Jews might themselves inherit. "My generation are men of thought, while they are men of deeds," he wrote in the 1930s. "It is like an architect who asked for stone and they gave him brick; for he intended to build a temple, while they intended to build themselves a house to live in." Joining a new society and "normal" community of Jews brought its own problems of survival and adjustment but resolved those of assimilation. If one lived, "In his own land, with his own people . . . who shared many of his qualities and many of whose qualities he shared, he felt that he no longer needed to strain to be like others, for he simply was like them," Agnon wrote. "Spiritual functions are very much like physical functions. A man who is thirsty to the point of madness finds water and drinks it, and his thirst is gone."[40]

In glorifying the intellectual value of that thirst, Koestler forgot that relatively few Jews in Europe had been intellectuals. Most of their parents were poor village people on a par with the immigrants to America, not the university graduate professionals of two generations later. Koestler disliked these new Jews both as being different from him and because he felt they represented a retreat from his image of Jews resting on the idea that security and creativeness were in conflict, while there was a link between persecution or alienation and spiritual or cultural achievement.

Koestler acknowledged, though, that in his day the alternative was murder; "the stink and filth and claustrophobia of the ghetto; the deterioration of the hereditary substance through the survival of the nimblest, the crookedest, into its final product, the flat-footed, shifty-eyed eternal tramp."[41] He frankly faced this trade-off as the price of creativity: In Buchenwald, Jews were being tortured. "Who would not swap all the formulae of Einstein" to save a single one? "But who, having completed the transaction, would rejoice about it?"[42] Yet people do not exist to be sacrifices for their intellectuals and artists. Einstein himself rejected Koestler's line of argument, "The best in a man can be brought out only when he belongs entirely to a human group. [A Jew] who has lost contact with his own national group and is regarded as an alien by the group among which he lives [often ends in] joyless egotism."[43]

Indeed, their situation had given assimilating Jews a sense of insecurity, dependence, and perennial struggle that remained a large element of whatever Jewish identity they possessed. No matter how mighty they felt as Americans or proud they were of Israel's achievements, Jewishness was associated with vulnerability. Since assimilation depended on an ability to please neighbors, they were obsessed with Israel's image, often deeming criticism of it to border on antisemitism while fervently hoping that country would do nothing to anger their own rulers or damage their own status.

Doubt that Jews were a people, derived from many decades of the assimilation process, made the implications of a Jewish state seem something of a mystery even to its assimilating supporters. In practice, Israel was most easily considered a refuge for Jews fleeing oppression in far-off lands. American Jews easily grasped this in the familiar form of helping endangered or impoverished communities. Flourishing as individuals in a multicultural society, they preferred that milieu. The psychology of assimilation made high concentrations of Jews simultaneously exciting and subliminally distasteful to them.[44] While assimilating Jews could easily reject the deeds of a society and government partly alien to themselves—taking advantage of their psychic duality—Israel's acts, or even existence, might seem to implicate them involuntarily in far more responsibility. Disassociation or—more commonly—a lack of interest in practice despite enthusiasm in theory showed one's successful assimilation and willingness to apply universally principles prized by intellectuals.

This American Jewish stance toward Israel, then, combined a willingness to cede it primacy while keeping some distance. Zev Chafets, an

American immigrant to Israel, tried to provoke Morris Abram, head of the U.S. Conference of Presidents of Major Jewish Organizations, by insisting that Israelis were like a team on the field, actually making Jewish history, while American Jews were merely spectators. Accepting this role, Abram agreed that American Jews were indeed watching and cheering. Similarly, an otherwise-cynical American Jewish intellectual could express awe even at being in an Israeli air force base's bathroom where pilots washed their hands before flying missions, and the next day tell Israeli leaders that he was quickly leaving because he did not want to be there when the 1991 Gulf War began, concluding, "I guess you don't have a choice."

"We do have a choice," replied an Israeli official. "We just happen to like it here."

Assimilating Jews had to develop a rationale for choosing not to be there. During over eighteen hundred years when Jews rarely physically returned to the land, they viewed themselves as in involuntary geographic exile. "Through a historical catastrophe—the destruction of Jerusalem by the Emperor of Rome," Agnon said in accepting the Nobel Prize, he was born abroad. "But I always deemed myself as one who was really born in Jerusalem."[45]

Now, however, this became a voluntary exile. *Diaspora* is a loaded term, a Greek word merely noting the fact of dispersion, in contrast to the Hebrew word *galut*, indicating exile from the land of Israel. It was easy to justify defining one's home in terms of staying at home by citing Israel's uncertain future and shortcomings, the diaspora's creativity, and America as a promised land. Philip Roth has an Israeli character in *The Counterlife* say, "In the Diaspora a Jew like you lives securely while we are living just the kind of imperiled Jewish existence that we came here to replace.... We are the excitable, ghettoized, jittery little Jews of the Diaspora, and you the Jews with all the confidence and cultivation that comes of feeling at home where you are."

These ideas were self-justifications for assimilating Jews who did not feel like exiles at all but as full residents in the civilization forming them. Still, they tended to express their "confidence and cultivation" in their character's "non-Jewish" side. Further, the America they inhabited was often a Jewish assimilationist variation. "The only life I can love, or hate is ... this American life of the twentieth century," said the novelist Saul Bellow, "the life of Americans who are also Jews." Bellow wrote that he was told, "Only as a Jew in Israel ... could I enter history again and prove the necessity and authenticity of my existence." But to do so, he continued, would actually invalidate his existence, "would wipe out me totally."[46]

Henry Roth felt "like a foreigner" in Israel yet almost equally alienated in America. "Here the land is not ours," he wrote about life in a trailer. "The dwelling is, but the space isn't."[47] Philip Roth's Portnoy found both shiksa girlfriend and Israelis adjusted because they had a clear identity while he did not. An Israeli woman told him, "The way you disapprove of your life! . . . Everything is ironical, or self-deprecating." He replies, "Self-deprecation is, after all, a classic form of Jewish humor." "Not Jewish humor! No! Ghetto humor," she answers. "Yes," Portnoy concludes, "I am a patriot too . . . only in another place! (Where I also don't feel at home!)"[48]

For those partly assimilated, to be at home was, in a sense, never to be at home but atop a high-wire of anxiety and marginalism; restless, insatiable alienation; rage, skepticism, and moralism infused with passion. Adrienne Rich evoked this situation in poetry: "By no means native, yet somewhat in love/With things a native is enamored of—/ Except the sense of being held and owned/By one ancestral patch of local ground." Yet the "ancestral patch" rejected was as much that of one's own ancestors as the one belonging to those who were truly, unselfconsciously, native.

Nevertheless, the high degree of success and security that Europe and America offered Jews in the late twentieth century was not merely attractive, it was phenomenal. In the United States, one-third of the billionaires, one-quarter of the multimillionaires, and between one-third and one-half of the elite professionals in law, journalism, medicine, and academia were Jews. They occupied the heights of almost every lucrative, glamorous, and creative field, enjoying the multiplier effect of having a huge audience in the world's most powerful country. Moreover, despite the fact that Jews were far more powerful and visible than in pre-1939 Europe, antisemitism was at very low levels.[49]

Still, the bottom line in philosophical and psychological terms remained the same as in earlier decades. The problems of their status as Jews—standing to some degree outside the society's mainstream—appeared inextricably entwined with the advantages that situation offered. The greatest of all the ironies of assimilation was that its participants' security was based on their insecurity, their centrality on marginality, their success drive on an inner unease, their complete triumph on a sense of incompleteness. When a friend warned Koestler that his method meant always remaining "a runaway and a fugitive," Koestler responded that if being alienated and insecure was inescapable, "It was just as well to know it and to accept it."⁵⁰

Many embraced such a fate. Even Groucho Marx's famous refusal to belong to any club that would have him was actually uttered in rebuffing a Jewish club that wanted him, not—as is commonly thought—a gentile one that didn't. What seemed a paradigm of independence from all groups was merely the denial of one's own and entrance into another. With membership so effortless, there seemed no good reason not to join completely; social tolerance eroded that old in-between status, making possible a unique assimilating Jewish culture and consciousness, a fact unchanged by some Jews trying to be so provocative as to re-create that atmosphere.

Jewish life was clearly not sustainable only in Israel but was unsustainable without it, generally more diluted and fragile outside it. New generations came who knew not shtetl, immigration, or Shoah. A more secure, prosperous Israel, the end of its long conflict with Arab neighbors in sight, was no longer an object for their protection or charity. Equally, formerly oppressed Jews had mostly emigrated to Israel or America, while antisemitism became too minimal to inspire fear or defiance. Some new basis for galut or diaspora Jewish life had to be found if it was going to endure.

Antisemitism's rout and the acquisition of equality—like an individual's achievement of basic subsistence—raises the question of what comes next, making it all the more pressing, as Philip Roth wrote, to find "a Jewish self-consciousness that is relevant to this time and place, where neither defamation nor persecution are what they were elsewhere in the past."⁵¹ But the new situation opened the door to total assimilation, against which there was little real defense outside of Zionism or religion. Confident of being fully American, unfamiliar with oppression or exclusion, Jews might discover that worldly advantage intensifies a need for spiritual fulfillment and psychological equilibrium.

There were two basic choices facing Jews in America and elsewhere: the paths offered by Heine or Hess; Lippman or Brandeis; Koestler or Herzl. They were no longer pariahs or recent arrivals, having to show they were loyal, altruistic, or identical to non-Jewish neighbors. Nor did they have to prove their apartness through cultural iconoclasm or political rebelliousness. They felt at ease and fully part of the society where they lived. At last they could afford to develop their duality or discard it.

The most common choice would be full integration into the majority society via intermarriage or gradual estrangement until—like the child in the Seder paradigm—forgetting that other answers even existed. Restoring a wholly Jewish national identity by immigration to Israel would be the rarest outcome. The challenge for those remaining would be to achieve a stable, permanent partial assimilation through some mix of ethnic identity—looking back to eastern Europe and across the ocean to Israel—and religious commitment. A network of Jewish groups, programs, and schools worked toward this goal of assuring Jews the right to be treated like everyone else without having to be like everyone else. It was still an open question, however, whether this balance could be sustained or whether it would inevitably slip away for a substantial portion of each subsequent generation.

As most Jews became normalized citizens of a Jewish state, non-Jewish citizens of other societies, or find some stable level of semi-integration, the assimilation era reaches its climax. The ideas absorbed in that process have made possible the Jewish people's revitalization in the twentieth century, yet its logical culmination will extinguish both that creative duality and Jewish identity among millions of people.

In this new situation, it is minimally necessary to understand the history of assimilation, the existence of choice, and an array of options offered by various blends between assimilation and Jewish identity. Those who do not fully accept the religion, tradition, and history into which they were born have all the more need to know them as a starting point from which to explore. At the same time, it is often precisely at the final moment before total immersion when one discovers what is about to be lost. Having given the world a great civilization does not mean that Jews should not also keep it for themselves.

NOTES

1. THE HOUSE OF BONDAGE: 1789–1897

1. Solomon Liptzin, *Germany's Stepchildren* (Freeport, NY, 1971), pp. 17–25.
2. Ahad Ha-Am was the pen name of Asher Ginzberg. Lewis S. Feuer, "The Sociobiological Theory of Jewish Intellectual Achievement: A Sociological Critique," in Joseph Maier and Chaim Waxman, *Ethnicity, Identity and History* (New Brunswick, NJ, 1983), p. 102; Ahad Ha-Am, *Selected Essays* (New York, 1962), pp. 198–99.
3. "What does it matter to us," wrote a French lawyer on the eve of that revolt, "what our fathers have done or how and why they have done it?" Simon Schama, *Citizens* (New York, 1989), pp. 299–300.
4. Ahad Ha-Am, op. cit., pp. 179–84, 198–99. A half-millennium earlier, after the terrible pogroms of 1391, when many Spanish Jews accepted conversion to Christianity rather than death, Solomon Alami attributed it to the widespread tendency to imitate gentile culture: "If a man should not be able to live by his faith, why should he suffer death for it and endure the joke and the shame of dispersion among the nations?" Jane Gerber, *The Jews of Spain* (New York, 1992), pp. 116–17.
5. Herzl, *Zionist Writings*, vol. 2.
6. Paul Mendes-Flohr and Jehuda Reinharz, *The Jew in the Modern World* (New York, 1980), p. 315; Ha-Am, op. cit., p. 272.
7. Eliezer Schach, the senior anti-Zionist, ultra-Orthodox rabbi in Israel, confirmed this point, saying, "[Orthodox] Jews used to be Zionists" but rejected the Enlightenment view that "it is possible to be Jewish without religion, that Israel is a nation like the rest of the world." *Jerusalem Post,* June 1, 1993. In short, religion was the nation's basis but not its sole quality.

8. Numbers 23:9; Exodus 19:6. Biblical quotations are taken from *Tanakh*, Jewish Publication Society (New York, 1985).

9. Deuteronomy 6:14–15. See also Exodus 23:24; Leviticus 20:1–5 and 26.

10. "And thou shall speak it diligently. . . . The Lord said of Abraham, For I have singled him out, that he may instruct his children and his posterity to keep the way of the Lord by doing what is just and right." Genesis 18:19.

11. Abraham Halkin, "The Judeo-Islamic Age," in Salo Baron, *Great Ages and Ideas of the Jewish People* (New York, 1956), pp. 236–37.

12. Genesis 41:50–52, 42:21–24. Louis Ginzberg, *The Legends of the Jews,* vol. 2 (Philadelphia, 1988), p. 72.

13. "A new king arose over Egypt who did not know Joseph. And he said to his people, 'Look the Israelite people are much too numerous for us. Let us deal shrewdly with them, so that they may not increase; otherwise in the event of war they may join our enemies in fighting against us,' and gain ascendancy over the country." Exodus 1:8–11.

14. Exodus 2:11–15.

15. "As Pharaoh drew near, the Israelites caught sight of the Egyptians advancing upon them. Greatly frightened . . . they said to Moses, 'Was it for want of graves in Egypt that you brought us to die in the wilderness? What have you done to us, taking us out of Egypt? . . . Let us be, and we will serve the Egyptians, for it is better for us to serve the Egyptians than to die in the wilderness.' " Exodus 14:10–12. See also Exodus 17:3; Numbers 14:1–4.

16. Numbers 25.

17. Exodus 22:20, 23:9; Leviticus 19:33–34. Miriam was even punished by God with temporary leprosy for criticizing her brother Moses for marrying a Cushite woman, Numbers 12.

18. Genesis 24:3 and 4; ibid., p. 327. See also the story of Dinah, Genesis 34; Yehezkel Kaufmann, "The Biblical Age," p. 53, and Gerson Cohen, "The Talmudic Age," p. 150, in Baron, op. cit.

19. *Midrash Ha-Gadol,* cited in Ginzberg, op. cit., vol. 1 (Philadelphia, 1988), p. 320.

20. Kaufmann, op. cit., p. 137.

21. Todd Endelman, *Jewish Apostasy in the Modern World* (New York, 1987), p. 6; Hans Bach, *The German Jew* (New York, 1984), p. 32.

22. Feuer, op. cit., p. 103.

23. Solomon Maimon, *An Autobiography* (New York, 1975), p. 7.

24. Ludwig Borne quoted in Liptzin, op. cit., p. 34.

25. Alexander Altmann, *Moses Mendelssohn* (London, 1973), p. 221.

26. Bach, op. cit., p. 98.

27. Mendes-Flohr and Reinharz, op. cit., pp. 95–99. Endelman, op. cit., pp. 71–72; Altmann, op. cit., p. 425.

28. Liptzin, op. cit., pp. 22–23.

29. Ibid., pp. 222–23.

30. Heinrich Heine, *The Poetry and Prose of Heinrich Heine* (New York, 1948), p. 448.

31. Mendes-Flohr and Reinharz, op. cit., pp. 104, 116–21; Paula Hyman, *From Dreyfus to Vichy* (New York, 1979), pp. 5–7.

32. Deborah Hertz, "Seductive Conversion in Berlin, 1770–1809," in Endelman, op. cit., pp. 49, 70. Hannah Arendt, *Rachel Varnhagen* (New York, 1974), p. 201.

33. Maimon, op. cit., p. 101.

34. Liptzin, op. cit., pp. 13–14; Arendt, op. cit., p. 86.

35. Arendt, op. cit., pp. 10, 13, 26.

36. Ibid., pp. 74, 85.

37. Arendt, "Privileged Jews," in Abraham Duker, *Emancipation and Counter-Emancipation* (New York, 1984), p. 74.

38. Mendes-Flohr and Reinharz, op. cit., pp. 224–25.

39. Ibid.

40. Liptzin, op. cit., pp. 41–42.

41. Seigbert Prawer, *Heine's Jewish Comedy* (Oxford, 1983), p. 3.

42. Gans, "A Society to Further Jewish Integration," in Mendes-Flohr and Reinharz, op. cit., p. 191.

43. Liptzin, op. cit., p. 71. Heine was far softer on himself: "My becoming a Christian is the fault of . . . Napoleon, who really did not have to go to Russia, or of his teacher of geography . . . who did not tell him that Moscow winters are very cold." In other words, he was merely responding to the victory of the reactionary forces that blocked emancipation. Mendes-Flohr and Reinharz, op. cit., p. 223.

44. Heine, op. cit., pp. 760–64.

45. Prawer, op. cit., pp. 12, 58, 263–67, 282–4.

46. Heine, op. cit., pp. 18, 285.

47. Ibid., pp. 760–64.

48. Ibid., pp. 165, 280, 349.

49. Ibid., pp. 765–69; Endelman, *Apostasy*, p. 109.

50. Heine, op. cit., pp. 604, 658, 703–705, and 660.

51. Ibid., pp. 593–94, 690, and 701.

52. Ibid., p. 485; Prawer, op. cit., pp. 57–58.

53. Heine, op. cit., pp. 23, 669–70.

54. Ibid., p. 700.

55. Shlomo Avineri, *Moses Hess: Prophet of Communism and Zionism* (New York, 1985), p. 43; Shlomo Avineri, *The Making of Modern Zionism* (New York, 1981), p. 40.

56. Duker, op. cit., pp. 159–63.

57. Ibid., p. 183; Baron, op. cit., p. 354.

58. Duker, op. cit., pp. 164–65.

59. Ibid., p. 181.

60. Sonia and V. D. Lipman, *The Century of Moses Montefiore* (Oxford, 1985), p. 52; Israel Finestein, "Jewish Emancipationists in Victorian England," in J. Frankel and Steven Zipperstein, (New York, 1992), pp. 41–42; Todd Endelman, *Radical Assimilation in English Jewish History 1656–1945* (Bloomington, IN, 1990), pp. 62–63.

61. Thom Braun, *Disraeli the Novelist* (Boston, 1981), pp. 118–24.

62. Ibid., pp. 126, 131.

63. Stephen Aris, *But There Are No Jews in England* (New York, 1971), pp. 47–50.

64. Martin Lovinson, in Monika Richarz, *Jewish Life in Germany* (Bloomington, IN, 1991), p. 117.

65. Liptzin, op. cit., p. 93.

66. Frankel and Zipperstein, op. cit., pp. 36–37; Baron, op. cit., p. 366. Reform adopted pre-

cisely the most unJewish features for its service. Instead of each person reading at his own pace—seen as disorder and chaos—Reform instituted a stage show, allowing—hence encouraging—a lower level of knowledge. With the congregation made into passive observers, no wonder many Jews felt that rituals were emptied of content, and hence no longer had any appeal.

67. Frankel and Zipperstein, op. cit., p. 37; Avineri, *Hess,* op. cit., p. 215.

68. Duker, op. cit., p. 182.

69. Liptzin, op. cit., p. 96.

70. *Jerusalem Post,* January 3, 1991.

71. Peter Gay, "Sigmund Freud: A German and His Discontents," in *Freud, Jews and Other Germans* (New York, 1978), pp. 111–13.

72. Richarz, op. cit., p. 25.

73. Berlin, *Personal Impressions,* p. 63; Robert Brym, *The Jewish Intelligentsia and Russian Marxism* (New York, 1978), p. 37.

74. Zygmunt Bauman, *Modernity and Ambivalence* (Ithaca, NY, 1991), p. 134.

75. Lucy Dawidowicz, *The Golden Tradition: Jewish Life and Thought in Eastern Europe* (New York, 1967), p. 83.

76. Avineri, *Making of Modern Zionism,* p. 58; Robert Wistrich, *The Jews of Vienna in the Age of Franz Joseph* (New York, 1989), p. 353.

77. Dawidowicz, op. cit., p. 129.

78. Quoted in Joan Comay, *Who's Who in Jewish History* (New York, 1974), p. 48.

79. Hannah Arendt, *The Origins of Totalitarianism* (New York, 1973), p. 117.

80. Theodor Herzl, *A Portrait for This Age* (New York, 1955), pp. 313–14.

81. Theodor Herzl, *Congress Addresses of Theodor Herzl* (New York, 1917), p. 5.

82. Ibid., p. 28.

83. Herzl and his colleagues did not ignore the Arab question, though in 1897 they underestimated it. They knew people lived in Palestine but thought them few in number and indistinguishable from the Ottoman Empire's other subjects. Arab nationalism would not appear for another quarter century and the early Zionists hoped that peaceful cooperation and economic development would bring coexistence. If they expected non-Jews would live peacefully and loyally as citizens in a Jewish state this had, after all, been the behavior demanded from and given by Jews in a score of Christian- and Moslem-ruled states over two millennia.

84. Herzl, *A Portrait for This Age,* p. 314.

85. Ibid., p. 5.

86. Ibid., pp. 24–25.

87. Ibid., pp. 21–22.

2. THE BURST COCOON: EUROPE 1897–1940

1. Gershom Scholem, *From Berlin to Jerusalem* (New York, 1988). See also Gershom Scholem, *On Jews and Judaism In Crisis* (New York, 1976), pp. 3–4.

2. Arthur Schnitzler, *The Road to the Open* (Evanston, IL, 1991), p. 109.

3. Isaiah Berlin, *Personal Impressions* (New York, 1981), pp. 70, 72.

4. Ibid., pp. 81, 152.

5. Dawidowicz, op. cit., pp. 361–62.

6. Ibid.

7. Only thirty years later, after fleeing Nazi Germany for Israel, did the man conquer his revulsion and reawaken the love for Hebrew felt in his childhood. Samuel Spiro in Richarz, op. cit., pp. 202–209.

8. Conrad Rosenstein, in Richarz, op. cit., p. 167. Scholem thought Reform services more like "an operatic production than a religious rite." *On Jews and Judaism,* p. 40.

9. Ibid., p. 100.

10. Walter Benjamin, *Reflections* (New York, 1978), p. ix.

11. Marsha L. Rozenblit, "Jewish Assimilation in Habsburg Vienna," in Frankel and Zipperstein, op. cit., pp. 235–37.

12. Endelman, *Jewish Apostasy,* pp. 10–13. Steven Beller, *Vienna and the Jews, 1867–1938* (New York, 1989), pp. 188–90, estimated nine thousand conversions between 1868 and 1903. The number climbed steadily thereafter, peaking in 1918.

13. Berlin, op. cit., pp. 147–48.

14. Schnitzler, op. cit., p. 68.

15. Wistrich, op. cit., p. 282.

16. Ibid., pp. 27–28.

17. Richarz, op. cit., pp. 1, 27–29.

18. Hugo Bettauer, *City Without Jews* (New York, 1991), p. 11. The author of this 1923 novel, predicting with startling accuracy the Nazi takeover fifteen years later, was himself murdered by an antisemite.

19. Wistrich, op. cit., p. 620.

20. Beller, op. cit., p. 163.

21. Ibid., p. 151.

22. Moritz Goldstein, cited in Bauman, op. cit., p. 125.

23. Schnitzler, op. cit., p. 78.

24. Peter Gay, *Freud: A Life for Our Time* (New York, 1988), pp. 16–17.

25. Beller, op. cit., p. 104.

26. Ibid., pp. 13, 33–35, 134.

27. Schnitzler, op. cit., p. 33.

28. Ibid., pp. 236–37, 239.

29. Beller, op. cit., p. 180.

30. Ibid., pp. 178–79, 216.

31. Ibid., p. 205.

32. Ibid., pp. 207, 211.

33. Benjamin, op. cit., pp. 251–54.

34. Ibid.; Beller, op. cit., pp. 76–77.

35. Schnitzler, op. cit., pp. xii, 9, 107–113.

36. Robert Alter, *After the Tradition* (New York, 1969), p. 28.

37. Ibid., p. 29.

38. "Gracchus," Franz Kafka, *The Complete Stories* (New York, 1971), p. 230.

39. Alter, op. cit., p. 73.

40. "Description of a Struggle," Kafka, op. cit., pp. 15–16, 34, 37, 40–41.

41. Ibid., pp. 255, 257.

42. Ibid., pp. 279–80.

43. Franz Kafka, *The Trial* (New York, 1953), p. 7.

44. Ibid., pp. 366, 367, 370–71.

45. Kafka, "The Problem of Our Laws," *Complete Stories,* p. 437.

46. "The Great Wall of China," ibid., p. 146.

47. Robert Alter, *Necessary Angels* (Cambridge, MA., 1991), pp. xix, 33.

48. Ibid., p. 116.

49. Albert Einstein, *About Zionism* (New York, 1931), p. 45. Avineri, *The Making of Modern Zionism,* pp. 104–5; Berlin, op. cit., pp. 147–48.

50. Bauman, op. cit., p. 169.

51. Jerry Diller, *Freud's Jewish Identity* (Rutherford, NJ, 1991), p. 118.

52. Gay, *Freud,* pp. 6, 27. See also Diller, op. cit., p. 79.

53. Diller, op. cit., p. 87.

54. Ibid., p. 75.

55. Gay, *Freud,* pp. 11–12.

56. Diller, op. cit., p. 75.

57. In a letter to Dr. David Feuchtwang.

58. Cited in William McGrath, "How Jewish Was Freud?" *New York Review of Books,* February 5, 1991, p. 27; Gay, *Freud,* p. 25.

59. Gay, *Freud,* pp. 172, 205, 598; Diller, op. cit., p. 117.

60. Diller, op. cit., p. 97; Gay, *Freud,* p. 448.

61. Gay, *Freud,* pp. 406, 549.

62. Ibid., pp. 204–5.

63. Ibid., pp. 205, 218, 231.

64. Diller, op. cit., p. 187; Gay, *Freud,* p. 241–42.

65. Diller, op. cit., p. 124; Gay, *Freud,* p. 566n.

66. Avineri, *The Making of Modern Zionism,* p. 101.

67. Meir Ben-Horin, *Max Nordau, Philosopher of Human Solidarity* (New York, 1956), p. 177.

68. Ibid., pp. 178, 184.

69. Ibid., pp. 180, 187.

70. Ibid., pp. 191–92, 195.

71. Benjamin, op. cit., p. 52.

72. Alter, *Necessary Angels,* p. 43.

73. Ibid., p. 8.

74. Gershom Scholem, *The Correspondence of Walter Benjamin and Gershom Scholem* (Cambridge, MA., 1992), p. xxviii.

75. Ibid., p. xxii.

76. Bach, op. cit., p. 133–34.

77. Liptzin, op. cit., pp. 234–35.

78. Ibid., pp. 231, 238.

79. Bach, op. cit., pp. 69, 196; Alexander Altmann, *Essays in Jewish Intellectual History* (Hanover, NH, 1981), p. 249.

80. Altman, *Essays,* op. cit., p. 255.

81. Ibid., p. 203.

82. Hans Morgenthau, "The Tragedy of the German-Jewish Intellectual," in Bernard Rosenberg and Ernest Goldstein, *Creators and Disturbers* (New York, 1982), p. 75; Paul Muhsam in Richarz, op. cit., pp. 252–53.

83. Richarz, op. cit., p. 236.

84. Scholem, *From Berlin to Jerusalem,* p. 78.

85. Ibid., pp. 27, 135–36.

86. J. Nedava, *Arthur Koestler* (London, 1948), pp. 37–38.

87. Arthur Koestler, *Arrow in the Blue* (London, 1952), pp. 209–10.

88. Arthur Koestler, *Thieves in the Night* (London, 1946).

89. Herbert Lottman, *The Left Bank* (Boston, 1982), p. 41.

90. Michael Kowal, "Arnold Schoenberg as Prophet," *Congress Monthly,* January 1991.

91. Liptzin, op. cit., p. 139, 144–45, 150.

92. Ibid., pp. 167–69.

93. Ibid., pp. 153, 177.

94. Ibid., pp. 180–81; Bauman, op. cit., p. 115; Gay, *Freud, Jews and Other Germans,* p. 150.

95. Liptzin, op. cit., pp. 198–201.

96. Ibid., p. 212; *Jerusalem Report,* March 12, 1992.

97. Berlin, op. cit., pp. 147–48.

98. Scholem, *On Jews and Judaism in Crisis,* p. 63.

99. Richarz, op. cit., pp. 306–7, 311–14.

100. Werner Cahnman, *German Jewry* (New Brunswick, NJ, 1989), p. 135.

101. Gay, *Freud,* p. 610.

102. Ibid., pp. 622, 629.

3. AMERICA'S FOUNDING IMMIGRANTS

1. Azriel Eisenberg, *The Golden Land* (New York, 1964), p. 73.

2. Jacob Katz, *Emancipation and Assimilation* (New York, 1972), pp. 79–80; Jerold S. Auerbach, *Rabbis and Lawyers* (Bloomington, IN, 1990), pp. 13–14.

3. For histories of American Jewry, see Arthur Hertzberg, *The Jews in America* (New York, 1989) and Howard Sachar, *A History of the Jews in America* (New York, 1992). Judah Benjamin, the secular scion of a religious family, married a devout Catholic, rose to the U.S. Senate in 1852 and became Confederate secretary of war and of state. Unlike Disraeli, he did not need to convert to reach high office. The Sephardic Jewish elite of the 1830s viewed newly arriving German Jews as the latter would see Eastern European immigrants a half-century later, finding them to be aggressive, ill-mannered, and crude, with unpleasantly "Jewish" features better left unnoticed by Christians: large noses, outlandish clothing, and speaking Yiddish, an "abominable garble of German and Hebrew." Milton Goldin, *Why They Give* (New York, 1976), p. 31.

4. Leon Harris, *Merchant Princes* (New York, 1979), pp. 29–30.

5. His son Lincoln was a Harvard graduate famous for supporting the ballet, and son George bought the crusading liberal magazine *The Nation.* Ibid., pp. 31–33.

6. Ibid., pp. 318–20; Goldin, op. cit., p. 141.

7. Stephen Birmingham, *Our Crowd* (New York, 1987), pp. 4–5.

8. Myron Berman, *The Attitude of American Jewry Towards East European Jewish Immigration 1881–1914* (New York, 1980), p. 505; Katz, op. cit., pp. 78, 81; Auerbach, op. cit., p. 78.

9. Salo Baron, *Steeled by Adversity* (Philadelphia, PA, 1971), pp. 395–96.

10. Goldin, op. cit., pp. 32–33; Birmingham, op. cit., pp. 17–18.

11. Harris, op. cit., pp. 46–48. Auerbach, op. cit., pp. 12–13; Goldin, op. cit., pp. 38–42.

12. Baron, op. cit., p. 358.

13. Goldin, op. cit., p. 52; Berman, op. cit., pp. 517–21; Stephen Birmingham, *The Rest of Us* (New York, 1984), p. 24.

14. Harris, op. cit., pp. 57–58; Birmingham, *The Rest of Us,* pp. 336–37.

15. Murray Baumgarten, *City Scriptures: Modern Jewish Writing* (Cambridge, MA, 1982), pp. 48–51.

16. Irving Howe in Rosenberg and Goldstein, op. cit., p. 270: Parents lost their children by entrusting "us to goyish schools with preponderantly Jewish teachers."

17. Henry Roth, *Shifting Landscape* (New York, 1987), p. 46.

18. In his works *Children of the Ghetto* and *Grandchildren of the Ghetto,* both popular in the early 1900s. Elsie Adams, *Israel Zangwill* (New York, 1971), pp. 54–59, 86, 434.

19. Hutchins Hapgood, *The Spirit of the Ghetto* (Cambridge, MA, 1967), pp. 18, 32, 34.

20. Howe in Rosenberg and Goldstein, op. cit., pp. 277–78; Eisenberg, op. cit., pp. 150–51.

21. Isaac Asimov, *In Memory Yet Green* (New York, 1979), pp. 44, 178.

22. Roth, "No Longer At Home," in *Shifting Landscape,* p. 170.

23. Baumgarten, op. cit., pp. 16–17.

24. Yip Harburg, pp. 137–38, Clurman, p. 180, Howe, pp. 277–78 in Rosenberg and Goldstein, op. cit.

25. George Burns, *The Third Time Around* (New York, 1980), pp. 26–27.

26. Ibid., p. 23.

27. Burns, *All My Best Friends* (New York, 1989), pp. 19, 34.

28. Burns, *The Third Time Around,* p. 35.

29. Arthur Miller, *Timebends* (New York, 1987), pp. 24–25.

30. *Jerusalem Report,* December 27, 1990.

31. Paul Cowan, *An Orphan in History* (Garden City, NY, 1982), pp. 3, 7, 47, 54, 59–60.

32. Ibid., p. 44.

33. Ibid., p. 50.

34. Ibid., p. 93.

35. Ibid., p. 16.

36. Golden, op. cit., p. 127.

37. Louis Brandeis, *Brandeis on Zionism* (Westport, CT, 1976), pp. 11–13, 18, 28–29. Einstein wrote in similar terms in 1926: "He who remains true to his origin, race and tradition will also remain loyal to the State of which he is a subject. He who is faithless to the one will also be faithless to the other."

38. Arthur Schlesinger, Jr., *The Disuniting of America* (New York, 1992), p. 35. I wish to thank Adam Garfinkle for calling my attention to these statements. When department store mogul Marshall Field was complemented for having "a very strong Jewish conscious-

ness," his wife replied, "That's exactly what I'm afraid of." Rosenberg and Goldstein, op. cit., p. 80.

39. Steven Blum, *Walter Lippmann and the American Century* (New York, 1981), pp. 10–12.
40. Lionel Abel, *The Intellectual Follies* (Buffalo, NY, 1984), p. 267.
41. Meryl Secrest, *Being Bernard Berenson* (New York, 1979), p. 57.
42. Ibid., pp. 118–19, 63, 86.
43. Ibid., p. 229.
44. Ibid., p. 395.
45. Ibid., pp. 48, 159, 357–58.
46. Ibid., pp. 354–58.
47. Ibid., pp. 395–96.
48. Thomas Edwards, "Underground Man," *New York Review of Books,* June 28, 1990.
49. "The Omnivorous Eye of Man Ray, *Washington Post,* December 2, 1988; Neil Baldwin, *Man Ray, American Artist* (New York, 1988), pp. 81, 177.
50. Marion Meade, *Dorothy Parker* (New York, 1988), pp. 38–42.
51. Ibid., pp. 85, 110.
52. Although not everyone in Hollywood was Jewish, the extent of that influence and presence is amazing. Even Italian-born director Frank Capra had Jewish writers, and Armenian-American writer William Saroyan had a Jewish wife.
53. A. Scott Berg, *Goldwyn: A Biography* (New York, 1989), pp. 5, 8, 10.
54. Ibid., p. 163. Ironically, the great love of her life was the Jewish homosexual director George Cukor.
55. Ibid., p. 293.
56. Rosenberg and Goldstein, op. cit., pp. 187–88.
57. Ben Hecht, *A Child of the Century* (New York, 1954), pp. 504–6. Chaim Weizmann spoke in similar terms of immigrants "guilt-ridden by their great fortune while brethren suffered and died in Europe," who sought atonement "in the form of contributions." Goldin, op. cit., p. 139. This fearful insecurity would also lead them to accept an anti-Communist blacklist.
58. *New York Observer,* June 7, 1993, p. 3.
59. Birmingham, op. cit., pp. 178, 180.
60. See Lawrence Bergreen, *As Thousands Cheer* (New York, 1990).
61. Angoff and Levin, op. cit., p. 10; Birmingham, *The Rest of Us,* op. cit., pp. 258–60. "If you want to pretend you're not a Jew, you may as well do it right. [Morgenstern sounds so] Jewish. Those overtones of potato pancakes, Friday-night candles, gefilte fish—that's what you don't like." Herman Wouk, *Marjorie Morningstar* (New York, 1957), p. 273.
62. Burns, *Third Time Around,* p. 201.
63. Burns, *All My Best Friends,* p. 180.
64. Rosenberg and Goldstein, op. cit., p. 194.
65. Robert Alter, *Defenses of the Imagination* (Philadelphia, 1977), p. 53.
66. Baumgarten, op. cit., pp. 21–22; Hecht, op. cit., p. 355.
67. Hecht, op. cit., pp. 354–55.
68. Ibid., p. 18; Harburg in Rosenberg and Goldstein, op. cit., p. 146. Compare this remark to

the imagery in that most remarkable film about assimilation, Woody Allen's *Zelig,* see chapter 5.

69. Hecht, op. cit., pp. 12–13.

70. Ibid., p. 15.

71. Ibid., p. 106.

72. Ibid., pp. 355, 76–77.

73. Ludwig Lewisohn, *The Answer* (New York, 1939), pp. 155–59.

74. Alan Dershowitz, *Chutzpah* (New York, 1991), pp. 294–95.

75. Berg, op. cit., pp. 345–47; Hecht, op. cit., pp. 486–87.

76. Harris, op. cit., pp. 54–55. For another example of a Jewish ambassador taking anti-Jewish actions, see the author's *Istanbul Intrigues* (New York, 1989), pp. 124–25; Stephen Birmingham, *The Rest of Us* (New York, 1984), p. 313.

77. Hecht, op. cit., pp. 516–18.

78. Cahnman, op. cit., p. 118.

79. Goldin, op. cit., p. 106.

80. Alfred Kazin, *New York Jew* (New York, 1978).

81. Hertzberg, op. cit., p. 245.

4. SELF-INVENTION, AMERICAN STYLE

1. Woody Allen, *Three Films of Woody Allen* (New York, 1987), pp. 145–46.

2. *Washington Post,* July 28, 1990.

3. Charles Fleming, "Arnie's Army," *Spy Magazine,* March 1992, p. 62.

4. Lewisohn, op. cit., p. 233.

5. Lenny Bruce, *The Essential Lenny Bruce* (St. Albans, VT, 1975), p. 56; Lenny Bruce, *The Almost Unpublished Lenny Bruce* (Philadelphia, 1984), p. 9.

6. Philip Roth, "The Anatomy Lesson," in *Zuckerman Bound,* pp. 445–46, 475–81.

7. Hecht, *Jew in Love,* pp. 45–46.

8. Rachel Brenner, *Assimilation and Assertion: The Response to the Holocaust in Mordechai Richler's Writings* (New York, 1989), p. 6.

9. Herman Wouk's novel *The Caine Mutiny* (New York, 1952) handled the issue in a different way, suggesting through a common Jewish concept that humanity must help God—especially at a time when the deity's competence as captain is questionable—and nation, which despite its faults is holding back barbarism. The intellectual who undermines this admittedly flawed order may bring disaster, a rejoinder to the revolutionary approach.

10. Brenner, op. cit., p. 89; Bruno Bettelheim, *Surviving, and Other Essays* (New York, 1979), p. 392.

11. Ted Solotaroff, "American-Jewish Writers: On Edge Once More," *New York Times Book Review,* December 18, 1988.

12. The country club problem has not become solely a metaphor, though changing mores or the pressure of state laws have made this rarer. In Palm Beach, Florida, where four of five clubs did not admit Jews, town council member Hemine Weiner asked, "A lot of Jews hate themselves, and they want to be where the other guy is. I don't see it. Why go where you're not wanted?" *Jerusalem Report,* March 5, 1992.

13. Robert Alter, *America and Israel* (New York, 1970), pp. 5–6.

14. Philip Roth, *Goodbye, Columbus and Other Stories* (New York, 1986), p. 146.

15. Eugene L. Meyer, "The Massacre at Volozhin," *Washington Post,* May 31, 1992.

16. Birmingham, *The Rest of Us,* op. cit., p. 309.

17. Eric Lax, *Woody Allen* (New York, 1991), p. 317; Diane Jacobs, *But We Need the Eggs* (New York, 1982), p. 14; Philip Roth, *Portnoy's Complaint* (New York, 1967), pp. 221–22.

18. Bruce, *The Essential,* pp. 53–54.

19. Wouk, *Marjorie Morningstar,* p. 59.

20. Roth, "The Anatomy Lesson," op. cit., pp. 483–84.

21. Philip Roth, *Patrimony* (New York, 1991), pp. 29, 92–97.

22. Bruce, *The Almost Unpublished,* p. 9. His mother, Sadie Kitchenberg, later went on, though, to be a professional dancer who, at age forty-nine, married a nineteen-year-old Chicano and had once changed her name to Boots Malloy.

23. Spitz, op. cit., pp. 17, 125, 197. For a similar story, see a review of the play *Sight Unseen* in *Jerusalem Report,* April 16, 1992, pp. 35–36.

24. Roth, *Patrimony,* p. 182; Thomas Edwards, "Vita Nuova," *New York Review of Books,* October 13, 1988.

25. Isaac Rosenfeld, *Passage from Home,* cited in Baumgarten, op., cit., p. 144.

26. Roth, *Shifting Landscape,* p. 182.

27. Roth, "The Anatomy Lesson," pp. 445–46, 475–81.

28. Roth, *Zuckerman Bound,* pp. 583–85.

29. Roth, *Portnoy's Complaint,* pp. 144–45.

30. Bruce, *The Essential,* p. 51.

31. Roth, *Goodbye, Columbus,* p. 110.

32. Lax, op. cit., p. 40.

33. Woody Allen, *Three Films,* p. 77.

34. Robert Alter, *America and Israel* (New York, 1970), p. 10.

35. Lax, op. cit., p. 234; Alter, *America and Israel,* pp. 5–6.

36. Jacobs, op. cit., p. 15.

37. See Stuart Schoffman, "Bugsy's Masquerade," *Jerusalem Report,* March 26, 1992.

38. Jane Horwitz, "The Strangers Among Us," *Washington Post,* July 19, 1992, subtitled, "Hollywood's Troubling Inability to Portray Jews as Real People," and *Jerusalem Report,* August 13, 1992, p. 45. For Jewish/non-Jewish romances see, for example, *Dirty Dancing* and *Baby, It's You.* A marvelous earlier tale of such a situation is I. L. Peretz's "Stories," in which an assimilating Jew seeks to attract a shiksa who is only drawn to him by the stories he tells. He is torn between his people's stories and fairytales more likely to win her favor, a situation also paralleling the choice between references and subjects that would win a Jewish audience but lose the larger one. See Samuel, op. cit., pp. 133–50.

39. Moshe Waldoks, "TV Jews," *Hadassah* Magazine, June–July 1991; *Newsweek,* October 12, 1992, pp. 88–89. *Washington Times,* July 21, 1993: "Fran Drescher stars in 'The Nanny,' a comedy in which she plays a young Jewish au pair who takes care of the children of a WASPy English widower." "We're writing the Christmas show now and having a great time doing it because of the idea of my character being in this authentic goyish house for Christmas," she said. "She becomes, like, the Christmas elf and has the Christmas that every Jew dreams of."

40. Allen, *Three Films,* pp. 20, 32, 110.

41. Roth, *Zuckerman Bound,* p. 397.

42. Brenner, op. cit., p. 153.

43. Ibid., p. 9.

44. Abraham Chapman, *Jewish-American Literature* (New York, 1974), pp. 627–28.

45. Jennifer Bailey, *Norman Mailer, Quick Change Artist* (New York, 1979), p. 30.

46. Mailer aspired to be a "White Negro." A hero of Woody Allen, Milton Mezzrow, was a Jewish jazz clarinetist who actually passed himself off as black. Richard Wagner and other European antisemites had often compared Jews with black Africans.

47. Goldman, op. cit., pp. 271–74. Ironically but coincidentally, the word *hep* had been an antisemitic insult in nineteenth-century Europe.

48. Carl Rollyson, *The Lives of Norman Mailer* (New York, 1991), p. 91.

49. Alpert said, "We were liberal Conservative. We only ate pork in Chinese restaurants." He changed his name to Ram Dass. *Jerusalem Report,* April 2, 1992, pp. 30–31. On Ginsberg, see Scholem, *On Jews and Judaism in Crisis,* p. 40.

50. Roth, *Zuckerman Unbound,* p. 404. Roth was so impressed by this theme that he also used it in *Portnoy's Complaint,* p. 248: "Home? I have none. Family? No!"

51. Bob Spitz, *Dylan: A Biography* (New York, 1991), pp. 528–32. After tiring of his Christian phase, Dylan visited Israel and returned to a more Jewish identity but continued to believe in Jesus. *Washington Post,* September 9, 1987; *Jerusalem Report,* May 30, 1991.

52. Lax, op. cit., 150–51.

53. Woody Allen, *God* (New York: 1975), p. 17.

54. Lax, op. cit., pp. 26–27.

55. Ibid., pp. 165–67.

56. Ibid.

57. Ibid., pp. 232.

58. Jacobs, op. cit., pp. 48–49, 67–68.

59. Brenner, op. cit., p. 125.

60. *Washington Post,* November 27, 1991.

61. Albert Goldman with Lawrence Schiller, *Ladies and Gentlemen, Lenny Bruce!* (New York, 1975), pp. 443–44.

62. Brenner, op. cit., pp. 151–53.

63. Bailey, op. cit., p. 91.

64. Roth, *Zuckerman Bound,* p. 393.

65. Roth, *Portnoy's Complaint,* pp. 3–4.

66. Goldman, op. cit., pp. 475, 536, 647.

67. Bruce, *The Essential,* pp. 51, 54–55; Bruce, *The Almost Unpublished,* p. 9.

68. *Jerusalem Post,* February 2, 1992; *Washington Post,* November 12, 1991; Howard Stern, *Private Parts* (New York, 1993), pp. 36, 68, 79, 237; Marty Jezer, *Abbie Hoffman, American Rebel* (New Brunswick, NJ, 1992), pp. 6–9.

69. Jacobs, op. cit., p. 14.

70. Goldman, op. cit., pp. 288, 783. Curtis sounds like "courteous" and Schwartz means "black," implying that a Jew is not a gentleman but the opposite of a White Anglo-Saxon Protestant. Bob Dylan, "It's Alright Ma (I'm Only Bleeding)."

71. Jacobs, op. cit., p. 25.

72. Megan Rosenfeld, "Dustin Hoffman, Big Little Man," *Washington Post,* October 1, 1992. His roles included a would-be assimilationist in Native American society, *Little Big Man,* and the leads in *Merchant of Venice* and *Death of a Salesman.*

73. Goldman, op. cit., p. 54. On the significance of such partial name changes, see Albert Memmi, *The Liberation of the Jew* (New York, 1966), pp. 34–37.

74. Bailey, op. cit., pp. 38, 55–58.

75. *Washington Post,* July 22, 1990; *Variety,* November 28, 1984.

76. Sandra Bernhard, *Confessions of a Pretty Lady* (New York, 1988), p. 1; *Washington Post,* July 22, 1990. The subjects of three of the four articles in the *Post*'s features section that day were Clay, Bernhard, and Allen Ginsberg.

77. Bernhard, op. cit., p. 1.

78. Cathy Horyn, "Ralph Lauren, Suiting Himself," *Washington Post,* May 24, 1992.

79. Ibid.

80. Ibid.

81. *New York Times,* January 30, 1994.

82. Scholem, *On Jews and Judaism in Crisis,* p. 255.

83. Jacobs, op. cit., p. 21.

5. THE MYSTERY PEOPLE

1. Wistrich, op. cit., pp. 292–93.

2. Schnitzler, op. cit., p. 252.

3. Ahad Ha-Am, op. cit., pp. 187, 192.

4. Scholem, *On Jews and Judaism in Crisis,* p. 89.

5. Maimon, op. cit., p. 61. Compare this image with Kafka's "A Hunger Artist." See chapter 3.

6. Maurice Samuel, *Prince of the Ghetto* (New York, 1959), p. 126.

7. Elias Canetti, *Auto Da Fé* (London, 1983), p. 225.

8. Memmi, op. cit., p. 120.

9. Ahad Ha-Am, op. cit., pp. 265–67.

10. David Ben-Gurion in Arthur Hertzberg, *The Zionist Idea* (New York, 1959), pp. 606–19; Arendt, *Origins of Totalitarianism,* op. cit., p. 67.

11. Isaiah Berlin, "Jewish Slavery and Emancipation," *Jewish Chronicles,* September 21, 1951.

12. Harold Bloom, *The Strong Light of the Canonical: Kafka, Freud, and Scholem as Revisionists of Jewish Culture and Thought* (New York, 1987), p. vi.

13. Arendt, op. cit., pp. 217–18, 222.

14. Bauman, op. cit., p. 114; Ahad Ha-Am, op. cit., pp. 265–67.

15. Léon Blum, *For All Mankind* (Gloucester, MA, 1969), pp. 24–25.

16. Samuel, op. cit., pp. 121–22.

17. Against the advice of the prophet Samuel, the Jewish tribes insisted that he anoint them a king so they would be like every other nation. Samuel acceded, with adverse results.

18. Alter, *Necessary Angels,* p. 72. Although "Talmudic" became a term of ridicule for petty,

disingenuous dispute, that field of study was equal to any other philosophical school, not an exercise in superstition or obfuscation but an intellectual enterprise of the highest order whose results established a leadership by the learned, governed the Jews' temporal lives, and preserved their society. Maimon, op. cit., p. 108: The Jewish people is "a perpetual aristocracy [of] learned men."

19. Avineri, *Hess,* p. 181. Jews were typical of the ancient world that formed them, but many contemporary nations also have had their own distinct religion. In east and southeast Europe, national Orthodox churches (Russian, Armenian, Greek); in Western Europe, Catholicism (Spain, Italy, France, Poland, Ireland) or specific Protestant sects (England/Anglican, Swedish/Lutheran); in Asia, Japanese Shintoism, and many other examples. In Middle Eastern and many other modern Third World nations, political community has generally been defined by religion. The question of noncommunicants being equal citizens frequently preoccupied Jews, which only reinforces the point.

20. Avineri, *Hess,* p. 102.

21. Ha-Am, op. cit., pp. 93–95, 183, 205–6.

22. In life, such types included Abraham Stavisky, Michael Milken, and Ivan Boesky; in literature, Abraham Cahan's *The Rise of David Levinsky,* Richler's *The Apprenticeship of Duddy Kravitz,* and Budd Schulberg's *What Makes Sammy Run?*

23. "The Jews were called to prove that the charges raised against them were untrue (or *no more* true), but the same people who brought forth the charges would pronounce on the cogency of the proofs." Bauman, op. cit., p. 113.

24. Ibid., op. cit., p. 118.

25. See the typology developed by the American Jewish sociologist David Riesman, *The Lonely Crowd* (New Haven, 1950).

26. Diller, op. cit., p. 118.

27. Wouk, op. cit., p. 488.

28. Philip Roth, *Reading Myself and Others* (New York, 1977), p. 3. On visiting a European castle, Arthur Miller's pleasure was vitiated by reflecting that the baron who had lived there would have oppressed or even tried to kill him. "The Jewish view of things is sometimes irritating." Miller, *Timebends,* p. 497.

29. Arendt, *Varnhagen,* p. 12.

30. Joel Colton, *Léon Blum: Humanist in Politics* (Cambridge, MA, 1974), p. 5.

31. Bloom, op. cit., p. 32.

32. Gay, *Freud, Jews, and Other Germans,* p. 76.

33. Ben-Horin, op. cit., p. 20.

34. John Gilbert, *Famous Jewish Lives* (Feltham, England, 1970), pp. 253, 256–57. One of his controversies was a bronze statue of Jesus. Epstein wrote, "A most hellish row broke out. The statue was reviled, attacked by the Press, the Clergy, and tamer artists."

35. See chapter 10.

36. Scholem, *On Jews and Judaism in Crisis,* p. 80. Privately, Jews often saw themselves as better and were proud of their history, a dichotomy perceived as hypocrisy by the later American generation of writers and by the political radicals.

37. Ha-Am, op. cit., p. 123.

38. Arthur Koestler, *The Invisible Writing* (London, 1954), p. 46; Philip Roth, *Zuckerman Bound,* p. 360.

6. IN DUBIOUS BATTLES: THE REVOLUTIONARY LEFT

1. Werner Cahnman, *German Jewry,* p. 105.
2. Memmi, *The Liberation of the Jew,* p. 231. This does not apply to socialist-Zionism and the Jewish Socialist Bund, see below.
3. Koestler, *Arrow in the Blue,* pp. 245–46.
4. Memmi, op. cit., p. 228. This gave two added incentives for Jewish radicals to discount their background: to conceal Marxism's own contradictions and the role of psychological factors in producing its adherents.
5. Antisemitism mixed with socialism from the start. "The Jew is the enemy of the human race," Proudhon wrote in 1847. "One must send this race back to Asia or exterminate it." William Cohen and Irwin Wall, "French Communism and the Jews," in Frances Malino and Bernard Wasserstein, *The Jews in Modern France* (Hanover, NH, 1985), pp. 82–84.
6. Avineri, *Hess,* pp. 70, 123.
7. Koestler, *Arrow in the Blue,* p. 52.
8. Auerbach, op. cit., pp. 15–16.
9. Lewisohn, op. cit., p. 121.
10. Avineri, *Hess,* p. 11.
11. Harry Ausmus, *Will Herberg, From Right to Right* (Chapel Hill, NC, 1987), pp. 53, 69.
12. Arendt, *Varnhagen,* p. 130.
13. Cited in David Bromwich, "The Poet's Burden," *New Republic,* November 8, 1993, p. 33.
14. Ibid., p. 35; Theodor Adorno, "Notes to Literature II," *The Jargon of Authenticity* (Evanston, IL, 1973), p. 215.
15. Hyman, op. cit., pp. 21–22. Compare Rolland's remark to that of Brentano, cited in chapter 5.
16. Daniel Burston, *The Legacy of Erich Fromm* (Cambridge, MA, 1991), pp. 146–47.
17. Leon Trotsky, *The Real Situation in Russia* (New York, 1928), p. 325.
18. Kim Chernin, *In My Mother's House* (New York, 1983), pp. 88, 91, 124, 268–69. After abandoning communism, she became a radical feminist.
19. Berlin, *Against the Current,* p. 269.
20. Ibid., pp. 225, 276–77.
21. Karl Marx, *Critique of Hegel's Philosophy of Right* (Cambridge, Eng., 1970), p. 141. Compare this statement with those of his comrades Heine and Börne cited in chapter 2.
22. Berlin, *Against the Current,* pp. 281–84.
23. Edward Bernstein, *Ferdinand Lassalle as a Social Reformer* (St. Clair Shores, MI, 1970), p. 16.
24. Ibid., pp. 17–19.
25. Avineri, *Hess,* p. 71.
26. Ibid., p. 42.
27. See, for example, Philipp Lowenfeld in Richarz, op. cit., p. 241.
28. Wistrich, op. cit., p. 333.
29. Stephen Bronner, *Rosa Luxemburg—A Revolutionary for Our Times* (New York, 1987), pp. 13, 22–23.
30. Robert Wistrich, "Rosa Luxemburg, Leo Jogiches and the Jewish Labour Movement,

1893–1903," in Ada Rapoport-Albert and Steven Zipperstein, *Jewish History* (London, 1989), pp. 529–30, 533.

31. Ibid., p. 542; Mendes-Flohr and Reinharz, op. cit., p. 225.

32. Duker, op. cit., p. 307; Wistrich, *Rosa Luxemburg,* in Rapoport-Albert and Zipperstein, op. cit., p. 541.

33. Beller, op. cit., pp. 132, 156–58.

34. A. L. Motzkin, "Ancestors," *New Republic,* April 13, 1992.

35. Dawidowicz, op. cit., p. 407; Duker, op. cit., p. 289.

36. Robert Brym, *The Jewish Intelligentsia and Russian Marxism* (New York, 1978), pp. 53, 73.

37. Ibid., p. 46.

38. Duker, op. cit., p. 288.

39. Brym, op. cit., p. 74.

40. Ibid., p. 45.

41. Ibid., pp. 38–44.

42. Juli Martov (Zederbaum), quoted in Duker, op. cit., pp. 290–92.

43. Ibid., p. 302.

44. Dawidowicz, op. cit., p. 381.

45. Ibid., p. 232.

46. Cited in *Jerusalem Report,* May 20, 1993.

47. Cohen and Wall, in Malino and Wasserstein, op. cit., pp. 88–91.

48. Birmingham, *The Rest of Us,* pp. 51–72.

49. Scholem, *From Berlin to Jerusalem,* pp. 144–6; Scholem, *On Jews and Judaism in Crisis,* p. 4.

50. Lottman, op. cit., pp. 268–69.

51. *New York Times,* November 29, 1987; Roth, *Shifting Landscape,* p. 47. An interesting case in a different setting was that of the Moroccan Jew Abraham Serfaty, a founder of the Communist Party there who quit, finding it inadequately radical, in 1970. Imprisoned from 1974 to 1991 for antiregime activity, he married a French Christian woman. Serfaty opposed Israel's existence, even alongside a Palestinian state, claiming only its destruction would "allow the Jews to rediscover their universality." *Forward,* September 20, 1991.

52. *Washington Post,* October 25, 1987.

53. Abel, *The Intellectual Follies,* pp. 261–62.

54. Irving Howe, "Range of the New York Intellectual"; Alexander Bloom, *Prodigal Sons: The New York Intellectuals and Their World* (New York, 1986), pp. 272–73; Rosenberg and Goldstein, op. cit., pp. 277–78. Ties within the Jewish community also contradicted Marxist theory. When the garment workers union was bankrupt in the 1930s, for example, it secured a no-interest loan from Jewish bankers.

55. Scholem, *Correspondence,* p. xxv.

56. Ibid., p. 131.

57. Adorno, *Jargon,* pp. xxi, 4, 66.

58. Ibid., pp. 5, 10, 21.

59. Grunfeld, p. 123.

60. Adorno, *Jargon,* pp. 76, 83.

61. Horkheimer/Adorno, "The Culture Industry: Enlightenment as Mass Deception," *Dialectic of Enlightenment,* pp. 166–67.

62. Ibid., p. 207.

63. Morgenthau, in Alexander Bloom, op. cit., p. 82.

64. Adorno, *Jargon*, p. 24.

65. Cohen and Wall, op. cit., pp. 95, 98. Dassault, France's leading warplane manufacturer, was a convert. See chapter 8.

66. Koestler, *The Invisible Writing*, p. 32.

67. Shimon Markish, "Officially Published Russian Literature," in Y. Roi and A. Becker, *Jewish Culture and Identity in the Soviet Union* (New York, 1991), p. 224. See Robert Wistrich, "Anti-Semitism in Europe Since the Holocaust," in David Singer and Ruth Seldin, eds. *American Jewish Yearbook 1993* (New York, 1993). Howard Sachar, *Diaspora* (New York, 1985), pp. 319–20; 344–46; cited in Josef Skvorecky, "The Theater of Cruelty," *New York Review of Books,* August 16, 1990, p. 42.

68. *Jerusalem Report,* October 7, 1993, p. 33; Abbie Hoffman, *Soon to Be a Major Motion Picture* (New York, 1980).

69. Raymond Aron, *Memoirs* (New York, 1990), p. 335.

70. Cohen and Wall, op. cit., pp. 98, 101.

71. Tom Sawicki, "My Uncle, the Butcher," *Jerusalem Report,* August 22, 1991.

72. Koestler, *The Invisible Writing*, p. 32.

73. Scholem, *On Jews and Judaism In Crisis,* p. 32.

7. THE LAST JEW

1. Dawidowicz, op. cit., p. 142.

2. Roth, *Portnoy's Complaint*, pp. 60–61.

3. Ginzberg, vol. 2, op. cit., p. 29.

4. Arendt, *The Origins of Totalitarianism*, p. 66.

5. Kafka, *The Complete Stories*, pp. 271–73, 277.

6. Franz Kafka, *Letter to His Father* (New York, 1966), pp. 75–81.

7. Endelman, *Jewish Apostasy,* pp. 88, 91, 93.

8. Harris, op. cit., p. 67.

9. David S. Landes, "Two Cheers for Emancipation," in Malino and Wasserstein, op. cit., p. 293.

10. Samuel, op. cit., p. 152, recalls James Joyce's character Leopold Bloom in *Ulysses*—"the most penetrating study ever made of a Jew assimilating into the non-Jewish world"—who when taunted replies that Mendelssohn, Marx, Spinoza, "and the Savior was a Jew." Samuel calls this "Stock Answer No. 1 of the Jew who knows little about Jewish things beyond those names and, knowing so little, has nothing else to fall back on."

11. Endelman, *Jewish Apostasy,* p. 98; Endelman, *Radical Assimilation,* p. 4.

12. Arthur Koestler, *Arrow in the Blue* (London, 1952), pp. 19–20.

13. Bruce, *The Essential*, pp. 58–59.

14. Endelman, *Jewish Apostasy,* pp. 94, 99.

15. Berlin, *Against the Current*, pp. 25–33.

16. Endelman, *Jewish Apostasy,* pp. 12–13; Dawidowicz, op. cit., p. 338.

17. Davidowicz, op. cit., pp. 344, 349.

18. Hyman, op. cit., p. 13.

19. Endelman, *Jewish Apostasy*, p. 117.

20. Richarz, op. cit., p. 249.

21. Ibid., p. 251.

22. Ibid., p. 252.

23. Ibid., pp. 160–61.

24. Ibid.

25. Ibid., p. 160.

26. Baumgarten, op. cit., p. 30.

27. *Washington Post,* November 7, 1991.

28. *The Economist,* December 7, 1991; *Washington Post,* November 11, 1991 and November 6, 1992.

29. Endelman, *Jewish Apostasy*, p. 85.

30. Harris, op. cit., pp. 61–63.

31. Ezekiel 18:1–20.

32. Baumgarten, op. cit., pp. 24–25.

33. Richarz, op. cit., pp. 256–57.

34. Ibid., p. 256.

35. Ibid., pp. 235–36.

36. Secrest, op. cit., pp. 49–55.

37. Erik Erikson, *Identity, Youth and Crisis* (New York, 1968), pp. 59–60.

38. Mary Morris, *Wall to Wall: From Beijing to Berlin by Rail* (New York, 1991), pp. 77–78, 240.

39. Secrest, op. cit., p. 16.

40. Goodman, op. cit., pp. 59, 74–75.

41. Ibid., pp. 93–94.

42. Comay, op. cit., p. 286; Jean Goodman, *The Mond Legacy* (London, 1982), pp. 72, 86.

43. Ibid., p. 96.

44. Ibid., pp. 156–62.

45. Ibid., pp. 210, 245; *Jerusalem Post,* May 21, 1993.

46. Donald Katz, *Home Fires* (New York, 1992), pp. 4, 19–21, 23.

47. Ibid., pp. 46–49.

48. Ibid., pp. 62, 161, 129–31.

49. Roth, *Portnoy's Complaint,* pp. 74–75.

50. Katz, op. cit., pp. 198–99.

51. Ibid., p. 150. See Woody Allen's comment on "God and carpeting" as his parents' main interests, chapter 5.

52. Ibid., p. 154, 196, 218.

53. Ibid., pp. 362–64, 378, 402, 438.

54. Ibid., p. 518.

55. Ibid., pp. 269–71.

56. Richarz, op. cit., pp. 256–57.

57. Clarence Brown, *Mandelstam* (Cambridge, Eng., 1973), pp. 19–21.

58. Ibid.

59. Ibid.

60. Maimon, op. cit., p. 109.

61. *The Economist,* February 8, 1992.

62. Chapman, op. cit., pp. 413–14.

63. David Bromwich, "The Poet's Burden," *New Republic,* November 8, 1993.

64. Brenner, op. cit., p. 100.

65. Lewisohn, op. cit., p. 146.

66. Marvin Liebman, *Coming Out Conservative* (New York, 1992).

67. Endelman, "German Jews in Victorian England," in Frankel and Zipperstein, op. cit., pp. 64–65.

68. *Jerusalem Report,* February 20, 1992; Iraq News Agency, May 1, 1989, (*FBIS,* May 2, 1989, p. 19). Other Jews also converted during the war, influenced by the trauma of the situation and by unscrupulous clerics. Jean-Marie Lustiger, grandson of an Orthodox rabbi, was concealed in a French Catholic boarding school by his mother, who was to die at Auschwitz. He became a priest and archbishop of Paris. Oswald Rufeisen, a Polish Jew who took refuge in a convent, became a Carmelite. Defining himself as a Christian Jew, he later moved to a monastery in Israel. See Nechama Tec, *In the Lion's Den: The Life of Oswald Rufeisen* (New York, 1990).

69. Endelman, *Radical Assimilation,* pp. 105, 128–29.

70. Harris, op. cit., pp. 22–23, 29. Her counterpart Gwen Cafritz was the Christian wife of real estate multimillionaire Morris Cafritz, whose three sons—Calvin, Carter, and Conrad—followed their father's trade but not his religion. On his death in 1964, Morris, an immigrant who had grown up above a grocery store, left $220 million to the family foundation. Despite his long-time role as president of the Jewish Community Council and a big giver to the United Jewish Appeal, on his death the foundation eschewed Jewish charities for the arts. Marjorie Williams, "Cafritz v. Cafritz," *Washington Post Magazine,* February 25, 1990.

71. Naomi Levine, *Politics, Religion and Love: The Story of H. H. Asquith, Venetia Stanley and Edwin Montagu* (New York, 1991).

72. Liptzin, op. cit., pp. 206–7. Alma tried desperately—and with partial success—to secure a Catholic funeral for her husband. The Jewish husband of the great French writer Collette, who she sustained by writing for collaborationist newspapers during the German occupation, was such a passionate Catholic that he demanded his freethinking wife have a Catholic funeral.

73. Richarz, op. cit., pp. 241–42.

74. Endelman, *Radical Assimilation,* pp. 128–29.

75. Ben Hecht, *A Jew in Love* (New York, 1931), p. 42.

76. Cowan, op. cit., pp. 112–13.

77. Philip Roth, "The Prague Orgy," in *Zuckerman Bound,* p. 718.

78. Memmi, op. cit., p. 93.

79. Goodman, op. cit., pp. 116–17, 137.

80. Edwards, op. cit.

81. Scholem, *From Berlin to Jerusalem,* p. 29.

82. Peter Donald, "Pro-Lifer Demoss' Stylish Wiles," *New York Observer,* October 19, 1992.

83. Ben-Horin, op. cit., pp. 86, 89. Lewis Namier followed a similar pattern.

84. Endelman, *Radical Assimilation,* pp. 83, 88.

85. Burns, *Third Time Around,* pp. 50, 57; Burns, *All My Best Friends,* p. 190.

86. Lenny Bruce, *The Essential,* p. 52. At one time, Bruce's mother married a Filipino. For a scene seemingly based on this experience, see the film, *My Favorite Year.*

87. Wouk, *Marjorie Morningstar,* pp. 175–77. For flattering characterizations of Jewish women, see Walter Scott's *Ivanhoe* and William Shakespeare's "The Merchant of Venice," both of which end with the heroine's conversion and intermarriage.

88. Erik Erikson, *Identity, Youth and Crisis,* pp. 21–22.

89. Koestler, *Arrow in the Blue,* op. cit., p. 28.

90. Roth, "The Anatomy Lesson," in *Zuckerman Bound,* pp. 586–87.

91. Kafka, *The Trial,* p. 250. Obviously, the Shoah is the great exception.

92. Stuart Schoffman, *Jerusalem Report,* October 17, 1991.

8. OTHER PEOPLE'S NATIONS

1. Dawidowicz, op. cit., p. 128.

2. Schnitzler, op. cit., p. 249.

3. Grunfeld, op. cit., p. 149; Kazin, op. cit., p. 11.

4. Avineri, *The Making of Modern Zionism,* p. 107.

5. Adams, op. cit., p. 28.

6. Mendes-Flohr and Reinharz, op. cit., p. 103–4.

7. Schnitzler, op. cit., p. 155. This statement has a fascinating similarity to Freud's view of the psychoanalytic process.

8. Charles Hannam, *Almost an Englishman* (London, 1979), p. 10.

9. Ibid., pp. 11, 20–21.

10. Ibid., pp. 150–51.

11. Ibid., pp. 202–6.

12. Aris, op. cit., p. 28.

13. Howard Sachar, *Diaspora* (New York, 1985), pp. 39, 42.

14. Aris, op. cit., p. 220.

15. Hyman, op. cit., p. 155.

16. Heine, op. cit., p. 39.

17. Julien Benda, *Treason of the Intellectuals* (New York, 1969), pp. 85–94, 114, 117. But he spoke at a French Communist rally in the 1950s to denounce Jewish victims of the East European Communist purge trials as traitors. Lottman, op. cit., p. 270.

18. Cahnman, op. cit., p. 26.

19. Wistrich, *Jews of Vienna,* pp. 30–31.

20. Edward Grossman, "A Romantic Grows Up," *Jerusalem Post International Edition,* September 5, 1987.

21. *Jerusalem Report,* January 2, 1992.

22. Simon Sebag Montefiore, "Curious Georgia," *The New Republic,* June 29, 1992, p. 18; *Jerusalem Report,* April 2, 1992, p. 31.

23. Hermann Giliomee, "Mandela's Mess," *New Republic,* October 19, 1992, p. 18.

>4>

24. Avineri, *Hess*, p. 194.
25. Duker, op. cit., p. 303
26. Quoted in Arendt, *Origins*, p. 117.
27. Mendes-Flohr and Reinharz, op. cit., p. 314.
28. Burston, op. cit., p. 13.
29. Endelman, *Jewish Apostasy*, p. 88.
30. Cahnman, op. cit., pp. 162–64.
31. Hyman, op. cit., pp. 8–9, 12.
32. Baron, "The Impact of the Revolution of 1848 on Jewish Emancipation," in Duker, op. cit., p. 156.
33. Scholem, *On Jews and Judaism in Crisis*, p. 87.
34. Betty Jean Lifton, *The King of Children: A Biography of Janusz Korczak* (New York, 1988).
35. Ilya Ehrenberg, *Memoirs: 1921–1941* (New York, 1964), pp. 33–34.
36. *Jerusalem Report*, April 2, 1992, p. 37.
37. Cited in Martin Peretz, "Cambridge Diarist," *New Republic*, February 10, 1992, p. 41.
38. Sachar, *Diaspora*, pp. 332, 336–37.
39. Anna Husarska, "Urban Blight," *New Republic*, December 9, 1991, pp. 11–12.
40. Michael Kaufman, "Poland's Plucky Activist," *New York Times Magazine*, April 26, 1987. See also Timothy Garton Ash, "Eastern Europe: Après le Deluge, Nous," *New York Review of Books*, August 16, 1990.
41. Heine, op. cit., p. 39.
42. Bauman, *Modernity and Ambivalence*, p. 123.
43. Baron, in Baron, op. cit., p. 340.
44. Cited in Richard Taruskin, "The Dark Side of Modern Music," *The New Republic*, September 5, 1988.
45. Avineri, *Hess*, p. 197.
46. Bach, op. cit., pp. 124–25.
47. Beller, op. cit., pp. 75, 86.
48. *Jerusalem Post International Edition*, September 28, 1991.
49. Romain Gary, *The Dance of Genghis Cohn* (New York, 1968), p. 3.
50. Michael Stanislawski, "Jewish Apostasy in Russia: A Tentative Typology," in Endelman, *Jewish Apostasy*, p. 189.
51. Brown, op. cit., pp. 12–13, 19; Alter, *Defenses of the Imagination*, p. 35.
52. Dawidowicz, op. cit., pp. 398–99.
53. Marc Chagall, *My Life* (New York, 1989), pp. 105, 170.
54. Walter Laqueur, "From Russia with Hate," *New Republic*, February 5, 1990.
55. Ludmilla Tsigelman, "The Impact of Ideological Changes in the USSR on Different Generations of the Soviet Jewish Intelligentsia," in Roi and Becker, op. cit., pp. 43–48.
56. *Washington Post*, March 7, 1992.
57. *Forward*, May 29, 1992.
58. *Jerusalem Report*, October 17, 1991, p. 7; January 2, 1992, p. 2.
59. Ahad Ha-Am, "Slavery in Freedom" (1891), *Selected Essays*, pp. 172–73.
60. Ibid.
61. Ben-Horin, op. cit., p. 175.

62. Michel Abitbol, "The Encounter Between French Jewry and the Jews of North Africa," Malino and Wasserstein, op. cit., pp. 34–35.

63. Raymond Aron, *Memoirs* (New York, 1990), p. 12. In the same way, two thousand years earlier, Josephus had justified his loyalty to the Roman Empire by insisting that antisemitism was a Greek product. Norman Bertwich, *Josephus* (Philadelphia, 1914), pp. 215–16.

64. Hyman, op. cit., pp. 42–52, 118–19, 132, 137, 139, 203.

65. Ibid., pp. 21–22, 156–57, 172, 227.

66. Léon Blum, *For All Mankind,* p. 166.

67. Ibid., p. 180.

68. William Cohen and Irwin Wall, "French Communism and the Jews," in Malino and Wasserstein, op. cit., pp. 84–85. Another French Jew wrote, "During the summer of 1940, I told myself that it was better to save 40 million Frenchmen than 500,000 Jews! The first racial restrictions reinforced my saddened acceptance. . . . I was even ready to accept the slaughter of the Jews if salvation for the rest of the French was to be bought at that price." Edgar Morin, cited in Memmi, op. cit., p. 233.

69. Natalie Zemon Davis, "A Modern Hero," *New York Review of Books,* April 26, 1990, p. 27.

70. Aron, *Memoirs,* pp. 444, 57.

71. Ibid., pp. 348–51.

72. Ibid., pp. 336–37, 341, 345, 347, 444.

73. Ibid., op. cit., pp. 442, 446.

74. Colton, op. cit., p. 477.

75. *Jerusalem Report,* January 27, 1994, p. 42.

76. Sachar, *Diaspora,* pp. 53–54, 63–65; Alexander Stille, *Benevolence and Betrayal: Five Italian Jewish Families Under Fascism* (New York, 1991).

77. Endelman, *Radical Assimilation,* p. 74.

78. Lewisohn, op. cit., p. 232.

79. Goodman, op. cit., pp. 97, 99–100, 145.

80. Einstein, op. cit., pp. 46–47.

81. Gerber, op. cit., p. 234.

82. Goodman, op. cit., p. 163.

9. THE CONTRARY CHILDREN

1. Schnitzler, op. cit., pp. 152–54.

2. Two cases known to the author. Perhaps this shows how membership in the club—as often happens with increasing integration into society—makes one both more secure and less awed by its luster.

3. Ernest Samuels, *Bernard Berenson: The Making of a Legend* (Cambridge, MA, 1967), p. 499.

4. Samuels, op. cit., pp. 130.

5. Baumgarten, op. cit., p. 54.

6. Berlin, *Against the Current,* pp. 232–33.

7. Samuels, op. cit., p. 16.

8. Feuer, in Maier and Waxman, op. cit., p. 104.

9. Cited in Barry Rubin, *Istanbul Intrigues* (New York, 1989), p. 125. See also Freud's other train story in chapter 2.

10. Schnitzler, op. cit., pp. 152–54.

11. Arendt, *Varnhagen*, pp. 216–17.

12. Berlin, *Against the Current*, p. 279.

13. Arendt, *Varnhagen*, pp. 217–18, 222.

14. Craig Horowitz, "Holy War," *New York*, February 14, 1994, p. 33.

15. Roth, *Shifting Landscape*, pp. 114–15.

16. *Jerusalem Report*, April 23, 1992, pp. 31–32.

17. Ibid.

18. Ha-Am, *Collected Essays*, p. 248.

19. Isaac Asimov, *Pebble in the Sky* (New York, 1950), pp. 43–44, 64, 221–22.

20. Dershowitz, op. cit., p. 328.

21. Koestler, *Thieves in the Night*, p. 278. While the words quoted come from a character in a novel, Koestler affirms such sentiments in his autobiography. See *Arrow in the Blue*, pp. 102–4.

22. Samuels, op. cit., p. 524.

23. Lewisohn, op. cit., p. 27.

24. Ibid., pp. 162–63.

25. Berlin, *Against the Current*, pp. 232–33.

26. Gilbert, op. cit., p. 252.

27. Arendt, *Varnhagen*, p. 219; Schnitzler, op. cit., pp. 152–54; Benda, *Treason of the Intellectuals*, pp. 11–12.

28. Schnitzler, op. cit., pp. 152–54.

29. Hecht, *A Jew in Love*, pp. 142–44.

30. Roth, *Portnoy*, p. 224.

31. G. W. Lewin, *Resolving Social Conflicts* (New York, 1948).

32. Dershowitz, op. cit., pp. 65–67.

33. Arendt, *Varnhagen*, pp. 216–18, 120, 208.

34. Ibid., p. 120.

35. Heine, op. cit., pp. 14–15.

36. Ibid., p. 26. Compare to Benjamin's sinking-ship analogy, chapter 6.

37. Samuels, op. cit., pp. 524–25, 536, 576. For parallel statements by Varnhagen, Heine, and others, see chapter 1.

38. Ibid., p. 576.

39. There have been various attempts to prove that leading antisemites were themselves partly Jewish and thus acting out of a sense of self-hatred. Adolf Hitler's father was illegitimate and it has been suggested that his grandfather was a Jewish employer of the dictator's grandmother. See Franz Jetzinger, *Hitler's Youth* (Westport, CT, 1976), pp. 19–25. There is some evidence that Hitler feared this possibility, and thus was acting psychologically like a self-hating Jew even if the story was untrue. Other antisemitic leaders were accused of being Jewish. For such associations see, for example, Frederick Busi, *The Pope of Antisemitism: The Career and Legacy of Edouard-Adolphe Drumont* (Lanham, MD, 1986), p. 11; Jacob Katz, *The Darker Side of Genius: Richard Wagner's Antisemitism* (Lon-

don, 1986), pp. 120–22; and Moshe Zimmermann, *Wilhelm Marr: The Patriarch of Anti-Semitism* (New York, 1986), p. 13.

40. Gay, *Freud, Jews and Other Germans*, pp. 202–28.

41. Beller, op. cit., pp. 221–22, 225; Liptzin, op. cit., pp. 184–94; Scholem, *On Jews and Judaism in Crisis*, pp. 84–85.

42. Endelman, op. cit., *Radical Assimilation*, pp. 136–39.

43. Gay, *Freud, Jews, and Other Germans*, p. 195. See chapter 2. Also Grunfeld, p. 80.

44. Michael Ignatieff, "The Limits of Sainthood," *The New Republic*, June 18, 1990. The fascination for Weil among intellectuals and leading Catholic theologians shows how much impact even the most bizarre assimilation experiences can have on a wider audience.

45. The American Jewish intellectual Lionel Abel recorded his mother's reaction on first seeing newsreels of the concentration camps, "I don't think the Jews can ever get over the disgrace of this." Abel, *The Intellectual Follies*, pp. 270–71. For a fuller picture of postwar European attitudes, see Wistrich in Singer and Selden, op. cit.

46. Markish in Roi and Becker, op. cit., pp. 214–22.

47. *Jerusalem Report*, May 7, 1992, p. 29.

48. Sachar, *Diaspora*, pp. 36–37; Wistrich, in Singer and Seldin, op. cit., p. 14.

49. See, for example, *Washington Post*, December 24, 1993. Zhirinovsky changed his name from Eidelstein in 1964 at the age of eighteen. He sought and obtained an invitation to emigrate to Israel in 1983 and worked with a Jewish group, Shalom, in Moscow. *Washington Post* and *Washington Times*, April 4, 1994.

50. *Washington Post*, December 13, 1993.

51. Dershowitz, op. cit., pp. 65–67; *Forward*, May 29, 1992; Frank Brady, *Bobby Fischer: Profile of a Prodigy* (New York, 1989), p. 2. On Rosenwald's background, see chapter 3.

52. This attitude was also partly a reaction against totalitarian ideologies that insisted that intellectuals must be ideologically committed instead of intentionally isolated.

53. Marjorie Williams, "The Long and the Short of Richard G. Darman," *Washington Post Magazine*, July 29, 1990.

54. Ibid., p. 27.

55. *Washington Times*, July 8, 1991.

56. Obviously, this analysis seeks neither to impugn a right to criticize Jews or Israel in a balanced or constructive way nor to equate criticism with antisemitism. The point here is that criticism may be a form of disassociation whose alternative is not praise or participation but silence.

57. Those involved were leaders of the Islamic fundamentalist groups Hamas and Islamic Jihad. The statement was an outburst in the midst of a scholarly article of literary criticism. Bruce Robbins in *PMLA* 107, October 1992, p. 1283. See also pp. 1280–82 and *PMLA* 108, May 1993, pp. 540–42.

58. Dershowitz, op. cit., pp. 234–35. Some intellectuals of diverse views, like professors Michael Walzer and Dershowitz, publisher Martin Peretz, and columnists William Safire, A. M. Rosenthal, and Charles Krauthammer, were outspoken as Jews on Jewish issues. Since this did not reduce their success it encouraged imitators. But they were also criticized and typecast for their role, a warning to those more thin-skinned or having different ambitions.

59. David Bromwich, *Politics by Other Means: Higher Education and Group Thinking* (New York, 1992), cited in *Washington Post Book World*, October 18, 1992.

60. Abel, op. cit., pp. 276, 279.

61. Liptzin, op. cit., p. 93.

10. PHILOSOPHY WARS

1. Ben-Horin, op. cit., p. 91.

2. Miller, *Timebends*, p. 314.

3. Marx, *Critique of Hegel's Philosophy of Right*, op. cit., p. 141.

4. Cited in Erik Erikson, *Identity, Youth and Crisis* (New York, 1968), pp. 21–22.

5. The worldview of America's political right seems potentially antisemitic, since it demonizes "humanism," "New York," "Hollywood," and liberals while exalting Christian values. But though these were anti-Jewish themes in Europe, antisemitism had little appeal for American conservatives since it was so discredited, other issues were far more salient, Jews were a small part of their enemies, and socially conservative Orthodox Jews were allies. Despite the movement's relative lack of antisemitism, however, most Jews saw it as a threat, given their historical experience and the symbols it invoked.

6. Bruce Feirstein, *New York Observer*, October 11, 1993.

7. Ben-Horin, op. cit., p. 82; Adams, op. cit., pp. 35–36.

8. Ha-Am, *Collected Essays*, pp. 177–79.

9. Richard I. Cohen, "Nostalgia and 'Return to the Ghetto' " in Frankel and Zipperstein, op. cit., pp. 144–45.

10. Burston, op. cit., p. 87: "Any norm of human development held in contrast to the prevailing cultural pattern is itself a cultural and historical product and is often modeled on the idealization of previous epochs or other cultures."

11. That is, women, nonwhite races, and subjected nations or classes.

12. Mendes-Flohr and Reinharz, op. cit., p. 191.

13. Roth, "The Anatomy Lesson," in *Zuckerman Bound*, p. 640.

14. Burston, op. cit., pp. 10–17, 94.

15. Ibid., p. 69.

16. Gershom Scholem, *On Jews and Judaism in Crisis*, pp. 31–33.

17. Elias Canetti, *Auto Da Fé*, pp. 377–78.

18. Alfred Kazin, *New York Jew* (New York, 1978), p. 27.

19. Leviticus 26:36–37.

20. William Chafe, *Never Stop Running* (New York, 1993), pp. xvi, xviii, 2, 16, 36–37, 44–45, 62, 79–81, 122, 127.

21. Samuels, op. cit., p. 483.

22. Lewisohn, op. cit., p. 38; Cowan, op. cit., p. 53.

23. A fairly typical American Jew with a burning sense of social injustice, Eli Tannen taught his daughters that books and ideas were more important than possessions and encouraged them to be nonconformist. "We learned the word 'iconoclastic' before we were 5,"

his daughter recalled. Barbara Matusow, "Talking With Deborah Tannen," *Washingtonian,* December 1993, p. 103.

24. Examples of this range from the multiethnic bomber crews of World War II films to that remarkable example of assimilating struggle, *Revenge of the Nerds,* in which misfits from different outgroups defeat the blond bullies of the most prestigious fraternity, but also get the pretty girl who resembles the latter.

25. Richard Cohen, "The Politics of Appearance," *Washington Post Sunday Magazine,* April 19, 1992, p. 3.

26. Martha Nussbaum, "The Softness of Reason," *New Republic,* July 13 and 20, 1992, p. 27.

27. See Michael Lewis, "The Speculator," *New Republic,* January 10 and 17, 1994.

28. Patricia Storace, "Look Away, Dixie Land," *New York Review of Books,* December 19, 1991, p. 31; Cowan, op. cit., p. 51.

29. Goldin, op. cit., pp. 216–17. For additional examples of such efforts and conflicts, see chapter 6.

30. David Samuels, "The Rap on Rap," *New Republic,* November 11, 1991. See also Arthur Kempton, "Native Sons," *New York Review of Books,* April 11, 1991, p. 58.

31. Henry Feingold, "Jewish Identity in America," in Gordis and Ben-Horin, *The American Jewish Experience,* p. 76.

32. Dershowitz, op. cit., p. 3.

33. Compare this to the contrasting Greek mythical hero Antaeus, who—as a more "normal" figure—was strengthened by contact with his native earth.

34. Shlomo Avineri, *The Making of Modern Zionism,* p. 106.

35. Lewisohn, op. cit., pp. 13–15; Jacob Neusner, *Understanding Rabbinic Judaism* (New York, 1974), p. 173.

36. Roth, *Portnoy's Complaint,* p. 247.

37. Jeremy Sher, *Washington Post,* April 22, 1992.

38. Brenner, op. cit., pp. 146, 150–53.

39. Celia McGee, "The Guru of Condé Nast," *New York Observer,* October 18, 1993.

40. Bloom, op. cit., p. 35.

41. Ibid., p. 16.

42. Sigmund Freud, *New Introductory Lectures on Psychoanalysis,* (London, 1932), p. 67.

43. Angoff and Levin, op. cit., p. 545.

44. S. Y. Agnon, *Shira* (New York, 1989), p. 218.

45. Review of Howard Jacobson, *Roots Schmoots: Journey among Jews,* in *Jerusalem Report,* January 13, 1994, p. 47.

46. Ellis Weiner, "Internettled," *Spy,* February 1994, p. 69.

47. Cited in *Jerusalem Report,* May 20, 1993.

48. Allen Ginsberg, *Collected Poems, 1947–1980* (New York, 1987), pp. 614–16.

49. *The New Yorker,* February 15, 1993; *New York Observer,* November 22, 1993.

50. Berlin, *Against the Current,* p. 240.

51. Lewisohn, op. cit., p. 121.

52. See Kinsley, *The New Republic,* February 24, 1992; Martin Peretz, "Cambridge Diarist," *New Republic,* February 10, 1992; and Leon Wieseltier, "Washington Diarist," *New Republic,* March 2, 1992.

53. Melvyn Hill, *Hannah Arendt* (New York, 1979), pp. 9, 222, 278.

54. Hannah Arendt, "Privileged Jews," in Duker, op. cit., pp. 58–60.

55. David Joroff, "Dark and Perverse," *Jerusalem Post,* March 18, 1989 weekly edition.

56. An interesting example is Mortimer Adler, *Truth in Religion* (New York, 1991).

57. The debate over the Chabad Hasidic movement's effort to display Hanukkah menorahs publicly posed interesting problems, with many Jewish groups questioning the legality of such a display.

58. Lear's column and Charles Krauthammer's response, *Jerusalem Post,* June 3 and 7, 1993. A similar case was Michael Lerner, who, despite his public pose as a religious Jew, also could not infuse any real content into his advocacy of the meaning of life as a political issue even when Hillary Rodham Clinton briefly took up the idea. The specter of Jews discussing the meaning of life with no reference to religion was all the more remarkable in its passing unnoticed by others.

59. Cited in Bromwich, op. cit., p. 37.

60. Philip Gourevitch, "Behold Now Behemoth," *Harper's,* July 1993, pp. 55–58, 62.

61. Aris, op. cit., pp. 120–21.

62. Roth, *Reading Myself and Others,* pp. 131–52.

11. NATIONHOOD, DIASPORA, GALUT

1. Ben-Horin, op. cit., p. 94.

2. Berlin, op. cit., p. 286; Abel, *The Intellectual Follies,* p. 260; Lewisohn, op. cit., p. 234.

3. Gay, *Freud,* pp. 117–18; Erik Erikson, *Identity, Youth and Crisis,* pp. 21–22. See also Baumgarten, p. 128.

4. Eisenberg, op. cit., p. 232.

5. David Singer and Ruth Selden, *American Jewish Year Book 1993* (New York, 1993). See Sergio Della Pergola, "Jews in the European Community," p. 49.

6. Ibid, p. 179. Irving Greenberg, "Aliyah, After All?" *Jerusalem Report,* March 26, 1992, p. 40.

7. Singer and Selden, op. cit., pp. 179–81.

8. Feingold, op. cit., p. 77.

9. Including large numbers of people with Jewish ancestors—but no such identity—will inflate future statistics.

10. Bauman, *Modernity and Ambivalence,* p. 159.

11. Avineri, *Making of Modern Zionism,* p. 58.

12. Memmi, op. cit., pp. 72, 119.

13. A high proportion of gay writers—Larry Kramer, Kushner, and Harvey Fierstein among them—were Jews. This cluster was similar to that in other movements of social rebellion. Homosexual self-doubt and concealment also had parallels with the assimilation process.

14. Memmi, op. cit., pp. 202–3.

15. Alter, *America and Israel,* p. 15.

16. Jonathan Sarna, "Jewish Identity in the Changing World of American Religion," in Gordis and Ben-Horin, op. cit., p. 91.

17. Lewisohn, op. cit., p. 125.

18. Scholem, *From Berlin to Jerusalem*, p. 26.

19. Ben Hecht, *Collected Stories* (London, n.d.), p. 164.

20. Scholem, *On Jews and Judaism in Crisis*, pp. 31–32: Reason "has had more notable successes in destruction [than construction]. The devotees of Reason have tried to build networks of positive thought—but these networks are far less enduring. . . . I know this is a very painful point and many admirers of Reason (of whom I am one) do not like to hear this. . . . I believe that morality as a constructive force is impossible without religion, without some Power beyond Pure Reason."

21. Ben-Horin, op. cit., pp. 85, 91, 113.

22. Roth, *Portnoy's Complaint*, pp. 78–79, 247.

23. See, for example, Isaiah Berlin, "On the Pursuit of the Ideal," *New York Review of Books*, March 17, 1988. The "Old" Testament is the main exception here but enters the canon through its effect on Christianity, and usually in a Christian translation at that.

24. *Forward*, books supplement, November 1991.

25. Gershom Gorenberg, "Their Sodom and Ours," *Jerusalem Report*, November 5, 1992, p. 55.

26. Roth, *Patrimony*, p. 238.

27. Kafka, *The Trial*, pp. 235–37.

28. Lewisohn, op. cit., pp. 164, 198–99.

29. Berlin, *Against the Current*, p. 239.

30. "The Menorah," for the Hanukkah issue of the Zionist newspaper *Die Welt*.

31. Avineri, *Moses Hess*, pp. 177–78.

32. Ibid., p. 220.

33. Avineri, *The Making of Modern Zionism*, p. 115.

34. Goodman, op. cit., p. 111.

35. Henry Roth, op. cit., p. 184.

36. Arthur Koestler, *Promise and Fulfillment* (New York, 1949), pp. 332–35.

37. *Jerusalem Report*, February 27, 1992. Naturally there are many exceptions to these and the following points.

38. S. Y. Agnon, *A Guest for the Night* (New York, 1968), p. 182.

39. Koestler, *Thieves in the Night*, pp. 152–53.

40. Agnon, *A Guest for the Night*, p. 101; Agnon, *Shira*, p. 547.

41. Ibid.

42. Koestler, *Thieves in the Night*, p. 154.

43. Einstein, *About Zionism*, p. 53.

44. Hence a Jewish joke that would be considered antisemitic if told by someone else: Jews are like fertilizer, more pleasant and productive when spread around than if concentrated in one place.

45. Comay, op. cit., p. 46.

46. His revealing title is, "I took myself as I was." *ADL Bulletin*, December 1976.

47. Henry Roth, op. cit., pp. 224, 185.

48. Roth, *Portnoy's Complaint*, pp. 250, 264.

49. Steven M. Cohen, "Undue Stress on American Antisemitism?" *Sh'ma,* September 1, 1989, p. 113.

50. Koestler, *Arrow in the Blue,* p. 306.

51. Roth, *Reading Myself and Others,* p. 150.

BIBLIOGRAPHY

Abel, Lionel. *Important Nonsense*. Buffalo, NY, 1987.
———. *The Intellectual Follies*. Buffalo, NY, 1984.
Adams, Elsie. *Israel Zangwill*. New York, 1971.
Adamson, Joe. *Groucho, Harpo, Chico, and Sometimes Zeppo*. New York, 1976.
Adler, Mortimer. *Philosopher at Large*. New York, 1977.
———. *A Second Look in the Rear View Mirror*. New York, 1992.
———. *Truth in Religion*. New York, 1991.
Adorno, Theodor. *The Jargon of Authenticity*. Evanston, IL, 1973.
———. *Notes to Literature*. New York, 1991.
Agnon, S. Y. *A Guest for the Night*. New York, 1968.
Alderman, Geoffrey. *Modern British Jewry*. New York, 1992.
Alfrey, Anthony. *Edward VII and His Jewish Court*. London, 1991.
Allen, Woody. *God*. New York, 1975.
———. *Three Films of Woody Allen*. New York, 1987.
Alter, Robert. *After the Tradition*. New York, 1969.
———. *America and Israel*. New York, 1970.
———. *Defenses of the Imagination: Jewish Writers and Modern Historical Crisis*. Philadelphia, 1977.
———. *Modern Hebrew Literature*. New York, 1975.
———. *Necessary Angels*. Cambridge, MA, 1991.
Altmann, Alexander. *Essays in Jewish Intellectual History*. Hanover, NH, 1981.
———. *Moses Mendelssohn*. London, 1973.
Angoff, Charles, and Meyer Levin. *The Rise of American Jewish Literature*. New York, 1970.

Arendt, Hannah. *Eichmann in Jerusalem.* New York, 1976.

———. *The Human Condition.* Chicago, 1958.

———. *The Jew as Pariah.* New York, 1978.

———. *The Life of the Mind.* New York, 1981.

———. *Origins of Totalitarianism.* New York, 1973.

———. *Rachel Varnhagen.* New York, 1974.

Aris, Stephen. *But There Are No Jews in England.* New York, 1971.

Aron, Raymond. *De Gaulle, Israel and the Jews.* London, 1969.

———. *Essai sur la condition juive contemporaine.* Paris, 1989.

———. *Memoirs.* New York, 1990.

Asimov, Isaac. *In Memory Yet Green: Autobiography, 1920–1954.* New York, 1979.

———. *Pebble in the Sky.* Garden City, NY, 1950.

Auerbach, Jerold. *Rabbis and Lawyers.* Bloomington, IN, 1990.

Ausmus, Harry. *The Polite Escape: On the Myth of Secularization.* Athens, OH, 1982.

———. *Will Herberg: From Right to Right.* Chapel Hill, NC, 1987.

Avineri, Shlomo. *The Making of Modern Zionism.* New York, 1981.

———. *Moses Hess, Prophet of Communism and Zionism.* New York, 1985.

Avni, Haim. *Argentina and the Jews.* Tuscaloosa, AL, 1991.

Bach, Hans. *The German Jew.* New York, 1984.

Bailey, Jennifer. *Norman Mailer: Quick-Change Artist.* New York, 1979.

Baines, Jennifer. *Mandelstam: The Later Poetry.* New York, 1976.

Baldwin, Neil. *Man Ray, American Artist.* New York, 1988.

Baron, Salo. *Great Ages and Ideas of the Jewish People.* New York, 1956.

———. *Steeled by Adversity: Essays and Addresses on American Jewish Life.* Philadelphia, 1971.

Bauman, Zygmunt. *Modernity and Ambivalence.* Ithaca, NY, 1991.

———. *Paradoxes of Assimilation.* New Brunswick, NJ, 1990.

Baumgarten, Murray. *City Scriptures: Modern Jewish Writing.* Cambridge, MA, 1982.

Bein, Alex. *The Jewish Question: Biography of a World Problem.* Rutherford, NJ, 1990.

Belle, Jean Michel. *Les folles années de Maurice Sachs.* Paris, 1979.

Beller, Stephen. *Vienna and the Jews 1867–1938.* New York, 1989.

Bellow, Saul. *Dangling Man.* New York, 1988.

———. *To Jerusalem and Back.* New York, 1976.

———. *The Victim.* New York, 1947.

Benda, Julian. *La fin de l'éternel.* Paris, 1977.

———. *The Treason of the Intellectuals.* New York, 1969.

Ben-Horin, Meir. *Max Nordau: Philosopher of Human Solidarity.* New York, 1956.

Benjamin, Walter. *Correspondence of Walter Benjamin and Gershom Scholem.* Cambridge, MA, 1992.

———. *Illuminations.* New York, 1986.

———. *Reflections.* New York, 1978.

Benny, Jack. *Sunday Nights at Seven.* New York, 1990.

Ben-Sasson, Haim H. *A History of the Jewish People.* Cambridge, MA, 1976.

Ben-Sasson, Haim H., and S. Ettinger. *Jewish Society through the Ages.* New York, 1972.

Berg, A. Scott. *Goldwyn: A Biography.* New York, 1989.

Bergreen, Lawrence. *As Thousands Cheer.* New York, 1990.

Berkley, George. *Vienna and Its Jews: The Tragedy of Success 1880s–1980s.* Cambridge, MA, 1988.

Berlin, Irving. *Everybody Knew But Me.* New York, 1945.

Berlin, Isaiah. *Against the Current.* New York, 1980.

———. *Conversations with Isaiah Berlin.* New York, 1992.

———. *Karl Marx: His Life and Environment.* New York, 1963.

———. *Personal Impressions.* New York, 1981.

———. *Trois essais sur la condition juive.* Paris, 1973.

Berman, Myron. *The Attitude of American Jewry towards East European Jewish Immigration, 1881–1914.* New York, 1980.

Bermant, Chaim. *The Cousinhood.* New York, 1972.

Berneri, Camillo. *Le juif anti-semite.* Paris, 1936.

Bernhard, Sandra. *Confessions of a Pretty Lady.* New York, 1988.

Bernhardt, Sarah. *My Double Life.* London, 1977.

Bernstein, Eduard. *Ferdinand Lassalle as a Social Reformer.* St. Clair Shores, MI, 1970.

Bernstein, Jeremy. *Einstein.* New York, 1976.

Bettauer, Hugo. *The City without Jews.* New York, 1991.

Bettelheim, Bruno. *Freud's Vienna and Other Essays.* New York, 1979.

———. *Surviving, and Other Essays.* New York, 1979.

Biale, David. *Power and Powerlessness in Jewish History.* New York, 1986.

Birmingham, Stephen. *Our Crowd.* New York, 1967.

———. *The Rest of Us.* New York, 1984.

———. *The Right People.* Boston, 1968.

Birnbaum, Pierre. *Un mythe politique: la "Republique juive".* Paris, 1988.

Biskin, Miriam. *My Life among the Gentiles.* South Brunswick, NJ, 1985.

Blake, Robert. *Disraeli's Grand Tour.* London, 1982.

Bloom, Alexander. *Prodigal Sons: The New York Intellectuals and Their World.* New York, 1986.

Bloom, Allan. *The Closing of the American Mind.* New York, 1988.

Bloom, Harold. *The Strong Light of the Canonical: Kafka, Freud, and Scholem as Revisionists of Jewish Culture and Thought.* New York, 1987.

Blum, Léon. *For All Mankind.* Gloucester, MA, 1969.

Blum, Steven. *Walter Lippmann and the American Century.* New York, 1981.

Blythe, Cheryl. *Say Good Night Gracie! The Story of Burns and Allen.* New York, 1986.

Boas, Franz. *Anthropology and Modern Life.* New York, 1928.

———. *Race, Language and Culture.* Chicago, 1982.

Bonner, Elena. *Mothers and Daughters.* New York, 1992.

Bottomore, T. B. *The Frankfurt School.* New York, 1984.

Bouganim, Ami. *Le juif égaré.* Paris, 1990.

Bowen-Moore, Patricia. *Hannah Arendt's Philosophy of Natality.* New York, 1989.

Bower, Tom. *Maxwell: The Outsider.* New York, 1992.

Brady, Frank. *Bobby Fischer: Profile of a Prodigy.* New York, 1989.

Brandeis, Louis. *Brandeis on Zionism.* Westport, CT, 1976.

Braun, Thom. *Disraeli the Novelist.* Boston, 1981.

Brenner, Rachel. *Assimilation and Assertion: The Response to the Holocaust in Mordecai Richler's Writings.* New York, 1989.

Bronner, Stephen. *Rosa Luxemburg: A Revolutionary for Our Times.* New York, 1987.

Brooks, Mel. *History of the World, Part I.* New York, 1981.

Brown, Clarence. *Mandelstam.* Cambridge, MA, 1973.

Bruce, Lenny. *The Almost Unpublished Lenny Bruce.* Philadelphia, 1984.

———. *The Essential Lenny Bruce.* St. Albans, VT, 1975.

———. *How to Talk Dirty and Influence People.* New York, 1991.

Brym, Robert. *The Jewish Intelligentsia and Russian Marxism.* New York, 1978.

Burns, George. *All My Best Friends.* New York, 1989.

———. *The Third Time Around.* New York, 1980.

Burns, Michael. *Dreyfus: A Family Affair, 1789–1945.* New York, 1991.

Burston, Daniel. *The Legacy of Erich Fromm.* Cambridge, MA, 1991.

Burt, Robert. *Two Jewish Justices: Outcasts in the Promised Land.* Berkeley, CA, 1988.

Butler, Pierce. *Judah P. Benjamin.* Philadelphia, 1907.

Cahnman, Werner. *German Jewry.* New Brunswick, NJ, 1989.

Canetti, Elias. *Auto Da Fé.* London, 1983.

Carlebach, Julius. *Karl Marx and the Radical Critique of Judaism.* Boston, 1978.

Carlier, Claude. *Marcel Dassault: The Legend of a Century.* 1993.

Chagall, Marc. *My Life.* New York, 1989.

Chapman, Abraham. *Jewish-American Literature.* New York, 1974.

Chernin, Kim. *In My Mother's House.* New York, 1983.

Chouraqui, Andre. *A Man in Three Worlds.* Lanham, MD, 1984.

Clark, Ronald. *Einstein: The Life and Times.* London, 1973.

Clingman, Stephen. *The Novels of Nadine Gordimer.* Amherst, MA, 1992.

Cohen, Edward. *Plays of Jewish Interest.* New York, 1982.

Cohen, Naomi. *American Jews and the Zionist Idea.* New York, 1975.

———. *Encounter with Emancipation: The German Jews in the United States.* Philadelphia, 1984.

———. *Jews in Christian America.* New York, 1992.

Cohen, Stephen M. *American Assimilation or Jewish Revival?* Bloomington, IN, 1988.

Coles, Robert. *Erik Erikson: The Growth of His Work.* New York, 1987.

Collier, Linda. *Lewis Namier.* New York, 1989.

Collins, John. *Between Athens and Jerusalem: Jewish Identity in the Hellenistic Diaspora.* New York, 1982.

Colton, Joel. *Léon Blum: Humanist in Politics.* Cambridge, MA, 1974.

Comay, Joan. *Who's Who in Jewish History.* New York, 1974.

Compton, Susan. *Marc Chagall: My Life, My Dreams.* New York, 1990.

Connerton, Paul. *Contemporary Jewish Religious Thought.* New York, 1987.

———. *The Tragedy of Enlightenment: An Essay on the Frankfurt School.* New York, 1980.

Corrin, Jay. *G. K. Chesterton and Hilaire Belloc: The Battle against Modernity.* Athens, OH, 1981.

Cowan, Paul. *An Orphan in History.* Garden City, NY, 1982.

Cuddihy, John Murray. *The Ordeal of Civility.* New York, 1974.

Davidson, Arnold. *Mordecai Richler.* New York, 1983.

Dawidowicz, Lucy. *The Golden Tradition: Jewish Life and Thought in Eastern Europe.* New York, 1967.

Day, Frank. *Arthur Koestler.* New York, 1987.

Derrida, Jacques. *Cinders.* Lincoln, NE, 1991.

———. *A Derrida Reader.* New York, 1991.

———. *The Ear of the Other.* Lincoln, NE, 1988.

Dershowitz, Alan. *Chutzpah.* New York, 1991.

———. *The Non-Jewish Jew and Other Essays.* New York, 1968.

Deutscher, Isaac. *The Prophet Unarmed: Trotsky, 1921–1929.* New York, 1970.

Diller, Jerry. *Freud's Jewish Identity.* Rutherford, NJ, 1991.

Disraeli, Benjamin. *Disraeli's Reminiscences.* London, 1985.

———. *Jerusalem by Moonlight.* Berkeley Heights, NJ, 1965.

———. *Letters,* vols. 1–4. Buffalo, 1989.

———. *Tancred.* Philadelphia, 1970.

Drew, Bettina. *Nelson Algren: A Life on the Wild Side.* New York, 1990.

Drew, Joseph. *An Examination of Kurt Lewin's Theory of "Jewish Self-Hatred" among Leaders from the Periphery.* Hilo, HI, 1976.

Dreyfus, Alfred. *The Dreyfus Case.* New York, 1977.

———. *Five Years of My Life.* New York, 1971.

Dukakis, Kitty. *Now You Know.* New York, 1990.

Duker, Abraham. *Emancipation and Counter-Emancipation.* New York, 1974.

Durkheim, Emile. *On Morality and Society.* Chicago, 1973.

———. *On Religion.* Boston, 1975.

———. *Professional Ethics and Civic Morals.* New York, 1992.

———. *Readings.* New York, 1985.

Dylan, Bob. *Bob Dylan in His Own Words.* New York, 1978.

———. *Lyrics, 1962–1985.* New York, 1985.

Edwards, Ruth. *Victor Gollancz.* London, 1987.

Ehrenberg, Ilya. *Memoirs: 1921–1941.* New York, 1964.

Einstein, Albert. *About Zionism.* New York, 1931.

———. *Essays in Humanism.* New York, 1983.

———. *Ideas and Opinions.* London, 1973.

———. *Living Philosophies.* New York, 1979.

———. *Out of My Later Years.* New York, 1989.

———. *Test Case for Humanity.* London, 1944.

Eisen, Arnold. *The Chosen People in America.* Bloomington, IN, 1983.

———. *Galut.* Bloomington, IN, 1986.

Eisenberg, Azriel. *The Golden Land.* New York, 1964.

Endelman, Todd. *Jewish Apostasy in the Modern World.* New York, 1987.

———. *Radical Assimilation in English Jewish History 1656–1945.* Bloomington, IN, 1990.

Erikson, Erik. *Dimensions of a New Identity.* New York, 1974.

———. *Encounter with Erikson.* Missoula, MT, 1977.

———. *Identity, Youth and Crisis.* New York, 1968.

———. *Selected Papers.* New York, 1987.

Evans, Eli. *Judah P. Benjamin: The Jewish Confederate.* New York, 1988.

Evans, Richard. *Dialogue with Erik Erikson.* New York, 1981.

Everman, Welch. *Jerzy Kosinski: The Literature of Violation.* San Bernardino, CA, 1991.

Fein, Leonard. *Where Are We?* New York, 1988.

Feingold, Henry. *A Midrash on American Jewish History.* Albany, NY, 1982.

Fiedler, Leslie. *The Collected Essays of Leslie Fiedler,* 2 vols. New York, 1971.

———. *An End to Innocence: Essays on Culture and Politics.* Boston, 1955.

———. *Fiedler on the Roof: Essays on Literature and Jewish Identity.* Boston, 1991.

———. *A Fiedler Reader.* New York, 1977.

———. *Freaks: Myths and Images of the Secret Self.* New York, 1979.

———. *The Return of the Vanishing American.* New York, 1968.

———. *To the Gentiles.* New York, 1971.

Fink, Carole. *Marc Bloch: A Life in History.* New York, 1989.

Finkelstein, Norman. *The Ritual of a New Creation: Jewish Tradition and Contemporary Litera-ture.* Albany, NY, 1991.

Finler, Joel. *Stroheim.* Berkeley, 1968.

Fishman, William. *Jewish Radicals.* New York, 1974.

Fittko, Lisa. *Escape through the Pyrenees.* Chicago, 1991.

Fleg, Edmond. *Brief Survey of Jewish Literature.* New York, 1963.

———. *The Jewish Anthology.* Westport, CT, 1975.

———. *Why Am I a Jew?* New York, 1975.

Fleming, Donald. *Intellectual Migrations.* Cambridge, MA, 1969.

Footman, David. *Ferdinand Lassalle: Romantic Revolutionary.* New York, 1969.

———. *Foundations of the Frankfurt School of Social Research.* New Brunswick, NJ, 1984.

Frankel, J. *Prophecy and Politics: Socialism, Nationalism and the Russian Jews 1862–1917.* Cam-bridge, MA, 1981.

Frankel, J., and Steven Zipperstein. *Assimilation and Community.* New York, 1992.

Franklin, Myrtle. *Sir Moses Montefiore 1784–1885.* London, 1984.

Fraser, Steven. *Labor Will Rule: Sidney Hillman and the Rise of American Labor.* New York, 1991.

Freedland, Michael. *Irving Berlin.* New York, 1974.

French, Warren. *J. D. Salinger, Revisited.* Boston, 1988.

Freud, Sigmund. *Jokes and Their Location to the Unconscious.* New York, 1989.

———. *Letters of Sigmund Freud.* New York, 1992.

———. *New Introductory Lectures on Psychoanalysis.* London, 1932.

Friedlander, Judith. *Vilna on the Seine: Jewish Intellectuals in France since 1968.* New Haven, CT, 1990.

Friedlander, Saul. *When Memory Comes.* New York, 1979.

Friedman, Lawrence. *Understanding Cynthia Ozick.* Columbia, SC, 1991.

Friedman, Thomas L. *From Beirut to Jerusalem.* New York, 1989.

Fromm, Erich. *Escape from Freedom.* New York, 1941.

Furbank, Philip. *Italo Svevo: The Man and the Writer.* Berkeley, CA, 1966.

Gabler, Neal. *An Empire of Their Own: How the Jews Invented Hollywood.* New York, 1988.

Gammond, Peter. *Offenbach: His Life and Times.* Tunbridge Wells, England, 1980.

Garland, Henry. *Lessing.* Norwood, PA, 1977.

Gary, Romain. *The Dance of Genghis Cohn.* New York, 1968.

———. *King Solomon.* New York, 1983.

———. *Madam Rosa.* New York, 1986.

———. *Promise at Dawn.* New York, 1961.

Gatt-Rutter, John. *Italo Svevo: A Double Life.* New York, 1988.

Gay, Peter. *The Berlin-Jewish Spirit.* New York, 1972.

———. *The Dilemma of Democratic Socialism: Eduard Bernstein's Challenge to Marx.* New York, 1979.

———. *Freud: A Life for Our Time.* New York, 1988.

———. *Freud, Jews, and Other Germans.* New York, 1978.

———. *A Godless Jew: Freud, Atheism, and the Making of Psychoanalysis.* New Haven, CT, 1987.

———. *The Rise of Modern Paganism.* London, 1973.

———. *Weimar Culture.* Westport, CT, 1981.

Giddens, Anthony. *Emile Durkheim.* New York, 1979.

Gilbert, John. *Famous Jewish Lives.* Feltham, England, 1970.

Giles, James. *Confronting the Horror: The Novels of Nelson Algren.* Kent, OH, 1989.

Gill, Brendan. *Here at The New Yorker.* New York, 1987.

Gilman, Sander. *Inscribing the Other.* Lincoln, NE, 1991.

———. *Jewish Self-Hatred.* Baltimore, 1986.

———. *The Jew's Body.* New York, 1991.

Ginsberg, Allen. *Collected Poems, 1947–1980.* New York, 1987.

———. *Journals: Early Fifties, Early Sixties.* New York, 1977.

Girgus, Sam. *The New Covenant: Jewish Writers and the American Idea.* Chapel Hill, NC, 1984.

Glatzer, Nahum. *The Judaic Tradition.* Boston, 1969.

Gold, Arthur. *The Divine Sarah: A Life of Sarah Bernhardt.* New York, 1991.

Goldberg, Anatol. *Ilya Ehrenburg.* New York, 1984.

Goldin, Milton. *Why They Give.* New York, 1976.

Goldman, Albert, with Lawrence Schiller. *Ladies and Gentlemen, Lenny Bruce!* New York, 1975.

Goldman, Emma. *Living My Life.* New York, 1982.

Goldman, L. H. *Saul Bellow's Moral Vision: A Critical Study of the Jewish Experience.* New York, 1983.

Gollancz, Victor. *More for Timothy.* London, 1953.

———. *Reminiscences of Affection.* New York, 1968.

Goodman, Jean. *The Mond Legacy.* London, 1982.

Gordon, Mary. *Good Boys and Dead Girls.* New York, 1991.

Gordimer, Nadine. *Burger's Daughter.* London, 1979.

———. *Conversations with Nadine Gordimer.* Jackson, MI: 1990.

———. *The Essential Gesture: Writing, Politics and Places.* London, 1988

Gordis, David, and Yoav Ben-Horin. *Jewish Identity in America.* Los Angeles, 1991.

Graetz, Michael. *On the Return of Moses Hess to Judaism.* Tel Aviv, 1987.

Grayling, A. C. *Wittgenstein.* New York, 1988.

Greenberg, Clement. *Art and Culture.* Boston, 1984.

Grenville, Bryan. *Kurt Tucholsky: The Ironic Sentimentalist.* Atlantic Highlands, NJ, 1981.

Grossman, Leonid. *Confession of a Jew.* New York, 1975.

Grunfeld, Frederic. *Prophets Without Honor.* New York, 1979.

Grunwald, Henry. *Salinger: A Critical and Personal Portrait.* New York, 1962.

Gurevitz, Baruch. *The Bolshevik Revolution and the Foundation of the Jewish Communist Movement in Russia.* Tel Aviv, 1976.

Guttman, Allen. *The Jewish Writer in America: Assimilation and the Crisis of Identity.* New York, 1971.

Gwynn, Frederick. *The Fiction of J. D. Salinger.* Pittsburgh, 1979.

Ha-Am, Ahad. *At the Crossroads.* Albany, NY, 1983.

———. *Selected Essays.* New York, 1952.

———. *Ten Essays on Zionism and Judaism.* New York, 1973.

Hall, Douglas. *Modigliani.* Oxford, 1984.

Halpern, Ben. *A Clash of Heroes: Brandeis, Weizmann, and American Zionism.* New York, 1987.

Halter, Marek. *Le fou et les rois.* Paris, 1976.

Hamilton, Ian. *In Search of J. D. Salinger.* New York, 1989.

———. *Koestler.* New York, 1982.

Handler, Andrew. *Dori: The Life and Times of Theodor Herzl in Budapest.* Tuscaloosa, AL, 1983.

Hannam, Charles. *Almost an Englishman.* London, 1979.

———. *A Boy in That Situation: An Autobiography.* New York, 1978.

Hanslick, Eduard. *Vienna's Golden Years of Music.* Freeport, NY, 1969.

Hapgood, Hutchins. *The Spirit of the Ghetto.* Cambridge, MA, 1983.

Harap, Louis. *Creative Awakening.* New York, 1987.

———. *The Image of the Jew in American Literature.* Philadelphia, 1974.

———. *In the Mainstream: The Jewish Presence in Twentieth Century American Literature.* New York, 1987.

Harari, Manya. *Memoirs.* London, 1972.

Harding, James. *Jacques Offenbach.* New York, 1979.

Hayes, Nelson. *Claude Lévi-Strauss: The Anthropologist as Hero.* Cambridge, MA, 1970.

Hayman, Ronald. *Proust.* New York, 1990.

Hecht, Ben. *A Child of the Century.* New York, 1982.

———. *A Jew in Love.* New York, 1931.

Heine, Heinrich. *Jewish Stories and Hebrew Melodies.* New York, 1987.

———. *The Poetry and Prose of Heinrich Heine.* New York, 1948.

Heller, Joseph. *Catch-22.* New York, 1961.

———. *Good as Gold.* New York, 1979.

Hellman, Lillian. *An Unfinished Woman: A Memoir.* Boston, 1969.

Herberg, Will. *From Marxism to Judaism.* New York, 1989.

Herbert, James. *The Political Origins of Abstract-Expressionist Art Criticism.* Stanford, CA, 1985.

Hertzberg, Arthur. *Being Jewish in America.* New York, 1979.

———. *The French Enlightenment and the Jews.* New York, 1968.

———. *Jewish Polemics.* New York, 1992.

———. *The Jews in America.* New York, 1989.

———. *The Zionist Idea.* New York, 1959.

Hickey, Des. *The Prince: The Life of Laurshka Mischa Skikne . . . Otherwise Known as Laurence Harvey.* London, 1975.

Hill, Melvyn. *Hannah Arendt.* New York, 1979.

Hoffman, Abbie. *Revolution for the Hell of It.* New York, 1968.

———. *Soon to Be a Major Motion Picture.* New York, 1980.

———. *Steal This Book.* New York, 1971.

Hoffmann, Banesh. *Albert Einstein.* New York, 1972.

Hofrichter, Laura. *Heinrich Heine.* Westport, CT, 1987.

Holtzman, William. *Seesaw: A Dual Biography of Anne Bancroft and Mel Brooks.* Garden City, NY, 1979.

Homer, William. *Alfred Steiglitz and the American Avant-Garde.* Boston, 1977.

Horowitz, David. *Destructive Generation: Second Thoughts about the Sixties.* New York, 1988.

———. *Isaac Deutscher: The Man and His Work.* London, 1971.

Howard, Leslie. *Trivial Fond Records.* London, 1982.

Howard, Ronald. *In Search of My Father.* New York, 1981.

Howe, Irving. *Jewish-American Stories.* New York, 1977.

———. *A Margin of Hope.* San Diego, CA, 1982.

———. *Selected Writings, 1950–1990.* San Diego, CA, 1990.

———. *World of Our Fathers.* New York, 1976.

Hughes, H. Stuart. *Prisoners of Hope: The Silver Age of the Italian Jews.* Cambridge, MA, 1983.

Hyatt, Marshall. *Franz Boas: Social Activist.* New York, 1990.

Hyman, Paula. *From Dreyfus to Vichy.* New York, 1979.

Jacobs, Diana. *But We Need the Eggs.* New York, 1982.

Jacobs, Jack. *On Socialists and "The Jewish Question" after Marx.* New York, 1991.

Jacoby, Russell. *The Last Intellectuals.* New York, 1987.

Jay, Martin. *Adorno.* Cambridge, MA, 1984.

———. *The Dialectical Imagination: A History of the Frankfurt School.* Boston, 1973.

Jenkins, Alan. *The Social Theory of Claude Lévi-Strauss.* London, 1979.

Josephus, Flavius. *The Works of Josephus.* Peabody, MA, 1987.

Jungk, Peter. *Franz Werfel.* New York, 1990.

Kadarkay, Arpad. *Georg Lukacs: Life, Thought, and Politics.* Cambridge, MA, 1991.

Kafka, Franz. *The Complete Stories.* New York, 1971.

———. *The Diaries, 1910–1923.* New York, 1988.

———. *I Am a Memory Come Alive: Autobiographical Writings.* New York, 1974.

———. *Letter to His Father.* New York, 1966.

———. *Letters to Felice.* New York, 1988.

———. *Letters to Milena.* New York, 1990.

———. *The Trial.* New York, 1985.

Kahler, Erich. *The Jews among the Nations.* New Brunswick, NJ, 1988.

Kaplan, Karel. *Report on the Murder of the General Secretary.* Columbus, OH, 1990.

Kaplan, Yosef. *From Christianity to Judaism: The Story of Isaac Orobio de Castro.* New York, 1989.

Karl, Frederick. *Franz Kafka: Representative Man.* New York, 1991.

Katz, Barry. *Herbert Marcuse and the Art of Liberation.* New York, 1982.

———. *Jewish Emancipation and Self-Emancipation.* Philadelphia, 1986.

Katz, Jacob. *Emancipation and Assimilation: Studies in Modern Jewish History.* New York, 1972.

Kaufmann, Donald. *Norman Mailer: The Countdown, the First Twenty Years.* Carbondale, IL, 1969.

Kautsky, Karl. *Are the Jews a Race?* Westport, CT, 1972.

Kazin, Alfred. *New York Jew.* New York, 1978.

———. *A Walker in the City.* New York, 1951.

Keats, John. *You Might as Well Live: The Life and Times of Dorothy Parker.* New York, 1970.

Keegan, Susanne. *The Bride of the Wind: The Life and Times of Alma Mahler-Werfel.* New York, 1993.

Kessler, Harry. *Walter Rathenau.* New York, 1975.

Kielsky, Vera. *Inevitable Exiles: Cynthia Ozick's View of the Precariousness of Jewish Existence in a Gentile Society.* New York, 1989.

Kiernan, Thomas. *The Roman Polanski Story.* New York, 1980.

Klein, Dennis. *Jewish Origins of the Psychoanalytic Movement.* New York, 1981.

Klingenstein, Susanne. *Jews in the American Academy, 1900–1940.* New Haven, CT, 1991.

Koestler, Arthur. *Arrival and Departure.* New York, 1943.

———. *Arrow in the Blue.* London, 1952.

———. *Astride the Two Cultures.* New York, 1976.

———. *Bricks to Babel.* New York, 1980.

———. *The Challenge of Our Time.* London, 1948.

———. *Dialogue with Death.* New York, 1967.

———. *Drinkers of Infinity.* London, 1968.

———. *The Ghost in the Machine.* New York, 1968.

———. *The Invisible Writing.* London, 1954.

———. *Promise and Fulfillment.* New York, 1949.

———. *Scum of the Earth.* New York, 1941.

———. *Thieves in the Night.* London, 1946.

———. *The Thirteenth Tribe.* New York, 1976.

Koestler, Mamaine. *Living with Koestler.* New York, 1985.

Kosinsky, Jerzy. *The Art of the Self: Essays.* New York, 1968.

———. *The Hermit of 69th Street.* New York, 1988.

Kosmin, Barry. *Intermarriage, Divorce, and Remarriage among American Jews, 1982–87.* New York, 1989.

Kracauer, Siegfried. *Orpheus in Paris.* New York, 1972.

Kraus, Karl. *Half-Truths and One-and-a-Half Truths.* Chicago, 1990.

———. *In These Great Times: A Karl Kraus Reader.* Chicago, 1990.

———. *No Compromise: Selected Writings of Karl Kraus.* New York, 1977.

Lavers, Norman. *Jerzy Kosinski.* Boston, 1982.

Lax, Eric. *On Being Funny.* New York, 1975.

———. *Woody Allen.* New York, 1991.

Laychuk, Julian. *Ilya Ehrenburg: An Idealist in an Age of Realism.* New York, 1991.

Lea, Henry. *Gustav Mahler: Man on the Margin.* Bonn, 1985.

Leftwich, Joseph. *Israel Zangwill.* New York, 1957.

Lessing, Doris. *The Memoirs of a Survivor.* New York, 1988.

Lessing, Gotthold. *Nathan the Wise.* New York, 1991.

Levi, Peter. *Boris Pasternak.* London, 1990.

Levi, Primo. *If Not Now, When?* New York, 1985.

Levin, Nora. *Jewish Socialist Movements, 1871–1917.* London, 1978.

Levin, Shmarya. *The Arena.* New York, 1975.

Levine, Naomi. *Politics, Religion and Love: The Story of H. H. Asquith, Venetia Stanley and Edwin Montagu.* New York, 1991.

Levy, Bernard Henri. *Barbarism with a Human Face*. New York, 1979.

———. *The Testament of God*. New York, 1980.

Lewin, Kurt. *Resolving Social Conflicts*. New York, 1948.

Lewisohn, Ludwig. *Anniversary*. Westport, CT, 1972.

———. *The Answer*. New York, 1939.

———. *The Island Within*. Philadelphia, 1968.

———. *Mid-Channel*. New York, 1975.

———. *Up Stream*. St. Clair Shores, MI, 1977.

Liebman, Arthur. *Jews and the Left*. New York, 1979.

Liebman, Charles. *The Ambivalent American Jew*. Philadelphia, 1973.

Lifton, Betty Jean. *The King of Children: A Biography of Janusz Korczak*. New York, 1988.

Lilly, Paul. *Words in Search of Victims: The Achievement of Jerzy Kosinski*. Kent, OH, 1988.

Lipman, Sonia, and V. D. Lipman. *The Century of Moses Montefiore*. Oxford, 1985.

Lipman, V. D. *A History of the Jews in Britain since 1858*. New York, 1990.

Lippmann, Walter. *Early Writings*. New York, 1970.

———. *A Preface to Morals*. New Brunswick, NJ, 1982.

Liptzin, Solomon. *Arthur Schnitzler*. New York, 1932.

———. *Germany's Stepchildren*. Freeport, NY, 1971.

Loewenberg, Peter. *Walter Rathenau and Henry Kissinger: The Jew as a Modern Statesman in Two Political Cultures*. New York, 1980.

Logue, William. *Léon Blum: The Formative Years, 1872–1914*. DeKalb, IL, 1973.

Lottman, Herbert. *Colette: A Life*. Boston, 1991.

———. *The Left Bank*. Boston, 1982.

Lourie, Arthur. *Serge Koussevitzky and His Epoch*. New York, 1971.

Lowenthal, Leo. *Critical Theory and Frankfurt Theorists*. New Brunswick, NJ, 1989.

———. *An Unmastered Past: Autobiographical Reflections*. Berkeley, CA, 1987.

Lowin, Joseph. *Cynthia Ozick*. Boston, 1988.

Lucid, Robert. *Norman Mailer: The Man and His Work*. Boston, 1971.

Lukes, Steven. *Emile Durkheim: His Life and Work*. Stanford, CA, 1985.

Lupack, Barbara. *Plays of Passion, Games of Chance*. Bristol, IN, 1988.

McCagg, William. *A History of the Habsburg Jews, 1670–1918*. Bloomington, IN, 1989.

———. *Jewish Nobles and Geniuses in Modern Hungary*. Boulder, CO, 1986.

McClellan, David. *Marx before Marxism*. New York, 1970.

———. *Utopian Pessimist: The Life and Thought of Simone Weil*. New York, 1990.

Mahon, Gigi. *The Last Days of the New Yorker*. New York, 1988.

Maier, Joseph, and Chaim Waxman. *Ethnicity, Identity, and History*. New Brunswick, NJ, 1983.

Mailer, Norman. *Advertisements for Myself*. New York, 1959.

———. *Cannibals and Christians*. London, 1967.

———. *The White Negro*. San Francisco, 1957.

Malamud, Bernard. *Conversations with Bernard Malamud*. Jackson, MI, 1991.

Malino, Frances, and Bernard Wasserstein. *The Jews in Modern France*. Hanover, NH, 1985.

Mamet, David. *Homicide: A Screenplay*. New York, 1992.

———. *Three Jewish Plays*. New York, 1987.

Manchel, Frank. *The Box-Office Clowns: Bob Hope, Jerry Lewis, Mel Brooks, Woody Allen*. Garden City, NY, 1979.

Mandel, Arthur. *The Militant Messiah: The Story of Jacob Frank.* Atlantic Highlands, NJ, 1979.

Mandelstam, Nadezhda. *Hope Abandoned.* New York, 1974.

———. *Hope against Hope.* New York, 1970.

Mann, Carol. *Modigliani.* London, 1980.

Markel, Michael. *Hilaire Belloc.* Boston, 1982.

Marks, Robert. *The Meaning of Marcuse.* New York, 1970.

Martin, Jay. *Nathanael West.* New York, 1970.

Marx, Alexander. *Essays in Jewish Biography.* New York, 1973.

Marx, Karl. *Early Writings.* New York, 1975.

Marx, Maxine. *Growing Up with Chico.* Englewood Cliffs, NJ, 1980.

Mason, Jackie. *How to Talk Jewish.* New York, 1991.

———. *Jackie Mason's America.* Secaucus, NJ, 1983.

———. *Jackie Mason's the World According to Me.* New York, 1987.

———. *Jackie, Oy!* Boston, 1988.

May, Derwent. *Hannah Arendt.* New York, 1986.

Mayer, Egon. *Children of Intermarriage.* New York, 1983.

Meade, Marion. *Dorothy Parker.* New York, 1988.

Meade, Robert. *Judah P. Benjamin: Confederate Statesman.* New York, 1943.

Mehring, Franz. *Karl Marx.* London, 1936.

———. *The Lessing Legend.* New York, 1938.

Memmi, Albert. *Albert Memmi.* Montreal, 1975.

———. *The Colonizer and the Colonized.* New York, 1965.

———. *Dominated Man.* New York, 1968.

———. *The Liberation of the Jew.* New York, 1966.

———. *The Pillar of Salt.* New York, 1955.

———. *Portrait of a Jew.* New York, 1962.

Mendelssohn, Moses. *Jerusalem and Other Jewish Writings.* New York, 1969.

———. *Selections from His Writings.* New York, 1975.

Mendes-Flohr, Paul. *Divided Passions.* Detroit, 1991.

———. *From Mysticism to Dialogue.* Detroit, 1989.

Mendes-Flohr, Paul, and Jehuda Reinharz. *The Jew in the Modern World.* New York, 1980.

Meredith, George. *The Tragic Comedians.* New York, 1975.

Merrill, Thomas. *Allen Ginsberg.* Boston, 1988.

Meyer, Michael. *Ideas of Jewish History.* New York, 1974.

———. *Jewish Identity in the Modern World.* Seattle, 1990.

———. *Response to Modernity.* New York, 1988.

Meyerowitz, Selma. *Leonard Woolf.* Boston, 1982.

Michalson, Gordon. *Lessing's "Ugly Ditch": A Study of Theology and History.* University Park, PA, 1985.

Mikes, George. *Arthur Koestler.* London, 1983.

Miklowitz, Gloria. *The Love Bombers.* New York, 1980.

Miles, Barry. *Ginsberg.* New York, 1989.

Miller, Ruth. *Saul Bellow: A Biographer of the Imagination.* New York, 1991.

Mills, Hilary. *Mailer.* New York, 1984.

Mintz, Alan. *"Banished from Their Father's Table": Loss of Faith and Hebrew Autobiography.* Bloomington, IN, 1989.

Moloney, Brian. *Italo Svevo: A Critical Introduction.* Edinburgh, 1974.

Monceau, Philippe. *Le dernier sabbat de Maurice Sachs.* Paris, 1979.

Morais, Fernando. *"Olga": The Gift to Hitler.* New York, 1990.

Morgenthau, Henry. *Mostly Morgenthaus: A Family History.* New York, 1991.

Morton, Frederic. *The Rothschilds: A Family Portrait.* New York, 1983.

Mosse, George. *German Jews beyond Judaism.* Bloomington, IN, 1985.

———. *Germans and Jews.* Detroit, 1987.

———. *The Jews and the German War Experience, 1914–1918.* New York, 1977.

———. *The Left Wing Intellectuals between the Wars, 1919–1939.* New York, 1966.

Muhlstein, Anka. *Baron James.* New York, 1982.

Nakhimovsky, Alice. *Russian-Jewish Literature and Identity.* Baltimore, 1992.

Namier, Lewis. *Facing East.* New York, 1958.

———. *In the Margin of History.* Freeport, NY, 1969.

———. *Skyscrapers and Other Essays.* Freeport, NY, 1968.

Nedava, Joseph. *Trotsky and the Jews.* Philadelphia, 1972.

Neier, Aryeh. *Defending My Enemy.* New York, 1979.

Neusner, Jacob. *Judaism in the American Humanities.* Chico, CA, 1981.

———. *Self-Fulfilling Prophecy.* New York, 1991.

———. *Stranger at Home.* Chicago, 1981.

———. *Struggle for the Jewish Mind.* Lanham, MD, 1988.

Nichols, Ray. *Treason, Tradition and the Intellectual: Julian Benda and Political Discourse.* Lawrence, KS, 1978.

Niehoff, Maren. *The Figure of Joseph in Post-Biblical Jewish Literature.* Leiden, Netherlands, 1992.

Niewyk, Donald. *The Jews in Weimar Germany.* Baton Rouge, 1980.

Nordau, Anna. *Max Nordau.* New York, 1943.

Nordau, Max. *The Conventional Lies of Our Civilization.* Chicago, 1884.

———. *Degeneration.* New York, 1895.

———. *The Dwarf's Spectacles, and Other Fairy Tales.* New York, 1905.

———. *The Interpretation of History.* New York, 1911.

———. *Paris Sketches.* Chicago, 1890.

———. *A Question of Honor.* Boston, 1907.

———. *The Shackles of Fate.* New York, 1897.

———. *Zionism and Anti-Semitism.* New York, 1904.

Norman, Dorothy. *Alfred Stieglitz: An American Seer.* New York, 1973.

Oncken, Herman. *Lassalle.* New York, 1971.

Ozick, Cynthia. *Art and Ardor: Essays.* New York, 1983.

———. *Metaphor and Memory: Essays.* New York, 1989.

Painter, George. *Marcel Proust.* New York, 1989.

Pawel, Ernst. *The Nightmare of Reason: A Life of Franz Kafka.* New York, 1984.

———. *Perspectives on Mordecai Richler.* Toronto, 1986.

Petrement, Simone. *Simone Weil.* New York, 1976.

Pickering, Stephen. *Understanding Doris Lessing.* Columbia, SC, 1990.

Pinsker, Sanford. *Jewish-American Fiction, 1917–1987.* New York, 1992.

———. *The Schlemiel as Metaphor.* Carbondale, IL, 1971.

———. *The Uncompromising Fictions of Cynthia Ozick.* Columbia, MO, 1987.

———. *Understanding Joseph Heller.* Columbia, SC, 1991.

Pissarro, Camille. *Camille Pissarro.* New York, 1954.

Polanski, Roman. *Roman.* New York, 1984.

Poor, Harold. *Kurt Tucholsky and the Ordeal of Germany.* New York, 1968.

Porter, Jack Nusan. *The Jew as Outsider.* Washington, DC, 1981.

———. *Jewish Radicalism.* New York, 1973.

Prawer, Siegbert. *Heine's Jewish Comedy.* Oxford, 1983.

Raczymow, Henri. *Maurice Sachs.* Paris, 1988.

Rajak, Tessa. *Josephus: The Historian and His Society.* London, 1983.

Raphael, Chaim. *A Coat of Many Colours.* London, 1979.

———. *Encounters with the Jewish People.* New York, 1979.

———. *Memoirs of a Special Case.* Chappaqua, NY, 1985.

———. *The Springs of Jewish Life.* New York, 1982.

Raphael, Marc. *Abba Hillel Silver.* New York, 1989.

Rapoport, Louis. *Stalin's War against the Jews.* New York, 1990.

Rapoport-Albert, Ada, and Steven Zipperstein. *Jewish History.* London, 1989.

Rathenau, Walter. *Notes and Diaries.* New York, 1985.

Reid, Randall. *The Fiction of Nathanael West: No Redeemer, No Promised Land.* Chicago, 1967.

Reinharz, Jehuda. *Chaim Weizmann: The Making of a Zionist Leader.* New York, 1985.

———. *Fatherland or Promised Land: The Dilemma of the German Jew 1893–1914.* Ann Arbor, MI, 1975.

———. *The German Zionist Challenge to the Faith of Emancipation, 1897–1914.* Tel Aviv, 1982.

———. *The Jew in the Modern World: A Documentary History.* New York, 1980.

———. *The Jewish Response to German Culture.* Hanover, NH, 1985.

———. *Living with Antisemitism: Modern Jewish Responses.* Hanover, NH, 1987.

Revah, Louis-Albert. *Un misanthrope juif dans la France de Maurras.* Paris, 1991.

Ribalow, Harold. *The Tie That Binds: Conversations with Jewish Writers.* San Diego, CA, 1980.

Rice, Emanuel. *Freud and Moses: The Long Journey Home.* Albany, NY, 1990.

Richarz, Monica. *Jewish Life in Germany.* Bloomington, IN, 1991.

Riesman, David. *The Lonely Crowd.* New Haven, CT, 1950.

Riner, Alexander. *Arnold Schoenberg: The Composer as Jew.* New York, 1990.

Robert, Marthe. *As Lonely as Franz Kafka.* New York, 1982.

———. *From Oedipus to Moses: Freud's Jewish Identity.* Garden City, NY, 1976.

Roberts, Adrian. *Arthur Schnitzler and Politics.* Riverside, CA, 1989.

Robertson, Richard. *Kafka: Judaism, Politics, and Literature.* New York, 1985.

Roi, Yaacov, and Avi Becker. *Jewish Culture and Identity in the Soviet Union.* New York, 1991.

Roiphe, Anne. *Generation without Memory.* Boston, 1982.

Rose, Gillian. *The Melancholy Science: An Introduction to the Thought of Theodor Adorno.* London, 1978.

Rose, Norman. *Chaim Weizmann: A Biography.* New York, 1986.

———. *Lewis Namier and Zionism*. New York, 1980.

Rosenberg, Bernard, and Ernest Goldstein. *Creators and Disturbers*. New York, 1982.

Rosenfeld, Isaac. *Alpha and Omega: Stories*. London, 1966.

———. *Passage from Home*. New York, 1988.

———. *Preserving the Hunger*. Detroit, 1988.

Roth, Henry. *Call It Sleep*. New York, 1964.

———. *Shifting Landscape*. New York, 1987.

Roth, Joseph. *Flight without End*. London, 1977.

———. *The Silent Prophet*. London, 1979.

Roth, Philip. *The Counterlife*. New York, 1991.

———. *The Facts*. New York, 1992.

———. *The Ghost Writer*. New York, 1989.

———. *Goodbye, Columbus and Other Stories*. New York, 1986.

———. *Patrimony*. New York, 1991.

———. *Portnoy's Complaint*. New York, 1967.

———. *Reading Myself and Others*. New York, 1977.

———. *Zuckerman Bound*. New York, 1985.

———. *Zuckerman Unbound*. New York, 1986.

Rothschild, Nathaniel. *Random Variables*. London, 1984.

Rothschild, Sylvia. *A Special Legacy*. New York, 1985.

Roy, Claude. *Modigliani*. New York, 1985.

Sachar, Abram. *A Host at Last*. Boston, 1976.

Sachar, Howard Morley. *The Course of Modern Jewish History*. New York, 1958.

———. *Diaspora*. New York, 1985.

———. *A History of the Jews in America*. New York, 1992.

Sachs, Maurice. *Chronique joyeuse et scandaleuse*. Paris, 1973.

———. *Le sabbat: Souvenirs d'une jeunesse orageuse*. Paris, 1979.

Salvadori, Massimo. *Karl Kautsky and the Socialist Revolution*. New York, 1990.

Sammons, Jeffrey. *Heinrich Heine*. Princeton, NJ, 1979.

Samuel, Maurice. *Prince of the Ghetto*. New York, 1959.

Samuels, Ernest. *Bernard Berenson: The Making of a Connoisseur*. Cambridge, MA, 1979.

———. *Bernard Berenson: The Making of a Legend*. Cambridge, MA, 1987.

Sanders, Ronald. *Reflections on a Teapot*. New York, 1972.

———. *Shores of Refuge*. New York, 1988.

Sassoon, Siegfried. *Diaries*. Boston, 1985.

———. *Letters to Max Beerbohm*. Boston, 1986.

———. *Memoirs of a Fox-Hunting Man*. London, 1977.

Schama, Simon. *Citizens*. New York, 1990.

———. *Two Rothschilds and the Land of Israel*. New York, 1978.

Schatz, Jeff. *The Generation*. Berkeley, CA, 1991.

Schechner, Mark. *After the Revolution: Studies in the Contemporary Jewish American Imagination*. Bloomington, IN, 1987.

———. *The Conversion of the Jews and Other Essays*. New York, 1990.

Schiff, Jacob. *His Life and Letters*. Grosse Pointe, MI, 1968.

Schmitt, Claude. *Le double jeu de Maurice Sachs*. Lausanne, 1979.

Schnitzler, Arthur. *Berta Garlan*. New York, 1987.

———. *Flight into Darkness*. New York, 1971.

———. *Illusion and Reality*. New York, 1986.

———. *My Youth in Vienna*. New York, 1970.

———. *Plays and Stories*. New York, 1982.

———. *The Road into the Open*. Berkeley, CA, 1992.

———. *Undiscovered Country*. London, 1980.

———. *Viennese Idylls*. Freeport, NY, 1973.

———. *Viennese Novelettes*. New York, 1974.

Scholem, Gershom. *From Berlin to Jerusalem*. New York, 1988.

———. *On Jews and Judaism in Crisis*. New York, 1976.

———. *Walter Benjamin*. New York, 1988.

Scott, Nathan. *Three American Moralists: Mailer, Bellow, Trilling*. Notre Dame, IN, 1973.

Seckerson, Edward. *Mahler: His Life and Times*. New York, 1982.

Secrest, Meryl. *Being Bernard Berenson*. New York, 1979.

Seed, David. *The Fiction of Joseph Heller*. New York, 1989.

Shaked, Gershon. *The Shadows Within: Essays on Modern Jewish Writers*. Philadelphia, 1987.

Shawn, Wallace. *Aunt Dan and Lemon*. New York, 1985.

———. *The Fever*. Boston, 1991.

———. *Marie and Bruce*. New York, 1980.

———. *Our Late Night*. New York, 1984.

Shelton, Madi Robert. *No Direction Home*. New York, 1986.

Sherwin, Byron. *Jerzy Kosinski: Literary Alarmclock*. Chicago, 1981.

Silberman, Charles. *A Certain People: American Jews and Their Lives Today*. New York, 1985.

Silverberg, Robert. *If I Forget Thee, O Jerusalem*. New York, 1970.

Sinclair, Andrew. *Spiegel: The Man behind the Pictures*. London, 1987.

Singer, David, and Ruth Seldin, eds. *American Jewish Yearbook 1993*. New York, 1993.

Sklare, Marshall. *The Jews: Social Patterns of an American Group*. Glencoe, IL, 1958.

Smith, Jeremy. *Religious Feeling and Religious Commitment in Faulkner, Dostoyevsky, Werfel, and Bernanos*. New York, 1988.

Solotaroff, Robert. *Bernard Malamud*. New York, 1989.

Sorkin, David. *The Transformation of German Jewry, 1780–1840*. New York, 1987.

Spater, George. *A Marriage of True Minds: An Intimate Portrait of Leonard and Virginia Woolf*. London, 1977.

Speaight, Robert. *The Life of Hilaire Belloc*. Freeport, NY, 1970.

Spiel, Hilde. *Fanny von Arnstein*. New York, 1991.

Spitz, Bob. *Dylan: A Biography*. New York, 1991.

Spivey, Ted R. *Religious Themes in Two Modern Novelists*. Atlanta, 1965.

Steel, Ronald. *Walter Lippmann and the American Century*. Boston, 1980.

Steenson, Gary. *Karl Kautsky*. Pittsburgh, 1978.

Steinberg, Stephen. *The Academic Melting Pot*. New York, 1974.

Stern, Selma. *The Court Jew*. New Brunswick, NJ, 1985.

Stewart, James. *Den of Thieves*. New York, 1991.

Stieglitz, Alfred. *Alfred Stieglitz.* New York, 1976.

Stille, Alexander. *Benevolence and Betrayal: Five Italian Jewish Families under Fascism.* New York, 1991.

Stone, Paulene. *One Tear Is Enough.* London, 1975.

Strauss, Leo. *History of Political Philosophy.* Chicago, 1972.

Strauss, Richard. *A Confidential Matter: The Letters of Richard Strauss and Stefan Zweig.* Berkeley, CA, 1977.

Strauss, Walter. *On the Threshold of a New Kabbalah: Kafka's Later Tales.* New York, 1988.

Sucher, Laurie. *The Fiction of Ruth Prawer Jhabvala.* New York, 1989.

Svevo, Italo. *Confessions of Zeno.* Westport, CT, 1973.

———. *Further Confessions of Zeno.* London, 1969.

Svevo, Livia. *Memoir of Italo Svevo.* Marlboro, VT, 1990.

Szajkowski, Zosa. *Jews and the French Revolutions of 1789, 1830 and 1848.* New York, 1970.

Talmon, J. L. *Israel among the Nations.* New York, 1971.

Tar, Zoltan. *The Frankfurt School.* New York, 1977.

Tec, Nechama. *In the Lion's Den: The Life of Oswald Rufeisen.* New York, 1990.

Terry, Megan. *Approaching Simone.* Old Westbury, NY, 1973.

Thane, Elswyth. *Young Mr. Disraeli.* New York, 1936.

Timms, Edward. *Karl Kraus: Apocalyptic Satirist.* New Haven, CT, 1986.

Toupounce, William. *Isaac Asimov.* Boston, 1991.

Tucholsky, Kurt. *What If?* New York, 1968.

Udelson, Joseph. *Dreamer of the Ghetto.* Tuscaloosa, AL, 1990.

Urofsky, Melvin. *Louis D. Brandeis and the Progressive Tradition.* Boston, 1981.

Vincent, John. *Disraeli.* New York, 1990.

Walden, Daniel. *On Being Jewish: American Jewish Writers from Cahan to Bellow.* Greenwich, CT, 1974.

Waldstreicher, David. *Emma Goldman.* New York, 1990.

Walter, Bruno. *Gustav Mahler.* New York, 1970.

———. *Theme and Variation: An Autobiography.* Westport, CT, 1981.

Walter, Herman. *Moses Mendelssohn: Critic and Philosopher.* New York, 1973.

Walton, John. *Disraeli.* New York, 1990.

Wasserman, Jacob. *Caspar Hauser.* New York, 1928.

———. *My Life as German and Jew.* New York, 1933.

Wasserstein, Bernard. *The Secret Lives of Trebitsch Lincoln.* New Haven, CT, 1988.

Weatherby, W. J. *Chariots of Fire.* New York, 1983.

Weinberg, Herman. *Stroheim: A Pictorial Record.* New York, 1975.

Weinberg, Steve. *Armand Hammer—The Untold Story.* Boston, 1989.

Weininger, Otto. *Sex and Character.* New York, 1975.

Weizmann, Chaim. *Trial and Error.* New York, 1966.

Wenke, John Paul. *J. D. Salinger.* Boston, 1991.

Werfel, Franz. *The Eternal Road.* New York, 1936.

———. *Jacobowsky and the Colonel.* New York, 1944.

———. *Paul Among the Jews: A Tragedy.* London, 1928.

———. *Twilight of a World.* New York, 1937.

Werner, Alfred. *Amedeo Modigliani.* London, 1967.

West, Nathanael. *Collected Works.* Baltimore, 1975.

Wexman, Virginia. *Roman Polanski.* Boston, 1985.

Whittaker, Ruth. *Doris Lessing.* New York, 1988.

Wiener Library. *German Jewry: Its History, Life, and Culture.* Westport, CT, 1975.

Wigoder, Geoffrey. *Dictionary of Jewish Biography.* New York, 1991.

Wilson, Derek. *Rothschild.* London, 1988.

Wilson, Duncan. *Leonard Woolf: A Political Biography.* London, 1978.

Wilson, Jonathan. *Herzog: The Limits of Ideas.* Boston, 1990.

Wilson, Nelly. *Bernard-Lazare: Anti-Semitism and the Problem of Jewish Identity in Late Nine-teenth Century France.* New York, 1978.

Winch, Peter. *Simone Weil: The Just Balance.* New York, 1989.

Winner, David. *Peter Benenson: Taking a Stand against Injustice.* Milwaukee, 1991.

Wise, Isaac Mayer. *Reminiscences.* Cincinnati, 1901.

Wistrich, Robert. "Anti-Semitism in Europe since the Holocaust." In David Singer and Ruth Seldin, eds., *American Jewish Yearbook 1993.* New York, 1993.

———. *Between Redemption and Perdition: Modern Anti-Semitism and Jewish Identity.* New York, 1990.

———. *The Jews of Vienna in the Age of Franz Joseph.* New York, 1989.

———. *Revolutionary Jews from Marx to Trotsky.* New York, 1976.

———. *Socialism and the Jews.* Rutherford, NJ, 1982.

———. *Trotsky: Fate of a Revolutionary.* New York, 1982.

Witte, Bernd. *Walter Benjamin: An Intellectual Biography.* Detroit, 1991.

Wolf, William. *The Marx Brothers.* New York, 1975.

Woodley, Richard. *The Jazz Singer.* New York, 1980.

Woolf, Leonard. *Beginning Again: An Autobiography, 1911–1918.* New York, 1964.

———. *Downhill All the Way, 1919–1939.* New York, 1967.

———. *Growing: An Autobiography, 1904–1911.* New York, 1962.

———. *The Wise Virgins.* New York, 1979.

Woollcott, Alexander. *The Story of Irving Berlin.* New York, 1983.

Wouk, Herman. *The Caine Mutiny: A Novel of World War II.* Garden City, NY, 1952.

———. *Marjorie Morningstar.* New York, 1957.

Wright, William. *Lillian Hellman.* New York, 1986.

Yerushalmi, Yosef Hayim. *Freud's Moses: Judaism Terminable and Interminable.* New Haven, CT, 1991.

Yezierska, Anzia. *How I Found America.* New York, 1991.

Young-Bruehl, Elisabeth. *Hannah Arendt: For Love of the World.* New Haven, CT, 1982.

Yovel, Yirmiyahu. *Spinoza and Other Heretics,* 2 vols. Princeton, NJ, 1989.

Yudkin, Leon. *Jewish Writing and Identity in the Twentieth Century.* New York, 1982.

Zangwill, Israel. *Children of the Ghetto.* New York, 1922.

———. *Ghetto Tragedies.* New York, 1919.

———. *The King of Schnorrers.* New York, 1987.

———. *Melting Pot.* New York, 1975.

———. *The Next Religion.* New York, 1913.

———. *Plaster Saints.* New York, 1915.

———. *They That Walk in Darkness.* Freeport, NY, 1970.

———. *The War for the World.* New York, 1917.

———. *Without Prejudice.* Freeport, NY, 1973.

Zweig, Stefan. *The World of Yesterday.* New York, 1943.

Zweigenhaft, Richard. *Jews in the Protestant Establishment.* New York, 1982.

ARTICLES

Bauman, Zygmunt. "Assimilation and Enlightenment." *Society* 27 (September–October 1990): 71–81.

Berlin, Isaiah. "Einstein and Israel." *New York Review of Books,* November 8, 1979.

———. "Jewish Slavery and Emancipation." *Jewish Chronicles,* September 21, 1951.

Bettelheim, Bruno. "The Holocaust: Some Reflections a Generation Later." *Encounter* 51 (December 1978).

Clark, Joseph. "Marx and the Jews: Another View." *Dissent* 28 (Winter 1981): 74–86.

Craft, Robert. "Jews and Geniuses." *New York Review of Books,* February 16, 1989.

Dinnage, Rosemary. "Fanning the Gemlike Flame." *New York Review of Books,* October 8, 1987.

Eder, Richard. "The Jewish Question in France." *New York Times Magazine,* November 30, 1980.

Edwards, Thomas. "Underground Man." *New York Review of Books,* June 28, 1990.

Friedman, Menachem. "The Haredim and the Holocaust." *Jerusalem Quarterly* 53 (Winter 1990): 86–114.

Harap, Louis. "The Meaning of Marx's Essay 'On the Jewish Question.'" *Journal of Ethnic Studies* 7 (Spring 1979): 43–56.

Hoffman, Stefani. "Soviet Jewish Intellectuals and the Russian Intelligentsia." *Soviet Jewish Affairs* 10 (February 1980): 23–38.

Ignatieff, Michael. "The Limits of Sainthood." *New Republic,* June 18, 1990.

———. "The Rise and Fall of Vienna's Jews." *New York Review of Books,* June 29, 1989.

Laqueur, Walter. "From Russia with Hate." *New Republic,* February 5, 1990.

McGrath, William. "How Jewish Was Freud?" *New York Review of Books,* February 5, 1991.

Solotaroff, Ted. "American-Jewish Writers: On Edge Once More." *New York Times Book Review,* December 18, 1988.

Tarushkin, Richard. "The Dark Side of Modern Music: The Sins of Toscanini, Stravinsky, Schoenberg." *New Republic,* September 5, 1988.

Index

ABOUT THE AUTHOR

BARRY RUBIN is a professor at the Hebrew University of Jerusalem and a senior fellow at Bar-Ilan University's BESA Center,
Hebrew University's Harry Truman Institute, and Haifa University's Jewish-Arab Center. His books include *Revolution Until Victory: The Politics and History of the PLO; Cauldron of Turmoil: America
in the Middle East; Istanbul Intrigues; Modern Dictators; Secrets of State:
The State Department and the Struggle over U.S. Foreign Policy; Paved
with Good Intentions: The American Experience and Iran; The Arab
States and the Palestine Conflict; Islamic Fundamentalists in Egyptian
Politics; The Great Powers in the Middle East, 1941–1947; International
News and the American Media;* and *How Others Report Us.*